Praise for

RIVER TOWN

by PETER HESSLER

"A perceptive and engrossing account of an outsider in fast-changing China. . . . Elegant." —*Business Week*

"Fascinating. . . . Vivid. . . . Penetrating. . . . A valuable book for anyone interested in assessing the progress and future of China." —*Washington Post Book World*

"A work of grace and profundity." —*Esquire*

"Tender, intelligent, and insightful, [this] is the work of a writer of rare talent; it deserves to become a classic."
—Simon Winchester, author of *The Professor and the Madman*

"Charming and insightful. . . . Poignant [and] hilarious. . . . Lively, intelligent. . . . You will learn a great deal about real life in contemporary China in *River Town*, and about how that vast country appears in the eyes of a sensitive, aware, rugged young American who keeps both his eyes and his mind open." —*New York Times*

"A vivid and touching tribute to a place and its people." —*Kirkus Reviews*

"If you should read only one book about China, let it be this. . . . Hessler is a marvellous writer. . . . I am not the only China-watcher who will wish he had written this book." —Jonathan Mirsky, *Literary Review* (London)

"An intimate, humorous, true-to-life portrait of modern China." —*Vanity Fair*

"*River Town* is at once profoundly insightful, sharply critical, deeply admiring, thoroughly unsentimental, precisely written, and often very, very funny." —Tim Cahill, author of *Pass the Butterworms* and *Road Fever*

"Richly nuanced. . . . Hessler tells his story in a prose that is both forceful and precise."
—*Los Angeles Times*

"With patience and trust, Hessler sees that it is possible to participate in and understand local life. . . . *River Town* is a poignant and beautifully written account of a backwater about to face the onslaught of socialist modernity."
—*Times Literary Supplement*

"Exquisitely reported. . . . Hessler describes the politics and the history of China in ways that I've never seen matched. . . . [He] writes beautifully and with balance."
—Gay Talese, *Brill's Content*

"Never is Hessler's complex China, or his book, anything less than magnificent."
—*Outside* magazine

"Moving, mesmerizing. . . . Transcends the boundaries of the travel genre and will appeal to anyone wanting to learn more about the heart and soul of the Chinese people."
—*Booklist*

"One of the most enchanting books I've read in a very long time. . . . The quality of the view is exhilarating."
—Anne Stephenson, *USA Today*

"Hessler writes beautifully. *River Town* is memoir, travelogue, and astute anthropological writing woven into a book that is difficult to put down."
—Abraham Verghese, author of *The Tennis Partner* and *My Own Country*

"Powerful. . . . Hessler makes poignant observations about the Chinese and the ways Communism and increasing openness affects them."
—Salon.com

"Suffused with candor, compassion, insights, and intimate knowledge, *River Town* is a wonderful read."
—Ha Jin, author of *Waiting*, winner of the National Book Award

Mark Leong

About the Author

PETER HESSLER is a regular contributor to *The New Yorker* and has also written for the *Wall Street Journal*, the *New York Times*, *Atlantic Monthly*, and *National Geographic*. Raised in Columbia, Missouri, he lives in Beijing.

River Town

Two Years on the Yangtze

PETER HESSLER

Perennial
An Imprint of HarperCollins*Publishers*

A hardcover edition of this book was published in 2001 by HarperCollins Publishers.

First Perennial edition published 2002.

Book Design by Nancy B. Field

Chinese Calligraphy by Dai Xiaohong

Map Design by Annie Lee

The Library of Congress has catalogued the hardcover edition as follows:

Hessler, Peter.
River town: two years on the Yangtze / Peter Hessler.—1st ed.
p. cm.
ISBN 0-06-019544-4
1. Fuling (Sichuan Sheng, China)—Description and travel. 2. Hessler, Peter, 1969– —Journeys—China—Fuling (Sichuan Sheng). I. Title.
DS796.F855 H47 2001
915.1'38—dc21 00-049872

ISBN 0-06-095374-8 (pbk.)

02 03 04 05 06 ❖/RRD 10 9 8 7 6 5 4

for my parents

CONTENTS

AUTHOR'S NOTE

THE CHAPTERS OF THIS BOOK describe my life in Fuling, while the interspersed sketches focus on the local landscape, its history, and the people. All of these sketches were written while I still lived there, and I've used this structure to give the reader some sense of the two roles that a foreigner plays in a town like Fuling. Sometimes I was an observer, while at other moments I was very much involved in local life, and this combination of distance and intimacy was part of what shaped my two years in Sichuan.

A few of the characters' names and other identifying features have been changed in cases where the subject matter is sensitive. I've relied on the standard *pinyin* romanization for most of the Chinese names and words, with exceptions for a few well-known names such as Yangtze and Hong Kong.

This isn't a book about China. It's about a certain small part of China at a certain brief period in time, and my hope has been to capture the richness of both the moment and the place. The place I know well—the murky Yangtze, the green well-worked mountains—but the moment is more difficult to define. Fuling was situated midriver both geographically and historically, and sometimes it was hard to see where things came from and where they were going. But the town and its people were always full of life and energy and hope, which in the end is my subject. Rather than an inquiry into a source or a destination, this is an account of what it was like to spend two years in the heart of the great river's current.

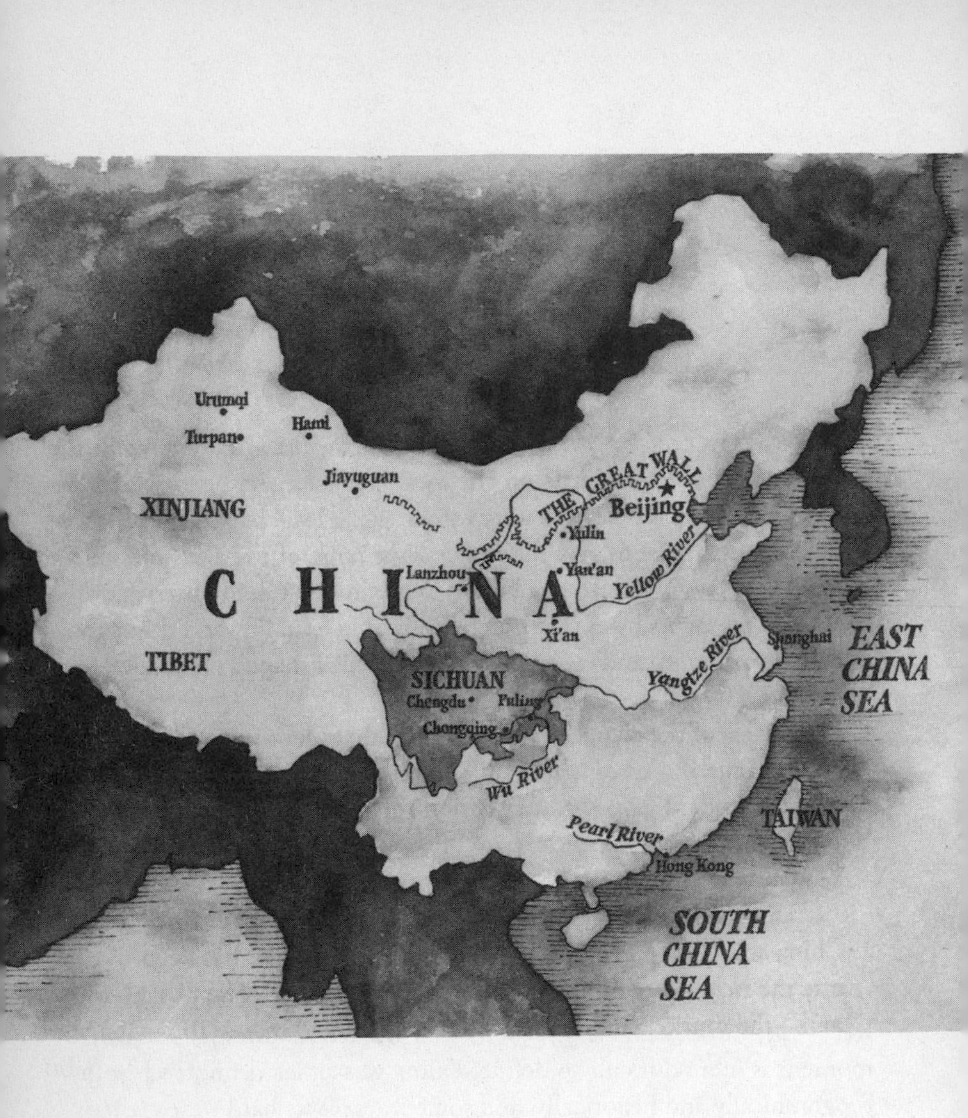
Urumqi
Turpan
Hami
Jiayuguan
XINJIANG
THE GREAT WALL
Beijing
Yulin
Yan'an
Yellow River
Lanzhou
CHINA
Xi'an
TIBET
SICHUAN
Chengdu
Fuling
Chongqing
Wu River
Yangtze River
Shanghai
EAST CHINA SEA
TAIWAN
Pearl River
Hong Kong
SOUTH CHINA SEA

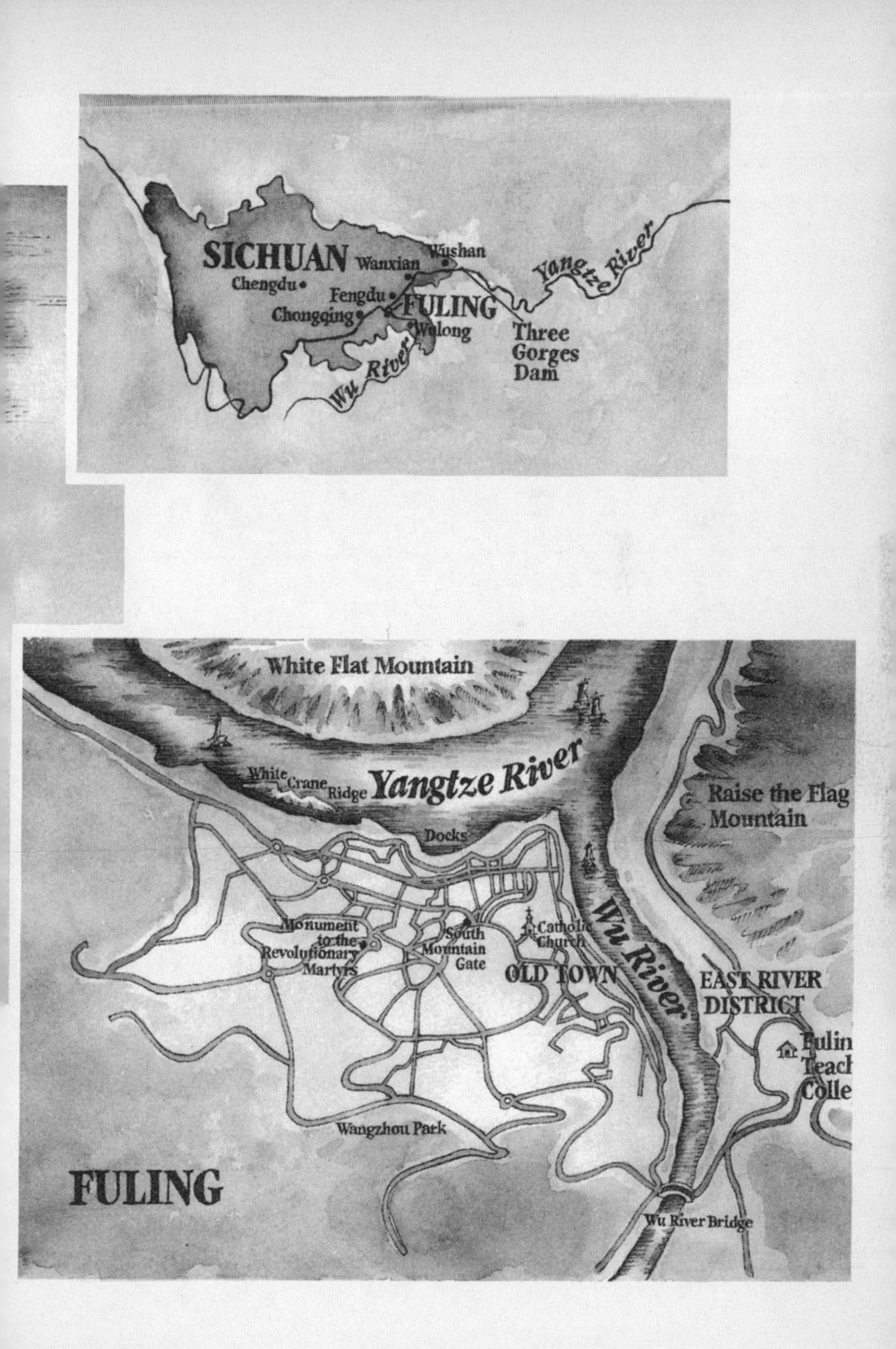
SICHUAN
Chengdu
Wanxian
Wushan
Fengdu
FULING
Chongqing
Wulong
Wu River
Yangtze River
Three
Gorges
Dam
White Flat Mountain
White Crane Ridge
Yangtze River
Raise the Flag
Mountain
Docks
Monument
to the
Revolutionary
Martyrs
South
Mountain
Gate
Catholic
Church
OLD TOWN
Wu River
EAST RIVER
DISTRICT
Fulin
Teach
Colle
Wangzhou Park
FULING
Wu River Bridge

PART · I

CHAPTER ONE

Downstream

I CAME TO FULING on the slow boat downstream from Chongqing. It was a warm, clear night at the end of August in 1996—stars flickering above the Yangtze River, their light too faint to reflect off the black water. A car from the college drove us along the narrow streets that twisted up from the docks. The city rushed past, dim and strange under the stars.

There were two of us. We had been sent to work as teachers, and both of us were young: I was twenty-seven and Adam Meier was twenty-two. We had heard almost nothing about Fuling. I knew that part of the city would be flooded by the new Three Gorges Dam, and I knew that for many years Fuling had been closed to outsiders. Other than that I had been told very little.

No Americans had lived there for half a century. Later, I would meet older people in town who remembered some American residents in the 1940s, before the 1949 Communist Liberation, but such memories were always vague. When we arrived, there was one other foreigner, a German who was spending a semester teaching at a local high school. But we met him only once, and he left not long after we settled in. After that we were the only foreigners in town. The population was about 200,000, which made it a small city by Chinese standards.

There was no railroad in Fuling. It had always been a poor part of Sichuan province and the roads were bad. To go anywhere you took the boat, but mostly you didn't go anywhere. For the next two years the city was my home.

A WEEK AFTER WE ARRIVED, everybody in the college gathered at the front gate. A group of students and teachers had spent the summer walking from Fuling to Yan'an, the former revolutionary base in northern Shaanxi province, and now they were returning to school.

It was the sixtieth anniversary of the Long March, the six-thousand-mile trek that the Red Army had made during the most critical part of the civil war, when the Kuomintang was on the verge of destroying Mao Zedong's forces. Against all odds the Communists had marched to safety, over the mountains and deserts of western China, and from Yan'an they had steadily built their strength until at last their revolution carried the nation, driving the Kuomintang to Taiwan.

All semester there were special events in the college to commemorate the anniversary of the march. The students took classes on the history of the Long March, they wrote essays about the Long March, and in December there was a Long March Singing Contest. For the Long March Singing Contest, all of the departments practiced their songs for weeks and then performed in the auditorium. Many of the songs were the same, because the musical potential of the Long March is limited, which made the judging difficult. It was also confusing because costumes were in short supply and so they were shared, like the songs. The history department would perform, resplendent in clean white shirts and red ties, and then they would go offstage and quickly give their shirts and ties to the politics department, who would get dressed, rush onstage, and sing the same song that had just been sung. By the end of the evening the shirts were stained with sweat and everybody in the audience knew all the songs. The music department won, as they always did, and English was near the back. The English department never won any of the college's contests. There aren't any English songs about the Long March.

But the summer walk to Yan'an was not a contest, and the return of the Fuling group was by far the biggest event of the Long March season. They had walked more than a thousand miles, all of it in the brutal heat of the Chinese summer, and in the end only sixteen had made it. Thirteen were students, and two were teachers: the Chinese department's Communist Party Secretary and the math department's Assistant Political Adviser. There was also a lower-level administrator, who had burst into tears in the middle of the walk and gained a measure of local fame for his perseverance. All of the participants were men. Some of the women students had wanted to come along, but the college had decided that the Long March was not for girls.

A week before the assembly, President Li, the head of the college, had traveled to Xi'an to meet the marching students, because at the finish of the trek they had run into trouble.

"The students have some kind of problem," said Dean Fu Muyou, the head of the English department, when I asked him what had happened. "I think they probably have no money left." And it was true—they had run out of cash, despite their sponsorship by Magnificent Sound cigarettes, the Fuling tobacco company. It struck me as a particularly appropriate way to honor the history of Chinese Communism, to march a thousand miles and end up bankrupt in Yan'an.

But President Li had been able to bail them out, and now the entire student body of the college met in the plaza near the front gate. It was a small teachers college with an enrollment of two thousand students, and it had been opened in 1977, one of many that were founded after the 1966-1976 Cultural Revolution had destroyed much of China's education system. On the spectrum of Chinese higher education, this type of teachers college was near the bottom. Courses took three years and the degree was considered lower than a bachelor's, and nearly all of the students came from peasant homes in the countryside of Sichuan province. After graduation they returned to their hometowns, where they became teachers in rural middle schools.

For many of the students, especially the freshmen, the college was an exciting place. Campus was just across the Wu River from the main city of Fuling, and few of the students had ever lived near a city that large. The college had movies, competitions, and dances on the weekends. Often there were political rallies and assemblies like the one to welcome the Long Marchers, and the students buzzed with anticipation as they milled around the plaza.

A group of eight women students stood at attention near the gate. They wore white blouses and black skirts, and across their chests were red sashes emblazoned with the name of the college. They were known as Hospitality Girls, and they had been carefully selected from the student body. All of the Hospitality Girls were tall and beautiful, and none of them smiled. They represented the college at official functions, standing in perfect formation, walking gracefully, pouring tea for dignitaries.

That was something else I had heard about Fuling: its women had a reputation for being beautiful. At least that's what I had been told in my Chinese class in Chengdu. One of my teachers was from Manchuria, a wisp of a woman with high cheekbones who had a gentle, skittish way of speaking. Even in summer she clutched a bottle of tea in both hands as if for warmth. Her name was Teacher Shang, and though she had never been to Fuling she said with conviction that the women there would be beautiful.

"It's because of the river and the mountains," she said. "All places with mountains and water have beautiful women."

And in Chengdu I had met a Fuling native who told me the same thing. "But sometimes the people there have bad tempers," she warned. "That's because it's so hot, and because they have mountains there." I often heard remarks like this, and they suggested that the Chinese saw their landscapes differently than outsiders did. I looked at the terraced hills and noticed how the people had changed the earth, taming it into dizzying staircases of rice paddies; but the Chinese looked at the people and saw how they had been shaped by the land. During my early days at the college I sometimes thought about this, especially since nearly all of my students had grown up close to the earth, and I wondered how the rugged Sichuan landscape had affected them. And at the same time I wondered what it would do to me in two years.

THE FULING MAYOR was the first to arrive. He was chauffeured to the college gate in a black Audi, and he stepped out of the car and waved briefly to the students' applause. The local TV news was there and they filmed him, a short pudgy man puffing in the September heat. Quickly he walked across the plaza and greeted Adam and me, shaking our hands and welcoming us to the city.

That was often the first thing that happened at events we attended in Fuling—the new Americans were greeted. On the day of the Long March rally we had been on our way to a hike, dressed casually in shorts and T-shirts, and we had stopped by out of curiosity. It was a foolish mistake to attend something of that sort without dressing appropriately, and we should have known better, because already we were learning that it was difficult to watch anything without becoming the center of attention.

Patriotic music blared from the campus loudspeakers as the Long Marchers arrived. They wore white T-shirts and camouflage fatigues. They were unshaven. Old canvas military packs hung from their shoulders. The leader carried a faded red banner that bore the name of the college and Magnificent Sound cigarettes, and he marched behind the Hospitality Girls, who were divided into two rows of four, walking in step, their heads steady, eyes straight ahead, arms swinging sharply. The rest of the Long Marchers followed in single file, smiling proudly and waving to the crowd. Everybody applauded, and the audience followed the procession into the auditorium, where a banner proclaimed:

Warmly Welcome the Fuling Teachers College Magnificent Sound Cigarette Ten-Thousand-Mile Long March Team as They Return from Victory!

Adam and I ducked into seats at the back of the auditorium, hoping to avoid attention. The students around us murmured and turned to stare. The attention spread, and soon everybody in the auditorium was craning their necks to see us—sinking in our chairs, baseball hats pulled low over our faces—and in a moment Vice President Dou was leading us onto the stage. Really he had no choice; otherwise the audience's attention would have been divided. This was one reason why we were so often incorporated into local events: it was a simple way to make sure people watched.

We were seated alongside the mayor and the Communist Party Secretary and the other cadres. The crowd roared as we took our seats; the Long Marchers applauded. The Hospitality Girls served us tea. I kept my head down and tried to hide my bare legs beneath the table. The cadres gave their speeches, praising the Long Marchers and reminding the crowd of the great history that was being honored. The speeches were delivered forcefully, like old films of dictators, and none of the speakers was better than Vice President Dou. He was a tiny man in his fifties who weighed perhaps 115 pounds, and there was a sparrowlike quality to his thin chest and delicate light-boned arms. But he worked the microphone brilliantly—at first softly, calmly, like a lecturer talking to a group of children; now louder, slowly quickening the gestures, a slender hand waving out over the crowd, almost as if scolding them; and finally he was shouting, arms pumping, eyes flashing, loudspeakers booming, the speaker and his audience now equal, united as comrades, patriots, servants of humanity; the crowd rising and erupting into cheers and a mad rush of applause.

I heard him say Adam's and my Chinese names, Mei Erkang and He Wei, and he announced that we had been sent to Fuling by the U.S.-China Friendship Volunteers, which was the Chinese term for Peace Corps. The crowd roared again—all of us were comrades now, together serving the people, building the country—and the Long Marchers stood proudly as each was pinned on the chest by a dignitary bearing a ribbon and a red plastic flower. Somebody handed me a flower and a ribbon; somebody else pointed me toward a Long Marcher waiting at the front of the stage. He smiled, bowed, and shook my hand fervently. I apologized and pinned him as quickly as possible, hoping to minimize the limelight on my shorts, but the crowd cheered again and I waved, the applause rising once more. I sat down, my face hot.

After the ceremony they took a photograph to commemorate the event. In the picture, the Long Marchers and the cadres are standing proudly in three rows, carefully spaced, and the faded red banner is unfurled in the style of the old revolutionary units. The Fuling Long Marchers wear clean white T-shirts and red ribbons on their chests. They are not smiling. The most important cadres stand in the front row, along with Adam and me. Vice President Dou and Communist Party Secretary Wei are smiling slightly while we grin in embarrassment. Adam is wearing sandals and I have on an old gray T-shirt, and our bare legs interrupt the row of neat trousers. None of the other cadres is smiling. There are no women in the photograph.

TWO YEARS LATER, after I returned to America, I would show that picture to friends and try to tell the story. But where to begin? To explain why the post-Cultural Revolution college was honoring the Long March was as difficult as telling how the mountains had been turned into terraces. Finally I would say: This was a political assembly at our college, and our participation was a surprise, because in most parts of the world Peace Corps volunteers are not welcomed with Communist Party rallies. And I left it at that—that was my story of the photograph.

Of course, none of it was that simple. I was a Peace Corps volunteer but I wasn't; China was Communist but it wasn't. Nothing was quite what it seemed, and that was how life went in those early days, everything uncertain and half a step off.

In Chinese, Peace Corps was *Heping Dui,* and there was more to those three simple characters than met the eye. During the Cultural Revolution, when anti-American propaganda reached a climax, the Chinese government had said much about the Peace Corps—that it was in league with the CIA, that it was an agent of Western imperialism, that America sent its young people overseas so their idealism would influence the Third World toward Capitalism (the toughest job you'll ever love). These things were no longer said, but the echoes still remained, and the word was hopelessly tainted. But the Chinese language, like the people, had learned to shift with the political winds, and another title was found when the Peace Corps came to China in 1993—*Meizhong Youhou Zhiyuanzhe,* U.S.-China Friendship Volunteers. The characters were more complicated but the connotations infinitely simpler. College authorities instructed our students never to use the term "Peace Corps," in English or Chinese, and most of them didn't. And so with a euphemism for a job title, I came to teach at a college that was built on the ashes of the Cultural Revolution, where history was never far away and politics everywhere you looked.

It was the Friendship that terrified all of us at the beginning. That was the part of the title that was difficult to translate or interpret. The college had had three foreign teachers the year before, an elderly Australian couple and a middle-aged man from Mexico, but that had been simpler because they were there for less than a year and rarely strayed far from campus. We were different—we were young, we were planning to live in Fuling for two years, and we had been sent by the American government as part of the third group of Peace Corps volunteers to come to China. The college gave us apartments in its best building, where the Communist Party Secretary and the other most important cadres lived, and for weeks they banqueted us almost every other night. There was a protocol to these affairs. We would sit down to a table full of Chinese appetizers—cashews, dried beef, string beans, lotus root—and often Teacher Han would make an announcement. He was the interim representative of the college *waiban,* or foreign affairs office, and he was twenty-seven years old. He had the best spoken English in the college, but he was an uneasy young man in a new position of authority. He asked us to call him Albert.

One evening in the first week, he turned to us before the banquet had begun.

"The college has decided," he said, "to buy you telephones that can call outside the college. You will be able to call anywhere in China."

We protested—it wasn't necessary, phones were expensive, volunteers at other colleges didn't have them. He waved us off. "Not a problem," he said. "Otherwise it's not convenient for you." Adam and I looked at each other and shrugged. We thanked him, and everybody began to eat, and the next day repairmen appeared to install our telephones.

A few days later there was another banquet, another announcement. "The college has decided," Albert said, "that it will buy Adam a washing machine."

"I already have one in my apartment," I said. "We can share that one—there's no need to waste money."

"It is inconvenient," Albert said. "The college has decided." Again our protests were ignored. And so we began to eat, and the next morning a new washing machine appeared at Adam's door.

A few days later, Adam was playing cards with some of the English department faculty members, and Party Secretary Zhang Yan mentioned that the college had received our résumés and biographical information from the Peace Corps.

"I see that you play tennis," said Party Secretary Zhang. "You must play very well."

Adam had coached at a tennis camp during college summers, and he was quick to shake his head. "I don't play that well," he said. "It's been a long time since I played seriously."

Party Secretary Zhang grinned and picked up his cards. He was a thin, sinewy man with crewcut hair, and it had taken us a week to establish two facts about him: he was the best basketball player on the English department faculty, as well as the best drinker of Chinese *baijiu*, or grain alcohol. He was also the highest-ranking cadre in the department, and as Communist Party Secretary he had authority over academic, disciplinary, and political issues. He was the sort of man who rarely spoke, but when he did speak, things happened. Now he examined his cards, leaned forward, and looked up at Adam.

"The college," he said softly, "has decided to *buy you tennis!*"

He sat back in his chair, waiting for the meaning of the declaration to sink in. But that was the problem—how exactly does one go about buying tennis? For a few moments Adam tried to decide how he should respond.

"That's very kind of the college," he said at last, speaking carefully. "I appreciate that you want to do something for us, but it isn't necessary. You don't have to buy me tennis, Mr. Zhang."

Party Secretary Zhang smiled as he discarded a card.

"Mr. Wei," he said, "is concerned that you might want to play tennis. He wants to make sure that you and Pete are happy."

Mr. Wei was the Party Secretary of the entire college, and as the highest-level Communist Party official on campus he undoubtedly had more important things to do than buy tennis for Peace Corps volunteers. Adam said something to this effect, emphasizing that he was quite happy without tennis. But Party Secretary Zhang was firm.

"It has been decided," he said flatly. "The college will buy you tennis. Now it is time to play cards."

THE NEXT MORNING, tennis did not appear at Adam's doorstep, but he didn't take any chances. He told me about the conversation, and together we made an attempt to communicate to the college, the sort of effort that over the next two years would be made again and again, with mixed results. Often our communication was indirect, and rarely was it simple. Sometimes it resulted in exactly the opposite of what we wanted.

We talked with Albert, we talked again with Party Secretary

Zhang, and we talked with Dean Fu and other English department faculty members. We said that tennis was very expensive, and I didn't know how to play it, and in fact Adam didn't even like it anymore. He had outgrown it in college and if anything he was looking forward to having a nice long break from tennis. It was a lousy game. Basketball was much better, and so was soccer. Tennis was a game of the exploiting classes. Actually, we never went quite that far, but we tried everything else, and for a week we campaigned steadily against the buying of tennis.

Next to our apartment building was a croquet court. It was without a doubt the nicest spot on campus, and perhaps it was the most peaceful patch of earth I ever saw in China. In a crowded country there weren't many places like that—a spot where the land was used for nothing but enjoyment. A ring of trees shaded the borders, and the packed dirt surface was perfectly smooth. It was well tended, but mostly it was smooth and beautiful because it was well played. Every morning, the retired teachers and workers in the college met in the croquet court, where they played all day long, with a break for lunch. They were impossibly good. They were so good that it almost didn't seem competitive—the ball went where it was intended to go, the way a magician's cards move according to the silent harmony of routine and skill. It was a daily exhibition, a game of trick shots; the retirees were artists—they had taken croquet to an entirely new level. And the whole affair was almost the exact same size as a tennis court.

For the first few weeks that was our great fear. Our balconies overlooked the court, and every morning we gazed out, afraid to see workers, shovels, picks, backhoes, dynamite—whatever was involved in the buying of tennis, we were deeply and sincerely afraid of it. The uncertainty was the worst part; it seemed an abstract notion, to buy tennis, but at the same time Fuling was clearly the sort of place where a great deal of work could be put into turning the abstract into reality. A glance at the plans for the Three Gorges Dam was enough to prove that.

But in the end tennis was not bought in Fuling. The banquets ended after four weeks. Within a month the college stopped buying things for our apartments. It wasn't long before we were complaining like spoiled children that our needs were neglected, but we grumbled lightly and to ourselves, high above campus in our cadres' apartments.

THE CROQUET SOUNDS drifted up to my apartment in the mornings—the gentle knock of the ball, the sound of shuffled footsteps on hard dirt, the soft chatter and laughter of the retirees as they played without hurry. These were some of the most soothing sounds I had ever heard, and often I sat out on my balcony and simply listened, the croquet sounds backed by the unsteady hum of the cicadas and the noise of the Wu River. Boat horns echoed across the narrow river valley, and motors sputtered against the current, and barges clanked as they unloaded sand onto rumbling trucks at the water's edge. A mile from my apartment, the Wu died in the brown rush of the Yangtze, and often I could hear a lonely horn booming out from the big river.

At the beginning, Fuling was mostly sounds to me. It was a loud city, but also the noises were different from anything I had known before—the steady clinking of chisels at construction sites, the crush of rock broken with a sledgehammer: these were the sounds of a place where much of the work was still done by hand. And it was the first time I had lived next to a river, listening to the boat noises and the way they echoed up and down the valley.

My apartment was on the top floor of a building high on a hill above the Wu River. It was a pretty river, fast and clean, and it ran from the wild southern mountains of Guizhou province. Across the Wu River was the main city of Fuling, a tangle of blocky concrete buildings rising up the hillside. Everywhere I looked, the hills were steep, especially due north, where the heavy shape of White Flat Mountain loomed sheer above the junction of the two rivers.

That was the view from my aerie—high on the sixth floor, far above the rivers and their town. Nothing blocked my view, which was another reason I heard so much. Long before the croquet sounds began every morning, I heard the rooster behind the building start to crow, and I heard the morning alarm go off all over campus at six o'clock. I heard the students as they jogged groggily to the small road that ran through campus, where they did their morning exercises. The exercise music started shortly after six, broadcast over the loudspeakers—morning-cheerful, workout-repetitive music, the same day after day. After exercises there were announcements, and propaganda, and the sound of students getting their breakfast; and then there were the bells for morning class and the first soft echoes rising up from the croquet court.

I lived next to the main teaching building and I heard those sounds as well. I heard students repeating their lessons, because in Fuling much was learned by rote. That was also a soothing sound; there was something satisfying about hearing their voices rise and fall in unison as they recited lessons that all of them had learned. And I liked hearing the teachers' voices once class started, and the jumbled noise of the ten-minute breaks, and the electronic bells and the eager rush of the lunch hour.

None of these noises bothered me. The early sounds woke me but that was fine, because they were part of the routine of the college and hearing them made me feel as if I were also in step. I wasn't, of course—and in some ways I never fell in. But during those early weeks I would have felt even more disjointed if it hadn't been for the steady routines that surrounded me.

Everything followed a strict timetable. There was the morning routine—the exercises, the bells, the classes—and often in the afternoons there was the whisk of brooms as the students did their mandatory campus cleaning. On Mondays and Thursdays they cleaned their classrooms. Sunday nights were political meetings, when the students gathered to give speeches and sing songs. Sometimes they sang patriotic anthems, but mostly they sang love songs, their voices echoing across the nighttime campus.

At the start of the year, the freshmen had military training. Each class formed a regiment, boys and girls together, and People's Liberation Army soldiers came to teach them how to salute, goose-step, execute turns, and stand at attention. During their military training they also learned songs—that seemed to be a way to make Communism fun. Our students were always singing patriotic songs for one organization or another.

For their military training, the freshmen wore the class uniform, which consisted of powder-blue Adidas-knockoff sweat suits. Their bright uniforms seemed incongruous next to the military stiffness of the camouflaged instructors, and so did the students. They were in their early twenties but most looked younger, fresh off the farm, and they cowered under the leaders' instructions. On hot days some of them fainted and were carried to the shade while the rest of the class continued goose-stepping. At the end of the two-week training, when they had their steps down, they marched out to the rifle range in a deep corner of Mo Pan Valley, where, as a punctuation to their initiation, they blew the hell out of targets with high-powered rifles. I heard that as well, the bursts of gunfire drowning out the sounds of the Wu River.

Campus quieted early at night. The dormitory lights went out at eleven o'clock sharp—all of them at once, a row of buildings going black as the electricity was cut. Sometimes I sat out on my balcony at night, watching the lights go out, and again there was something soothing about the regularity of it all.

From my balcony the city was beautiful at night. During the day Fuling was a dirty river town, and you could see that much of it had been built too quickly, but at night all of the flaws disappeared. It was only water and lights—the brilliant lights and the dark water, the deep black mirror of the Wu River streaked with red and yellow and white. Sometimes a night boat slipped upriver, steadily pushing a triangle of light ahead of its prow, the motor coughcoughcoughing in the darkness of the valley. And every half hour or so there would be a big passenger boat on the Yangtze, a bright band of lights floating past in majestic silence.

I didn't really understand any of the routines. I didn't know where the boats were going and I didn't know why the college was regulated the way it was. They played croquet differently than we do in America, but I never bothered to figure out the Fuling rules. I simply liked their playing every day—the regularity was what mattered. Nor did I ever think much about the military training, until I read one of my students' journal as she described a typical afternoon in the college:

> It's sunny, the first year students are doing their military training. They walked again and again. Although the sweat is dropping down from their head, they can't stop without the permission of their leader.
>
> Of course, in this way, they know how hard the army life is. Their spirits can be discouraged.
>
> Everyone should have a strong sense of patriotism, especially the college students. Our state costs a lot of money to educate them. They should be faithful to their motherland. Army force is a symbol of the power of a country, so it's necessary to have some knowledge about military. In 1989, there was a student movement in Beijing. For the

> youth, their thoughts don't ripe and they don't have their own ideas, so the surroundings can influence them easily. Also they can't tell the truth for the fault. Where there is exciting thing, they turn up. After the movement, our state decides to have military training in college, to make them understand that it is not easy to obtain our present life.

That was what I had actually been hearing—the marching and the distant gunshots were the echoes of the Tiananmen Square protests. I realized that there was more to the routines of the college than I had first imagined, and after that I began to listen more carefully to the sounds that filtered up to my aerie high above the Wu River.

MUCH OF WHAT I LEARNED in the early days was from the students. My Chinese wasn't yet good enough to talk with the people in town, which made the city overwhelming—a mess of miscommunication. And so I listened to my students, reading what they wrote in their journals for class, and parts of Fuling slowly began to draw into focus.

The first thing I saw was myself and Adam. This was intimidating, because never in my life had I been watched so closely that every action was replayed and evaluated. Everything we did was talked and written about; every quirk or habit was laid bare. Students wrote about the way I always carried a water bottle to class; they wrote about how I paced the classroom as I taught; they wrote about my laugh, which they found ridiculous. They wrote about my foreign nose, which impressed them as impossibly long and straight, and many of them wrote about my blue eyes. This was perhaps the strangest detail of all, because my eyes are hazel—but my students had read that foreigners had blue eyes, and they saw what they wanted to see.

Mostly they wanted to see all of the outside world condensed into these two young *waiguoren,* which was what foreigners were called in Fuling—"people from outside the country." One afternoon, Adam and I threw a Frisbee around the front plaza after dinner, and by the next day, when I read one student's journal, the lazy game had become Olympian:

When I was writing my composition, someone shouted at the classes: 'Pete and Adam are playing Frisbee!' At once, I put down my pen and rushed out the classroom. Really, they are! I wanted to see it clearly and didn't want to miss any scene. I ran into the classroom and put the glasses on my nose, then dashed to the classroom again. I can see it clearly now! . . . The two sports men stood far away from Frisbee each other and began to play. How wonderful it looked! The Frisbee was like a red fire, flying person to person between the two men. I have seen it for a long time. Foreigners are so versatile.

Other descriptions were less heroic. My favorite was written by a student named Richard, in an essay entitled "Why Americans Are So Casual":

I'm a Chinese. As we all know, the Chinese nation is a rather conservative nation. So many of us have conservative thinking in some degree. I don't know whether it is bad or good.

Our foreign language teachers—Peter and Adam—came to teach us this term. It provides a good opportunity of understanding the American way of life. In my opinion, they are more casual than us Chinese people. Why do I think so? I'll give you some facts to explain this.

For example, when Mr. Hessler is having class, he can scratch himself casually without paying attention to what others may say. He dresses up casually, usually with his belt dropping and dangling. But, to tell you the truth, it isn't consider a good manner in China, especially in old people's eyes. In my opinion, I think it is very natural.

Last week, when Miss Thompson [another Peace Corps volunteer who visited Fuling] gave us a lecture on the American election, she took off her woolen sweater and tied it to her waist. To us Chinese people, it's almost unimaginable. How can a teacher do that when she/he is having a lesson! But thanks goodness, we major in English and know something about America, it didn't surprise us. But if other people saw this, they might can't believe their own eyes.

It was an easy place to make mistakes, and plenty were made. But the locals tended to be forgiving—usually they gave us a hint, a nudge in the right direction. During the first week of class, Adam had his students introduce themselves, and a girl named Keller stood up. She told the name of her hometown, and she explained that she had chosen her English name in honor of Helen Keller. This was a common pattern; some of them had taken their names from people they admired, which explained why we had a Barbara (from Barbara Bush), an Armstrong (Neil Armstrong), and an idealistic second-year student called Marx. A few had translated their Chinese names directly—House, Yellow, North. There was one boy whose English name was Lazy. "My name is Lazy," he said, on the first day of class. "I am very lazy. I do not like to play basketball or football or do many things. My hobbies are sleeping."

Other names made less sense. There was a Soddy, a Sanlee, a Ker. Some were simply unfortunate: a very small boy called Pen, a very pretty girl named Coconut. One boy was called Daisy, a name that greatly dismayed Dean Fu. The dean was a handsome man with blue-black hair, and he was our main liaison with the English department—a position whose weight of responsibility often gave him a mournful air. He seemed particularly morose when he called me into his office to talk about Daisy.

"That's a girl's name, isn't it?" Dean Fu asked.

"Yes," I said. "Except now in America even girls don't like that name."

"I remember it from *The Great Gatsby,*" Dean Fu said, smiling sadly. As a student his specialty had been American literature, and he was familiar with virtually all of the great twentieth-century novelists. He sighed and shook his head.

"Last year that student had a boy's name," said the dean. "He changed it over the summer. I don't know why."

I didn't know either—I never talked with Daisy about it. He wasn't easy to speak with, and all I ever learned about him was that his lifelong goal of being a soldier had been crushed when the People's Liberation Army turned him down because of bad eyesight. This was a failure that illuminated the mystery of Daisy's existence; he was a tall, taciturn boy with an air of deep sadness, and every day he wore a full camouflage uniform to class. Whether it was consolation or a form of self-punishment, I never knew. I simply liked having a tall camouflaged boy named Daisy sitting in the back of my class, and I never would have asked him to change either his name or his uniform. I didn't tell that to Dean Fu, of course.

But Keller's name was very straightforward. Helen Keller was a common heroine among the students—even some of the boys listed her as a role model, partly because she had had Communist sympathies. On the day that Keller introduced herself, she explained the reasons for her name, and then she smiled.

"Thank you," Adam said. "You have very nice freckles, Keller."

The classroom suddenly became very still. Keller's face fell and she sat down quickly. In the awkward silence Adam floundered for a moment, and then he hurriedly explained that in America freckles are considered attractive. Which, it turned out, is not the case in China—his compliment was like saying "You have a nice birthmark." But there was nothing to do except continue the lesson, and in a few minutes the awkwardness had passed.

But it wasn't forgotten. A week later two students mentioned the incident in their journals, trying, in the Chinese way, to communicate the message indirectly:

> I have heard of that there are so many American women have freckles on their faces. In China, women especially girls who have freckles on their faces do not like other people to mention it. It's bad manner. I want to know what do the American women who have freckles think of it?

> Some of their [the foreign teachers'] teaching methods are acceptable. . . . We should affirm their achievements. But sometimes they also make some students embarassed due to their absence of Chinese custom. We Chinese have our own taboos. We never make frivolous remarks about people's appearanc. But one of these two American teachers broke this taboo once in class. But I think, with the time on, up their knowledge of Chinese daily life, would some embarransements be avoided.

AND SO WE BUMBLED ON. We were naive, of course—we trusted good intentions and hard work, and we thought that soon we would slip into the routines of the city without much problem. But like most parts of the country, Fuling had a complicated past, and I had no real understanding of this history, regardless of how many books I had read about the Great Leap Forward and the Cultural Revolution.

More specifically, I didn't recognize what it meant for this particular part of China to finally have American residents. Later I would learn that much of the local industry had been moved here from Shanghai as a direct result of the American nuclear threat in the 1950s and 1960s, when Mao Zedong dispersed China's military factories throughout the remote mountains of the southwest. It was inevitable that such a past would have some effect on the way locals viewed us, but we knew nothing about this chapter in history.

Probably it would have been harder if we had known more. One of my favorite students was a girl named Anne, whose family lived on the ground floor of our building. Her father was a math professor, the highest-ranking faculty member on campus, and this was an honor that had earned him a place in our exclusive building. It had also earned him a job in a remote Sichuan coal mine for eight years of the Cultural Revolution. Like so many other talented Chinese, he had been banished as an intellectual, or *chou laojiu,* "the Old Stinking Ninth", the lowest of the low, the ones who could be saved only by the basest and most tedious labor.

Those years seemed to sit lightly on Professor Liang—he was a cheerful man, undoubtedly happy to have been politically rehabilitated. Even in the coal mine he had made the best of the situation, winning the locals' admiration by showing them how to balance their accounts. But I thought that perhaps the past had somehow affected his daughter more, even though she had not lived through his experience. She was one of the brightest students in the class, and also one of the few who stood apart. Her ideas were different—she liked being alone, and she made up her own mind; she was capable of veering away from the political cant that most of them rehashed. Of all my students, I expected her to be the most open-minded to me as a foreigner. And yet after her graduation she wrote a letter and explained honestly how it had been at the beginning:

> Not long after you became my teacher, I read a piece of old news comment that said Mr. Clinton took presidency, one of the reasons

[why the Americans had elected him] was that he would take stronger measure on China. Those days, I hated to see you and Mr. Meier.

In the first few months I never would have guessed that such feelings were so strong, although there were occasional signs that my students still viewed the outside world with mistrust. I treated these moments as isolated incidents—I responded, usually gently, and then I tried to think no more about it. One day a female student named Catherine wrote about the differences between women in the East and the West:

> People in the west like the girl who is elegant or the girl who is sexuality? But I always heard a view that girl in the east is famous for her elegance and the girl in the west is famous for her sexuality.
>
> The girls in China, most of them are elegant, refined, and kind. They always do something following rules. It's the Chinese tradition.
>
> But the girls in the west are very open to outside. They can marry anyone and get divorced whenever. Don't mind the appraise of others. They can do everything that she wants to do, not concern about whether it's wrong or right. They lead a loose life.
>
> I think I like the statue and virtue of the girl in the east. They are elegant, refined.

Catherine was a lovely girl, a quiet student with eager eyes and a friendly smile, and I couldn't be harsh. Below her journal entry, I simply wrote that in America I had three sisters—and I left it at that. In Fuling that sort of communication was enough; a day later she apologized.

She wrote about being "open," which was a watershed issue for the people in Fuling, and, in turn, for all of China. People everywhere talked about *Gaige Kaifang,* Reform and Opening, which included both increased contact with the outside world and the Capitalist-style economic reforms that Deng Xiaoping had initiated in 1978. To a certain degree, Reform and Opening was similar to the Russian concepts of Perestroika and Glasnost, with one critical difference: the Chinese term lacked an explicit political component, as the country's leaders had no intention of opening the political system in the manner of Gorbachev. Nevertheless, Reform and Opening resulted in massive social changes, ranging from increased mobility between regions to new styles and attitudes that were influenced by foreign cultures. Most Chinese people saw these as positive developments, because they were accompanied by rising living standards, but there were still quiet fears that lurked in people's minds. And simply having the first American teachers in Fuling was enough to trigger these uncertainties.

I was too overwhelmed to dwell on such matters during that first semester. I was studying Chinese, preparing lessons, and writing in my journal; I didn't have time to worry about the political implications of our arrival. But still there were moments that shook me—like the time I read part of an entry in a student journal, three short sentences that echoed in my mind long after the grading was finished:

> Today's China has been opened to the foreign countries. The criminals have been increased. It's important to maintain public order.

NONE OF THAT seemed too important in the early months. I copied the interesting remarks in my journal, and then I moved on. I sensed that I simply couldn't judge the students for anything they thought, at least in the beginning. Their backgrounds were too far removed from what I had known before coming to Fuling, and, like all young Chinese, they were surrounded by the aura of a troubled past. It was easy to forget this—it was easy to laugh at their ridiculous names, or smile at their childlike shyness, and it was easy to dismiss them as simple young people from the simplicity of the countryside. But of course nothing was farther from the truth—the Sichuan countryside is not simple, and my students had known things that I had never imagined. Even if appearances were deceiving, the truth always came through in the way they wrote about their homes and families:

> In real life, I think my father is a hero. Once he told us his past. When he was about ten years old, his elder brother and sisters had been married and worked far from home. At that time, China was following a road of collectivization, and people were taking a collective productive labour. They couldn't have their own property.
>
> Before those days, my grandparents made a lot of property through hard work, but when the collective productive labour began, the

> property of my family were all destroyed by the "revolution group." They said all things belonged to the public, then they took some good things away. My grandma wanted to stop them, but failed. They hanged up and beat her and refused to give her something to eat. Later she died from starving, then they forced my father to weed in water field in winter. My father didn't complain, just worked hard.

Most of their grandmothers had had bound feet; few of their grandfathers had been able to read. Their parents had come of age during one of the most horrible periods in Chinese history. All of this affected my students and shaped who they were, but at the same time they were something entirely different. They were educated, and although few of them had much money, they weren't desperately poor. They could buy things—fashionable clothes, books, radios. They went to college. They had studied English for seven years. They had seen great changes, both political and economic. Perhaps by my standards they were politically brainwashed, but compared to the past they were remarkably free.

They were a watershed generation, in the same way that "opening" was a watershed issue for China. I sensed that a great deal depended on the people of this age group—in some ways it was like the American generation of my parents, who grew up on stories of the Depression and World War II, and who built the America of today, for better or worse. There was the same sense of future glory in China, but the past was far more brutal than anything that had ever happened in America, which complicated things. My students had difficulty criticizing anything Chinese, and this was not surprising, because they were constantly being indoctrinated by the Communist Party. Occasionally some of my better students wrote about China with a mixture of cool accuracy and blind optimism that gave me some sense of how wonderful and difficult it was to be a young Chinese:

> I think, in the history of the People's Republic of China, there are two great men: Mao Zedong and Deng Xiaoping. We should mention the two men if we want to point out the difference between two generations' views on China.
>
> When my parents were at my age, China wasn't rich. Even the people couldn't live the type of dressing warmly and eating there fill. The

situation was very hard at that time. Because of lack of experience, the leaders of China didn't solve some questions very well. Maybe, that period was the hardest within the progress of China. But, there is a fact that is beyond all question: it was Mao Zedong and his comrades that founded the People's Republic of China, and brought the Chinese people independence and democracy which is a long cherished goal for the Chinese. So, people admired him from the bottom of their heart. This kind of admiration led to people's profound love to China to a great extent. My parents did the same. It was the Great Cultural Revolution then; there were many wrong things in life. But they thought China was the best and perfect country and had splendid position. In their minds, China would reach its great goal only by performing planned economy because it was a socialist country. Anything about market economy was Right deviation. My parents only did what they were ordered to do and didn't consider whether they were true or false.

Today, when we see those days with our own sight, we'll feel our parents' thoughts and actions are somewhat blind and fanatical. But if we consider that time objectly, I think, we should understand and can understand them. Each generation has its own happiness and sadness. To younger generation, the important thing is understanding instead of criticising. Our elder generation was unlucky; they didn't own a good chance and circumstances to realize their value. But, their spirit, their love to our country set a good example for us.

IT WAS HARD for me to imagine a better job. My students were eager and respectful, and they were bright. The college was not prestigious, but in China less than 2 percent of the population attend any schooling beyond high school, which meant that even Fuling's students were a very select group. In fact I was glad to be at a lower-level school, because there was an unpolished quality to the students that I had never seen before. Everywhere else I had been, education rounded off the edges much earlier—in America, even high school students were cagey, cynical, suspicious. Education was a game and students played it, but in Fuling they hadn't yet reached that point. Their intelligence was still raw—it smelled of the countryside, of sweat and muck, of night soil and ripening rapeseed and everything else that composed the Sichuanese farmland. And in their thoughts were flashes of the land, glimpses of the same sort of hard beauty that surrounded the teachers college, where the campus ended in terraced fields that ran steep up the side of Raise the Flag Mountain.

It shone through brightly in some of them. We had one student named Ker—like so many of the students' English names, his was a puzzle. He was one of the quietest boys in class and he looked like a middle-aged peasant: short, stocky, his face tanned and weathered by the Sichuan sun. He had a peasant's quiet smile, and a peasant's modest politeness, and he had been a peasant until the day the government sent a letter informing him that his examination scores had won him admission to Fuling Teachers College. Now he was twenty-one years old, the youngest student in his section, and one day Adam assigned a fifteen-minute free writing. Ker put his head down and wrote:

> I'm working in the fields. The ox suddenly becomes a machine with an ox head. So I finish my task ahead of time. Because of that I am recommended to be the leader of our town. Then I go to Beijing by air to report my deeds to President Jiang Zemin. He doesn't believe it's true, because he's never seen a machine with an ox head. He orders that I be sent to prison. On my way to prison, my ox appears. It becomes a train with an ox head and . . .
>
> My fortune and my changing ox is closely connected.
>
> Fortunately I get back with the help of the train-like ox. I go into the town government office. The ox, now it is really an ox, follows me and murmurs something. I can't catch what it said. It turns into a computer which looks like an ox head. The screen shows: My young master, you are not suitable for politics. What you should do now is to go to school to learn more knowledge. Especial your English is too poor. Only in this way can you do your job better and live a more happy life . . . .
>
> Perhaps for the ox's advice I will abandoned farmwork for study.

There was a great deal of Sichuan in those two hundred words, and yet it seemed so effortless—but of course there was more to it than met the eye. The first time Adam had assigned a free writing, it had not gone according to plan. He explained to the class that they would have fifteen minutes, and then he told them to "write about anything you want."

The students wrote. At the end of the hour Adam collected their papers. They had written about anything they wanted, and what he had was forty-five shopping lists. I want a new TV, a new dress, a new radio. I want more grammar books. I want my own room. I want a beeper and a cell phone and a car. I want a good job. Some of the students had lists a full page long, every entry numbered and prioritized.

It wasn't exactly what Adam had intended, but nevertheless there was a great deal of Sichuan in those lists as well. The next time, Adam explained very carefully that they should "write about any subject you want to write about."

That worked better. Ker put his head down and wrote. And Adam and I kept plugging away, learning from our mistakes and trying to fit into the local routines.

THE CITY

THERE ARE NO BICYCLES in Fuling. Otherwise it is similar to any other small Chinese city—loud, busy, dirty, crowded; the traffic twisted, the pedestrians jostling each other; shops overstaffed and full of goods, streets covered with propaganda signs; no traffic lights, drivers honking constantly; televisions blaring, people bickering over prices; and along the main streets rows of frightened-looking trees, their leaves gray with coal dust, the same gray dust that covers everything in the city.

There are no bicycles because Fuling is full of steps, and the city is full of steps because it is squeezed close on the mountains that press against the junction of the Wu and Yangtze Rivers. Narrow streets also rise from the riverbanks, switchbacking up the hills, but they are cramped and indirect and too steep for bicycles. Automobile traffic tangles on the sharp corners. And so the long stone staircases are the true boulevards of Fuling, carrying most of its traffic—shoppers descending the stairs, pausing to browse in stores; porters climbing up, shoulders bowed under the weight of crates and bundles.

Virtually every necessary good or service can be found along these stairways and their landings. There are shops and restaurants, cobblers and barbers. One of the lower stairways is lined with Daoist fortune-tellers. Another staircase is home to a group of three dentists who work at a table covered with rusty tools, syringes in mysterious fluids, and pans of cruelly defeated teeth—a sort of crude advertisement. Sometimes a peasant will stop to have his tooth pulled, after haggling over the price, and a crowd will gather to watch. Everything is public. A haircut comes with an audience. The price of any purchase is commented on by the other shoppers who pause as they pass. For medical problems one can sit in the open air and see a traditional Chinese physician, who has a regular stand near the top of one of the stairways. His stand consists of a stool, a box of bottles, and a white sheet with big characters that say:

To Help You Relieve Worries and Solve Problems!
Particular Treatments: Corns, Sluggishness, Black Moles, Ear Checks.
Surgery—No Pain, No Itching, No Bloodletting, No Effects on Your Job!

Fuling is not an easy city. Old people rest on the staircases, panting. To carry anything up the hills is backbreaking work, and so the city is full of porters. They haul their loads on bamboo poles balanced across their shoulders, the same way freight was carried in the south of China in the 1800s, when the English referred to such laborers as "coolies"—from the Chinese *kuli*, or "bitter strength." Here in Fuling, as in all of the eastern Sichuan river towns, the porters are called *Bang-Bang Jun*—the Stick-Stick Army. They have uniforms (the simple blue clothes of the Chinese peasantry), and the weapons of their trade (bamboo poles and loops of cheap rope), and they tend to gather in packs, in companies, in battalions. To bargain with one stick-stick soldier is to bargain with a regiment. Their jobs are difficult enough without cutthroat competition, and they look out for each other; there is no formal union but the informal bond of hard labor is much closer. During midday, when most people rest, the stick-stick soldiers can be seen along the midtown streets, sitting on their poles, smoking, chatting, playing cards; and in their leisure there is an air not so much of relaxation as of a lull in the battle.

Most of them are peasants who have farms in the mountains outside of Fuling, and usually there is a wife or a brother tending the land while they try their luck carrying loads on the docks. There is always an especially heavy flood of stick-stick soldiers during the winter, because that is the light season in the countryside. But never is there any shortage of these men, and there is something eerie in their silent ubiquity. They stand five deep in front of television stores, staring at the wall of screens. If a foreigner eats at a streetside stand, ten stick-stick soldiers will gather to watch. If there is an argument on the docks, they will cluster close, all of them dressed in blue, holding their bamboo poles and listening intently. Occasionally a small variety show will stop in Fuling and pitch its tent on the river flats, fronted by an advertisement featuring more or less undressed dancing girls, and invariably there is a lost regiment of stick-stick soldiers gaping at the marquee. An auto accident is not truly an auto accident unless a company of stick-stick soldiers arrives to gaze at the damage. They are quiet men—even the most grisly wreck sometimes fails to inspire them to words—and they never interfere. They simply watch.

But to see them work is to understand why they so often rest, because in a hard city there is no harder job. For a load they generally make one or two yuan—there are slightly more than eight yuan to the American dollar—and routinely these workers carry more than one hundred pounds up the staircases. They are short, stocky men, their bodies shaped by the hilly city and the nature of their work. In summer, when they go without shirts, you can see where the bamboo poles have burnished the skin along their shoulders like leather. In hot weather they are drenched in sweat; in winter their bodies steam. Below rolled-up trousers their calves bulge as if baseballs have been tied to the backs of their legs.

Fuling is a city of legs—the gnarled calves of a stick-stick soldier, the bowed legs of an old man, the willow-thin ankles of a *xiaojie*, a young woman. You watch your step when climbing the stairways; you keep your head down and look at the legs of the person in front of you. It is possible, and very common, to spend a morning shopping in Fuling and never once look up at the buildings. The city is all steps and legs.

And many of the buildings are not worth looking at. There is still an old section along the banks of the Wu River, where beautiful ancient structures of wood and stone are topped by gray tiled roofs. But this district is shrinking, steadily being replaced by the nondescript modern buildings that already dominate the city. There are a few tall ones, seven or more stories, but they are cheaply made of blue glass and white tile like so many new structures in China. And even if you built a beautiful new building in Fuling, it would quickly fade beneath the gray layers of dust.

The city is different from the land in that, apart from the small old district, there is no sense of the past. To travel through the Sichuan countryside is to feel the history, the years of work that have shaped the land, the sheer weight of humanity on patches of earth that have been worked in the same way for centuries. But Sichuanese cities are often timeless. They look too dirty to be new, and too uniform and ugly to be old. The majority of Fuling's buildings look as if they were dropped here about ten years ago, while in fact the city has existed on the same site for more than three thousand years. Originally it was a capital of the Ba Kingdom, an independent tribe that was conquered by the Chinese, and after that nearly every dynasty left it with a different name, a different administrative center: it was Jixian under the Zhou Dynasty, Fuling under the Han, Jixian under the Jin, Hanping under the Northern Zhou, Liangzhou under the Sui, Fuzhou under the Tang, Kuizhou under the Song, Chongqing under the Yuan and Ming, Fuzhou under the Qing, Fuling under the Republic of China that was founded in 1912.

But all of those dynasties have passed with hardly a mark left behind. The buildings could be the buildings of any Chinese city whose development has swallowed its history. Their purpose is simply to hold people, the more than 200,000 people who spend their days climbing the staircases, fighting the traffic, working and eating, buying and selling.

DAWN. A cool morning, the city covered in haze. Retirees practice *taiji* in the small park near South Mountain Gate, the central intersection. Fuling is relatively quiet—as quiet as it gets. There is a steady stream of traffic, and already many of the drivers are honking their horns; but the roads are not congested and the noise of the city is not yet overpowering. It is a pleasant morning.

The retirees are lined up neatly in rows. A radio plays traditional Chinese music, and the old people move slowly, gracefully. The park is tiny—not so much a park as a lull in the city. There are stunned bushes and exhausted flowers and broken-hearted patches of grass. But all of it is well cared for—vandalism of public property is not a problem in Fuling. The problem is the air, the coal dust that blankets the city and chokes the greenery. Few things are more pathetic than a tree in Fuling, its leaves gray and dull as if it were just taken out of the attic.

The roar of the city rises as sunshine fills the haze in the eastern sky. It is a mottled medley of sounds: honking horns, roaring television shops, blaring cassette tape stands, the uneven buzz of streetside salespeople calling out to the passersby. East of South Mountain Gate there is a sudden reprieve, a completely different strain, the soft but piercing music of an *erhu* played by a blind man.

Erhu means "two strings"—that is all. It is a simple name for a simple musical instrument: a cylindrical wooden sound box covered by python skin and topped by an upright handle with two strings stretched taut along its length. It looks something like a crude two-stringed violin. But that pair of strings has a rich soulful range and the *erhu*, played well, makes haunting music.

Today the blind man is playing well. He is about forty years of age, but his face looks older: tanned and creased, his eyes pinched shut. He wears dirty blue clothes and green army surplus sneakers. He sits on a low stool, and next to him is a cloth covered with poorly written characters. His nine-year-old daughter stands nearby with a glass jar half full of money. A small crowd has gathered, because the *erhu*'s music, despite the blaring horns and the noise of rushing passersby, is powerful enough to make people stop and listen. They read the words on the cloth:

A Brief Story of a Household

At twenty years I was married, and at twenty-two I lost the sight of both eyes. Eleven years after marriage I had a boy child, and then on December 2 of 1988 I had my second child, a daughter. My wife and I shared the care of the two children, tried to survive on the land of our household. But our family was short of hands, and we had trouble, because grain and money were unreliable. The woman had to drag all of these people behind her by the strength of her own effort, and indeed finally she was unable to continue living. For this reason, we were forced to flee on January 8 of 1996.

Because of my two lost eyes, I was not able to live from day to day! On March 2 of 1996 I was forced to send my son to live with his mother's father. My son was fourteen years old, and without money we could not send the boy to school. I hope that all of you uncles and aunts, fathers and mothers, brothers and sisters, will extend your warm hands to help me! My heart extends ten thousand thanks! I wish you success in your work! Happiness and a long life!

Above all of this the *erhu* plays. Effortlessly the music rises and falls, the voice flowing from the snakeskin-bound box, never drowned out by the rushing cars, the stream of pedestrians, the nearby televisions. At last the man stops. Gently he lays down the *erhu* and takes out his pipe. With his fingers he feels the rough roll of tobacco, and then he calls for his daughter. She lights the pipe, carefully. The blind man inhales deeply and sits back to rest, surrounded by the rising roar of the morning city.

CHAPTER TWO

Shakespeare with Chinese Characteristics

IN FULING I taught English and American literature. I also had classes in writing and speaking, but most of my time was spent teaching lit. There were two sections of third-year students, and I taught each of them four hours a week. Our textbooks started with *Beowulf* and continued through twelve centuries and across the ocean to William Faulkner's "A Rose for Emily."

It was a great deal of ground to cover. The Peace Corps suggested that we not be too ambitious with such courses, given our students' backgrounds and the fact that many of them had relatively low levels of English comprehension. It was recommended that we use literature to introduce important grammatical points, but this was an idea I didn't like. I knew that I was an uninspired teacher of the language's technical aspects, and I also knew that Shakespeare is an even worse grammar instructor than me. And I had studied literature for too long to use it as a segue to the present perfect tense.

But I still had some concerns. The students, after all, were from the countryside, and it was true that their English—and especially their spoken English—was sometimes poor. On the first day of class I asked them to jot down the titles of any English-language books they had read, either in the original or translation, and I asked what they would like to study in my course:

I enjoyed Hai Ming Wei, The Old Man and the Sea. I mostly want to study Hai Ming Wei.

I mostly want to study Helen Keller's and Shakespeare's work.

I've read Jack London and his The Call of Wild, Dicken and his The Tale of Two Cities, O. Henry and his The Last Leaf, Shakespeare and his King Lear (and that made me burst into tears).

I'm most interested in Jane Eyre by Charlotte Bronte. I don't know which periods it belonged to. I like Jane. I think she is a very common women, but she has a uncommon seeking. She dared to resist wife of mother's brother and brother of cousinship. She is a progressive lady.

Shakespeare was the greatest of all English authors. I had read some of his works. Romeo and Juliet is a dire story. Romeo and Juliet love each other. But there was revengefulness between their families.

And I have read "Farewell, Weapons," which was written by Hemingway. He was a tough man, but he killed himself.

I looked at their responses and thought: I can work with this. For the first week I assigned them *Beowulf*.

I TAUGHT on the fifth floor of the main teaching building. There were forty-five students to a class, all of them pressed close together behind old wooden desks. The room was their responsibility. They washed the blackboards between classes, and twice a week they cleaned the floor and windows. If the cleaning wasn't adequate, the class was fined. That was how everything worked at the college—students were fined for missing morning exercises, for skipping class, for failing examinations, for returning late to their dormitories at night. Very few of them had extra money to spend in this way, and so twice a week the classrooms were diligently and thoroughly cleaned.

Each room contained about fifteen more students than could comfortably fit, and it would have been claustrophobic if I hadn't been able to teach with the door open. Fortunately, there was plenty of space outside the classrooms were high above the Wu River, the same view that I had from my apartment's balcony: the fast-running Wu, the jumbled city, the muddy Yangtze and the dark shape of White Flat Mountain.

That was what I saw to my left as I taught, and at the beginning it was distracting. But there was always a good breeze coming off the rivers, which kept the room from becoming unbearably hot. If things got quiet—if I had the class doing a writing assignment, or if they were working smoothly in small groups—I'd gaze out the door at the traffic on the rivers: the little two-man fishing sampans, the crowded ferries crossing from one bank to the other, the barges bringing coal and gravel north from the upper Wu, the big white tourist boats slipping down the Yangtze toward the Gorges. There was something deeply satisfying about teaching with that view, and I liked watching the routines of the city in the same way that I liked listening to the routines of the college. During class I used to look down at the traffic teeming on the rivers, at all of the fishermen and barge captains and dock workers, and I'd think: I'm working, too. The city was moving and I was a small part of it.

At the beginning we read very little from the literature textbooks, because even the summaries were difficult, but it wasn't hard to get at the material from other angles. Often I told the stories, acting them out with reluctant students I grabbed as "volunteers," and the classes loved this—in a country where foreigners were often put on television simply because they were *waiguoren*, a room full of students was completely entranced by a foreigner performing *Gawain and the Green Knight*. Other days I gave them writing assignments; for *Beowulf* we talked about point of view, and they wrote about the story from the perspective of Grendel, the monster. Almost without exception the boys wrote about what it was like to eat people, and how to do it properly; while the girls wrote about how cold and dark the moor was, and how monsters have feelings too. One student named Grace wrote:

> The warriors said I am a monster, I can't agree with them, but on the contrary I think the warriors and the king are indeed monsters.
>
> You see, they eat delicious foods and drinking every day. Where the foods and drinking come from? They must deprive these things from peasants.

> The king and the warriors do nothing but eat delicios foods; the peasants work hard every day, but have bad foods, even many of them have no house to live, like me just live in the moor. So I think the world is unfair, I must change it.
>
> The warriors, I hate them. I will punish them for the poor people. I will ask the warriors build a large room and invited the poor people to live with me.

In college I had been taught by a few Marxist critics, most of whom were tenured, with upper-class backgrounds and good salaries. They turned out plenty of commentary—often about the Body, and Money, and Exchange—but somehow it didn't have quite the same bite as Grace's vision of Grendel as Marxist revolutionary. There was honesty, too—this wasn't tweed Marxism; Grace, after all, was the daughter of peasants. She didn't have tenure, and I had always felt that it was better if people who spoke feelingly of Revolution and Class Struggle were not tenured. And I figured that if you have to listen to Marxist interpretations of literature, you might as well hear them at a college where the students clean the classrooms.

The truth was that politics were unavoidable at a Chinese college, even if the course was foreign literature, and in the end I taught English Literature with Chinese Characteristics. We followed *Gawain* with a ballad about Robin Hood, and I asked them to write a story about what would happen if Robin Hood came to today's China. A few followed the Party line:

> Robin Hood comes to and settles in China, leaving his own country. On landing in the territory he is impressed by the peaceful country and friendly, industrious Chinese. He knows that the bright pearl of the east is distinct from England in many aspects. Englishmen have no freedom, no rights. They are oppressed deep by their masters and exploiters and live a dog's life. Moreover, the gap between the rich and the poor is widening. He hates such exploiting classes who lead a luxurious life based on plundering the poor cruelly. But he does not seem to be adequate to overthrowing the rule.
>
> However, in China people are masters of the country, serving country is serving people. Some of the people are allowed to get wealthy first through honest and lawful labour [which] does not

> widen the gap between the rich and the poor, but leads the people to common prosperity. Robin Hood knows deeply the fact that it is unnecessary to take something away from the rich by force as he did in England, but China still needs justice and bravery. Cultural and ethical construction should be fastened to development.

But most of them kept Robin Hood busy stealing from corrupt cadres and greedy businessmen. Often they put him in the booming coastal regions, in Shenzhen and Guangzhou and Xiamen, where reforms had freed the economy and materialism was king. In their stories, Robin Hood stole from the rich and gave to the peasants, and almost invariably he ended up in prison. Sometimes he was executed. One student had him successfully reeducated over a fifteen-year prison term (upon his release he became a detective). But almost always Robin Hood was caught; there were no illusions about the idealized green world of Sherwood Forest. There are few trees in China and the police always get their man.

I had them debate about whether Robin Hood was a good role model for today's China, which split them right down the middle. Some said that he was like Mao Zedong, a revolutionary against injustice; they compared him to the heroes of the Long March and said that China would be nowhere without people like Robin Hood. Others answered that he was a Counter-Revolutionary, the sort of person who would stir up trouble and disturb the economy. They pointed at what had happened during the Cultural Revolution—do you want constant Class Struggle with Robin Hood in the middle?

Within ten minutes they were no longer debating about Robin Hood. They were arguing about China, and they were arguing about the political dogma with which all of them had been indoctrinated. Things quickly became heated. I sat in the back, listening to the mess of contrary ideas they had been taught. Revolution was good—all of them knew that. Mao was a hero and the Long March had led to Liberation, which was the greatest moment in Chinese history. But Counter-Revolution was bad—Tiananmen Square protesters, pro-democracy activists; anything that agitated for change was bad and against the Revolution. To be faithful to the Revolution, you should support the status quo and the Communist Party—that was how you remained Revolutionary. Or was it? Robin Hood tangled them for an exhausting hour, every student speaking at least once, some of them angrily, and sitting in the back I wondered how you could ever make sense of it all.

ONE THING that I came to understand very early was that Fuling Teachers College served a dual purpose. It trained teachers, but like any Chinese school it was also an educational extension of the Chinese Communist Party. Each Fuling student carried a red identity card at all times, and on the front page of the card were eight "Student Regulations." The first three were as follows:

1. Ardently love the Motherland, support the Chinese Communist Party's leadership, serve Socialism's undertaking, and serve the people.
2. Diligently study Marxism-Leninism and Mao Zedong Thought, progressively establish a Proletariat class viewpoint, authenticate a viewpoint of Historical Materialism.
3. Diligently study, work hard to master basic theory, career knowledge, and basic technical ability.

It wasn't by accident that academic study came third. The top priority was political: these students were being trained to be teachers, and as teachers they would train China's next generation, and all of this training was done within the framework of Chinese Communism. Everything else was secondary—and if it contradicted basic theory, it wasn't taught.

First-year students of all departments studied Marxism-Leninism, and during their second year they took a course in law. Third-year students studied Building Chinese Socialism, oblivious that the city across the Wu, with its booming private businesses and bankrupt state-owned enterprises, was a testimony to the Dismantling of Chinese Socialism that was happening all across the country. This was the strangest part of it all, the way students could study and believe in Communist courses while free-market contradictions sprang up all around the college. And they did believe in what they were taught—most of the students were patriotic and faithful in the way they were trained to be. They took their political meetings and rallies seriously, and they coveted the chance to join the Communist Party. In every class perhaps 10 percent would have that opportunity; in the English department, there were eight Party Members out of ninety third-year students. They were some of the best in the class—the brightest, the most talented, the most socially adept.

The second rule, which emphasized their duty to "authenticate a viewpoint of Historical Materialism," explained a great deal about how political theory worked in China. I never gained more than a vague understanding of what Historical Materialism means—it has something to do with Class Struggle—but authenticating was the key. Not investigating, or contemplating, or analyzing—simply authenticating. They did whatever was necessary to prove the theories correct, ignoring complications and contradictions, and in the process they carefully used the appropriate terms. A few times I asked students to explain what some of these phrases meant—Historical Materialism, the People's Democratic Dictatorship, Socialism with Chinese Characteristics—but they were never able to answer in clear and simple language. It was, as Orwell would say, a case in which words and meaning had parted company. All that mattered was that students used the correct terminology and the correct political framework as they viewed the world around them.

Often it was difficult to see exactly where Adam and I fit into this vision of education. Adam taught American Culture, which used an English-language textbook entitled *Survey of Britain and America.* The book had been published in 1994, and often its portrait of America was hardly recognizable—for example, the chapter on American religion didn't mention charities, communities, or schools, but said quite a bit about the Jonestown mass suicide. Another particularly vivid chapter was called "Social Problems." Part of it read as follows:

> The American society is developing very fast scientifically, while the spirit of the society is becoming more and more hollow, and the society itself more and more corrupted. . . . Many social scientists claim that premarital sexual relations were not unusual among both young men and young women before 1960's. But what is different

> today is the open acceptance by many young people of a single standard for both sexes before marriage. Some Americans say this is only casual behavior; others may find such an excuse that premarital relations are the natural result of romantic love. This sounds even more ridiculous. The "new morality" is nothing but "immorality." This is the so-called "American civilization."
>
> Homosexuality is a rather strange social phenomenon that most people can hardly understand. It widely spreads. One reason for this may be the despair in marriage or love affairs. Some people fail in marriage and become disappointed with it. So they decide no longer to love the opposite sex, but instead begin to love a person of the same sex as a return of hatred to the opposite. Another reason may be that some people just want to find and do something "new" and "curious," as the Americans are known as adventurous. So they practised homosexuality as a kind of new excitement. Through this, we can see clearly the spiritual hollowness of these people and the distortion of the social order.

The chapter outlined a number of additional problems—racism, sexism, drugs, religious fanaticism—and then it gave the fundamental reason for America's flaws:

> However, the most important reason is the capitalist system of America. In this capitalist society, although science and technology is highly advanced, some people are suffering from spiritual hollowness. Thus they start to look for things curious and exciting. Therefore, only when the American capitalist system is ended, can all these social problems be solved.

It was not an easy book to teach from. The biggest problem was separating the wheat from the chaff: it was important to tell the students that things like racism and sexism were indeed major problems in America, but at the same time they needed to know that for many people homosexuality was not an issue (and it was also good if they realized that Capitalism does not cause homosexuality). In the students' minds, though, the book was either correct or it was wrong. There was no middle ground, and they had been taught not to question official texts.

Teaching as a foreigner was a matter of trying to negotiate your way through this political landscape. It was an acquired skill—over time, Adam and I gradually learned how to minimize the politics, to find subjects and ways to approach them that didn't trigger the standard knee-jerk reactions. It was easier for me in literature class, especially when we started working on poetry, which simplified everything.

By rights it shouldn't have been simple—the first poem we studied was Shakespeare's, and I didn't make it particularly easy. I defined the form of a Shakespearean sonnet and gave them Sonnet Eighteen in pieces, broken apart line by line. We reviewed poetic terms and archaic language, and I divided them into groups and told them to put the poem in order. Even though I gave them the first line, I figured it was an impossible task; my goal was simply to make them struggle with the bare bones of the poem until its form felt somewhat familiar. But they were never suspicious of impossible tasks, which was part of what made it so easy to teach in Fuling. The students would work at anything without complaint, probably because they knew that even the most difficult literature assignment was preferable to wading knee-deep in muck behind a water buffalo. And so the groups studied their broken sonnets while I gazed out at the sampans and barges on the Wu River.

Within an hour they had it. Some of the groups were merely close, but in each class there were two or three who nailed it:

Shall I compare thee to a summer's day?
Thou art more lovely and more temperate.
Rough winds do shake the darling buds of May,
And summer's lease hath all too short a date.
Sometime too hot the eye of heaven shines,
And often is his gold complexion dimmed;
And every fair from fair sometimes declines,
By chance, or nature's changing course, untrimmed;
But thy eternal summer shall not fade,
Nor lose possession of that fair thou ow'st,
Nor shall Death brag thou wand'rest in his shade,
When in eternal lines to time thou grow'st.
So long as men can breathe or eyes can see,
So long lives this, and this gives life to thee.

And they understood the form of the poem; just as they had put it together, they could take it apart. They could scan its rhythm—they knew where the stresses were in each line, and they could find the inconsistencies. They read the poem to themselves and softly beat time on their desks. They *heard* the sonnet. This was something that few American students could do, at least in my experience. We didn't read enough poetry to recognize its music, a skill that educated people lost long ago. But my students in Fuling still had it—nothing had touched that ability, not the advent of television or even the pointed devastation of the Cultural Revolution.

As time went on it almost depressed me. The Chinese had spent years deliberately and diligently destroying every valuable aspect of their traditional culture, and yet with regard to enjoying poetry Americans had arguably done a much better job of finishing ours off. How many Americans could recite a poem, or identify its rhythm? Every one of my Fuling students could recite at least a dozen Chinese classics by heart—the verses of Du Fu, of Li Bai, of Qu Yuan—and these were young men and women from the countryside of Sichuan province, a backwater by Chinese standards. They still read books and they still read poetry; that was the difference.

Verse never seemed to bore or frustrate them. The only stumbling block was language, the new vocabulary and the English archaisms, and with these they had infinite patience. We reviewed Sonnet Eighteen carefully, until at last we distilled it to the notion of poetic immortality, and I asked them: Was Shakespeare successful? Did the woman live forever? Some of them shook their heads—it was four hundred years ago, after all—but others hesitated. I asked them where the woman had lived.

"England," said Armstrong, who answered most of my questions.

"And when was that?"

"Around 1600."

"Think about this," I said. "Four centuries ago, Shakespeare loved a woman and wrote a poem about her. He said he would make her beauty live forever—that was his promise. Today the year is 1996, and we are in China, in Sichuan, next to the Yangtze River. Shakespeare never came to Fuling. None of you has ever been to England, and you have not seen the woman that Shakespeare loved four hundred years ago. But right now every one of you is thinking about her."

There was absolute silence. Usually Fuling was a riot of horns and construction projects, but at that moment in that classroom it was completely quiet. There was respect and awe in that silence, and I shared it. I had read the poem countless times, but I had never heard it truly until I stood in front of my class in Fuling and listened to their stillness as they considered the miracle of those fourteen lines.

A moment later I asked them to describe what they saw in that silence, Shakespeare's woman through Chinese eyes:

> Her skin is as white as snow and as smooth as ice. Her long hair is like waterfall; her eyes are so attractive you will never forget after you see her. She is plentiful, she is tall. Her little mouth as red as roses, and her eyebrow is like the leaves of willow. Her fingers are so slender that scallions can't compare with them.

> She looks like a slim and graceful lotus that is beginning to blossom. Her long hair is like a waterfall. Her elbow is like a crescent moon. Her mouth is like a red cherry. She has bright eyes. She is as gentle as water.

> She is slim, with long black hair. Her eyes are big and bright, full of soft and shyness. Her brows are like two leaves of willow. Her lips seem very active. Her skin is white and soft, like cooked fat.

> Her hair is just like golden wave. Her skin is so smooth that you will suspect it is made of marble. Her waist is as soft as watergrass and her fingers are slim as the root of onion.

> She has natural, plain beauty as a woman in the countryside. She is as pure as crystal. She looks like a floating poem.

> In our imagination, she is very beautiful and have something of melancholy. In Chinese history, there are four beauties, maybe, she looks like one of them—Wang Zhaojun. For us, we can't find some description about their beauty, because their beauty is beyond description. We can only say: they are very beautiful.

THERE WAS AN INTENSITY and a freshness to their readings that I'd never seen before from any other students of literature, and partly it was a matter of studying foreign material. We were exchanging clichés without knowing it: I had no idea that classical Chinese poetry routinely makes scallions of women's fingers, and they had no idea that Sonnet Eighteen's poetic immortality had been reviewed so many times that it nearly died, a poem with a number tagged to its toe. Our exchange suddenly made everything new: there were no dull poems, no overworked plays, no characters who had already been discussed to the point of clinicism. Nobody groaned when I assigned *Beowulf*—as far as they were concerned, it was just a good monster story.

This was the core of what we studied in that cramped classroom, and on the good days we never left. But there was always a great deal that surrounded us: the campus and its rules, the country and its politics. These forces were always present, hovering somewhere outside the classroom, and it reached the point where I could almost feel the moments when they pressed against us, when some trigger was touched and suddenly the Party interfered. Occasionally students wrote about how Shakespeare represented the Proletariat as he criticized English Capitalism (because of this theory, many Chinese are familiar with *The Merchant of Venice*), and several pointed out that Hamlet is a great character because he cares deeply about the peasantry. Other students told me that the peasants in *A Midsummer Night's Dream* are the most powerful figures in the play, because all power comes from the Proletariat, which is how Revolution starts.

I had mixed reactions to such comments. It was good to see my students interacting with the text, but I was less enthusiastic about Shakespeare being recruited for Communist Party propaganda. I found myself resisting these interpretations, albeit carefully—in light of my students' backgrounds, I couldn't bluntly say that the peasants in *A Midsummer Night's Dream* are powerless buffoons who provide comic relief. But one way or another I always tried to answer the readings that I felt were misguided. I argued that Hamlet is a great character not because he cares deeply about the peasantry, but rather because he cares deeply and eloquently about himself; and I pointed out that Shakespeare was a Petty Bourgeois Capitalist who made his fortune by acquiring stock in a theater company.

For the first time I came to understand why literature so often slides away toward politics. I had struggled with this before; at Princeton I had majored in English, and after graduation I had spent two years studying English language and literature at Oxford. My original plan had been to become a professor of literature, but over time I became less enamored of what I saw in English departments, especially in America. Part of it was simply aesthetics—I found that I couldn't read literary criticism, because its academic stiffness was so far removed from the grace of good writing. And I could make very little sense of most criticism, which seemed a hopeless mess of awkward words: Deconstructionism, Post-Modernism, New Historicism. None of it could be explained simply and clearly—just as my Fuling students stumbled when asked to define Historical Materialism or Socialism with Chinese Characteristics.

But mostly I was disturbed by the politicization of literature in the West: the way that literature was read as social commentary rather than art, and the way that books were forced to serve political theories of one stripe or another. Very rarely did a critic seem to react to a text; rather the text was twisted so that it reacted neatly to whatever ideas the critic held sacred. There were Marxist critics, Feminist critics, and Post-Colonial critics; and almost invariably they wielded their theories like molds, forcing books inside and squeezing out a neatly-shaped product. Marxists turned out Marxism; Feminists turned out Feminism; Post-Colonialists turned out Post-Colonialism. It was like reading the same senseless book over and over again.

And I resented the way that English departments constantly tinkered with the canon, hoping to create a book list as multicultural as the fake photographs they put on the covers of their undergraduate brochures. It had always seemed to me that with regard to literature there was some value in establishing and respecting a cultural foundation, and now in China I saw what happened when these roots were completely ripped up. For years the Chinese had mined literature for its social value, especially during the Cultural Revolution, when all operas were banned except for a handful of political works like *The Red Detachment of Women*. Even today there was much that had been lost. All of my students knew Marx; none of them knew Confucius.

But at the same time I came to see the reason for such politicization in a more human light. I realized that part of the power of great literature is its universality: the daughter of Sichuanese peasants can read *Beowulf* and make connections to her own life, and a classroom of Chinese students can listen to a Shakespeare sonnet and see the flawless features of a Tang Dynasty beauty. But along with this power there is a fragility, because it is always tempting to misappropriate the force of a great writer. It's natural to want Shakespeare on your side—and if he doesn't fit perfectly, you can twist his words to serve your purpose. Or, if he absolutely refuses to come to heel, you can expel him from the canon.

All of this was commonly done in China, and yet I was surprised to find that in some ways my students did a better job of avoiding politics than students at Princeton and Oxford. As the semester went on, the political forces outside the classroom seemed to drift farther and farther away, probably because the material was foreign. The literature was so fresh and different that the students usually forgot their standard political guidelines, and we also skirted the hassles of English departments in America. None of my students seemed to care that in the fall semester we read strictly dead white males, just as they didn't care that a live white male taught the class. As far as they were concerned, all of us were simply *waiguoren.*

Instead of worrying about politics, their energy was focused on understanding the material. They listened to the way the poetry sounded, and they weighed the characters in the stories. They took this seriously—to them, literature wasn't simply a game, and its figures were like real people who should be judged accordingly. They studied a summary of *Hamlet*, and after reading it a student named Lily responded in her journal:

> Mr. Hessler, do you like Hamlet? I don't admire him and I dislike him. I think he is too sensitive and conservative and selfish. He should tell the truth to his dear, Ophelia, and ask her to face and solve the problem together. After all, two lovers should share wealth and woe. What's more, I dislike his hesitation. As a man he should do what he wants to do resolutely.

You couldn't have said something like that at Oxford. You couldn't simply say: I don't like Hamlet because I think he's a lousy person. Everything had to be more clever than that; you had to recognize Hamlet as a character in a text, and then you had to dismantle it accordingly, layer by layer, not just the play itself but everything that had ever been written about it. You had to consider what all the other critics had said, and the accumulated weight of their knowledge and nonsense sat heavily on the play. You had to think about how the play tied in with current events and trends. This process had some value, of course, but for many readers it seemed to have reached the point where there wasn't even a split-second break before the sophistication started. As a student, that was all I had wanted—a brief moment when a simple and true thought flashed across the mind: I don't like this character. This is a good story. The woman in this poem is beautiful and I bet her fingers are slim like scallions.

This was what I was looking for as a student—some sign that literature was still enjoyable, that people read for pleasure and that this was important in and of itself, apart from the politics; but often it was hard to tell if this was happening. In Fuling, however, there was no question that the students enjoyed what they read, and I realized that for the rest of my life I would try to think of literature as they saw it. Sometimes, when they were working on an assignment and I was looking out at the Wu River, I'd smile and think to myself: We're all refugees here. They've escaped from their classes on Building Chinese Socialism, and I've escaped from Deconstructionism. We were happy, reading poetry while out on the rivers all of Fuling went about its business.

WE STUDIED *HAMLET* IN OCTOBER, when the weather was still warm but the autumn rains were beginning to settle in the river valley. I divided my classes into eleven groups and they spent a day preparing their scenes, and then they performed the play in the classroom. They pushed the teacher's podium to the side of the room and swept the floor, which was the stage. All of the students crowded their stools and desks into the back and from there they watched.

Acting transformed them entirely—in class they could be painfully shy, but drama changed all of that. Every gesture was overblown, every emotion overdone; they were incorrigible overactors, and after growing accustomed to their shyness it was strange to watch them shout and cry on the bare stage of the classroom. Sometimes I thought that perhaps it had something to do with the influence of traditional Chinese opera, in which the action is exaggerated and stylized, but more likely it was simply a release in a society where emotions were rarely open. Regardless, it was a strange experience to watch them perform; they were half-recognizable, like the play itself, and both the students and *Hamlet* became something new in my eyes.

Roger played the dead king's ghost, a writhing, howling spirit in a brightly painted cone-shaped Chinese emperor's crown that he had made of papier mâché. In any performance of *Hamlet* it is the ghost that sets the tone for the play, and so it was with Roger in his imperial crown—a touch of China in the class's Denmark.

In the second scene, Hamlet went before Gertrude and Claudius, who were played by Jane and Sally. Romance was always a knotty issue for my students; even the most casual public contact between sexes was taboo, and to play a wife or a girlfriend was too embarrassing for most of the female students. Often they simplified it the way Jane and Sally did, by making the couple the same sex, because in Fuling it was common for friends to be openly affectionate with each other. And so Sally stroked Jane's hair, and Jane fondled the other girl's arm, and then, realizing that Hamlet was glaring at them, Sally said imperiously,

> How is it that the clouds still hang on you?

And Hamlet—played by Barber, a nervous misnamed boy in thick glasses and a cheap tan suit—replied,

> Not so, my lord. I am too much in the sun.

Jane ran her hand along Sally's thigh. Both of them were pretty girls, their long hair brushed smooth like black silk. Barber scowled. Languidly Jane pressed close against Sally, and then she purred,

> Good Hamlet, cast thy nighted color off,
> And let thine eye look like a friend on Denmark.
> Don't continue to be sad for your father,
> You know that every man must die.

They wrote most of the dialogue themselves—the language of the play was too difficult and they used only the most famous lines, writing the rest in colloquial speech. Hamlet's Act III soliloquy was performed by Soddy, the class monitor, who stood alone in front of the class and said,

> To be, or not to be: that is the question:
> Whether it's better to do nothing and suffer,
> Or whether I should struggle against Claudius
> And end these troubles. To die, to sleep—
> No more—and by sleeping to end all of
> These terrible problems! To die, to sleep—
> To sleep—perchance to dream: ay, there's the rub. . . .

He was a big kid with a lazy eye from the countryside of northern Sichuan, and the other students called him *Lao Da*—Big Brother, a nickname from Hong Kong gangster films, a term of respect that reflected Soddy's authority. But despite his high position in the class hierarchy, he was a relatively poor student. His writing was fine, but his spoken English was bad and he had no confidence in class. Rarely did he speak out or answer questions.

I had never understood why the students respected Soddy so much until the day he stood in front of us and played Hamlet. His English was still poor—he stumbled over the soliloquy, and some of it was unintelligible. But that didn't matter, because now his talent was suddenly palpable; it was as if he had reached out and caught hold of his gift in the palm of his hand, turning it over once or twice, holding it as surely as he held our attention. He was slow, deliberate. He paced the room, and in his movements there were traces of Sichuan opera—a cloak folded just so over the crook of his arm; a wooden stool laid on its side and used as the focus of his wanderings, until he made a palace of that simple prop. But mostly his voice was perfect—he controlled the pace and tone of his speech, the way Hamlet's emotions rise and ebb like a hot uncertain sea. And Soddy knew how to use both noise and silence, to shout in frustration and then let the words resound in the classroom that he cleaned every week. He paced restlessly; he crouched on the stool; he buried his head in his hands; he roared and shouted; he kicked at the chair; and suddenly he was silent—and then, after the silence was complete, he said, quietly,

> Thus conscience does make cowards of us all,
> And thus we want to do something
> But our thoughts prevent us
> And lose the name of action—

He was Hamlet and he was *Lao Da;* there was no longer any question in my mind. The students watched with rapt attention and at the end they applauded madly. For the rest of the year, whenever I looked at Soddy, at his square jaw and his cockeyed gaze and his dark peasant's complexion, I saw the Prince of Denmark. That was exactly what Hamlet would have looked like in the countryside of Sichuan province.

IN THE OTHER CLASS'S PERFORMANCE, Rosencrantz and Guildenstern marched before the king, kowtowed until their foreheads nearly grazed the floor, and stood there holding hands while they listened to Claudius's instructions. In Sichuan it was common for male friends to hold hands like that—and certainly you would want to hold somebody's hand if you were being sent off unknowingly to your death.

They loved the characters of Rosencrantz and Guildenstern. Some of them were annoyed by Hamlet, and they found Ophelia pathetic, but everybody loved Rosencrantz and Guildenstern. They loved their hapless prying and they loved their demise, the way the servants are tricked into carrying their own death warrants to the King of England. That was a good touch by Shakespeare—another bit of China in the Bard's Denmark. It was a little like Miao Ze in the Chinese classic *The Romance of the Three Kingdoms,* who betrays his brother-in-law Ma Teng in order to win the graces of the powerful Cao Cao. But Cao Cao, after killing Ma Teng, turns to the expectant Miao Ze and says, "A man so faithless does not deserve to live," and promptly executes him and his entire family in the public square. Or maybe it was like Mao's general Lin Biao, who had tried to turn the Cultural Revolution to his purposes but in the end became one of its victims. In any case, my students knew Rosencrantz and Guildenstern—they had seen those characters many times in many ages. Even today you could sometimes still find them in the cadres' offices.

The play ended in a flurry of swordplay and kung-fu kicks, Laertes and Hamlet and Claudius involved in what could have been the climax of a Hong Kong martial arts film, until at the end only Hamlet and Horatio crouched in front of the class. They were played by Vic and Lazy, both of them dressed in cheap Western-style suits, and before their scene they carefully spread newspaper across the floor so the Prince could die without getting dirty. The class giggled—but then the scene began, and Lazy leaned against the wall and held the dying Hamlet, and everybody hushed.

Lazy cradled him close, like a child, and yet the contact was natural because Chinese men were allowed to touch each other in that way. Hamlet groaned, tried to speak, coughed out his dying words; Horatio stammered farewell and rocked his friend tenderly in his arms. The class was silent, watching. The actors were small men and alone on the floor they looked even smaller, crouched below the peeling paint and the dusty blackboard. Hamlet coughed again and said,

> I cannot live to hear the news from England,
> But I support Fortinbras. He has my dying voice.
> So tell him that—the rest is silence.

And so Hamlet died—and for a moment I almost forgot that I was in a cheerless Chinese classroom, and that Horatio was in fact a peasant's son who liked to sleep and called himself Lazy, holding Hamlet tenderly and saying softly, sadly, Lazily,

> Good night, sweet prince,
> And flights of angels sing thee to thy rest.

THE LATE-AUTUMN MISTS fell over White Flat Mountain and the classrooms grew colder. They weren't heated—few public buildings in Fuling were—and finally I took to closing the door when I taught. The students started wearing coats, scarves, gloves; their fingers swelled with chilblains and their ears turned red. I could see their breath in the cold crowded room. We read Swift, Wordsworth, Byron. The verses resounded with sweet regularity as we recited them aloud—iambic puffs of steam rising toward the ceiling. Outside, the unmetered wind blew hard from the Yangtze. Beneath their desks the students stamped their feet in the cold.

They begged me to assign another Shakespeare play, and at last I did, partly to keep warm. I summarized *Romeo and Juliet* and they played it. Soddy and his classmates built a balcony out of desks, an unstable tower upon which Lucy stood bravely while Soddy courted her from below. Five scenes later, Grace gave Juliet's soliloquy as she prepared to take the Friar's sleeping potion. Her family was against her, and Romeo had been exiled, and in the middle of the scene Grace began to cry. She was a beautiful, lively girl, one of my favorite students because she always spoke her mind without fear of embarrassment. Chinese girls weren't supposed to be like that—but Grace didn't care. On the day she played Juliet her long black hair was pulled back smooth past her shoulders, and her eyes shone bright with tears, and her breath came out white in the cold classroom.

A few days earlier, when they had been preparing the play, I had noticed one boy standing apart from his group. His English name was Silence Hill. "I am always silent," he had explained back in September, when I first asked him about his name. But he wrote beautifully, a thoughtful young man from a village of 250 people, and he always had a soft smile on his worn face. On the day that I noticed him standing alone, he was smiling and staring fixedly at the text of the play. I asked him what he was looking at, and without a word he pointed at two of Juliet's lines:

> My only love, sprung from my only hate!
> Too early seen unknown, and known too late!

"Do you understand what that means?" I asked, thinking he had a question.

"Yes," he said. "I think it's very beautiful."

I paused and looked at the lines again.

"I think you're right," I said, and for a moment neither of us said anything. Together Silence Hill and I stood there looking at the poetry.

掛旗山

RAISE THE FLAG MOUNTAIN

THE MOUNTAIN HAS TWO NAMES, Peach Blossom Mountain and Raise the Flag Mountain, and it rises green above the college and the junction of the rivers. In spring and fall and winter, the peak often fades into the river-valley fog, and in summer, when the days burn bright under a violent sun, the groves of peach trees near the summit seem to shiver in the heat.

The blossoms appear in late March or early April, two brief pink-flowered weeks that give the mountain its first name. But almost nobody in Fuling calls it Peach Blossom Mountain, although the origins of the other title are even more fleeting—a single instant during the nineteenth-century Taiping Rebellion, when China's history came to Fuling, marched up the mountain, and then moved on. This was perhaps the only time when Fuling was close to the center of China's affairs, and after more than a century the echo still remains, the mountain's name a memorial to a strange and violent revolution.

The Great Taiping Rebellion was started in the mid-1840s by Hong Xiuquan, a poor man from Guangxi province who, frustrated by failing the Chinese civil service examination four times, decided that he was the Son of God and the younger brother of Jesus Christ. After that, things happened very quickly. By 1851, Hong Xiuquan was leading twenty thousand armed followers, and he declared that he was the Heavenly King of a new dynasty. His soldiers let their hair grow long, fought without fear of death, and believed a sort of bastardized fundamentalist Protestantism that was based loosely on foreign missionary tracts. In 1853, they captured the eastern city of Nanjing, calling it their New Jerusalem, and in time Hong Xiuquan ruled almost half of China.

The Heavenly Kingdom of Great Peace—Taiping Tianguo—was opposed to opium, foot binding, prostitution, gambling, and tobacco, and it had some support from the Chinese peasants, who had no affection for the corrupt Qing Dynasty rulers. But Hong Xiuquan and the other revolutionary leaders lacked the vision and experience to run a country, and power tempted most of them into luxury and infighting. They began to acquire the trappings of the dynasty they hoped to overthrow: robes of yellow silk, hordes of sycophants, endless concubines. But they were still too powerful to be defeated by the Qing, and the Taipings held Nanjing even while engaging in increasingly bloody internecine power struggles.

Hong Xiuquan's greatest general was Shi Dakai, who was known as the Wing King, Lord of Five Thousand Years. Of all the original leaders, he was the most capable, and his disillusionment with the Taiping infighting finally pushed him to leave Nanjing in 1857. Leading 100,000 soldiers, he embarked on a military campaign that spanned six years and foreshadowed the sweeping troop movements of the Communist Long March. His Taiping army zigzagged across eastern and southern China, arriving eventually at the Yangtze River valley. In time they came to Fuling, where Shi Dakai and his soldiers marched up the long even slope of Peach Blossom Mountain, and there, at the summit, they raised the flag of the Heavenly Kingdom.

FROM THE SUMMIT of Raise the Flag Mountain, all of Fuling can be seen on a clear day. But in the fall, when the seasonal rains and mists sit heavy above the rivers, there are days when the view is blocked by clouds, and the city across the Wu is nothing but sound: horns and motors and construction projects echoing up through the heavy white fog. Sometimes the mist will stay for days or even weeks. But then something clears the valleys—a shift in temperature, a stiff breeze—and suddenly the view opens.

Southward the mountain falls away steeply to valleys of terraced cropland, and near the Wu River the land is broken by the settlements of the East River district: the college, looking small with the distance;

the ceramics factory, its stacks spewing yellow dust into the air; the long concrete pier and the old ferries that traverse the Wu. The river lies slack, like a long thin bolt of gray silk unrolled between the hills.

In the mist the city looks dirty and old, its buildings flung carelessly across the hills, and it also looks big. Seen from ground level it is impossible to gain perspective on Fuling's size, but from Raise the Flag Mountain the scale of the city is suddenly apparent. The gray buildings are piled off far into the horizon, past the distant needlelike spire of the Monument to the Revolutionary Martyrs. And yet by Chinese standards it is a small city—a town, really—and all around the jumbled buildings the mountains are green and impressive.

But none of them is truly wild. The view from Raise the Flag Mountain extends for perhaps six miles in every direction, and in that range nearly every inch of useful soil is under cultivation. The same is true for the mountain itself: the peak is an orchard, a garden, an enormous farm lying on its side, the slope broken into steps and terraces that turn the hillside into level land.

Peach and orange groves are planted along the summit, where the mountain is too steep for terracing. A bit lower, the slope decreases and the peasants have carved the land into short shelves for vegetables—cabbage, potatoes, soybeans, radishes. Even lower, the terraces broaden enough for grain crops, and now in the fall it is almost time to plant the winter wheat. The peasants will sow the crop in November and December, and between every two or three rows they will leave a space of two feet. In March, two months before the wheat is harvested, they will plant corn in the spaces between the rows. No land is wasted, and nothing is rushed or delayed; everything has its season, and every season rests on the simple work that the peasants do with their hands.

Farther down the mountain, the rice paddies were harvested weeks ago; now the fields are dry, and yellow stubble pokes up from the dirt. Most of the paddies sit in the low valley of the mountain's southern flank, where the land flattens enough to be shaped into broad sweeping terraces that can hold water. Of all the mountain's crops, rice has the most intricate routines. It is sowed in March, planted densely in seedbeds, and then the following month the green shoots are uprooted and moved by hand to flooded paddies. In July and August, the crop is harvested and threshed, and the dry paddy can be used for vegetables or winter wheat. And so the cycle continues, season after season, year after year, and sometimes a single plot of land will see a full year's crops: rice to vegetables, vegetables to wheat, wheat to rice once more.

The lower mountain is cut by a dusty road near the Wu River. Below the road, the hillside falls away steeply, but even this floodland is used for winter potatoes and mustard tuber. The small plots continue all the way to the rocky banks of the Wu, where an old rusted boat approaches the junction of the rivers. The craft's low front deck is empty of cargo, and from the cabin flutters a red Chinese flag. The boat reaches the Yangtze, spinning to face the river's flow. Its motor wheezes. For an instant it pauses, fixed by the current—below the mountain, in front of the city, caught in the junction of the two rivers. Then the propeller catches hold of the fast-moving Yangtze and the boat putters upstream.

SHI DAKAI AND HIS MEN followed the river valley west from Fuling. They marched past Chongqing and Luzhou, and then they left the Yangtze and entered the mountains of western Sichuan. By now it had been years since the march began, and in Nanjing the Heavenly Kingdom was in shambles, and finally the brave expedition became a retreat.

The army followed the banks of the Dadu, a mountain river in western Sichuan whose water runs green with glacial melt. The river had seen great battles before—critical campaigns were pitched there in the Three Kingdoms Period, sixteen centuries earlier. And now the Qing government forces were in close pursuit, hoping to trap Shi Dakai and his men in the narrow valleys. The year was 1863.

They paused for three days on the banks of the river to mark the birth of Shi Dakai's son. The rituals were elaborate, because the boy was a prince in the Heavenly Kingdom—the son of the Wing King, the Lightning of the Holy Spirit, the Lord of Five Thousand Years. But the Heavenly Kingdom was already fading into history, and Shi Dakai's five thousand years would be cut short. The delay at the Dadu proved fatal; the Qing army cornered the rebels, and Shi Dakai surrendered after making sure that his five wives and children had been put to death as painlessly as possible. He begged his captors to execute him instead of his faithful followers, whose ranks had already shrunk from the original 100,000 to two thousand men. The Qing commanders listened patiently to Shi Dakai's request, and then they massacred the Taiping troops and dismembered the Wing King, slowly.

Seventy-two years later, Mao Zedong led his Communist forces to the same river during the heart of the Long March. The Kuomintang was on the verge of destroying the Red Army, and the lessons of history taught Mao not to delay. His troops moved steadily northward, until at Luding they came to an ancient iron bridge across the Dadu that was well defended by Kuomintang forces. The situation appeared hopeless.

Thirty Red soldiers volunteered. Under machine-gun fire they crawled across the bridge, hand over hand, iron link by iron link, and against all odds they succeeded in capturing the enemy gun nests. The entire Communist army crossed the river victoriously, having survived what turned out to be the most critical battle of the Long March. Later that year, eight thousand of Mao's men, all that remained from an initial force of eighty thousand, finished their trek in northern Shaanxi province. They established a base and steadily grew in power, conquering the nation village by village, province by province; and in every town they spread their doctrine, which was a sort of bastardized Marxism based loosely on the Soviet model. Fourteen years later, in 1949, Mao Zedong established the People's Republic of China.

The Communists opposed opium, foot binding, prostitution, and gambling, and they had a great deal of support from the Chinese peasants, who had no affection for the grasping landlords and the corruption of the Kuomintang. But Mao lacked the vision and experience necessary to run a country effectively, and power inspired him to build a cult of state-worship around his image. The leading cadres began to acquire the luxurious trappings of the corrupt reign they had overthrown: great mansions, hordes of sycophants, endless concubines.

But even in the late 1990s, as stories of corruption are rife and the country's economy quickly privatizes, the official view of history holds steady. The Communist vision of the past idealizes peasant revolts like the Great Taiping Rebellion, until even a remote place like Fuling has a stone statue of Shi Dakai in the public park. Some aspects of the movement, in contrast, have been allowed to fade—Chinese history books say little about the Taipings' strange brand of Christianity, and many students in a place like Fuling don't know that Hong Xiuquan believed himself to be the younger brother of Jesus Christ. But students know that he was a peasant revolutionary, and that Mao succeeded where Hong Xiuquan failed. Such echoes are seen as evidence of legitimacy rather than signs that Chinese history, like the land, sometimes follows a pattern of cycles.

The Dadu River runs south to Leshan, where it enters the Min River under the sightless gaze of the largest carved Buddha in the world. The Min flows southwest to Yibin, where it enters the Yangtze, and from there the river runs west and north for three hundred miles until it passes the green terraced slopes of Raise the Flag Mountain. Today there is no flag on the rounded peak. The two-named mountain looms large above the river, its solid bulk recalling the words that the Sichuan poet Du Fu wrote more than a thousand years ago:

> The state is shattered;
> Mountains and rivers remain.

CHAPTER THREE

Running

IN THE MORNINGS I often ran to the summit of Raise the Flag Mountain. As I ran, I studied the propaganda signs along the route, although at the beginning there wasn't much about them that was recognizable. There were three signs on the road out to the mountain, and to me they looked like this:

建设精神 **Cultu** 更新生育观念

控制 **People Mouth** 增长，促进社会进步

教育 **Is** 立 **Country** 基础

I finished my runs back in the center of campus, not far from the teaching building, where a stone wall served as a backdrop for an inscription of three-foot-high characters:

教书育 **People,** 管理育 **People,** 服务育 **People,** 环境育 **People**

That was how Chinese appeared in my first few months. I arrived in Fuling able to recognize about forty characters, all of them simple: people, middle, country, above, below, long, man, woman. There hadn't been time for more; the Peace Corps had given us an intensive course during our two months of training in Chengdu, but the emphasis was on learning enough spoken Mandarin to function. We had to study written Chinese on our own, and until I got to Fuling I simply hadn't had enough time.

I came to Sichuan because I wanted to teach, but I also had two other motivations: I thought the experience would make me a better writer, and I wanted to learn Chinese. These were very clear goals, but the way to achieve them was much less obvious. I hoped the writing would take care of itself—I would keep my eyes open and take notes, and eventually, when I felt I was ready, I would start to write. But Chinese was a different matter altogether and I had never undertaken something like that before.

That was one reason I had decided to come to China with the Peace Corps, because I knew they would try to teach me the language. Their Chengdu training course had been excellent; the classes were small and the teachers experienced, and it had been easy to make progress. In Fuling, though, language study was my own affair. The Peace Corps would pay for tutors, but I had to find them myself, and I had to decide which textbooks I would use and how I would structure my studies. It was a daunting task—essentially, I had to figure out how to learn Chinese.

For the first few weeks, Dean Fu searched for tutors who could help Adam and me. He was as lost as we were—he had never known a foreigner who was trying to learn the language, and I suspected that secretly he felt the project was hopeless. *Waiguoren* couldn't learn Chinese—everybody in Fuling knew that. Our students found it hilarious that we even tried. They would ask me to speak a little Chinese, or write a character or two, and then they would laugh at my efforts. At first this didn't bother me, but quickly it became annoying. They thought I was dabbling in the language when in fact I was serious: I knew that studying Chinese was one of the most important things I could do in Fuling. So much depended on knowing the language—my friendships, my ability to function in the city, my understanding of the place.

I also wanted to learn Chinese out of stubbornness, because as a *waiguoren* you weren't expected to do that. Such low expectations had a long tradition; even as late as the early 1800s it had been illegal for a

Chinese to teach the language to foreigners, and a number of Chinese were imprisoned and even executed for tutoring young Englishmen. This bit of history fascinated me: how many languages had been sacred and forbidden to outsiders? Certainly, those laws had been changed more than a century ago, but China was still ambivalent about opening to the outside world and language was still at the heart of this issue. In good conscience I could not live there for two years and not learn to speak Chinese. To me, this was as important as fulfilling my obligations as a teacher.

But this need wasn't nearly as obvious to everybody else. Dean Fu took a long time finding tutors, and perhaps he was hoping that we'd forget about it. We didn't need Chinese to teach, after all, and we already knew enough to buy groceries and eat at local restaurants. That should be adequate, people figured. In some respects, we were seen as English-teaching machines, or perhaps farm animals—expensive and skittish draft horses that taught literature and culture. We were given cadres' apartments, and we had our own Changhong-brand color televisions with remote. Our bedrooms were air-conditioned. Each of us had a good kitchen and two beautiful balconies. Our students were obedient and respectful. It didn't matter that, even as we were given all of these things, the leaders also gave quiet instructions to our colleagues and students that they should avoid associating with us outside of class. *Waiguoren* were risky, especially with regard to politics, and in any case we didn't need close friends in the college. We could teach during the day and return to our comfortable cages at night, and, if we needed friendship, we always had each other. They even gave us telephones so we could call Peace Corps volunteers who lived in other parts of Sichuan.

Some of the more insightful students sensed that this did not make a full life. In his journal, Soddy wrote me a short note, politely addressed in the third person:

> Pete and Adam come to our college to teach our English without pay. We are thankful for this behavior. But we are worried about Pete and Adam's lives. For example: Pete and Adam know little Chinese, so they can't watch Chinese TV programmes. I think your lives are difficult. I want to know how you spend your spare time.

It was a good question. My teaching and preparation time rarely took much more than thirty hours a week. I ran in the mornings, and sometimes I went for walks in the hills. Adam and I played basketball and threw the Frisbee. I wrote on my computer. I planned other diversions for the future—subjects I wanted to cover in class, possible travel destinations. Mostly, though, I knew that there was plenty of exploring to be done in the city, but at the beginning this was the hardest place of all to open up.

Downtown Fuling looked good from my balcony. Often I'd gaze across the Wu River at the maze of streets and stairways, listening to the distant hum of daily life, and I'd think about the mysteries that were hidden in the river town. I wanted to investigate all of it—I wanted to go down to the docks and watch the boats; I wanted to talk with the stick-stick soldiers; I wanted to explore the network of tangled staircases that ran through the old part of town. I longed to figure out how the city worked and what the people thought, especially since no foreigner had done this before. It wasn't like living in Beijing or Shanghai, where there were plenty of *waiguoren* who had discovered what the city had to offer. As far as foreigners were concerned, Fuling was our city—or it would be once we figured it out.

But once I got there it didn't look so good. Partly this was because of the dirt and noise; the main city of Fuling was an unbelievably loud and polluted place. There wasn't as much heavy industry as in other parts of China, but there were a few good-sized factories that spewed smoke and dust into the air. The power plant on the banks of the Wu River burned coal, as did all of the countless small restaurants that lined the city's streets, and automobile emissions were poorly regulated. In winter the air was particularly dirty, but even in summer it was bad. If I went to town and blew my nose, the tissue was streaked with black grease. This made me think about how the air was affecting my lungs, and for a while I wondered what could be done about this. Finally I decided to stop looking at tissues after I blew my nose.

Noise was even more impressive. Most of it came from car horns, and it is difficult to explain how constant this sound was. I can start by saying: Drivers in Fuling honked a lot. There weren't a great number of cars, but there were enough, and they were always passing each other in a mad rush to get to wherever they were going. Most of them were cabs, and virtually every cabby in Fuling had rewired his horn so it was triggered by a contact point at the tip of the gearshift. They did this for convenience; because of the hills, drivers shifted gears frequently, and with their hand on the stick it was possible to touch the contact point ever so slightly and the horn would sound. They honked at other cars, and they honked at pedestrians. They honked whenever they passed somebody, or whenever they were being passed themselves. They honked when nobody was passing but somebody might be considering it, or when the road was empty and there was nobody to pass but the thought of passing or being passed had just passed through the driver's mind. Just like that, an unthinking reflex: the driver honked. They did it so often that they didn't even feel the contact point beneath their fingers, and the other drivers and pedestrians were so familiar with the sound that they essentially didn't hear it. Nobody reacted to horns anymore; they served no purpose. A honk in Fuling was like the tree falling in the forest—for all intents and purposes it was silent.

But at the beginning Adam and I heard it. For the first few weeks we often complained about the honking and the noise, the same way we complained about blowing our noses and seeing the tissue turn black. But the simple truth was that you could do nothing about either the noise or the pollution, which meant that they could either become very important and very annoying, or they could become not important at all. For sanity's sake we took the second option, like the locals, and soon we learned to talk about other things.

I realized this in early November, when a college friend of mine named Scott Kramer came to visit. For five years he had lived in Manhattan, and yet the noise in Fuling absolutely stunned him; he heard every horn, every shout, every blurted announcement from every loudspeaker. When he left, we took a cab from the college to the docks, and Kramer, who worked on Wall Street and had a mathematical turn of mind, counted the honks as our driver sped through the city. It was a fifteen-minute ride and the driver touched his contact point 566 times. It came to thirty-seven honks per minute.

If Kramer hadn't been counting, I wouldn't have noticed, and I realized that I had stopped hearing the horns long ago, just like everybody else in town. In fact, Kramer was the only person in the whole city who heard them, which explained why he was so overwhelmed. The entire city had been honking at him for a week.

For me it wasn't the same, and after a month or so the discomforts of Fuling weren't important enough to deter me from going into town. Despite the noise and the pollution, it was still a fascinating place, and I still wanted to explore its corners and learn its secrets. But the language was an enormous problem, and in the beginning it made the city frustrating and even frightening.

Mandarin Chinese has a reputation as a difficult language—some experts say it takes four times as long to learn as Spanish or French—and its characters and tones are particularly challenging to a Westerner, because they are completely different from the way our languages are structured. In Sichuan, things are further complicated by the provincial dialect, which is distinct enough that a Chinese outsider has trouble understanding the locals in a place like Fuling. The variations between Mandarin and Sichuanese are significant: in addition to some differences in vocabulary, Sichuanese slurs the Mandarin reflexive sounds—*sh* becomes *s*, *zh* becomes *z*—and certain consonants are reversed, so that the average person in Sichuan confuses *n* and *l*, and *h* and *f*. A word like "Hunan" becomes "Fulan." The Sichuanese tonal range is also shorter, and most significant, two of the four Mandarin tones are reversed in Sichuan. If Mandarin is your starting point, it seems that the entire language has been flattened and turned upside down.

In addition, Sichuan is an enormous province where lack of development, particularly with regard to road and rail links, has resulted in vast regional differences. The Chengdu dialect is distinct from that of Chongqing, which is also different from that of Leshan, and so on. The town of Fengdu is less than thirty miles downstream from Fuling, and yet occasionally the residents of these places have difficulty understanding each other. At a Fuling restaurant, if you want the dish known as *hundun* in Mandarin—translated in English as "wonton"—you have to ask for *chaoshou*, but if you go another thirty miles to Fengdu you'll have to call it *baomian*. Or, more accurately, *baomin*, because the folks in Fengdu slur the *ian* sounds.

The result is a hell of a mess that I hadn't expected. I came to China hoping to learn Chinese, but quickly I realized there was no such thing. "Chinese" was whatever it took to communicate with the person you happened to be talking with, and this changed dramatically depending on background and education level. Educated people usually could speak Mandarin, especially if they were from the younger generation—the walls of our classrooms had enormous signs that commanded: "Use Mandarin!" But the vast majority of Fuling's population was uneducated and functioned only in the dialect. It made going to town a frustrating experience, because even the simplest conversations were difficult, and it also made my goal of learning Chinese seem impossible: I couldn't imagine learning both Mandarin and Sichuanese in two years. In fact, all I needed to do was improve my Mandarin, which would naturally enable me to handle the dialect, but in the early months I didn't know that. It seemed that I was in hopelessly over my head, and every trip into town was a reminder of that failure.

And Fuling was a frightening place because the people had seen so few outsiders. If I ate at a restaurant or bought something from a store, a crowd would quickly gather, often as many as thirty people spilling out into the street. Most of the attention was innocent curiosity, but it made the embarrassment of my bad Chinese all the worse—I'd try to communicate with the owner, and people would laugh and talk among themselves, and in my nervousness I would speak even worse Mandarin. When I walked down the street, people constantly turned and shouted at me. Often they screamed *waiguoren* or *laowai*, both of which simply meant "foreigner." Again, these phrases often weren't intentionally insulting, but intentions mattered less and less with every day that these words were screamed at me. Another favorite was "hello," a meaningless, mocking version of the word that was strung out into a long "hah-loooo!" This word was so closely associated with foreigners that sometimes the people used it instead of *waiguoren*—they'd say, "Look, here come two hellos!" And often in Fuling they shouted other less innocent terms—*yangguizi*, or "foreign devil"; *da bizi*, "big nose"—although it wasn't until later that I understood what these phrases meant.

The stresses piled up every time I went into town: the confusion and embarrassment of the language, the shouts and stares, the mocking calls. It was even worse for Adam, who was tall and blond; at least I had the advantage of being dark-haired and only slightly bigger than the locals. For a while we adopted the strategy of going into town together, thinking that between the two of us we could more easily handle the pressure. This was a mistake, though, because adding another *waiguoren* only increased the attention, and after a month of that we started making our trips solo. Finally, as the fall semester wore on, we did everything possible to avoid going to town. When I did go, I wore headphones. That was the only way I could handle it; I listened to the loudest and most offensive rap music I had—Dr. Dre, Snoop Doggy Dogg, the Beastie Boys—and it was just enough to drown out the shouts as I walked down the street. It made for surreal trips downtown, listening to Snoop rap obscenities while I dodged the crowds, but it kept me sane.

And so Soddy's question remained: How do you spend your spare time? When I finished teaching I would sit at my desk, which looked out across the Wu River to the city, and I would write:

学 学 学 学 学 学 学 学 学 学

While I wrote, I pronounced the word over and over, as carefully as I drew it:

"Xue xue xue xue xue xue xue xue xue xue xue xue xue xue xue xue xue xue xue xue."

I would write the same character about a hundred times total, and then I would think of ways in which it was used: *xuexi, xuesheng, xuexiao.* I would write it on a flash card and put it on a stack that grew steadily on my desk—between five and ten a day, usually. I listened to language tapes and reviewed the text that we had used during Peace Corps training. I flipped through the flash cards. By early October, when Dean Fu finally found two Chinese tutors, I had learned 150 characters. The signs on the way to Raise the Flag Mountain were still unintelligible, but the one in the center of campus had changed slightly:

Teaching 育 **People,** 管理育 **People,**

服务育 **People, Environment** 育 **People**

OUR TUTORS were Kong Ming and Liao Mei, and we came to know them as Teacher Kong and Teacher Liao. They taught in the Chinese department, and neither of them spoke any English. They had never known a *waiguoren* before. Dean Fu had been unable to find tutors who spoke English, and at last we told him it wasn't important. We wanted to get started and we knew that Chinese department teachers had good Mandarin.

Teacher Kong was a short man who wore glasses and smelled of Magnificent Sound cigarettes. He was thirty-two years old, and he taught ancient Chinese literature. By Chinese standards he was slightly fat, which meant that by American standards he was slightly thin. He smiled easily. He was from the countryside of Fengdu, which was famous for its ghosts—legend said that spirits went to Fengdu after death.

Teacher Liao was a very thin woman with long black hair and a reserved manner. She was twenty-seven years old, and she taught modern Chinese. She smiled less than Teacher Kong. Our students, who also had some courses in the Chinese department, considered Teacher Liao to be one of their better instructors. She was from the central Sichuan city of Zigong, which was famous for its salt. Every city and small town in Sichuan claimed to be famous for something. Fuling was famous for the hot pickled mustard tuber that was cured along the banks of the rivers.

That was essentially everything we knew about Teachers Kong and Liao for months. We also knew about their Mandarin, which was very clear except for a slight Sichuanese tendency to confuse the *n* and *l* sounds. Other than that we knew nothing. To us they were like Chinese-teaching machines, or perhaps farm animals—a sort of inexpensive and bored draft horse that corrected bad tones. And to them we were very stupid *waiguoren* from a country whose crude tongue had no tones at all.

My first tutorial with Teacher Liao was scheduled for two hours, but I lasted less than sixty minutes. I went home with my head reeling—had a human being ever compressed more wrongness into a single hour? Everything was wrong—tones, grammar, vocabulary, initial sounds. She would ask me a question and I would try to process the language to respond, but before I could speak she was answering it herself. She spoke clearly, of course, and it was also true that during that hour not a word of English had been spoken. That was what I wanted, after all—a Chinese tutor. But I couldn't imagine doing that for seven hours a week and maintaining my sanity, and I looked at the pathetic stack of flash cards on my desk and thought: This is hopeless.

For a solid month it looked that way. I was too self-absorbed to even imagine what it was like from the other side, but later I realized that it was even worse for my teachers. They weren't under threat of execution for teaching the sacred tones to a *waiguoren*—that law, at least, had been changed since Qing Dynasty days. But theirs wasn't an enviable job. First of all, we underpaid them. This wasn't intentional; Adam and I had been given wrong information about the standard rate for tutors. Teachers Kong and Liao, of course, were far too polite to set us straight, which meant that for the entire first year they worked for two-thirds of what they deserved. Even worse, though, they were underpaid for seven weekly hours of boredom and frustration. The lessons in the book were simple—taking a train, going to a restaurant—and yet I botched everything, and they had no idea how to steer me in the right direction. How do you teach somebody to speak Chinese? How do you take your knowledge of ancient poetry and use it to help a *waiguoren* master something as basic as the third tone?

We were all lost, and that failure seemed to be the extent of our relationship. Other Peace Corps volunteers had tutors who spoke English, so at least they could chat together after class. They heard about their tutors' families; they ate dinner together; they became friends. My tutors didn't seem like real people—it was months before I learned that Teacher Liao was married and that Teacher Kong had a son. Here the language problem was compounded by the fact that at the beginning they were somewhat cagey and distant; they had never known a *waiguoren* before, and they weren't at all certain how to approach us.

Chinese teaching styles are also significantly different from western methods, which made my tutorials even more frustrating. In China, a teacher is absolutely respected without question, and the teacher-student relationship tends to be formal. The teacher teaches and is right, and the student studies and is wrong. But this isn't our tradition in America, as my own students noticed. I encouraged informality in our classes, and if a student was wrong I pointed out what she had done right and praised her for making a good effort. To them, this praise was meaningless. What was the point of that? If a student was wrong, she needed to be corrected without any quibbling or softening—that was the Chinese way.

I couldn't teach like that, and it was even harder to play the role of student. Actually, this became worse after my Chinese classes started to feel productive, which happened more quickly than I expected. The characters in my book's lessons had always been elusive, odd-shaped scratches of black that drifted in and out of my head, calling up arbitrary allusions that were misleading. They were pictures rather than words: I would look at 卡 and think of K-mart, and the twenty-seventh radical— 阝 reminded me of the letter B, or perhaps an ax hanging on a wall. 大 looked like a man doing jumping jacks. 点 was a marching spider carrying a flag across the page. I stared so long at those odd figures that I dreamed about them—they swarmed in my head and I awoke vaguely disturbed and missing home.

But at a certain point it was as if some of the scratchings stood up straight and looked me in the eye, and the fanciful associations started slipping away. Suddenly they became words; they had meaning. Of course, it didn't happen all at once, and it was work that did it—I was studying madly in an effort to make the classes less miserable. But I was so busy that I hardly had time to realize that progress was being made.

One day after more than a month of classes, I read aloud a paragraph from my book, recognizing all of the characters smoothly except for one. I sat back and started to register the achievement: I was actually reading Chinese. The language was starting to make sense. But before this sense of satisfaction was half formed, Teacher Liao said, "*Budui!*"

It meant, literally, "Not correct." You could also translate it as no, wrong, nope, uh-uh. Flatly and clearly incorrect. There were many Chinese words that I didn't know, but I knew that one well.

A voice in my head whined: All of the rest of them were right; isn't that worth something? But for Teacher Liao it didn't work like that. If one character was wrong it was simply *budui.*

"What's this word?" I asked, pointing at the character I had missed.

"*Zhe*—the *zhe* in *zhejiang.*"

"Third tone?"

"Fourth tone."

I breathed deeply and read the section again, and this time I did it perfectly. That was a victory—I turned to Teacher Liao and my eyes said (or at least I imagined them saying): How do you like me now? But Teacher Liao's eyes were glazed with boredom and she said, "Read the next one." They were, after all, simple paragraphs. Any schoolchild could handle them.

It was the Chinese way. Success was expected and failure criticized and promptly corrected. You were right or you were *budui*; there was no middle ground. As I became bolder with the language I started experimenting with new words and new structures, and this was good but it was also a risk. I would finish a series of sentences using vocabulary that I knew Teacher Liao didn't expect me to know, and I would swear that I could see her flinch with unwilling admiration. And yet she would say, *"Budui!"* and correct the part that had been wrong.

I grew to hate *budui*: its sound mocked me. There was a harshness to it; the *bu* was a rising tone and the *dui* dropped abruptly, building like my confidence and then collapsing all at once. And it bothered me all the more because I knew that Teacher Liao was only telling the truth: virtually everything I did with the language was *budui*. I was an adult, and as an adult I should be able to accept criticism where it was needed. But that wasn't the American way; I was accustomed to having my ego soothed; I wanted to be praised for my effort. I didn't mind criticism as long as it was candy-coated. I was caught in the same trap that I had heard about from some of my Chinese-American friends, who as children went to school and became accustomed to the American system of gentle correction, only to return home and hear their Chinese-minded parents say, simply, *budui*. That single B on the report card matters much more than the string of A's that surrounds it. Keep working; you haven't achieved anything yet.

And so I studied. I was frustrated but I was also stubborn; I was determined to show Teacher Liao that I was *dui*. Virtually all of my spare time went to studying Chinese, and the stack of flash cards on my desk grew rapidly. By the first week in November I knew three hundred characters. I had no clear idea what I was shooting for—I had a vague goal of reading a newspaper, which would require between two and three thousand. But mostly I knew that I needed more knowledge than I had, and I needed it quickly.

In the mornings I ran to the summit of Raise the Flag Mountain, charging hard up the steps, my lungs burning high above the Yangtze. The effort was satisfying—it was challenging but uncomplicated, and at the finish I could look down on the city and see where I had gone. It was different from the work of learning Chinese, which had no clear endpoint and gave me more frustration than satisfaction.

There was a skill to running, and in some ways it was the only skill I had in Fuling. Everybody else seemed to have found something that he or she was good at: the owner of the dumpling restaurant made dumplings, the shoeshine women shined shoes, the stick-stick soldiers carried loads on their leathered shoulders. It was less clear what my purpose was—I was a teacher, and that job was satisfying and clearly defined, but it disappeared once I left campus. Most people in town only saw my failures, the inevitable misunderstandings and botched conversations.

And they always watched carefully. The attention was so intense that in public I often became clumsily self-conscious, which was exacerbated by my suddenly becoming bigger than average. In America I was considered small at five feet nine inches, but now for the first time in my life I stood out in crowds. I bumped my head on bus doorways; I squeezed awkwardly behind miniature restaurant tables. I was like Alice in Wonderland, eating the currant-seed cakes and finding her world turned upside down.

Mostly I longed to find something that I could do well. This was part of why the simple routines of the city fascinated me; I could watch a stick-stick soldier or a restaurant cook with incredible intensity, simply because these people were good at what they did. There was a touch of voyeurism in my attention, at least in the sense that I watched the people work with all of the voyeur's impotent envy. There were many days when I would have liked nothing more than to have had a simple skill that I could do over and over again, as long as I did it well.

Running was repetitive in this way, and it was also an escape. If I ran on the roads, cars honked at me, people laughed and shouted, and sometimes a young man would try to impress his friends by chasing after me. But crowds couldn't gather around, and none of the young men followed for long. I ran alone, and in a crowded country that sort of solitude was worth something. There was nobody in the city who could catch me.

Usually I ran in the hills behind campus, following the small roads and footpaths that wound around Raise the Flag Mountain. I ran past old Daoist shrines, and atop the narrow walls of the rice paddies, and I followed the stone steps that led to the mountain's summit. I liked running past the ancient stone tombs that overlooked the rivers, and I liked seeing the peasants at work. On my runs I watched them harvest the rice crop, and thresh the yellowed stalks, and I saw them plant the winter wheat and tend their vegetables. I first learned the agricultural patterns by watching the workers as I ran, and I studied the shape of the mountain by feeling it beneath my legs.

The peasants found it strange that I ran in the hills, and they always stared when I charged past, but they never shouted or laughed. As a rule they were the most polite people you could ever hope to meet, and in any case they had more important things to do with their energy than scream at *waiguoren.* And perhaps they had an innate respect for physical effort, even when they didn't see the point.

The air in the countryside was often bad, because the Yangtze winds blew the city's pollution across the Wu River, and I knew that running did my health more harm than good. But it kept my mind steady, because the fields were quiet and peaceful and the activity felt the same as it always had. That old well-known feeling—the catch in my chest, the strain in my legs—connected all the places where I had lived, Missouri and Princeton and Oxford and Fuling. While I ran through the hills, my thoughts swung fluidly between these times and places; I remembered running along the old Missouri-Kansas-Texas railroad pathway, and I recalled the rapeseed blooming gold on Boar's Hill, and the old shaded bridge of Prettybrook. As the months slipped past I realized that even these Sichuan hills, with their strange tombs and terraces, were starting to feel like home.

But still the signs on the way to Raise the Flag Mountain were foreign, and even as they slowly became familiar they reminded me how far I still had to go:

Build 精神 Culture, New Give Birth 观念

Population Increase, 促进 Society 进步

Education Is a Powerful Country's 基础

DURING THAT SEMESTER there was a volatility to the written language; it constantly shifted in my eyes, and each day the shapes became something other than what they had been before. Spoken Chinese was also starting to settle in my ears, and soon I could make simple conversation with the owners of the restaurants where I ate. The same slow shift was also happening with regard to my tutors, who finally started to change from tone machines into real people.

As this happened, I began to sense an edge to Teacher Liao that I couldn't quite figure. It wasn't simply her tendency to say *budui*; she seemed slightly uncomfortable around both Adam and me, and there were moments when I almost thought she disliked us (which, given that we didn't pay her enough, would have been understandable). Later, I would come to recognize other reasons for this discomfort, but during that first semester I only sensed that there were complications in our relationship.

Once we had a tutorial the day after I had played in the faculty basketball tournament, and she asked what I had thought of the game. In fact, it had gone very badly—Adam and I were starting to realize that there was a great deal of resentment over our participation, because the English department team was now suddenly very good. To the other participants, the games were taking on a patriotic significance; it was a matter of China vs. America, an issue of saving face for the Motherland, and the games grew steadily rougher and rougher. The referees also took sides; they allowed our opponents to foul us while constantly whistling us for phantom violations. In the game before our tutorial, I had been whistled more than fifteen times for double-dribble—by the end of the game I only had to touch the ball and the whistle would blow. Adam and I were considering pulling out of the tournament, which we eventually did. It seemed the best solution for everybody involved.

I knew that Teacher Liao had been at the game, and I assumed that she felt the same way I did. My students had been embarrassed by the poor sportsmanship, and they told me that the referee had a horrible reputation on campus. He was notorious for getting into fights—once he even threatened an administrator with a knife. His wife had recently divorced him; the rumor was that he had beaten her. And yet the college was unable to fire him, because of the job security that was promised to all state workers under the traditional Communist system.

I answered Teacher Liao's question honestly, telling her that I hadn't found the game much fun.

"That referee," I said, "is a *huai dan.*" It was a common insult: bad egg.

"Budui!" said Teacher Liao. "It wasn't his problem—you were wrong. And you should not criticize the referee."

To me this seemed insult upon injury. I wanted to tell her: There are no tones in basketball and you have no jurisdiction over it. But she had more to say.

"You were dribbling wrong," she said. "That's why he kept penalizing you. You were doing this—" And she gestured, showing me that I had carried the ball.

"Budui!" I said. "That's not what I was doing. I was dribbling the same way I always do in America. That referee just doesn't like *waiguoren.* And he doesn't understand basketball."

"*Budui!* Here you can't dribble the same way that you do in America, because they have different rules in the NBA. That's the problem—you're accustomed to playing the American way."

She said it in hopes of ending the argument tactfully, because she saw that I was annoyed. But I had already heard too many explanations about "the Chinese way," and I did not want to be lectured about Basketball with Chinese Characteristics.

"Basketball is an American sport," I said. "We made the rules and I understand them. That referee just doesn't like *waiguoren.*" After I spoke, I realized how stupid my words sounded, and I might as well have continued: And we Americans can study a language for only four months and already convey our arrogance. But I didn't have the vocabulary for that, and in any case it was clear that both of us wanted to talk about something else. We reviewed a lesson about going to the airport and nobody mentioned basketball again.

Classes were simpler with Teacher Kong, who alternated weeks with Teacher Liao. He was slightly less inclined to say *budui*, partly because he had a lazy streak, but also because the struggles of that semester were slowly teaching us to recognize each other as people. Eventually he would become my first real Chinese friend—the first friend who saw me strictly in Chinese. And even in those early months, before we developed a true friendship, I could see his interest growing. He sometimes asked me about America, within the limits of my vocabulary, and I sensed there were many questions he would ask once he had the chance. Certainly I had a few of my own that were waiting for the language to catch up with my thoughts.

We had classes in my dining room, where the morning light was warm after the sun rose above the shoulder of Raise the Flag Mountain. We drank tea while we studied—jasmine flower tea, the tiny dried petals unfolding like blooming lilies on the surface of the hot water. Before he drank, Teacher Kong blew softly over the cup, so the loose leaves and flowers floated to the far side, and this was something else I learned in those classes. If he sipped a leaf by mistake, he turned and spat lightly on the floor. I learned that, too—I liked living in a cadre's apartment and still being able to spit on the floor.

One sunny afternoon in December, I was preparing for class when I heard loud music blaring from the plaza below. There wasn't anything unusual about that—the campus loudspeakers were always vomiting noise. But today I looked down from my balcony and saw a crowd assembling in front of the auditorium, and I knew that some sort of important event was about to take place.

My balcony looked straight down to the plaza and I could see everything clearly. A banner had been unfurled and stretched above the steps. I couldn't make out most of the characters, but a few were recognizable: "Safety," "Environment," "Peace." A row of chairs materialized below the banner. The crowd grew larger. Tables were set in front of the chairs. A blue cloth was laid upon the tables; teacups were put on the cloth. Microphones appeared.

I had seen this sort of arrangement before—it was a nesting area for cadres. Soon six of them marched up the steps and took their places at the table. I strained to see who they were, but I couldn't recognize their faces, and all I saw was that some were in uniform. But many people in Fuling wore uniforms and that never told you anything.

The speeches began, echoing up to my balcony. A crowd gathered at the bottom of the auditorium steps—mostly students, but also people from the neighborhood outside the gates, old peasants and women with their babies. They listened quietly, and in their silence I could see that it was a serious event. The speeches reverberated in the plaza and I couldn't understand what they were saying.

Teacher Kong arrived for class and set his books on the dining-room table. "It's very loud," he said, smiling, and I agreed—too loud to concentrate on Lesson Thirty-one and its mindless description of a train ride to Guilin. We stepped out onto the balcony and watched the crowd. There were hundreds of people listening to the speeches now, and I could see groups of students hurrying down from the teaching building.

"All of the students have been excused from class," Teacher Kong said, and I asked him what the event was. "They're going to *panjue* two people," he said. "It's a public *panjue*."

I hadn't studied the word, and he explained its meaning until I was nearly certain I understood. I went into the dining room to double-check with the dictionary—"*panjue*: bring a verdict; judgment." They were having a public sentencing in front of the auditorium.

"Are they students?" I asked.

"No. They're from East River."

I asked what they had done, and he explained that there had been a series of fights between East River people and students in the physical education department. East River was a rough part of town, a seedy riverfront section of small shops and dusty warehouses. After the Three Gorges Dam was built, much of East River would disappear underwater, and few people would probably miss it. The dirty streets were depressing, and the residents, most of whom were poor, saw the students as privileged outsiders—spoiled kids who lived six or seven to a bare room, cleaned their unheated classrooms, and woke up at six o'clock every morning for mandatory exercises. Sichuanese town-and-gown tension was, like anything else, a matter of relative conditions.

Recently this animosity had turned ugly; some of the East River men had used knives and sticks in the fights, and a couple of students had been hurt. I heard about it from my own students, who wrote in their journals about a weekend night when two physical education boys had been injured and their friends returned to the dormitory for reinforcements. They were collecting weapons of their own when the police arrived.

"None of the injuries was too serious," said Teacher Kong. "But they want to show the students that the college is safe, so today they're having a public *panjue*."

The cadres finished their speeches, the crowd waiting in expectant silence. Two men appeared, flanked by policemen. They wore cheap suits and their hands were cuffed behind their backs. The police marched them halfway down the steps of the auditorium, where they stood between the cadres and the crowd. The two men's heads were bowed. The students had pressed to the front; at the back stood the peasants and the mothers with their babies. Everybody was quiet. In the background, from the Wu River, I heard the low growl of riverboat horns.

One of the cadres read from a sheet of paper. His voice echoed over the plaza, and in response the crowd shifted and murmured. The two men kept their heads down.

"A few days," Teacher Kong said. "Only a few days in jail. Not very serious."

And in that instant it was over: the cops took the handcuffed men out the front gate, where a bus was waiting; the cadres disappeared; the tables were whisked away; the banner was taken down; the students returned to class. The people in Fuling were extremely organized with public events and their rallies could materialize and disappear in the space of an hour. Within fifteen minutes there was no sign that anything had happened in the plaza.

Teacher Kong and I reviewed some vocabulary from the trial, and then we moved on to Lesson Thirty-one. There was something strange about returning so quickly to class after having watched the sentencing from high above, as from a luxury box at a stadium, turning somebody's public humiliation into a vocabulary lesson. But many things were public in Fuling and few locals would have found it unusual. I had Peace Corps friends at another Sichuan teachers college who, the following spring, had their classes canceled one afternoon for a pre-execution rally in the school's sports stadium. Student attendance at the event was mandatory, because the criminals were young drug dealers and their deaths would provide a valuable lesson for the spectators. The college gathered in the stadium, where the police paraded the condemned prisoners in front of the students. Afterward the criminals were taken away to the countryside and shot. Classes resumed as normal the next day.

NOT LONG AFTER the sentencing, I came back from a run and realized that the sign in the center of campus had become completely intelligible. This was a moment I had always looked forward to—from the beginning, I had seen that string of characters as a benchmark, and I traced my progress in the way those words became meaningful. And one day all of it finally made sense:

Teaching Educates the People, Administration Educates the People, Service Educates the People, Environment Educates the People

I stopped and took a long look. I read the sign again, waiting for the sense of achievement. But nothing was there—it was simply propaganda, the same sort of trite phrase that could be found in the students' textbooks or on billboards all across the city. I would react the same way when the other messages on the way to Raise the Flag Mountain came into focus:

Construct a Spiritual Civilization, Replace the Old Concept of Giving Birth
Controlling Population Growth Promotes Social Development
Education Is the Foundation upon Which a Powerful Nation Is Built

All of it was the same old cant. Every time one of the signs became intelligible, I felt very little of the satisfaction that I had once imagined. Instead I heard Teacher Liao's voice in my head: Read the next one. You haven't achieved anything yet. And so I kept writing the characters over and over again at my desk, gazing out my window at the city.

LATE ONE AFTERNOON in December, Adam and I were summoned to the English department office, where we were informed that there would be a banquet tonight. These announcements were always made at the last minute, and they meant that the evening was effectively finished, because it was impossible to go to a banquet and not get hopelessly drunk.

A good part of our Peace Corps medical training had involved preparation for these moments. Even though we were only the third Peace Corps China group, the Sichuan countryside was already littered with tales of volunteers who had become banquet casualties. There were stories of fights, of vandalism, of volunteers who had become so dangerously intoxicated that they forever swore off drinking at such occasions. Our medical officer strongly recommended that after arriving at site we establish ourselves as nondrinkers, at least as far as banquets were concerned.

The most frequently performed procedure in Sichuanese emergency rooms was stomach-pumping. The vast majority of these patients were male, because drinking, like smoking, was an important part of being a man. This was true in many parts of China, especially in the more remote regions, and Sichuan drinking wasn't simply a casual way to relax. Often it was competitive, and usually it involved *baijiu,* a powerful and foul-tasting grain alcohol. Men toasted each other with full shots, and there was a tendency for this drinking to turn into a kind of bullying, the participants goading each other until somebody got sick. One of our Peace Corps training sessions had involved personal testimony from a Sichuanese man, who shrugged sheepishly and explained that even good friends were perfectly willing to drink each other into the hospital. Like the medical officer, he recommended that we use our *waiguoren* status to avoid this ritual entirely.

It was a typical Peace Corps scenario: having been told a wealth of horror stories about the pointless machismo of Sichuanese drinking, Adam and I were promptly sent down the river to the most remote Peace Corps site in the province. At our welcoming banquet, when we were served our first shot of *baijiu,* neither of us hesitated for even a second. Our training had repeatedly emphasized that this was critical to whatever it took to be a man in a place like Fuling, and as far as we were concerned this was part of our job. We hadn't come all this way just to be *waiguoren.* We downed the shot, and we downed the next one, too.

During that first month we had two or three banquets a week, and soon I could see that all of the drinking was organized with remarkable intricacy. The faculty took it easy on us at the beginning, no doubt because the Peace Corps had given all the colleges a stern warning about responsibility. But eventually our colleagues came to the same conclusion that we had: the Peace Corps was far away. Steadily the pressure to drink increased, and as time passed I realized that the English department had an alcoholic leaderboard. This wasn't a literal leaderboard in the sense of being written down, but it was completely public and accepted. You could ask any teacher where his alcohol tolerance stood in relation to everybody else's in the department, and he would answer with well-tested precision. Party Secretary Zhang was at the top, followed by Albert, then Dean Fu, and so on through the ranks until you came to Teacher Sai, who was such a lightweight that people referred to him scornfully as "Miss Sai" during banquets.

Within three weeks Adam was the undisputed number one drinker in the English department. I was ranked second; Party Secretary Zhang slipped to third. In truth I wasn't much of a drinker at home, but Fuling tolerance levels tended to be low, because many residents have a genetic intolerance of alcohol that is common among Asians. Even Party Secretary Zhang, despite his lofty ranking, turned bright red after a few drinks. This was one reason why local drinking patterns were so abusive with relatively light consequences; most people were genetically unable to become alcoholics. Once or twice a week they might be able to drink heavily, but they got too sick to do it all the time. It was a ritual rather than a habit.

In a pathetic way, drinking became one small thing that Adam and I were good at, although it was difficult to take much pride in this. If anything, it said a great deal about our troubles adjusting to Fuling life, because the banquets and the drinking, despite their strange childishness, represented one of our more comfortable environments. We gained instant respect for our tolerance levels, and to a certain degree this was how the department authorities communicated with us. If they had something important to tell us, or if a request needed to be made, it was handled at a banquet. Our colleagues, who usually seemed stiff and nervous around the *waiguoren*, loosened up once the *baijiu* started flowing. These events were strictly all-male—the only women involved were the waitresses who served the *baijiu*.

Before the December banquet, Adam and I were escorted into the English department office to meet our hosts for the evening. Two men stood up and shook our hands, smiling. One of them was a tall handsome man in his forties and the other was a short older man of perhaps sixty years. The tall man wore a new sweater, and from the way he carried himself it was clear that he was important—a cadre. It was also just as obvious that they were here to make some request of us, because they were sponsoring the meal. Teacher Sai and Dean Fu were there to translate.

"This is Mr. Wang from the Chinese department," Teacher Sai said. "Mr. Wang came to the college in 1977—he was part of the first class when the college opened after the Great Cultural Revolution. He was the best English student, but English was not a preferred subject in those days. So he became a Chinese professor instead. But he is still very interested in English."

Adam and I shook Teacher Wang's hand again. Teacher Sai seemed to have forgotten the other man, who didn't appear to be offended. Obviously he was accustomed to moving in the bigger man's wake.

All of us sat down. Adam and I waited for the request; cynically I assumed that Teacher Wang wanted English lessons. Already I could imagine myself sitting in this cadre's office, bored to tears while he said, slowly, "How-are-you?"

"Mr. Wang has heard that you studied literature," Dean Fu said. "He wants to ask you some questions about American literature."

This took me by surprise. I asked him what he meant.

"Mr. Wang is the editor of the college literary magazine," said Dean Fu. "He has more than ten thousand books."

He paused to let the number sink in. Then he leaned forward and spoke in a low voice. "Mr. Wang," he said, "has the most books of anybody in Fuling Teachers College."

A proud smile flickered across Teacher Wang's face and I could see that he understood what had been said. I wondered if Sichuanese men had book rankings as well as alcohol rankings, and what the relationship might be between these two sources of prestige. This was all uncharted territory—in Peace Corps training nobody had warned us about books.

I said that I knew less about American literature than English literature, but I'd try to answer his questions. Teacher Wang nodded and shot off his first query in Chinese to Dean Fu, who translated.

"Mr. Wang has a question about Saul Bellow," he announced. "Does the average American understand his books?"

I said that I had read very little of Bellow's work, but my impression was that his style was accessible, and that he was considered one of the best Jewish American writers and a voice of Chicago. Teacher Wang nodded, as if this was what he had expected to hear. He had another question ready.

"What about Joyce Carol Oates?" Dean Fu said. "Do you think that she follows in the tradition of Virginia Woolf?"

"Not really," I said. "Most people say that Joyce Carol Oates isn't a feminist writer. Actually, some feminists criticize her."

This led us to a discussion on feminism, followed by Toni Morrison and black women writers, and then we came to southern literature. After that we talked about Hemingway and the "Dirty Realism" of authors like Raymond Carver and Tobias Wolff. All of it was translated through Dean Fu, and as we talked I realized that he had an even more impressive knowledge of American literature than I had thought. I also realized that I was a jackass for assuming that the ten-thousand-book Teacher Wang needed my help to say "How-are-you."

After half an hour we moved to the banquet hall. The first toast was a general one, for everybody at the table, and then Teacher Wang gave Adam and me a special toast. Party Secretary Zhang followed with another shot for the entire party. When the next toast came around, Teacher Sai pushed his cup away and grinned nervously.

"I can't drink any more," he said. "That is enough."

"Drink it," said Party Secretary Zhang. "All of it."

"You know that I do not drink," Teacher Sai said. He brought his hands together and bowed his head quickly in a pleading gesture. Teacher Sai was one of the brightest of the department teachers, a pudgy man in his forties who was always smiling. Tonight his face was already bright red after two shots. He shook his head again.

"No, no, no," said Party Secretary Zhang. "You must do it for our guests."

"I can't."

They were speaking English for our benefit, but then they shifted to Chinese. While arguing they fought over the cup—Teacher Sai tried to push it away while Party Secretary Zhang held it firmly on the table. Dean Fu and Teacher Wang grinned. They joined in, scoffing at Teacher Sai until at last he picked up the shot glass. Everybody watched.

It took him a long time to drain the cup. He drank it in three painful sips, and after the last one he gasped and coughed. He put the cup back down on the table. Within seconds the waitress was there to refill it. Teacher Sai quickly put his hand over the cup, shaking his head.

"That is enough," he said.

Party Secretary Zhang tried to pry Teacher Sai's hand away. The waitress stood by patiently, bottle in hand. It was a quintessentially Sichuanese scene—for every scroll painting of a lovely river they could have had ten depicting *baijiu* arguments, two men scrabbling over a cup while a young woman waited with a bottle.

"Seriously," Teacher Sai said. "That is enough for me."

"Miss Sai," taunted Party Secretary Zhang, pulling at his hand.

"Miss Sai," echoed Dean Fu, grinning.

Teacher Wang said something and everybody laughed. For a few minutes the entire table was focused on Teacher Sai's cup. It was hard to believe that less than an hour ago we had been talking about Saul Bellow and Joyce Carol Oates. Finally Teacher Sai relented.

"Only one more," he said. "This is the last one."

The waitress filled his cup. Teacher Wang smiled and turned his attention toward Adam and me. He made a quick gesture, holding up his cup, and the three of us drank. Teacher Wang downed the *baijiu* easily and he was not turning red.

The food came and for a while the shots slowed. When they resumed, everybody had forgotten about Teacher Sai, who was only good entertainment at the start and finish of a banquet. He was too much hassle once the serious drinking started and now he sat sipping tea while the *baijiu* flowed in earnest.

There was strategy to this part of the banquet and usually the shots were preceded by low murmurings, the teachers speaking the Sichuan dialect while Adam and I muttered English back and forth. The trick was to get a two-for-one—if Party Secretary Zhang toasted both Adam and me, then we would both drink and immediately afterward Dean Fu could do the same. Our response was to hit them with a preemptive strike; if we sensed that they were plotting, one of us would toast the pair, or the entire table, and then they would have to recover before resuming the attack. Occasionally they tried to focus on me, sensing weakness, but when that happened Adam would step in and cover me. That was acceptable in Sichuan—a friend could take a shot for you. Sichuanese drinking was a lot like war.

Every banquet had a leader, a sort of alcoholic alpha male who controlled the direction of the *baijiu.* Party Secretary Zhang always led the English-department events, but tonight he deferred to Teacher Wang. The big man worked quickly and with surprising fairness, toasting the entire table until the other teachers started to weaken. After that he focused on Adam and me, scorning the usual two-for-one as he traded personal shots between the two of us. It was a remarkable exhibition. After half an hour the three of us were still the most sober at the table, but I was fading quickly and Teacher Wang showed no signs of slowing. I heard Dean Fu and Party Secretary Zhang asking him to ease up, because they were afraid I would get sick, and at last the flurry of toasts ended.

Teacher Wang began to tell a long story. It was about a pedicab and he told it in Sichuanese while Teacher Sai translated. The story moved slowly and I was too drunk to listen carefully. My gaze wandered across the table until I found myself looking at the little man who had come with Teacher Wang. I had forgotten entirely about him and now he smiled. He said something, but I couldn't understand; he was a dialect speaker and in any case the *baijiu* had not improved either of our language abilities. Finally he concentrated very hard, pronouncing four Mandarin syllables clearly.

"Sha shi bi ya," he said.

"I'm sorry," I said in Chinese. "What did you say?"

"Sha shi bi ya."

I shook my head and he repeated it a few more times, gesturing as if he were reading a book. Finally something clicked in my mind.

"Shakespeare?" I said.

He laughed and gave me the thumbs up. *"Di gen si."*

"Dickens?"

He nodded and laughed again.

"Ma ke tu wen."

"Mark Twain."

Slowly we made our way through Melville, Norris, O'Connor, and Cheever. It took me a long time to guess Norris and Cheever. There wasn't anything else that we were able to talk about and I never learned the little man's name, although he was able to communicate that he especially liked the Norris novel *McTeague*, which is perhaps the only great American novel about a dentist. Nowadays hardly anybody in America reads Norris but there was at least one fan along the Upper Yangtze.

Teacher Wang finished with the pedicab story. Even though I had missed most of it I could gather that it was about a time when he was very drunk and spent half an hour negotiating with a pedicab, only to realize that he was already in front of his hotel. All of the men laughed at the story. Listening to its translation reminded them that Teacher Sai was still there.

"Drink," said Party Secretary Zhang, pointing at Teacher Sai's cup.

"I can't."

"Drink."

"I can't."

"Yes."

"No."

"Drink!"

"I'm sorry."

"Miss Sai!"

"Miss Sai!"

Finally he shuddered through another shot. It was clear that the banquet was breaking up, and Teacher Wang held his cup up to Adam and me. We raised our glasses.

"To books," I said.

But Teacher Wang had something else in mind. He spoke to me, seriously now, and Teacher Sai translated.

"Mr. Wang," he said, "wants you to write something for the college magazine."

Our cups were frozen above the table.

"What do you mean?"

"He wants you to write an article about literature."

"American or English? And how long?"

They discussed this quickly. Our three cups were still in midair; it was without question the most favorable instant for a request.

"American is better," said Teacher Sai. "Only about ten thousand words."

I caught my breath. "I don't know American literature well enough for that," I said. "Tell him I can do either Elizabethan poetry or Charles Dickens, because that's what I studied at Oxford. Or Shakespeare. But otherwise it would be difficult. I don't have many notes here."

There was another discussion. My arm was growing heavy. Teacher Wang nodded.

"Dickens," said Teacher Sai. "Ten thousand words."

We drank the shot. The *baijiu* was starting to taste dangerously foul and I shuddered after it was down. A good banquet was like a good short story: there was always a point, but you didn't quite understand it until the very end. Now I realized why we had been invited tonight, but I wasn't resentful; at least now I knew how a Sichuanese literary journal recruited new material. The table bullied Teacher Sai for a few more minutes and then all of us staggered out.

I HOPED THAT EVERYBODY would forget about the promised essay, but within a week the quiet reminders started. I delayed, explaining that I was busy with teaching, but then I began to receive messages about Teacher Wang's impending deadline. Finally I sat down and wrote what he wanted, which was an essay about Dickens' relationship to political reform.

I wrote it as quickly as possible. I argued that Dickens was essentially a middle-class figure who liked writing about social problems not because he wanted revolutionary change, but rather because these subjects made for good creative material. I knew the Marxists wouldn't like this approach, so I added a line that accused Dickens of being a Capitalist Roader. I liked being able to use that term in a literary essay. Otherwise the article was not very enjoyable to write, and I loaded the descriptions in order to jack up the word count. Teacher Sai had to translate it into Chinese. For a solid week he struggled with the damn thing, coming into my office with questions about my inflated prose, holding his head in his hands.

ON THE SECOND DAY of January, the city of Fuling held a road race in the center of town. It was the Twenty-second Annual Long Race to Welcome Spring, and all of the city's schools and *danwei*, or work units, competed against each other. Two weeks before the race, Dean Fu asked if I would run on the college team. He was obviously nervous, because it hadn't been long since the problems of the faculty basketball tournament.

"You must understand," he said, smiling uncomfortably. "There will be many peasants and uneducated people. They don't know anything about sportsmanship, and perhaps some of them will be rough. Also, in twenty-one years they have never had a foreigner in the long race. They welcome you to participate, but I think it will be different from in America."

I could see that Dean Fu thought it would be simpler if I didn't run, and I knew he was right. For a while I considered not taking part, because the basketball tournament had been a low point in an otherwise good semester. All of the difficult parts of my life were already public; there wasn't any reason to seek out more crowds.

But there are no referees in running, and it is not a contact sport. There would be crowds but I figured that at least I would be moving. It couldn't be much different from a race in America—and even if it was, I was curious to see what it was like, at least once. I told Dean Fu that I wanted to participate.

He explained that every runner had to have a physical exam, and a week before the race I visited a doctor in the college infirmary. It was a low tile-roofed building next to the croquet court, one of the old structures on campus that remained from the pre-Cultural Revolution days when the college had been a high school.

The doctor checked my pulse and blood pressure. After each test he smiled and told me that I was very healthy, and I thanked him. Then he led me to a side room where a dirty white box-shaped instrument hung on the wall. Dean Fu said, "Now you will have a chest X ray."

I stopped at the entrance to the room. "I don't want to have a chest X ray," I said.

"It's no problem," said Dean Fu, smiling. "It's very safe."

"I don't want a chest X ray," I said again, and I looked at the dirty box and thought: Especially I don't want *this* chest X ray. "Why is it necessary?"

"Everybody in the race must have one. To make sure they are healthy."

"Everybody?" I asked, and he nodded. I asked how many people would be running.

"More than two thousand and five hundred."

"And all of them must have a chest X ray before they can run?"

"Yes," he said. "That is the rule. It is very safe."

It struck me as a ludicrous notion—that a city with a per capita income of about forty American dollars a month would require a chest X ray from each of the 2,500 participants in a four-kilometer road race. I had my suspicions about what was really happening: some administrator in the college was probably worried about me dropping dead in the middle of the race, and they wanted to cover their tracks. It was always Dean Fu's job to convey such commands to the *waiguoren*, and occasionally he served as a filter as much as a translator. It was a lousy job and I always felt sorry for him when I sensed that this was happening, but there was nothing to do about it except try to find a tactful solution.

We were at an impasse. Dean Fu could see that I was serious about refusing to have an X ray, and I knew that he couldn't simply back down and say that the procedure wasn't in fact required. We stood there for a moment, the doctor watching expectantly. Finally I told Dean Fu that I would go to my apartment and call the Peace Corps office in Chengdu.

I tried to call but the medical officer wasn't in. I sat in my bedroom for ten minutes, reading a book, and then I returned to the infirmary.

"I'm very sorry," I said, "but the Peace Corps told me I can't have a chest X ray. I don't know what we can do about this."

"It's no problem," Dean Fu said. "I just talked to some of the people in charge of the race, and they said it is fine if you do not have an X ray. They will give you an exception because you are a foreigner."

I thanked him and apologized for the hassle, and he apologized back. Both of us shook the doctor's hand. He walked us to the door, smiling and waving as we left.

THERE WAS NO SCHEDULED TIME for the race to start. The runners assembled in a disorderly mob at the starting area, and at nine o'clock the cadres began their speeches. The race would begin whenever the speeches finished, and thc officials droned on and on while the starting line repeatedly broke and surged. A small section would make a false start and the rest of the crowd would react, and then the police would call everybody back. I tried to jog in place to stay warm, fighting with my elbows to keep position.

The starting line was spread across a massive construction site where a new public park was being built. The entire left side of the line headed directly toward a six-foot drop—a small, crumbling cliff. On the far right was a narrow dirt road that provided the only safe exit for the runners, but it was so close to the start—less than forty yards—that it would be impossible for the crowd to funnel in such a short distance. And even for the runners who did make it safely, the course immediately took a ninety-degree turn that would claim more victims.

Without question it was the most dangerous starting arrangement I had ever seen in a lifetime of racing. I was tempted to pull out, partly for my safety but mostly because I wanted to be able to watch the disaster from the perspective of a spectator. Rob Schmitz, another Peace Corps volunteer, was visiting us that week, and he and Adam took their cameras and gleefully waited across the road.

The college team had staked out a spot on the right side of the line, directly in front of the exit. Most of them were physical education students, and usually we were the best team in the race, along with the Taiji medicine factory. All of us squeezed together, waiting for the start. It was a cool morning and the winter smog hung low over the city.

Five minutes passed, then ten. The cadres kept talking, and the police were having trouble holding everybody back. Either they were going to start the race or it was going to start itself, and finally one of the cadres must have realized this. He fired the gun.

It was China. Chaos, noise, adrenaline; fear and surprise and excitement; a mass of bodies, everybody yelling, horns sounding, the earth pounding; all of us running madly, arms outstretched to clear room; legs pumping, dashing, sprinting, trying to keep the back kick low to avoid being tripped; some runners shouting as they stumbled over the cliff, others skidding around the first turn, dodging the few unfortunate ones who fell and skidded below the rush of legs. The seconds slid past, each moment an eternity of concentration and effort. We flew down the street in a wild charging mob, hit the second turn, and headed west on Xinghua Road.

The course began to climb uphill. The scene was still shaky with adrenaline but I realized that the eternity of the start was over, and that I was no longer a part of the starting mob. After the beginning of a race there is always that moment of disengagement, when the euphoria of being a part of something massive is over and you realize that you are alone, and that you have your own race to run.

I slowed down. Suddenly I felt tired; the adrenaline evaporated and everything slipped into focus. I checked myself—no scrapes, no bruises; no memory of exactly how I had made it safely off the line. I glanced around me. I was in the lead pack, a group of perhaps fifty, and the others were also settling in after the rush of the start. We were climbing steadily now and the pace was slowing. I felt my legs come back to me, the numb excitement replaced by the rhythm of a long hard run—steady steady steady steady, up on my toes as the hill steepened. Police cars rolled their lights in front of the pack. Far ahead, groups of school kids were trying to cheat, jumping into the race with a lead of a hundred yards, but the cops pulled them out as they drove past.

The entire first half was uphill, and by the time I took the lead, perhaps two minutes into the race, I could see that the others were finished. It was a varied field—college students and *danwei* workers and a few athletes who clearly could have been good runners with more training—but all of them were done. Quickly I slipped ahead.

To lead any big race is a strange feeling. People speak of the loneliness of running, but I've always felt that the sport is lonely only in the races, and especially when the pack breaks and you find yourself alone in front. In the pack you usually feel some solidarity with the other athletes, even though you are still competing, but in front there are no illusions. That's when the race becomes a chase—one man against the rest of the field—and I've always felt that this is the loneliest feeling in the world. And it's even lonelier when you are the only foreigner in a field of more than two thousand, and all along the course spectators are calling out *"Waiguoren, waiguoren, waiguoren."* Out-of-country person, out-of-country person, out-of-country person.

I looked back. Behind me I could see the rest of the field—an endless stream of people, a black-haired mob. The main pace car had slowed and I was following a few strides behind its flashing lights. I looked back again, so I would remember the strangeness of the scene. The hill was steep now, climbing toward the pointed tower of the Monument to the Revolutionary Martyrs. The street was lined with spectators and I could hear the wave of surprise as I passed; they were talking excitedly and exclaiming with amazement. *"Waiguoren, waiguoren, waiguoren."*

And I thought: Not today. If you're looking for people who are out of their country, out of place, out of step, out of shape, awkward, clumsy; if that's what you're looking for, look back there. Look for the ones who started too fast, or the men who have smoked too many Magnificent Sound cigarettes, or the people who are wearing too many clothes and are choking with heat and sweat. Don't look at me—I've done this for many years in many places, and always it has been exactly the same. There are no referees, no language barriers, no complicated rules of etiquette. All you do is run.

By the turnaround I had more than thirty seconds on the next runner, and I took it easy from there. The second half was all downhill, and because it was an out-and-back course I passed the rest of the field. The ones who weren't too exhausted joined in the chorus: *"Waiguoren, waiguoren, waiguoren."* But it didn't bother me a bit, because for those four kilometers I felt completely at home.

FOR THE VICTORY I won two pairs of polyester sports uniforms, both too small, with the characters for Fuling City inscribed proudly on the chest. I also received a certificate testifying that "Comrade He Wei," my Chinese name, had won the Twenty-second Annual Long Race to Welcome Spring. The race organizers awarded me twenty yuan, and the college gave me five for participating on its team. They also gave me one and a half yuan for undergoing the medical exam, which made me wonder how much I could have made if I had agreed to the chest X ray. All told I cleared twenty-six and a half yuan, which paid for two weeks of noodle lunches.

I was on the local TV news for the following week, and the next day's paper featured a front-page story about the race. They reported that an American teacher from Missouri named H.Essler had participated, and there was a detailed description of the way I had warmed up before the start. They reported the excitement of the college representatives when I finished in first place, and they quoted one of the other top finishers, a young man from the medicine factory who said, "If this race had been right after my military training, I definitely would have beaten that foreigner." The end of the article read:

> The competition also succeeded in establishing patriotism in sports. When our reporter asked, "What are your thoughts about a *waiguoren* finishing first," a Trade School student named Xu Chengbo said: "To have a sports competition in a Chinese area and allow a *waiguoren* to take first place, I feel very ashamed. This gives us a wake-up call: our students and adults need to improve the quality of their bodies, because if we improve our strength, we can be victorious!" . . . A Southwest Military School teacher said: "The *waiguoren* took the initiative, and that sort of spirit deserves to be studied. Only if we plunge into developing our bodies, and have more diligent and scientific training, will we see the day when we achieve the championship!"

It wasn't exactly the reaction I had hoped for, although I wasn't surprised. There was a great deal of patriotism in Fuling, and sports always made these feelings particularly intense. That was why the basketball had been such a failure, and sometimes I wondered if it had been a bad idea to run in the race. A few of my Peace Corps friends thought that at least I shouldn't have tried to win. But I liked running races hard, just like many others in the competition, and I saw no reason to treat the people in Fuling like children. I wanted them to know that *waiguoren* were living in their city, and I wanted them to see that despite all my struggles with the language, there was at least one thing I could do well. If they reacted with shame, that was unfortunate, but perhaps when they grew to know me better it would be different. I figured it was a good sign that my certificate read "Comrade He Wei."

A few days after the race, I had class with Teacher Liao, who beamed when we started the lesson.

"I saw on the department message board that you won the long race in Fuling!" she said. "I hadn't heard—why didn't you tell me?"

"It's not important," I said. "In fact, I didn't run very fast at all."

"Yes, you did!" she said, doubly pleased by my false modesty, which followed the appropriate Chinese custom. "That's a very big race—in all of Fuling City, you are the fastest person!"

"There are probably better athletes who didn't participate," I said. "And you know, Wang Junxia is still faster than me."

Wang Junxia was the Chinese woman distance runner who had recently won gold and silver medals in the Atlanta Olympics, and this reference made Teacher Liao even happier. She praised me again, and finally we settled down to a chapter on how to say goodbye. Either I did unusually well or she was in a particularly forgiving mood; on that day she hardly said *budui* at all.

白鶴梁

THE WHITE CRANE RIDGE

TODAY THE YANGTZE RIVER is two inches higher than it was in midwinter 1,234 years ago. The intervening years have witnessed other changes—the passing of five imperial dynasties; the arrival and departure of the Mongols, the Manchus, the British, the Japanese; the construction of the Great Wall and the destruction of the Cultural Revolution; the Great Leap Forward and the Reform and Opening; the development of the Three Gorges Dam from a half-formed dream to the biggest building project in China—but despite all of these changes the level of today's Yangtze is exactly two inches higher than it was in 763. Two inches in 1,234 years.

This is the story that is told by the White Crane Ridge, an eighty-yard-long strip of sandstone that sits like a temporary island in Fuling's harbor. At most the ridge emerges from below the muddy skin of the Yangtze for five winter months, in the heart of the dry season, and the ridge does not appear at all if the year is unusually wet. When it does emerge, the sandstone speaks—twenty-two pictures and over 300,000 characters are engraved on its surface. Along the nearly four thousand miles of the Yangtze's length, there is no other place where man has left such a vivid record of the river's life.

Nobody knows for certain when the ridge was first used in this way, but virtually all of the carvings refer to a pair of stone carp that are engraved at the bobbing waterline of the river. Each fish is nearly two feet long and they swim one after the other, heading westward, their bellies forming a line that represented the low-water mark at the time of their engraving. In the hooked mouth of the forward carp is a lotus blossom. These fish were carved sometime in the Tang Dynasty before the year 763, which is the date of the first engraved reference to their appearance. This afternoon, the level of the Yangtze is just a touch higher than the line of the carp.

The original purpose of the fish was practical rather than artistic. Never was the Yangtze more dangerous to boats than in winter, when low water exposed shoals and crags. Pilots passing Fuling could study the White Crane Ridge, note the water level in comparison to the twin carp, and predict the condition of the river ahead. The fish swam in place; the river constantly fluctuated; the locals understood this relationship and it became part of the Yangtze's annual pattern.

Over the years, other dynasties left their own engravings on the ridge, most of which note the return of the Tang fish. Just above the two carp, a Northern Song Dynasty carving greets their appearance in the year 971: "The water of the river retreats. The stone fish are seen. Next year there will be a bumper harvest." Ten feet higher on the ridge, time suddenly leaps three and a half centuries to 1333, when Yuan Dynasty officials note the Tang carp's return: "In Fuling the appearance of the stone fish indicates a great harvest, guarding the prefecture for the next year."

Most of the carvings follow this ritualized form—the date of the carp's sighting, followed by a harvest prediction, all of which is inscribed in the name of the emperor. Central to this ritual was the belief that the appearance of these Tang fish was associated with harvests, and eventually the White Crane Ridge shifted from a navigational tool into an oracle of the mysterious and vital cycles of the natural world. And pinned through these never-ending cycles was the straight line of human history, as the representatives of emperor after emperor left their marks on the rock.

The ridge was only one of dozens of annual signs that were recorded in this way by the emperor. He was the Son of Heaven, a representative of the unspeakable forces of nature, and yet the manifestation of these same forces—an earthquake, a flood, a famine—could signal that heaven had turned against a ruler and his dynasty. The emperor embodied what he could not control and did not understand. As a result, he sought refuge in ritual, and the Fuling government officials regularly engraved the stone in the name of their ruler, despite the broken and weathered paragraphs of old that testified to lost dynasties and forgotten emperors. And the springtime rising of the Yangtze, the swollen river sweeping over the characters, gave evidence that there were forces the emperor could only watch, and that his glorious titles, like the inscriptions, were nothing more than words.

And so it goes with the Yuan. The 1333 inscription speaks optimistically of a bumper harvest, but the dynasty is already on the decline, having slipped from what was the largest empire the world has ever known—the empire of Kublai Khan, the Mongol-ruled China that Marco Polo visited. But by 1333, Marco Polo is long gone, and Kublai Khan is dead, and the power of the Yuan is fading. Their officials carve bravely onto the stone, but the dynasty has only thirty-five more years before the wash of time covers it forever.

DOCKED ON THE SOUTH SIDE of the White Crane Ridge are three sampans. The boats are wood, with arched roofs of bamboo and woven reeds. Each roof is less than three feet tall at the highest point, reducing wind drag and avoiding a structure that could tip the craft, which has no keel. The boats are light and narrow, low-gunneled, with virtually no freeboard, and they are easily maneuvered in the river's current. Their design has not changed greatly since people first began carving on the rock to which the sampans are tethered.

Four women chat in the prow of a boat. All of them wear simple jackets of blue, and their clothes, like the boats, are dirty. They are river people who live on their sampans; for most of the year they depend on fishing, but winter fish are sluggish and the owners of these crafts spend the season on the ridge. They rely on tourism, using small rowboats to ferry visitors back and forth from shore.

Today is a holiday and more than fifty visitors are wandering up and down the sandstone, gazing at the inscriptions. Occasionally they will ask a question of one of the eight workers stationed on the ridge, who have been sent here by the Fuling City Cultural Relics Administration. Two of these staff members have some formal education in archaeology, while the others are common workers whose job is to sell snacks, oversee the rowboats, and, for two yuan, take photographs of visitors next to the ridge's biggest carved fish.

A cold wind runs down the corridor of the river valley, and the workers huddle around their snack table, shivering and drinking hot tea. They watch the Yangtze closely, measuring its level every day. Undoubtedly they dream of the river rising, because whenever it covers the carvings they can return to the indoors work of their government office in town. For them, the appearance of the stone carp augurs nothing more than long cold days of exile out on the river.

To a certain degree this is appropriate, because a number of inscriptions were made by government officials who for various infractions had been exiled to Fuling. It was the sort of place that made for a good punishment—a lonely river town far from the heart of the empire, a post where communications broke down and the civilized world slipped away. One carving was mistakenly made in the name of an emperor who had actually already died. News of his passing had not yet made its way down the Yangtze, and so local officials didn't realize that they were the subjects of a new ruler.

And while Fuling sometimes represented the end of a political career, the ridge is testimony that other pursuits could flourish here. Poetry and calligraphy were the traditional pastimes of the lonely exile, and many of the local officials left inscriptions that are works of beauty. Toward the western edge, four characters are inscribed with particular style: "The River Runs Forever." This carving's exact date is unknown; it was made sometime during the Kuomintang period, in the 1930s or 1940s, and the calligraphy's distinctive loops and curves are of the "running grass" script style. The last character, *nian*, trails off in a long straight line that points like a dagger at the river below.

Perhaps the ridge's most famous calligraphy consists of four large characters less than twenty feet from the Tang carp. These words are stacked one on top of the other, and they follow the flowing form of the "running hand" style. Moss grows green in the ruts of the inscription, which says, "Pillar Rock in Midstream."

The author, Xie Bin, was a celebrated calligrapher in the Fuling area, where his skills earned him the nickname Sacred Hand. He carved the phrase in 1881, during the Qing Dynasty, and the elegant inscription calls to mind that period more than a century ago, when the pillar rock holds steady but China is in trouble. The Opium Wars have been fought and lost; the Great Taiping Rebellion has been put down at enormous expense. European powers control ports all along the Chinese coast. Government money to modernize the navy is being diverted to build a new pleasure palace for Cixi, the Empress Dowager. Thirteen years from now; the Japanese will invade Korea, taking both the peninsula and southern Manchuria. But the White Crane Ridge emerges as it always has, and Fuling's Sacred Hand leaves his graceful mark.

A Russian-made hydrofoil streaks past the north side of the rock, heading toward Chongqing. The boat's wake rises and swamps the lower section of the ridge. Tourists scamper to higher ground, laughing, and the water breaks white over the characters and engraved fish. Then the waves subside, and the carvings are clear once more, and the river runs the same way it has run forever.

CHAPTER FOUR

The Dam

I TAUGHT MY WRITING CLASS from a Chinese-published text called *A Handbook of Writing.* Like all of the books we used, its political intent was never understated, and the chapter on "Argumentation" featured a model essay entitled "The Three Gorges Project Is Beneficial."

It was a standard five-paragraph essay and the opening section explained some of the risks that had led people to oppose the project: flooded scenery and cultural relics, endangered species that might be pushed to extinction, the threat of earthquake, landslide, or war destroying a dam that would hold back a lake four hundred miles long. "In short," the second paragraph concluded, "the risks of the project may be too great for it to be beneficial."

The next two sentences provided the transition. "Their worries and warnings are well justified," the essay continued. "But we should not give up eating for fear of choking." And the writer went on to describe the benefits—more electricity, improved transportation, better flood control—and concluded by asserting that the Three Gorges Project had more advantages than disadvantages.

I had some moral qualms about teaching a model persuasive essay whose topic had been banned from public debate in China since 1987—this seemed a slap in the face to the very notion of argumentation. At worst it was an exercise in propaganda, and at best it didn't seem particularly sporting. But I had nothing else to work with, and the truth was that the essay, apart from its political agenda, provided a good structural model. My job was to teach the students how to write such a composition, and so I went ahead and taught it. I reckoned there was no sense in giving up eating for fear of choking.

I was punished by having that transition sentence infect my students' papers for the rest of the term. They were accustomed to learning by rote, which meant that they often followed models to the point of plagiarism. They were also inveterate copiers; it wasn't uncommon to receive the exact same paper from two or three students. There wasn't really a sense of wrong associated with these acts—all through school they had been taught to imitate models, and copy things, and accept what they were told without question, and often that was what they did.

When I told them that the Three Gorges essay was a good model, they listened carefully and adopted its nuances in future work. I assigned argumentative essays on whether students should be required to do morning exercises, and many of them opened their compositions by describing the benefits of the morning routine. After that was finished, they made their shift: "But we should not give up eating for fear of choking." Even students who were writing on opposite sides of the issue used that same transition. Later I assigned an argumentative essay on Hamlet's character, and they listed his shortcomings—indecisiveness, cruelty to Ophelia—and many of them seemed like good papers until suddenly that cursed sentence came from nowhere and boomed out, "But we should not give up eating for fear of choking." I came to loathe the phrase, and repeatedly I told them that it was a horrid transition, but it always reappeared. At last I gave up, consoling myself by thinking darkly of the day when the river was dammed, and the Yangtze would rise up and carry away all of the *Handbooks of Writing* and smash them in the dam's seven-hundred-megawatt turbines.

That was only fancy, of course—the new reservoir would cause the river to rise, but it wouldn't climb as high as the teaching building. Some of my students said it would hardly reach the middle of the East River district, while others said it would flood the entire neighborhood, rising all the way to the college's front gates. None of them knew for certain, but they didn't seem to care. They had been told that the dam was beneficial, and that was enough.

IN TOWN I KNEW EXACTLY where the waterline of the new Yangtze would be, because there were signs that marked its future rise. One was in the old part of Fuling, painted in red on the side of a snack shop. There was another in downtown's Mid-Mountain Road, which was the second big street above the docks.

Both of these signs said the same thing in huge red numbers: "177m." This figure represented the future water level of the reservoir, which at its maximum could be filled to an elevation of 177 meters (581 feet) above sea level. There were red signs like this in all of the Yangtze settlements, and heading downstream the numbers marched steadily up the hillsides, until at last you came to low-lying towns like Wushan, where the signs were so far above the city that nothing would be left once the dam reached full capacity in 2009.

Because Fuling lies three hundred miles upstream from the dam site, the rise of the river here won't be nearly as dramatic as in places like Wushan. But even in Fuling the red numbers foreshadow what will be a massive change: taking the White Crane Ridge as Fuling's traditional winter benchmark, the surface of the new reservoir will be more than 130 feet above the Tang Dynasty twin carp.

Sometimes when I was in town I'd stop and watch the 177m signs for a few minutes on an average morning. Outside the snack shop, children would be playing, and stick-stick soldiers would be carrying loads up the steps, and the woman who owned the shop would have a yellow pot of bean curd steaming in her doorway. On Mid-Mountain Road there would be unemployed laborers standing with bow saws and paintbrushes, looking for work, and shoeshine men and small-time entrepreneurs would have their stands set up next to the sign. Everywhere I looked, it was typical, everyday life; and yet in a decade all of it would be below the level of the new reservoir. And by walking downhill I could see just how much more of the city would be affected: the majority of the old town with its buildings of tile and wood, and the entire shop district of Mid-Mountain Road and Riverside Road. They were lively parts of the city, and the people always seemed too busy to look twice at those signs. The river wasn't scheduled to start rising until 2003, which for the residents of Fuling was a long time away. They had other things to worry about.

They also had the government's promise that it would build a dike around Fuling to protect these low-lying districts. Whenever I asked people about the Three Gorges Project, they always shrugged and said that the city was going to build a 150-foot-high *shuiba,* a water-wall, which meant that the new dam wouldn't affect their homes. But the details of this dike seemed awfully vague. Would it surround the entire city? When would it be built? If they built a 150-foot high wall next to your home, wouldn't that be awfully dark and unpleasant? And what about safety—could you really trust the *shuiba?* Whenever I asked these questions, nobody had any answers, and it seemed that none of them entertained such doubts. There was going to be a *shuiba*—that was all they knew and all that mattered. Even when I left Fuling, in the summer of 1998, construction of the dike hadn't yet begun, but still I didn't hear of any worries or concerns.

Mostly I heard the advantages of the dam, which followed the three points of my textbook's essay: electricity, flood control, and transportation. These are important issues for people in a place like Fuling, and with regard to all three the new dam will make a substantial difference. By far it will be the largest hydroelectric dam in the world, its wall roughly six times the length of the Hoover Dam's, and the Three Gorges Dam's twenty-six massive turbines will produce 18,100 megawatts of electricity—the equivalent of ten nuclear reactors, enough energy to boost China's national output by 10 percent. The Yangtze's summer floods, which in the past six decades have killed more than 330,000 people, will be better controlled by the dam. In effect, it will turn Chongqing into a seaport, as ten-thousand-ton ships—three times the size of the current limit—will be able to navigate the upper river.

This last point was of particular interest to Fuling, because the largest ships will not be able to go all the way to Chongqing in all seasons. There are some narrow river passages between the two cities, and speculation is that Fuling will become a major port to serve boats too large to reach Chongqing. This will be a significant change, as Fuling, with its lightly populated Wu River, has previously played a relatively small role in Sichuan's transportation network. More important, this new status will end the city's isolation. When I arrived in Fuling, construction had already begun on a high-speed expressway that would run to Chongqing, and there was talk of building a railroad sometime after the year 2000. For the people of Fuling these were long-awaited changes: soon their city would become something more than a forgotten river town, and they would no longer be at the mercy of the Yangtze and its slow boats.

But at the same time this begged another obvious question: Can one really believe that all of the people along the Yangtze—the boat captains, the businessmen, the flood-fearing peasants—will no longer be at the mercy of the river? Or will the river still be in control, with the stakes of disaster raised by the effort to harness the Yangtze? The dam is being constructed on an earthquake fault, and the unstable Gorges have a long history of enormous landslides that cause massive waves. And the Yangtze isn't just water; the river carries a thousand times as much silt as the muddy Mississippi. Cities like Chongqing and Fuling spew their sewage more or less untreated into the river, as well as waste from their factories, and there is speculation that all of this filth and silt will back up behind the dam. A ten-thousand-ton ship won't be of much use in a four-hundred-mile-long bog.

For these and other reasons, the project has long inspired apocalyptic visions from a host of experts, both Chinese and foreign. They envision a broken dam, a silt-filled reservoir; they warn that the rising river will carry new poisons that previously had been stored on its banks. The reservoir will flood thirteen cities, 140 towns, and 1,352 villages; it will swamp 650 factories and 139 power stations. For more than ten thousand years the river valley has been home to human civilization, and all of man's endless traces, the garbage dumps and the chemical deposits, will be held stagnant in the new reservoir. And the river isn't something to be tinkered with lightly—over 350 million people live in the Yangtze's watershed, more than in America and Canada combined, one person out of every twelve on earth.

Experts warn that mercury, lead, and other poisons from the flooded areas could be carried into people's water supplies, and they fear the outbreak of endemic infections along the soggy new valley: malaria, leptospirosis, Japanese B encephalitis. The dam's forty thousand construction workers, all of whom are living temporary lives in temporary housing, will spread gonorrhea via the prostitutes who flock to the workers' cities. AIDS could run the same course. And where will these workers go when the dam is finished?

And what about the nearly two million people, mostly peasants, who will be displaced by the new reservoir? The government has promised them benefits of jobs and land, which will cost one-third of the entire project's price tag—thirty billion dollars, according to conservative estimates. But eastern Sichuan has long been an isolated part of the country, and local officials have little direct contact with the central government. Sending huge sums of money down the river is far more likely to lead to corruption rather than efficient population transfer.

There are countless tombs, dozens of ancient temples, and many priceless cultural relics like the White Crane Ridge. What will be done with those? The ridge would be a major historical monument in most parts of the world, but there is so much history in the Three Gorges region that Fuling's carvings don't even make the A-list of threatened artifacts. Downstream is Shibaozhai, a stunning twelve-story pagoda from the eighteenth century, and beyond that is Yunyang's seventeen-hundred-year-old temple to Zhang Fei, a hero from the Three Kingdoms era. Both will be lost if expensive preservation measures aren't undertaken. And there are tombs of the Ba people, who lived in Fuling and the other Yangtze regions more than two thousand years ago, and whose remains have never been thoroughly studied. Little is known about them, and nothing more will be learned after their relics are flooded forever.

The dam also threatens wildlife: the Siberian crane, the cloud leopard, the finless porpoise, the Chinese alligator, the Chinese white river dolphin, the Chinese sturgeon, and 172 other species of fish. Already the development of the Yangtze, which carries 80 percent of China's river traffic, has been environmentally costly, and there are but one hundred river dolphins left. This is one of five freshwater dolphin species in the world, and for millennia it adapted to the muddy waters of the Yangtze until now it is virtually blind, relying on highly developed sonar capabilities. But today the river is full of boats, with the racket of engines growing louder every year, and the dolphin, deafened by technology and blinded by evolution, is already having trouble avoiding danger and finding mates. Ten-thousand-ton ocean vessels might finish off the species.

These points have been made throughout the decades that the dam has been considered by Chinese leaders. The project was first conceived by Sun Yat-sen in 1919, and it was seriously considered by both Chiang Kai-shek and Mao Zedong. For the dictators it had a classic Chinese appeal, at once pragmatic and grandiose—a way to modernize a poor country while rallying national pride, a modern-day infrastructure project on the scale of the Great Wall and the Grand Canal. Mao's engineers completed a full-scale survey in 1955, and they might have started construction if not for the distractions of the Great Leap Forward and the Cultural Revolution.

But there were always voices of dissent. Even in the 1980s, as Deng Xiaoping and Premier Li Peng moved closer to beginning actual work on the dam, it was one of the few major issues in China that could be debated publicly. Criticism was accepted, and there was no shortage of it; many experts believed that constructing a series of smaller dams on the Yangtze and its tributaries would have many of the same benefits without the risks. The debates continued until finally in 1987 the government tired of this version of democracy and silenced it. If China's leaders wanted the largest dam in the world, it would be built, regardless of the risks. None of the difficulties mattered—the silt, the earthquakes, the lost relics, the extinct species, the displaced peasants. The experts could be ignored, just as they had been ignored so many times in the past: when Mao encouraged high birth rates in the 1950s and 1960s; when the Great Leap Forward was launched; when the Cultural Revolution began. Sometimes you need decision rather than debate. There's no sense in giving up eating for fear of choking.

BUT STILL THE CRITICAL VOICES wouldn't go away. Dai Qing, a Chinese journalist who was one of the project's most vocal opponents, spent ten months in prison after publishing a 1989 book condemning the dam. In 1992, Premier Li Peng pushed the National People's Congress to take a final vote on the project, which was duly approved. This was no surprise—the NPC wasn't much more than a rubber-stamp assembly—but nevertheless there were signs of strong opposition, as a third of the representatives either opposed the project or abstained from voting.

China's first environmental lobby group was formed in response to the dam, and careful criticism continued even as work began in 1993. In August of 1996, the month I arrived in Fuling, a number of archaeologists and other professors publicly requested President Jiang Zemin to step up efforts to preserve the flood region's cultural relics. Protection work had been scheduled to begin in 1996, but nothing had yet been done, and the petitioners asked that $230 million be spent on various necessary measures: excavations, relocated temples, new museums. There were proposals to protect the island pagoda of Shibaozhai with a dike, and there was a plan to move Zhang Fei's temple, piece by piece, to higher ground. Tianjin University proposed building an underwater museum to house Fuling's White Crane Ridge. Tourists would access the museum via a tunnel on shore, and the roof of the building would rise above the new reservoir in a shape that recalled the ancient strip of sandstone.

All of these plans and complaints greatly annoyed the forces that were pushing the dam forward. Wei Tingcheng, the seventy-year-old chief engineer who had spent virtually his entire professional life developing the project, scoffed at the "palaces" that archaeologists were proposing. "To tell you the truth," he said, in a 1996 interview with the *New York Times,* "the common people of China have such a low education level that they will not be able to enjoy these cultural relics, and only some of these experts will go to these museums."

It wasn't a particularly tactful remark, but in some ways it addressed an important issue: a country like China is accustomed to making difficult choices that Americans might not dream of considering. I thought of this every time I visited the White Crane Ridge, where I was always amazed to see the conjunction of the ancient carvings and the timeless river. Nowhere else had I felt so strongly that there are two types of history, nature's and man's, and that one is a creature of cycles while the other, with mixed results, aims always at straightness—progress, development, control. And I sensed that on the Yangtze it was a particularly dangerous violation to force these together, pressing the river's cycles into stagnancy behind the long line of the dam.

But this was a poetic turn of thought, and most people in Fuling couldn't afford it. They didn't have the time or interest to visit the White Crane Ridge, and they didn't worry much about the relationship between man and nature. Often there were no other tourists on the ridge besides me, and the only time I ever saw a big crowd was the day I researched my story about the carvings, which was on a weekend during the Spring Festival holiday in 1998. Most people in Fuling had difficulty reading the inscriptions—the characters were of the traditional sort that had been simplified after Liberation, and all of the carvings followed the formal language that had been used by the Chinese intelligentsia before twentieth-century linguistic reforms. Even educated people often weren't interested. If you wanted to see local history, it wasn't necessary to go to the hassle of taking a boat—you could wander into the countryside and stumble upon Qing Dynasty tombs without even searching.

I was impressed that the city sent so many caretakers out to the ridge, especially since many of these workers were well enough trained to answer almost any question about the carvings' content and history. This was far more than I would have expected in a city with essentially no outside tourism, and at a historical site where often there weren't any visitors at all. It wasn't like America, where an empty and featureless late-Qing Dynasty battlefield might receive millions of dollars in funding, simply because some soldiers had fought and died there during a civil war. There was a great deal of history in China and if you protected all the ancient sites the people would have nowhere to grow their crops.

The final government decision on the proposed underwater museum hadn't yet been made, but approval seemed unlikely. The issue was sometimes covered in the *Chongqing Evening Times,* and this government-run newspaper was always careful to note that officials were also considering another option, which involved preserving the carvings by making a complete set of rubbings before the dam was built. To them, this would undoubtedly be the more practical solution—the region simply didn't have the sort of resources necessary to build an underwater exhibition chamber, and the White Crane Ridge didn't mean much to the average Fuling resident. It seemed most likely that the rubbings would be made and sent off to a distant museum, and then the flood would cover the ridge forever. Experts estimated that within ten years of the dam's completion the silt and sand of the new reservoir would erase all twelve centuries' worth of carvings.

It didn't surprise me that protecting the ridge wasn't high on the list of local priorities, but it was more striking that people in Fuling seemed just as passive about the dam's other issues, including resettlement. Apart from the downtown area, where the dike would be constructed, there were still large numbers of people who would be displaced by the new reservoir: the residents of lower East River, the peasants at the base of White Flat Mountain, and the people who lived on the lower slopes of Raise the Flag Mountain. They were called *yimin*—immigrants—and some of them would be moved to the new apartments that were being constructed behind our campus. This had originally been farmland, and the peasants whose fields had been taken for the construction project were compensated with discount prices on new apartments, as well as the choice between a government job and a cash settlement. The ones I spoke with had been offered six thousand yuan, and all of them had taken the cash—it was a lot of money in Fuling, a year's wages at a decent salary. They were also provided with a living stipend of seventy yuan a month, and as far as they were concerned it was a sweet package. After all, the last decade had seen plenty of Chinese leave the countryside in search of city jobs, and it didn't take a great deal of money to persuade a peasant not to be a peasant anymore. Every time I walked through the half-built complex I saw shops full of ex-peasants, playing mah-jongg and smoking Magnificent Sound cigarettes, waiting patiently for the day when the flood would drive their new neighbors up from the river's banks.

There were reports of immigrants who had not yet received their compensations, often because of corrupt officials who embezzled funds, which seemed to be a particularly serious problem in downriver cities like Wanxian. But even in these instances the most common reaction seemed to be one of quiet complaint rather than open protest. The truth is that the disruption of the dam, which seems massive to an outsider, is really nothing out of the ordinary when one considers recent history in the local context. Within the last fifty years, China has experienced Liberation, the radical (and disastrous) collectivization of the 1958-1961 Great Leap Forward, the Cultural Revolution, and Reform and Opening.

Fuling and the other Yangtze River towns have the additional experience of being a focal point of Mao Zedong's Third Line Project, which had an especially large influence on the region during the 1960s. The early preparations for this project started in 1950, when Mao sent Deng

Xiaoping to the southwest so he could research the feasibility of moving Shanghai's military industry to remote mountain areas in Sichuan and Guizhou provinces. The American atomic bomb triggered this plan, as Mao became increasingly concerned that China's heavily concentrated defense industry was too susceptible to a U.S. attack. The Korean War accelerated the project, and eventually three-quarters of China's nuclear weapons plants were incorporated into the Third Line, as well as more than half of its aeronautics industry. The project was, as Harrison Salisbury describes it in his book *The New Emperors,* "something like that of picking up the whole of California's high-tech industry and moving it bodily to the wilds of Montana as they existed, say, in 1880."

In comparison it seems a small matter to turn the river into a lake. Much of Fuling's economy had originally come via the Third Line Project, which made the locals accustomed to massive changes. The local Hailing factory, which now produces combustion engines for civilian use, had formerly been a defense industry plant moved from Shanghai. A few miles upstream from Fuling is the Chuan Dong boat factory, which in the old days made parts for nuclear submarines. All of the local Chang'an-brand cabs—the name means Eternal Peace—are made by a Chongqing factory that originally produced firearms for the military.

Many of the old Third Line factories had been converted in this way since Deng Xiaoping came to power and started dismantling the project in 1980. With China's foreign relations rapidly improving, the American threat seemed less serious (and, in any case, it was clear that there wasn't much protection in putting factories in places like Fuling). The Third Line had always been a huge drain on the economy; in some years as much as 50 percent of China's capital budget was spent on the project. Never before had such a massive country reorganized its economy on such a scale—even Stalin's first Five-Year Plan couldn't compare—and according to some estimates, the Third Line did more damage to China's economy than the Cultural Revolution.

Despite its enormous scale, the project had been developed and dismantled in remarkable secrecy, as few locals in Fuling and the other Third Line towns ever had a clear notion of what was going on. They knew that commands were coming in from Beijing, and that these commands were bringing factories from Shanghai; and they also knew that all of this had a military sensitivity that required secrecy. It wasn't something you asked questions about, and after four decades of that it seemed natural enough not to ask questions about the dam. These things just came and went—just as the Chuan Dong factory, which arrived to build nuclear submarines, was subsequently converted to a boat plant, and eventually would disappear forever beneath the waters of the new Yangtze.

But even with all of this history in mind, I still found the lack of interest and concern about the dam to be remarkable. People were much better educated now than they had been in the past, and to some degree one would expect China's historical disasters to provide lessons that prevented their blind repetition. Nevertheless, it seemed clear that the dam and the fate of the lowland immigrants were not the concern of the average citizen. Once Teacher Kong and I talked about the dam during class, and I asked if the coming changes worried him.

"No," he said, and I could see he thought it was a strange question.

"Well, is anybody worried?"

He thought for a moment. "If you're an immigrant," he said, "then maybe you'd be worried. But for most people it doesn't make any difference."

The longer I lived in Fuling, the more I realized that this was a characteristic response. It was strange, because foreign newspapers routinely printed scathing reports on the project, and there were angry critics in cities like Beijing and Shanghai. But in Fuling, where the dam would affect the people directly, there was no sign of unhappiness. In the two years I lived there, I never heard a single resident complain about the Three Gorges Project, and I heard gripes about virtually every other sensitive subject.

But there wasn't a strong sense of community in Fuling, as remarks like Teacher Kong's illustrated. Recent history had taught the people to be disengaged from public affairs, and this separation was compounded by a simple lack of awareness. Fuling residents didn't have access to reliable information about important local issues, which, combined with the restrictions on public protest, made it difficult for citizens to be involved in any direct capacity. Most important, they neither expected nor demanded information of this sort.

In my opinion, this disengagement was so complete that it

couldn't be blamed simply on post-Liberation patterns. The past fifty years had taught the people not to meddle in public affairs, but to some degree Communism merely built on the foundations of traditional Chinese collectivism, which had shaped social patterns for centuries. This characteristic can be difficult to define, especially with regard to its effects. My students often wrote about how the Chinese were collective-minded, which inspired them to help each other through Socialism, while the individualistic Americans followed the selfish road of Capitalism.

I didn't agree that our countries' political differences were so neatly (and morally) explained by these contrasting attitudes toward the individual and the group. But I felt that the stereotype was more accurate with regard to close social networks of families and friends. The families I knew in Fuling were arguably closer than the average in America, because individual members were less self-centered. They were remarkably generous with each other, and often this selflessness extended to good friends, who were also drawn into tight social circles. Collective thought was particularly good for the elderly, who were much better cared for than in America. In Fuling I never saw older people abandoned in retirement homes; they almost always lived with their children, caring for grandchildren and doing what they could to help out around the family farm, business, or home. There was no question that their lives had more of a sense of purpose and routine than I had seen among the elderly at home.

But such collectivism was limited to small groups, to families and close friends and *danwei,* or work units, and these tight social circles also acted as boundaries: they were exclusive as well as inclusive, and the average Fuling resident appeared to feel little identification with people outside of his well-known groups. In daily life I saw countless examples of this sort of thought. The most common was the hassle of ticket lines, which weren't lines so much as piles, great pushing mobs in which every person fought forward with no concern for anybody else. It was a good example of collective thought, but not in the way my students said. Collectively the mobs had one single idea—that tickets must be purchased—but nothing else held them together, and so each individual made every effort to fulfill his personal goal as quickly as possible.

Another striking example of this brand of collectivism involved the reaction to pickpockets on Fuling's public buses. Once Adam was on a bus from East River and a shifty-looking passenger stepped off, and the person sitting next to Adam nudged his arm.

"You should be careful," he said. "That was a pickpocket."

"Why didn't you tell me before he got off?" Adam asked, but there was no answer other than a shrug. I saw the same thing happen a number of times, with people gesturing that I should watch my wallet, but never did they confront the thief. When I asked my students about this, they said that everybody knew there were pickpockets who worked the buses, but nobody did anything about it. According to my students, the people were afraid to resist, but it seemed there was more to it than that. As long as a pickpocket did not affect you personally, or affect somebody in your family, it was not your business. You might quietly alert the *waiguoren,* because he was a foreign guest, but even here you didn't take any risks. Sometimes it was safest to warn him after the pickpocket had already left the bus.

This same instinct led to the mobs that gathered around accident victims, staring passively but doing nothing to help. Crowds often formed in Fuling, but I rarely saw them act as a group motivated by any sort of moral sense. I had witnessed that far more often in individualistic America, where people wanted a community that served the individual, and as a result they sometimes looked at a victim and thought: I can imagine what that feels like, and so I will help. Certainly there is rubbernecking in America as well, but it was nothing compared to what I saw Fuling, where the average citizen seemed to react to a person in trouble by thinking: That is not my brother, or my friend, or anybody I know, and it is interesting to watch him suffer. When there were serious car accidents, people would rush over, shouting eagerly as they ran, *"Sile meiyou? Sile meiyou?"*—Is anybody dead? Is anybody dead?

In the end, the divide between crowd and mob was extremely fragile in Fuling. Something would happen—an accident, or, more likely, a public argument—and a crowd would appear, gathering its own momentum, swollen by people with one simple reason for being there: something was happening. And occasionally the sheer weight of a mass of people behind this single idea was indeed enough to make something happen; an argument would escalate, driven by the audience, or somebody from the crowd would start to participate and spur the action on.

I was both disturbed and fascinated by Fuling crowds, partly because they so often gathered around me. If I stumbled upon an argument or any other public event that had attracted a crowd, I invariably stopped to watch. But usually I watched the faces of the crowd rather than the actors themselves, and in their expressions it was hard to recognize anything other than that single eager observation: something was happening.

FULING IS NOT THE ONLY PLACE IN CHINA where crowds have an edge, and countless writers, both Chinese and foreign, have remarked this tendency. Lu Xun, probably the greatest Chinese literary figure of the twentieth century, wrote with intense feeling and frustration about the pre-Communist tendency of the Chinese to ignore their fellow men in times of need. I recognized this same frustration in the writing of my own students, especially when they created stories about Robin Hood coming to China. Many of their tales featured Robin stealing from corrupt officials, but another common theme involved Robin acting in situations where the crowd was passive. One student wrote:

> One day, haunting the street, he [Robin Hood] espied a pickpocketer reaching for money. At the same time he noticed that people around the woman saw the pickpocketer's deed, but what disappointed him was that no one stood out and prevented the young man. They pretended to see nothing. . . .

I was struck by how many stories described scenes of this sort, and always they continued with Robin coming to the aid of a person who was abandoned by the crowd—a victim of thieves, or somebody publicly beaten by bullies, or a person drowning in a river while the mob watched. To my students, this was the quintessential vision of true heroism, to act while the crowd did nothing, and their holding it up as the ideal suggested that it rarely happened in real life.

I sensed that this was a small part of what contributed to the passivity with regard to the Three Gorges Project in Fuling. The vast majority of the people would not be directly affected by the coming changes, and so they weren't concerned. Despite having large sections of the city scheduled to be flooded within the next decade, it wasn't really a community issue, because there wasn't a community as one would generally define it. There were lots of small groups, and there was a great deal of patriotism, but like most patriotism anywhere in the world, this was spurred as much by fear and ignorance as by any true sense of a connection to the Motherland. And you could manipulate this fear and ignorance by telling people that the dam, even though it might destroy the river and the town, was of great importance to China.

The dam was an issue for the people who were unfortunate enough to live along the banks, but even they weren't likely to cause trouble. Like most Chinese, they had been toughened by their history, and this was especially true in a remote place like Fuling. All of the big changes that had ever touched the city came from somewhere else—the Taiping warriors had wandered in from the east, and the Kuomintang had come from Nanjing, and the Communist land reforms had been initiated in the north before working their way south to the river valley. The Third Line Project had come and gone, sweeping everything in its wake. In recent years, fancy new products had started making their way down the Yangtze from Chongqing, along with the legal changes that allowed the new free-market economics. Even *waiguoren* were now starting to appear on the streets of downtown Fuling. You accepted all of these developments and adjusted to them, because they weren't under your control. It was like the Yangtze itself, which came from another place and went somewhere else. Someday in the future it would rise 130 feet, and you would cope with that as well. Once I asked a friend if there would be any problems associated with the river's future rise, and, like Teacher Kong, he seemed surprised at the question. "Well," he said at last, "the boats will all float, so they'll be fine."

There was also a sense that the dam was simply a good idea. It meant electricity, which represented progress, and this was the most important issue for the vast majority of Fuling's residents. The completed dam would supposedly create enough electricity to replace the burning of fifty million tons of coal a year, which was no small benefit in a horribly polluted country where one of every four deaths was attributed to lung disease. There were days when I stood on my balcony and felt a touch of sadness as I looked at the Yangtze, because I knew its days as a rushing river were numbered. But there were many other days when the smog was so thick that I couldn't see the river at all.

I also gained new perspective on this issue during the winter, when there were periodic power cuts to conserve electricity. My apartment had only electric heating, and sometimes these blackouts lasted for hours—long, cold hours, the dark apartment growing steadily more uncomfortable until my breath was white in the candlelight. I found that during these periods I didn't think too much about whether Fuling's new dike would hold, or if the immigrants would be well taken care of, or whether the White Crane Ridge would be adequately protected. What I thought about was getting warm. Cold was like hunger; it had a way of simplifying everything.

And a lot of people in China still think in these terms. It's different from America, where there is an average of three thousand watts of electrical power for every citizen—enough for every single American to turn on an oven and a hair dryer at once. In China, there are 150 watts per head, which is enough for everybody to switch on a light bulb or two. But even one light isn't possible for the sixty million Chinese who have no electricity at all.

The history of such projects in China has two different aspects. The country has been controlling and harnessing water for centuries—no other civilization on earth has such a long and successful history of turning rivers to man's use. The development of central Sichuan province was originally sparked by the construction of Dujiangyan, a brilliantly designed irrigation project that was constructed twenty-three centuries ago and even today still functions perfectly, turning the Chengdu Basin into one of the most fertile rice-growing regions in the country. Even the Yangtze has been tamed before, albeit on a much smaller scale; the Gezhou Dam was completed in 1981 on a site downstream from the location of the current project.

But there is also the history of Henan province, where heavy rains in 1975 caused sixty-two modern dams to fall like dominoes, one after another, and 230,000 people died. Although the scale of that particular disaster was unique, the poor engineering was less unusual: 3,200 Chinese dams have burst since 1949. In this century, the failure rate of Chinese dams is 3.7 percent, compared to 0.6 percent in the rest of the world.

In the end I was like most people in Fuling—I passively watched the preparations for the project, and I tried not to be too judgmental. I was, after all, an outsider. But I figured it was better to be there before the dam than afterward, and it was good to see the White Crane Ridge and the Three Gorges before the river was tamed. There was man's history and there was the Yangtze's, and I didn't particularly want to be there when they clashed, changing the place forever.

THE SEMESTER FINISHED near the end of January, and we had four weeks off for the Spring Festival Holiday. Adam and I could go anywhere we wished—other volunteers were going to Japan, Thailand, Laos—but for us it was easiest to go downstream, which was where we went.

We bought tickets on the afternoon Jiangyu boat because we had been told not to. Our colleagues had warned us against those ships; they were dirty and crowded and served primarily as transportation for people who lived along the river. They didn't stop at the temples and interesting sights, like the tourist ships, and there wouldn't be other *waiguoren.* All of that sounded good—I had already seen enough temples, and the cliffs of the Gorges would look the same from any boat. Mostly I was interested in catching a glimpse of average life on the river.

Previously the Jiangyu line had been called "The East is Red," in honor of the song praising Mao Zedong, but now there was a great deal of competition on the Yangtze and it was better not to remind potential customers of the sort of service they had received in the past. The boat we took was named the *Monkey King,* taken from a character in the classic *Journey to the West,* which describes a seventh-century pilgrimage to India. That had been during the Tang Dynasty, and the people along the Yangtze had no bad memories associated with travel in those days.

Our boat swung away from the docks on a beautiful afternoon, the sun shining bright on the White Crane Ridge. The *Monkey King* was everything we had hoped for—pleasantly grimy, bustling with passengers, and there were no *waiguoren* besides the four of us who were traveling together. In addition to Adam, there was another Peace Corps volunteer, Craig Simons, and a boyhood friend of mine named Mike Graham, who was teaching English and studying Chinese in Xi'an. We settled on the back deck, standing in the sunshine and watching the river scenery.

The old familiar landscape slipped behind—White Flat Mountain disappeared behind a bend, and Raise the Flag Mountain faded into the distance. Strange new hills rolled eastward along the Yangtze. To me they were nameless, without history, and every time we passed a pagoda-topped mountain or a riverside hamlet I wondered what had happened there. Had Shi Dakai and his army passed through? Were there any echoes of the lost dynasties, any carved stones or ancient tombs? Had a sad-eyed calligrapher with a steady hand ever been exiled to those shores? I was accustomed to being the one standing still; so often I had sat on my balcony, gazing down on the ships and wondering where they were going; but now I was looking at the land and thinking about what might have happened there. I realized that this was how most passing tourists saw Fuling: a dirty harbor, a long sloping mountain, a wandering thought—did anything ever happen here?—and then the river town was gone and new scenery came into view.

The sun glanced off the silver-brown water; hawks glided overhead. Men rode unsteady bamboo rafts along the river's edge. Coal boats puttered past. Workers quarried limestone along the shore, the clink of their chisels echoing clear above the winter river. We docked briefly at Fengdu, a long narrow city stretched across the river flats. Fengdu was low, too low; in a decade all of it would be flooded. There was a pagoda on a hill just beyond town and that was where the sun set, glowing orange for a moment and then disappearing below the green slope.

A worker with a cigarette clenched between his teeth took down the Chinese flag and put it in a box on the stern. Mike chatted with a former biology student from Beijing, who explained that in 1989 he had taken part in the student demonstrations; the subsequent crackdown had prevented him from pursuing an academic career. Instead he went into business with some friends, producing fire alarms for boats, and this journey was both a business trip and a victory tour. "Every boat on the Yangtze has our alarms," he said proudly. There were still dissidents in prison for the political crimes of 1989, but there was also a whole generation of young Chinese like this man, whose political record had pushed him to the relative freedom of business.

The hills were rising now, blue-green with the coming darkness, and often they were too steep for farming. On the north bank we passed a long wild hillside, empty except for two small white graves pressed close together. They were completely alone and the *fengshui* was good; they faced south, overlooking the river, and perhaps they were high enough to foil the coming reservoir.

The boat cut its motor, coasting with the current. The air was still. Except for us the river was empty; almost nobody was on deck. Everything was quiet as the heart of the Yangtze swept us onward. And in that moment I felt the power of the river, its massive silent strength pushing us downstream as night crept over the valley.

The two lonely tombs slipped past in the twilight. The hills loomed black against the sky. Stars began to appear, faint and cold in the distance. And then the motor rumbled to life once more, and darkness came, and I went to my bunk in our third-class cabin.

There were ten beds and eleven people in our cabin; a young man and a woman were sharing the bunk below Adam. On Chinese boats and trains it was common for passengers to do that, because couples rarely paid for two separate bunks, and often friends did the same to save money. Nobody would look twice at two men lying together on a cramped berth.

The woman in our cabin was shy and she kept her eyes on the floor. She was bundled in sweaters and her long black hair hung straight down her back. Her companion was also quiet; he asked politely where we were going, and then he arranged their bunk and lay down to sleep.

The narrow beds had a thin bamboo matting and dirty old blankets. I slept restlessly, waking while we docked at Wanxian and the city lights filtered into the cabin. After an hour the boat set off once more, and at last I fell asleep, lulled by the steady hum of the motor.

I woke again in the unknown darkness of the river. I had been dreaming, and for an instant I was lost—was I at home in Missouri? Or Chengdu? Fuling? I recognized the Yangtze sounds and remembered, and I was starting to fall back asleep when I heard the noise.

A creak; a muffled gasp. Steady deep breathing and a sound that was soft and wet but not riverine. What was that? More creaks; the breathing deeper, less steady. I listened until I was fully awake, and then I realized what it was. The couple on the bunk below Adam, the shy woman and the young man, were having quiet but determined sex as the boat rocked its way toward the Gorges.

They didn't make much noise. The young Chinese were accustomed to that—small rooms, crowded apartments, furtive moments in shady park corners. Some of our students went in pairs down to the banks of the Wu River on Friday nights. On the boat I tried not to listen too closely, and finally I fell asleep again. The next morning I would learn that Craig had also been awake, listening in disbelief, but Adam had slept soundly, oblivious to what was happening below him. And the next morning the woman again looked shyly at the floor, brushing her hair away from her face as she prepared to disembark at Wushan.

WE SLEPT THROUGH THE FIRST GORGE. It was called the Qutang Gorge and was reputed to be the most dramatic of the three, the Yangtze narrowing to 350 feet as it rushed beneath two-mile-high mountains. There was some uncertainty among the *Monkey King*'s staff as to what time we would reach the Qutang, but the general consensus was that we would pass through the gorge at daybreak, so I woke up early and waited on deck. Old people were already doing their *taiji* exercises on the stern, and an enormous yellow moon followed us down the river. The valley was deeper now, the bare hills breaking into red cliffs of stone. The river flowed swift between the mountains. Mike joined me on deck, and together we watched the sunrise, waiting for the gorge, until a passenger informed us that Wushan, our stop, was just ahead. In the darkness we had slipped through the Qutang without knowing it.

"Oh, well," Mike said, disappointed, and then he brightened. "Hey, at least we still have two more left."

The town of Wushan was named after the mountain that loomed above its harbor, and the mountain was named after its resemblance to the character *wu*—"witch" or "wizard." The town's name meant Witch Mountain, and its winding streets were decorated with Three Gorges water-level signs, foreshadowings of the hydroelectric wizardry yet to come. This was what Mao Zedong had envisioned during a visit to Wushan in 1956, when he composed the poem "Swimming," which describes how man can overcome nature through the glory of the dam:

Walls of stone will stand upstream to the west
To hold back Wushan's clouds and rain
Till a smooth lake rises in the narrow gorges.

In the center of town, a billboard gave a detailed schedule for the county's future. In 2003, when the first stage of the dam will be completed, the river will rise 52.72 meters in Wushan, and then by 2009, when the project is finished, the water will climb another 40 meters. By 2003, 37,908 people will be transferred to new homes; another 18,545 by 2009. All of this was reported impassively by the billboard, which also noted the total area of moved housing (1,026,082 square meters by 2003! An additional 530,094 by 2009!), and the sign itself, with its dizzying flood of statistics, will be drowned in a decade, mercifully.

Wushan was a classic river town, a larger version of Fuling's old section, all tiled roofs and grimy steps and tiny alleys. The traffic was bad, taxis honking their way angrily through the twisted Qing Dynasty streets, but that wouldn't be a problem for long. They'd have a chance to start over, and undoubtedly the new Wushan would be better designed for automobiles. But in the meantime it was a good place for wandering and we spent two days there, sleeping in the Red Flag Hotel and exploring the hills above the Daning River.

The Daning was cold and clear, rushing in angry rapids below sheer cliffs of limestone, and peasants above the cliffs were harvesting hay with scythes. They tied the harvest into braids so it could be carried easily on metal-tipped staves, which they used to haul the hay down to the river's edge. On the banks of the Daning they piled the hay onto wood flat-bottomed boats that rode the rapids down to

Wushan and the Yangtze. It was a wild ride—a boatsman standing in the prow, using all his weight to steer an enormous sweep oar while another man worked a long oar to port. The hay would be taken down the Yangtze to the city of Wuhan, where factories would churn it into paper, and for their efforts the peasants made the equivalent of 2.4 American cents per pound, or forty-eight dollars for every ton of hay that was cut and braided and steered down the rushing river.

We spent a day hiking in the mountains, where the cliffs were so steep that we couldn't see the Daning far below, and the peasant children dropped their scythes and laughed in surprise whenever they saw us. Following the hay paths, we made our way down to the river, where we waved boats over to the rocky shore to ask for rides. That was what we wanted—to ride the hay harvest down the cold clear Daning—but the peasants had been instructed that *waiguoren* were contraband and they laughed and told us it was too dangerous. We bartered with one boatsman for a ride that everybody knew was impossible, and he complimented us on our fledgling Chinese, and we praised the beauty of his countryside.

"This place?" he said, cocking an eyebrow. "This place is too poor!"

"But your scenery is very famous—that's why we came."

"There aren't any roads here," he said. "Look at those people working in the mountains—life here is too *xinku,* difficult. Every place with mountains like this is poor."

He shook his head and arranged the load on his boat. He was a small wiry man in his thirties and his eyes were hard and dark beneath a shock of black hair. When everything in the boat was ready, he lit a cigarette and set off for the work of the rapids. But there was a gleam in his eye as he watched the river, and when he hit the fast water his body grew taut, his face glowing with concentration and skill and joy, the stubborn cigarette somehow surviving the spray of the mountain river.

THE NEXT DAY we rode the Daning the way tourists were supposed to, on the authorized boats that charged eighty yuan and came with a guide. He showed us the rock formations we had paid to see—the Pig God Praising Buddha, the Dragon's Head, the Horse's Ass, the Lying Beauty—and the rest of the tourists, all of whom were Chinese, squealed in delight as they tried to recognize the shapes in the broken cliffs. This was a ritual at every Chinese nature site; there seemed to be no value in the natural world unless it was linked to man—some shape that a mountain recalled, or a poem that had been written about it, or an ancient legend that brought the rocks to life.

The guide also pointed out the tiny square holes that had been carved into the cliff twenty feet above the river, where in ancient days there had been a plank road for the trackers who hauled the boats upstream. Legend said that it was along this route that the Tang Dynasty concubine Yang Guifei had her favorite lichees transported in the late ninth century, heading north to the capital of Chang'an. In those days, Fuling's lichees were considered the best in China—even today that is still one of Fuling's nicknames, the Lichee City—and for Yang Guifei the fruit was carried down the Yangtze and up the Daning. She was one of Chinese history's Four Great Beauties, the sort of woman for whom lichees travel great distances, and her charms so beguiled the Emperor Xuanzong that his control over the country's affairs loosened until at last rebellion broke out. The emperor fled to Sichuan, and Yang Guifei tried to follow, but soldiers captured her and forced her to hang herself. The heartbroken emperor died in exile, and his son's effort to maintain control failed, and the Tang Dynasty, after ruling for nearly three centuries, collapsed—all for the love of a beautiful woman who liked Fuling lichees.

We cruised north through the Daning's Small Three Gorges, the river clear and bright in the morning sunshine. The empty hay boats were making their way back upstream, the peasants wading in the shallows and towing their craft by rope through the rapids. Golden monkeys scrambled over the cliffs of the Bawu Gorge, swinging heavily from bushes and calling out on the banks behind us.

Several times the boat stopped at concrete docks, where we disembarked and were ushered along new-built walkways, bordered by stand after stand of peasants selling the same goods: Three Gorges postcards, Three Gorges videos, painted rocks, grinning Buddhas, fake jade bracelets, fake ancient compasses, fake old coins. There weren't many tourists, because it was winter, but still it was easier to sell fake things than cut hay and ride it down the river for 2.4 cents a pound.

And they knew the crowds would come in summer. All across

China and overseas, a major advertising campaign was exhorting tourists to see the Gorges before they were flooded, and the concrete walkways were part of the preparation for the mobs. There was something cynical about these ads: Come and see this place before we destroy it. But the campaign was effective: in 1997 Wushan would draw more tourists than any other Chinese county.

The peasants were aggressive salespeople, shouting and shoving their wares in our faces. By the third stop, I imagined the coming waters inundating the tourist walkways and their stalls, and I thought: Good. This was how I sometimes felt on bad days in Fuling, when there was a hassle on the docks and I became a sort of Chinese Noah. Let the waters come and wash all of this away.

But these dark thoughts disappeared once I was back on the river, gazing at the clear fast-flowing water. That would disappear as well—the Daning was doomed to rise nearly three hundred feet, its gorges half filled, and these rapids would run clear no more. It would be part of the new reservoir, with the same stagnant water as the Yangtze. Probably that would make things easier for the hay boats, but I suspected that the gleam in the boatsmen's eyes would also fade away.

I felt the same sense of loss the next day, when we caught another slow boat down through the big gorges on the Yangtze. Again it was a lovely morning, cold and bright, the wind whipping between the cliffs of the Wu Gorge. We passed the Xiangxi River, home of Qu Yuan, the third-century-B.C. poet, and the home of Wang Zhaojun. She was another of the Four Great Beauties, married off to the Huns for diplomatic reasons during the Han Dynasty. As a girl she had washed her handkerchiefs in the river; or perhaps she had washed the river in her handkerchiefs, because finally the water ran fragrant, sweetened by the beauty on its banks, which was how it came to be called the Xiangxi—the Fragrant River.

There was so much history along the Yangtze that one couldn't harbor illusions about untouched nature. Every rock looked like something; every tributary carried its legends; every hill was heavy with the past. With all of this history, it was impossible to say that the new dam was an entirely new sort of violation: Wang Zhaojun had turned her river into perfume, and now Li Peng and the engineers would turn theirs into electricity. Even the relic of the White Crane Ridge had started as a sort of vandalism—Tang Dynasty boatsmen scratching onto a perfectly innocent piece of sandstone—and if the man-made dam destroyed the man-made carvings, there was perhaps something appropriate about that. The engravings had been made to serve boatsmen, just as the river had always served man in so many ways.

But to have it simply stop—to turn the river into a lake—for some reason that bothered me more than anything else. In a selfish way, I didn't mind so much the lost temples, or the scenery's lessened magnificence, or even the displaced people. The part that bothered me the most was all that stagnant water; I didn't want to see the Daning and the Xiangxi and the Yangtze slow down. I couldn't explain it other than that they were clearly meant to rush forward; that was their essential nature. There was power and life and exuberance in those rivers, and in a decade all of that would be lost.

We came out of the Xiling Gorge and cruised into the construction site of the dam. It was absolutely indescribable—too many cranes, too many dredging boats, too many piles of dirt and stone on the river's banks. I had my notebook out but I wrote nothing; the size of the thing overwhelmed me. Across a distant mountain an enormous propaganda sign proclaimed in twenty-foot-high characters: "Build the Three Gorges, Exploit the Yangtze." Even those eight characters, although they said a great deal, didn't describe very much.

The only describable part of the scene was our boat. It slowed as we reached the construction site, and every passenger came shivering onto the deck. There were People's Liberation Army soldiers, young couples with their babies, and old peasants in military surplus coats. Many of them had stayed in their cabins when we went through the Wu and Xiling Gorges, because it was so cold, but now everybody stood entranced on deck as we passed the cranes and trucks and piles of stone. They snapped pictures. They pointed at the cranes. The Chinese flag flapped in the wind. I looked closely at the faces around me, and what I saw was awe and determination—awe at the massive scale of the dam, and determination to withstand the cold and see every inch of the project that they could. Even the babies seemed to have that look in their eyes.

烏江

THE WU RIVER

THE OLD FISHERMAN has no real hope of catching anything. "The fishing's no good now," he says. "In the winter it's too cold; the fish don't move much. Mostly I come here because I'm retired—I come just to play." He smiles and looks out over the green water of the Wu River. The old man is perched on a rock, and beside him his rod is also sitting upright, anchored under a stone. For hours at a stretch they sit beside each other, the old man and his fishing rod, and on cold days like today they are as silent and still as the rocks themselves, until the fixed points of the scene—the rocks, the rod, the old man—seem a world apart from the cold green water that rushes past on its way to the Yangtze.

Everything seems slow next to the current of the Wu. At the river's mouth even the great Yangtze appears to stand still, its muddy water sluggish in comparison to the quick-moving tributary. The waters of the two rivers are so different that on a day like today their junction is defined by a line that looks as sharp and straight as a border on a map: the Yangtze is brown, the Wu green, and they meet like two slivers of painted glass that have been pressed neatly together below the rough-browed peak of White Flat Mountain.

The Wu is a mountain river. It starts in the heart of Guizhou province, where the hills are wild and the people few, and it falls east and north to Sichuan. There are only a handful of cities along its length, none bigger than Fuling, and so the water stays green and clear until it meets the Yangtze. The Wu isn't wide enough for big river cruisers—many of its navigable channels narrow to thirty or forty feet during the dry season—and in any case there is no reason for the big boats to follow the green track upstream. Even here on the banks of the East River district, where the heart of the city lies just across the Wu, one can look upriver and see wild steep mountains in the distance. They crowd against the narrow airspace above the river, and their rugged blue shapes give some sense of the remoteness of the upper Wu.

All rivers have distinct personalities, intangible traits that go beyond width and length and swiftness, and the two rivers in Fuling are so dissimilar that their conversation is limited to the terse color line at the Wu's mouth. The Yangtze is peopled—it has been channeled, prodded, diverted, dammed; buoys mark its shallows and boats of all sizes crest its polluted waters. It goes to Shanghai. The Wu—clear, green, lightly traveled—comes from the mountains. One river is all about origin; the other, destination: this is what defines the contrast in their personalities. The Yangtze in its size and majesty seems to be going somewhere important, while the Wu in its narrow swiftness seems to have come from someplace wild and mysterious; and the faint forms of its distant hills suggest that the river will keep its secrets. You can fish all day long and the Wu will give you nothing.

Carp are a slow-water fish and they are all the old man is hoping for, along with the other eight fishermen who sit here with their rods. They are spread across a rocky inlet that breaks the river's flow, their lines trailing off into a dead spot where the water bulges slightly as the current rebounds from the rocks. "The carp around here can be from one to eight pounds," the old man says. "In town you'd pay seven or eight yuan a pound, but we don't sell them—we eat them ourselves. You can also catch black carp, but usually that's in the faster current. The river has yellow croaker, too—that's the best fish in the Wu, but you can't catch it here on the banks. It sells for twenty to thirty yuan a pound! And in the summer there's grass carp, but in the summer, when the fishing's better, there are so many more people here."

The fisherman is sixty-five years old, and for more than a decade he has been retired from the Chongqing factory where he used to work. He wears heavy-rimmed glasses and a dirty worn suit, and he is bent by age. They are a contrast, this pair—the fragile-looking old man and his brand-new eight-foot-long collapsible aluminum rod. "It cost one hundred and fifty yuan," he says proudly. He is smoking, like all of the other men on the bank, and he smells faintly of alcohol. He talks about another kind of fish, perhaps the best fish in the river, the fish nobody ever catches. He says its name, but he is a dialect speaker and the word—something like *sanyu*—is hard to understand, and he doesn't know how to write it. In any case, great fish are often nameless. "It's very rare and very good to eat," he says, "but our government protects it. It costs one hundred yuan a pound! If you catch it and nobody else is around, you can walk away. But if anybody else is there you have to throw it back." He says this with a certain seriousness, as if he were quoting from a law that explicitly gives such instructions. He clears his throat and spits on the rocks, and then he looks down his empty line to the dead spot in the river.

乌

THE CHARACTER for *Wu* is shaped vaguely like a bird—a tiny tuft on top, a square head with a hooked beaklike notch, a single straight line that represents a wing. Like some Chinese characters, its form echoes part of the meaning: "crow." It also means black, or dark, and perhaps the name refers to the color of the river, the way it swells an angry blue-black when storm clouds roll in over the valley, their heavy shadows bruising the water long before a drop has struck the surface.

But nobody in Fuling seems to know for certain the origin of the river's name, and its color is as quicksilver as the brown Yangtze is unchanging. In summer, when the rains are frequent and the snowmelt steady, the swollen Wu tends to run a smooth brown, its color fading indistinctly into the muddy Yangtze. As the dry season begins in late autumn, the river shifts from brown to gray to deep blue-green, until at last in winter it stretches like a narrow band of jade scratched white by the rapids.

Now the dry season is past its midpoint but the spring rains have yet to come, and for weeks the Wu has run blue-green without change. It is late afternoon; the rapids near the bank flicker in the setting sun. Beyond the old fisherman, slabs of sandstone are jumbled into the very heart of the river, and a pair of students have leaped from rock to rock until they stand on a stony island in the midst of the rushing current.

It is a beautiful spot—so close to the water that one can feel the cold air pushed by the current, the uneven chill that the river has swept north all the way from Guizhou. The students sit on the rock, gazing at the scenery, listening to the river. For a moment in the heart of the Wu there is no sound other than the fluid voice of its current.

North of the students, a boat is docked near the road that runs down from the East River district, and five men chat on the deck while the sun sets. Their boat is eighty feet long, its deck half covered with barrels of ferric oxide. Tomorrow there will be more cargo to load, but today's work is finished, and the men smoke cigarettes while they rest and watch the sun drop.

Soon they will be bound for the city of Jiangyin in Jiangsu province, a thousand miles down the Yangtze. They will float under the cliffs of the Three Gorges, past the lowlands and lakes of central China, and on toward the country's far east. The journey will take seven days.

"Usually we don't go that far," says the owner of the boat. "Usually we go to Hunan—we take these barrels downriver and then we bring back feldspar for the ceramics factory. It takes about five days to get to Hunan. That's Chairman Mao's home province, did you know? We usually stop about half an hour from his hometown of Shaoshan. No, I've never been there. But Hunan is good—it's better than here. The transportation is more developed, and so is the economy. It's flatter there—it's not a mountainous region like this. Fuling has bad transportation. Most places I've seen in China are more developed than here."

The man is forty-three years old, and without talking to him it would be difficult to guess that he is the owner of the boat. He wears a dirty gray suit and tennis shoes, and he squats on the deck, smoking Magnificent Sound cigarettes. He smokes the cheap ones, the four-yuan packs that are the standard for Fuling's *laobaixing*, Old Hundred Names, the common folk. His hands are dirty. His shoulders are broad and strong. He is a hands-on boss; he supervises the loading, and he rides down the Yangtze with the other eight workers who make up his crew. Clearly he is close to the other men, and he carries himself more or less as one of their equals—in fact, he is slow to acknowledge that the boat is his. But the others treat him with a quiet respect, and when a stranger approaches it is the boss who does most of the talking.

"Two of the workers can drive," he says. "I can't, but you only need two—one to drive and one to rest. It's harder to drive a boat than a car, you know. It only takes two or three months of studying to learn to drive a car, but on the river it takes five years before you're ready for the examination. A license costs ten thousand yuan. It takes so much money and trouble because if you make a mistake with the boat, it's very dangerous.

"The Three Gorges aren't too risky if you understand the river, though. Of course, if you don't know the river, it's difficult, but we've been through there many times. And after all those trips it's not so interesting anymore. The scenery is beautiful, of course, but I've seen it many, many times."

His remarks echo the words of another boatsman, written long ago: "Now when I had mastered the language of this water, and had come to know every trifling feature that bordered the great river as familiarly as I knew the letters of the alphabet, I had made a valuable acquisition. But I had lost something, too. I had lost something which could never be restored to me while I lived. All the grace, the beauty, the poetry, had gone out of the majestic river!"

And undoubtedly Mark Twain, who also lamented the construction of wing dams along the Mississippi, would have been even more saddened to see a river like the Yangtze trapped behind huge walls of concrete. But this Fuling boatsman is still a boatsman; his interest is shipping, not the lore and history and poetry of the river. He shrugs when asked about the new dam; it won't have much effect on his trade. The major change will be that he'll have to traverse the new locks, an eight-step process that will likely take six or seven hours. But that won't be a problem, and in any case he is a man who has struggled against the river as often as he has been borne by its current. In a small way he tames the Yangtze every month, and the taming of it on a larger scale does nothing but impress him.

"That dam is very big," he says. "Have you seen it? Since they diverted the river it's very wonderful. Now we go through a side channel like this—"

With his finger he sketches on the deck of the boat: the bend of the new diversion, the dry riverbed, the construction site. The other men watch, interested. The sun has dipped below the western hills; the air is growing colder. There are no boats on the Wu now and the twilit water has a purple tint.

The boat's cabin glows white in the dying light. The men continue talking, and the boss explains how most of his working life was spent as a technician for the local television broadcasting company. "It was a good job," he says. "The working conditions were good, but the salary was too low, so I decided to change. I bought this boat in 1993, for more than four hundred thousand yuan. Most of the owners of this kind of boat are like me—we're independent, without a *danwei.* The owner decides where it goes and how long it will take. That's good—we have freedom. Usually we make about one trip a month, and then we rest here in Fuling. This is our hometown, myself and all the workers. It's good to see other parts of China, but this is where we live."

He motions broadly with his Magnificent Sound cigarette—to the hills of the East River district, to the fading blue mound of Raise the Flag Mountain, to the gray downtown buildings and their early-evening lights. The lights streak orange across the dark rapids of the untamed Wu, illuminating the cold clean water that rushes into the brown Yangtze and then runs eastward—past the Three Gorges, past Mao's home province, past Jiangyin, where the men will finish their next journey, past Shanghai to its muddy mouth and the emptiness of the East China Sea.

CHAPTER FIVE

Opium Wars

I LEARNED ABOUT DENG XIAOPING'S DEATH from Anne, one of my students. I had just returned from vacation; it was the heart of the dry season and the Wu River was low. Children along the shoreline flew kites, the way they did all across China after the Spring Festival.

On February 20, I noticed that the Chinese flag on the teaching building was at half-mast. But I didn't think much of it until I went to get my spare key from Anne, who lived downstairs and had been watching my apartment.

"Have you heard what happened?" she asked.

"Here in the college?"

"No, in Beijing," she said. "Deng Xiaoping is dead."

I said that I was sorry, and I asked when he had passed away.

"Yesterday. They told us on the television today before noon. When I heard, I felt like crying."

She smiled as she spoke, but it was the Chinese smile that served as a mask against deeper feelings. Those smiles could hide many emotions—embarrassment, anger, sadness. When the people smiled like that, it was as if all of the emotion was wound tightly and displaced; sometimes you caught a glimpse of it in the eyes, or at the corner of a mouth, or perhaps in a single wrinkle stretching sadly across a forehead. Anne had high cheekbones and deep dimples, and today I thought I saw a trace of her sadness wavering along her cheek.

"The funeral will be on Tuesday," she said. "They will cancel class in the college."

"Well," I said, "he had a very long life."

"He was ninety-three years old. I think that everybody in China is sad today. Especially here in Sichuan—you know that Deng Xiaoping was from Sichuan."

She smiled once more, but now the sadness at her dimple shivered away into pride. I took my key and thanked her, heading back upstairs to my apartment.

I thought about Anne's father, the math professor who had spent eight years of the Cultural Revolution working in a Sichuan coal mine, and I knew that Deng Xiaoping had suffered hardships of the same kind. He had been purged twice, and his son had been paralyzed after a mysterious fall from an upper-story window during an interrogation by Red Guards. And yet Deng had survived to lead the country out of the Cultural Revolution, and he was responsible for the recovery of people like Anne's father.

There had been no other modern Chinese leader quite like Deng Xiaoping. His appearance was unassuming; he was short, and as a young man he hadn't been handsome like Zhou Enlai and Mao Zedong. He had grown up in the countryside northeast of Chongqing, where he acquired the tastes and habits of a peasant. His spitting was famous, at least overseas—virtually every foreign description of Deng Xiaoping noted that he spat loudly during important meetings. But he was capable of what the Chinese called "eating bitter"—enduring hardships—and he had a practical, hard-headed intelligence, which was why he was able to turn China away from the disasters of a state-run economy. He was blunt, too, which was one reason why the pro-democracy demonstrations in 1989 had been suppressed with such violence. Much of what was good and bad about the Sichuanese could be seen in the character of Deng Xiaoping.

Many of my students were from Guang'an, the same region where Deng had grown up. During the first semester I had asked Anne's third-year class to write about their heroes, and, apart from the eleven students who chose people in their families, the results were as follows:

Seven wrote about Mao Zedong.
Four wrote about Deng Xiaoping.
Four wrote about Zhou Enlai.

Three selected Napoleon, because he "broke the system of feudalism in Europe."
One chose Kong Fansen, a Chinese worker-martyr who died in Tibet.
One chose George Washington.
One chose Nathan Hale, "an American revolutionary."
One chose Muhammad Ali.

They had a taste for heroes who made Revolution. Even Ali was a revolutionary of sorts, a man who gave up his livelihood to protest against the Vietnam War. I admired Ali myself, but it bothered me that so many of my students idolized Mao Zedong. Wendy, who was one of the brightest in the class, wrote:

> Though [Mao] is responsible for the Great Cultural Revolution, we mustn't deny his achievements. As everyone knows, no gold is pure, no man is perfect. So we must look at things dialectically. He is the savior and the Red Sun of China, and he is my hero, too.

Seth wrote along the same lines:

> Of course, Mao had a lot of mistakes, but one flaw cannot obscure the splendor of the jade. He is still respected by Chinese people. His body blend with China's mother earth. It can be asserted that if there is no Mao, Chinese revolution would be much inferior. So I think Mao Zedong fully deserve a worthy [spot] in the world's history. I am afraid only Lenin and Churchill can compare with him.

Teaching in Fuling forced me into something approaching a personal relationship with China's past leaders, which was strange considering that they had meant nothing to me during the first twenty-seven years of my life. But now I encountered them everywhere—the entrance of the college library had a wall-sized replica of Mao's calligraphy, and his portrait hung in the building where I taught. Taxi drivers dangled Deng icons from their rearview mirrors. Students talked about China's politicians all the time; their writing was heavy with Mao quotes, and they referred constantly to Deng Xiaoping and Zhou

Enlai. To the people in Fuling, these men were much more than political leaders, and in turn I found myself developing strong feelings about each of them. It was like living in a new land and coming to grips with the gods they worshiped there.

I disliked Mao intensely. This was not unusual for a *waiguoren;* there weren't many reasons to like him when you came from outside. Much of Mao's appeal lay in his inspiring the Chinese to be proud of themselves and their country, but to a foreigner most of this pride seemed hollow—ignorance and jingoism, smoke and mirrors. In Fuling I came to dislike the sight of his fat smug face, and I disliked his pithy sayings and neat theories that were so easily memorized. Especially I disliked Mao's story "The Foolish Man Who Moved the Mountain," which was a favorite of my students'. It was a simple fable: An old man lived near an inconvenient mountain, and he tried to convince the other villagers to help him move it. Of course, everybody scoffed at him; you can't move a mountain! But the old man was stubborn, as well as dedicated, and every day he shoveled alone at the mountain. At last he moved the entire thing all by himself, and the villagers realized they had been wrong.

Perhaps it was a useful story for children, but Mao had made this sort of nonsense the foundation of economic policies that affected hundreds of millions of people. The 1958-1961 Great Leap Forward had been about old men moving mountains: peasants were told to smelt iron in their backyards so that China's industrial production could overtake Britain's, and the result was massive deforestation and the worst famine in mankind's recorded history, killing between 30 and 45 million people. Yet less than four decades later, my students still wrote about how they were inspired by "The Foolish Man Who Moved the Mountain." Every time I read a student's summary of the story, something inside of me tightened and I nearly responded: Leave the mountain alone, you old jackass. But of course I refrained, the same way I was careful not to let my students know that I hated Mao Zedong.

Zhou Enlai baffled me—he was the most foreign of the Chinese gods. He was also the most respected; nationwide polls showed that he was by far the biggest hero of the younger generation. They admired him because he was a master diplomat, and because he had softened the damage of the Cultural Revolution. These points were true—there was no doubt that his skills had deeply impressed every foreign dignitary he ever met, and it seemed clear that the Red Guards would have done even worse damage if Zhou had not reined them in at key points. But unlike Deng Xiaoping, Zhou had never openly opposed the destruction, and even at the height of the madness he could be found onstage at the rallies, waving his Little Red Book along with all the other fanatics.

I thought there was something slippery about him—he was handsome and brilliant, and he was good at saving his own skin. I felt that a mature politician who had maintained a high position throughout the Cultural Revolution could not be an entirely good man, just as any adult German who had risen in the Nazi hierarchy was at least partly complicit in its crimes. But for the Chinese, this was an oversimplification; they were more likely to see a politician like Zhou as an Oskar Schindler—a man who recognized the system as wrong but worked from within to temper its ill effects. There is a sort of pragmatic heroism in such figures, and the Chinese have always been pragmatists, much more so than Westerners.

I was much more sympathetic, though, to Deng Xiaoping's brand of pragmatism. He had his share of flaws—he had been prominent in the Anti-Rightist campaigns of the late 1950s, when Mao solidified his hold on the country, and of course Deng had approved the violent repression of the 1989 protests. But at least he was capable of departing from the Party line, which he proved during the Cultural Revolution, when he stepped away from the fawning example of Zhou Enlai and criticized the movement. As a result, Deng was purged, his family was punished, and his son was thrown out of a window. His criticism wasn't very political, but he wasn't the sort of man who was interested in politics for its own sake. And he was a survivor—albeit in a very different way from Zhou Enlai. I liked this about him, and especially I liked Deng Xiaoping because he reflected what I admired most about the Sichuanese—their toughness and their lack of pretension. In the end he was the only Chinese god that I understood, and I felt a touch of sadness at his passing.

ON THE TUESDAY MORNING after Deng Xiaoping died, there was a memorial service in Beijing's Great Hall of the People. It was broadcast live on China Central Television, and every *danwei* in the country was expected to gather and watch the ceremony together. All flags were flown at half-mast, and at ten o'clock, when the service began, there was a three-minute period of nationwide mourning during which factories, boats, warships, cabs, trucks, and trains blew their whistles and horns. In China, that kind of memorial was much easier to organize than a moment of silence.

Our morning classes were canceled, and all of the students and teachers in the English department met in a lecture hall to watch the service. The teachers gathered at the front of the room. Adam and I took places at the back, because we were uncertain of the protocol and didn't want to draw attention. Horns echoed up from the rivers as everybody stood solemnly.

Party Secretary Zhang led the ceremony in the classroom. He followed the televised service and gave sharp commands to the students and teachers: we stood when the dignitaries in the Great Hall of the People stood, and we kowtowed when they kowtowed. Together we bent forward at the waist three times, slowly, and then Party Secretary Zhang told us to sit down for the memorial speech.

President Jiang Zemin spoke for fifty minutes. At the start he was broken up, wiping his face and sobbing, and I could see that some of the students were also crying. A handful of freshmen boys in the back started to giggle. But they kept quiet and most of the group was sober, and after ten minutes everybody was simply bored. From outside I could hear the sounds of laborers working on the new dormitory behind my apartment. I thought that of all the memorials, Deng would have liked that one the most—the steady homage of clinking chisels as yet another building was constructed in China.

After the service was over, Adam and I walked home with Teacher Liu. She was one of the highest-ranking teachers in our department, a fifty-three-year-old woman who was married to Party Secretary Wei, the top Communist Party cadre in the college. They lived on the third floor of our building, but I had rarely spoken with Teacher Liu—like most of the cadres, she seemed slightly uncomfortable around us. But today for some reason she was eager to talk as we made our way around the empty croquet court.

"I am almost the same age as New China," she said. "I was six years old when they started New China. So in some respect I saw New China grow up—we were both young at the same time. You probably have heard that in the early years after Liberation there were many political campaigns. Especially in the 1960s and the 1970s—in those years there were always political campaigns."

The three of us came to our apartment building. As a sign of mourning she wore a white paper flower on her chest, and she fiddled with it when we stopped at the entrance. She looked up at me with a tight blank smile but her eyes glistened full of tears.

"The political campaigns didn't stop until Deng Xiaoping came," she said. "We were so happy."

For a few seconds she fumbled with her words. She held everything carefully—the smile frozen on her face, the tears hanging stubbornly in her eyes. She gathered herself and spoke again.

"Now we have so much freedom," she said, in a sort of fierce whisper. "We are so free. We have so much freedom now."

I stood there awkwardly, nodding as if I understood. I couldn't imagine thinking that life in the college was any sort of true freedom, although I knew that I would feel differently if I had spent the Cultural Revolution in China. And perhaps I also would have felt differently if I were married to the highest-ranking Communist official in the college. I knew this thought was inappropriate but still I couldn't push it away.

She seemed to sense this—not so much my different concept of freedom as my inability to imagine the horrors of China's past.

"You can't know what it was like," she said. "In those days we had so little. Half a *jin* of meat." She said it hungrily, her eyes fixed on me. A *jin* was slightly more than a pound.

"Half a *jin* of meat for one month," she said. "Every month we had twenty-seven *jin* of rice. That's all—twenty-seven *jin!* Do you know how little that is? Now a family might eat that much in a week; for us it was a month. An entire month! In those times we were always hungry." She held her stomach, her eyes still glistening, and I realized that true hunger was even harder for me to imagine than being overjoyed at the freedom of Fuling Teachers College.

"When I finished university," she said, "I was sent to the remote countryside. It was near the Wu River, almost to Guizhou. I was a peasant. You must remember that my home was Chongqing; I was not from the countryside. I was not a peasant. But I could not go back to my home. For three years I was a peasant, and then for three years I taught in a country school. Middle school. I taught the students to read.

"You cannot imagine those times. Jiang Qing"—she hissed the name, the way I'd heard other Chinese say it—"Jiang Qing, Mao's wife, she said no need to learn, no reason to learn the ABCs. No ABCs!" And she repeated it a few times, her voice rising angrily—no ABCs, no ABCs, no ABCs. She seemed to realize that it sounded almost silly to be crying and saying that, but there was no other way to express what it was like to have been an educated city woman in the countryside, a teacher with nothing to teach. Even now there was no way to tell us what it was like to be fifty-three years old and still burn with the memory of time wasted like that. Adam and I stood there in silence. I thought that I should say something, and finally I asked her how today had been different from the services when Mao died in 1976.

"At that time, every *danwei* had a committee in charge of mourning," she said. "We wore white, we made wreaths, and for a week there was mourning. Everybody worked for the funeral. Students, teachers, workers, peasants—everybody worked. Everything was stopped. This time it is very different."

She swept the air with her arm, gesturing out to the teaching building, the city, the boats on the rivers. "This," she said, "is cheap."

She spat out the word, and then she wiped her eyes and went inside the building. I had seen more emotion from her in five minutes than I usually saw in weeks of Fuling conversations. I passed her in the street the next day and she smiled but said nothing, the same way she always had in the past. Over the next year and a half we never had another serious conversation.

FOR THE FIRST SIX WEEKS of term, all of the third-year students returned to their hometowns to do practice teaching, and I only had four hours of class a week. They were first-year speaking classes and the preparation work was not difficult. My job took perhaps five hours a week.

By now Adam and I were spending less time together, although usually we met for a meal at least once a day. We had always been concerned about relying too much on each other, which was a common pattern for Peace Corps volunteers in China. Living as a foreigner in a small town in Sichuan was often difficult, and the temptation was to withdraw into the foreign community—even if it was a community of only two.

This was an easy way to miss whatever the town had to offer, and it was also an easy way to ruin a friendship. Somehow, most of the Peace Corps pairings worked out, but there were a few that didn't, sometimes spectacularly. Occasionally volunteers could hardly speak to each other after a year. This wasn't what either Adam or I wanted from our experience in Fuling, and so that was our balancing act—to be friends without the claustrophobia, to support without leaning.

Probably it helped that in certain respects we were similar. Adam was from Minnesota; I was from Missouri; both of us had gone to university on the East Coast. Our parents taught in colleges. We had lived overseas before. Each of us was independent—that was crucial. And each of us had an analytical turn of mind, which was often how we dealt with Fuling, talking with each other as we tried to figure out why things happened the way they did.

But we spent most of our time together doing what the Chinese call *chui niu*—"blowing the bull." We told old stories and talked sports; we joked around and created our own mythology of Fuling, composed of the places and people we saw every day: Rat Girl, Jackson, Left Eye, Copy Girl, the Club, the Karaoke Boat, the Hepatitis B Barber Shop. None of it would have made sense to anybody else, like our language itself. Really we had four languages: Chinese; Special English, which we used when speaking slowly with the students; Normal English, for the rare times when we happened to go someplace where there were other *waiguoren;* and Fuling English, which was what we spoke when we were together. Fuling English consisted of a combination of slang from our previous lives, references to the local mythology, and a sort of pidgin Chinese: certain useful Chinese words and phrases, spoken without tones, and often corrupted with an English "s" at the end (there are no plurals in Chinese and words never end in an "s" sound). In our Fuling English, *guanxi* meant "relationship"; *xiaojies* were "young women"; *mafan* was "trouble." When you spent that much time with a person it was inevitable that you developed your own language—and part of that language was that there were many things that didn't have to be said at all.

The need for space was one of those unspoken understandings, and during the start of the second semester we began to drift into more independent lives. I focused on studying Chinese, and I also started to spend more time in the city, which was slowly becoming less intimidating. I realized that the key was finding places I went to regularly—it was no good just to wander around downtown Fuling, because that way I attracted too much attention and the passersby shouted at me. It was better to go to the same places at the same times every week, and then the people became accustomed to me and it was easier to have conversations.

Often I stopped by the South Mountain Gate Park, where there was a photographer named Ke Xianlong who was interesting to talk with. He was a dialect speaker but he was very patient, and three or four times a week I'd talk with him and then make my way up to the Wangzhou Park at the top of Fuling City.

The park had a nice teahouse where I'd sip tea and study my textbook. There was a friendly *xiaojie* named Song Furong who worked there, along with some other girls whose names I never learned, and we'd kid each other and they'd teach me words I shouldn't know. I always used the words innocently, as if I had no idea what I was saying, and the *xiaojies* would cover their mouths and howl with laughter.

I started to realize that in a place like Fuling it actually wasn't so difficult to learn spoken Chinese once you had the foundation. Virtually nobody knew English, and there was so much curiosity about *waiguoren* that people constantly approached me, and once we started talking there seemed no limit to their interest and patience. The most important part of my study routine was simply making myself available—I sat in the teahouse with my textbook, and whoever was walking past would stop to see what the *waiguoren* was reading. We'd start talking and if it was a good conversation it would last for thirty minutes, and then somebody else would stop. I'd spend three hours there, the *xiaojies* refilling my cup whenever it cooled, and in that time I'd have conversations with more than a dozen people. The city was teaching me Chinese.

Above the teahouse was a karaoke bar where they had prostitutes, and sometimes young men would walk past me on their way upstairs. Often they were drunk, moving in packs with their beepers and cigarettes, and sometimes they'd stop to talk. Usually I could tell they just wanted to give the *waiguoren* a hard time and I'd pretend I didn't understand, and they'd laugh and move on. Song Furong thought that was funny, and after the young men had left we'd talk about why I hadn't liked them. That was something else I realized that semester: One of the benefits of being a *waiguoren* was that nobody could tell how much you knew.

I had finished the language lessons about catching trains and saying goodbye, and now my new textbook dealt with Chinese history and politics. It was a Chinese-published book with a Chinese political agenda, which made the classes much more interesting, because the vocabulary was useful and I could watch the way my tutors reacted to the material. One chapter featured a political debate between two fictional American students of Chinese, one of whom asked how it was possible that China could be a democratic country when it was led by only one party. The other American student, named John, answered:

> Why can't a country led by a single party achieve a high level of democracy? The Chinese Communist Party represents the interests of every group, and the Chinese people enjoy wide-ranging democratic rights.

When we reviewed that lesson one day in class, Teacher Kong paused and ran his finger over the paragraph. "Some people," he said, "would not agree with that."

I said that I didn't know much about it, although most Americans had their own opinions about Chinese politics.

"What do most Americans think?" he asked.

"Most Americans think that China is not a democratic country."

I wouldn't have said that to any of my students, or anybody on the street, but it was different with Teacher Kong. I knew he wasn't a dissident—and indeed he would join the Communist Party himself the next year—but he was slow to judge and he could listen to ideas without either flatly accepting or refuting them. In Fuling those were rare qualities.

"Our China is different from America, I think," he said. "The education level in America is higher. Most of the Chinese are peasants, and if they chose our leaders directly it would be dangerous, because anybody could lie to them, or trick them. China isn't ready for that yet. But that's just my opinion—I don't know if it's correct or not."

He appeared to be slightly uncomfortable with the subject and I didn't pursue it. And in truth I wasn't certain about my own notion of democracy, which had broadened considerably since my arrival in China. Part of this was because the Chinese government also claimed the word, which made me consider how it was sometimes abused in America. Teacher Kong's remark was cynical, but at the same time there was a strain of idealism in the way he looked at American-style democracy, because he didn't realize that in fact the poor and uneducated rarely bothered to vote in the United States. Sometimes that was how I felt about democracy—regardless of whether it was the Chinese or the American government claiming to be empowered by the common man, part of it was dishonest wordplay. But even at my most cynical I recognized that there was an enormous difference in the degree of dishonesty.

Living in Fuling taught me that democracy is as much a matter of tolerance as of choice. After talking with Teacher Kong, I thought about my own participation in America's system, and I realized just how shallow my involvement had been. I had never cast a vote that truly made a difference, and I never would; elections are not decided by a single tally. Nor had I ever played a major role in organizing a demonstration, and I had yet to react to an injustice by writing letters or alerting the press. Essentially, this was the extent of my role in American democracy: casting meaningless votes and accepting the results. But still I didn't feel particularly powerless, because I knew that my role resulted from my own decisions, and I could always increase my involvement if something struck me as intolerable. In the past I had simply chosen not to be involved, and this choice was just as democratic as any positive act.

Many of these democratic options had been made extremely difficult in Fuling, where the price of dissent was high. Or at least I assumed that it was, because I had read about Chinese dissidents; I certainly didn't meet very many in Fuling. It was far more common to meet people like

Teacher Kong, who seemed uninspired by the notion of democracy. Of course, such citizens were the natural by-product of a system like China's, but this worked both ways: the Chinese system could also be seen as the natural creation of people who had little faith in their own power. As to which had come first, the people or the system, that was hard to say. But it was striking that while most Fuling residents were completely disengaged from public affairs, there wasn't a strong sense of powerlessness that accompanied this condition. Rather they didn't seem to care very much, and it wasn't much different from the way I felt in America. In the end, Fuling struck me as a sort of democracy—perhaps a Democracy with Chinese Characteristics—because the vast majority of the citizens quietly tolerated the government. And the longer I lived there, the more I was inclined to see this as the silent consent of people who had chosen not to exercise other options.

The week after my class with Teacher Kong, I reviewed the same chapter in my textbook with Teacher Liao. When we came to John's response, I asked her what she thought.

"That's correct," she said. "China is a democratic country."

"But some Chinese think it's a problem that there's only one party, don't they?" I asked.

"No," she said. "All of us support the Communist Party. And we have elections all the time—we had one recently. China is a democratic country."

"Do you think that China has any Capitalist Characteristics?" I asked, because this was something else that Teacher Kong and I had discussed. We had talked about the way capitalism was taking hold as Chinese state-owned enterprises were privatized, and how the reforms allowed people to own private businesses. But everything was different with Teacher Liao—the language was the same, but its political parameters shifted dramatically whenever I changed between my two teachers.

"China has no Capitalist Characteristics," she said flatly. "It is Socialism with Chinese Characteristics."

It was pointless to argue with Teacher Liao, at least with regard to politics, where she strictly followed the government line. And it was remarkable how far this line stretched; in Fuling bookstores you could buy a copy of the Constitution of the People's Republic of China, which included Article 35, Section II:

> Citizens of the People's Republic of China enjoy freedom of speech, of the press, of assembly, of association, of procession, and of demonstration.

That was almost as good as the slave-owning American revolutionaries writing about equality. My favorite part of the Chinese Constitution was Article 32, Section 1:

> The People's Republic of China may grant asylum to foreigners who request it for political reasons.

Newspapers were the same way, and anybody in Fuling who wanted real news relied on either the Voice of America, itself a propaganda organ, or *xiaodao xiaoxi,* which translated as "small alley news," or word of mouth. It seemed incredible that in a modernizing country of China's size many people turned to rumor as the most reliable source for information about current events. To me, this was the most substantial political distinction between America and China—even though much of what America believed about itself was also fraudulent, at least the press and publishers could express unorthodox views. It wasn't until I went to China that I realized a person could become homesick for conspiracy theories.

At the start of the spring semester, an English-speaking teacher from another department asked if he could borrow some literature books, and I invited him to stop by my apartment. I showed him my small collection—Hemingway, Jack London, Mark Twain, a Norton Anthology. I also had some political books about China, which he examined carefully.

"Those books all criticize China," I said. "I don't know if they are true or not, but probably you wouldn't like them."

His eyes lit up. He was a tiny man with thick glasses and a jutting jaw, and he took my copy of *China Wakes* and looked at the back cover. "In China we can't get books like this," he said.

"That book is very negative," I said. "It was written by two reporters for the *New York Times.* Some of it is about the student protests in 1989."

"Can I borrow it?" he asked.

I saw no harm in that and I gave him the book. I asked him how he usually found out about things that were forbidden, and he mentioned the small alley news. Recently the foreign press had carried reports of ethnic unrest in the far-western province of Xinjiang, and out of curiosity I asked if he had heard anything.

"I've heard that there are some problems there," he said. "Or actually, they said on the television that there are no problems there. But if there were no problems, why would they say so on the television? So I knew there must be something wrong. But I don't know exactly what is happening."

I gave him a recent copy of *Newsweek* that included an article about Xinjiang, and he took his book and left. Over the semester he came periodically to borrow my books, although he never said much about what he thought of them. He was a shy, quiet man who never seemed comfortable talking with me, and it was the same way with a couple of young English teachers who occasionally stopped by my apartment. I sensed that these men were searching for friendship, but something seemed to be holding them back. Perhaps it was their own uncertainty, but more likely it was the warnings of the college; I never learned for sure. To me they were nothing more than shadowy figures who seemed to be groping for something that couldn't be found in Fuling.

Teacher Liao was different—she had no patience for the foreign view of China. In some ways I couldn't blame her; the American press tended to portray a China that was overwhelmingly negative and Beijing-centered. And yet like any *waiguoren* in China, I knew that I had access to a great deal of information that was unavailable to the Chinese, and as a result I often felt as if I understood the political situation better than the locals. It was impossible to avoid this type of arrogance, even though I realized that it was misleading and condescending, and I was careful not to voice my opinions openly. But Teacher Liao obviously noticed my skepticism about the material we studied, and I, in turn, sensed her suspicion of what I had been taught in America. She liked that I was learning Chinese fairly quickly, and I could see that she respected my efforts to study the language. But as my Chinese improved we began to see each other more clearly, and soon there was no avoiding the central issue in our relationship: that I was a *waiguoren* and she was Chinese.

During the spring semester our relationship grew increasingly unhealthy, fueled by the political and historical lessons in my book, and often there was a definite tension as we prodded each other carefully. When the textbook discussed the Opium Wars, she quietly pointed out that America had also benefited from the unequal treaties that were forced upon the Chinese, and she lingered over the description of the *waiguoren* looting and burning the Summer Palace. During our review of the chapter on science and technology, she was careful to note that although the American experts had said there were no major oil reserves in China, native scientists had discovered the vast Daqing fields after Liberation. This pleased Teacher Liao immensely—she pointed out that the Chinese were now self-sufficient in oil, whereas America had to rely on the Middle East.

I had never been a patriot, and certainly I had never been patriotic about oil, but things were different now—I was a *waiguoren*, and I was developing a *waiguoren*'s sensitivity to any sort of slight. The second time Teacher Liao bragged about China's oil self-sufficiency, I noted that China had actually become a net oil importer in 1995. Although Teacher Liao distrusted my sources (*Newsweek*), I could see that she was annoyed by the readiness and precision of my statistics. And I pointed out that Americans don't worry much about being self-sufficient in things like oil, because we have good relations with many countries and have never made an effort to close ourselves to the outside world. More sensible voices sounded in my head—what about Pat Buchanan? America First? the anti-Chinese laws in the nineteenth century?—but balance was not my goal. I was fighting fire with fire, and I responded to propaganda with more of the same.

Those were our Opium Wars—quiet and meaningless battles over Chinese and American history, fueled by indirect remarks and careful innuendo. The same thing was happening in Adam's classes, and sometimes we discussed the best way to react when Teacher Liao started to needle us about the unequal treaties or the loss of Hong Kong. It was difficult because she always had the advantage; the book was on her side, and so was the language. In Chinese, the Korean War is known as the "War of Resistance Against the Americans and in Support of the Koreans," and it is difficult to discuss a war with that name and make the Americans look good. And the Chinese use personal pronouns when they speak of national affairs—it's "our China" and "your

America." I found this to be a small but critical quirk in the language; every political discussion quickly became polarized, and every aspect of America—both its successes and its failures—became my personal affair.

In response, Adam and I learned to attack Teacher Liao's soft spots. It was always effective to mention innocently how rich Hong Kong had become under British rule, and we knew that we could get a rise out of her by talking about Premier Li Peng. He wasn't popular in China—in particular, many Chinese intellectuals hated him, because of his old-style conservatism and because he had supported the use of violence in quelling the Tiananmen Square protests. And it was no secret that the foreign press criticized him mercilessly. One day there was a lull in class and I brought up the subject, just to see how Teacher Liao would react.

"What do the Chinese people think of Li Peng?" I asked.

"All of us like Li Peng," she said quickly. Invariably her responses were like that—all or nothing, white or black.

I nodded and continued, "He had some *guanxi* with Zhou Enlai, didn't he?"

"What do you mean?"

"I don't know how to say it—I read in a history book that Li Peng didn't have parents." I was trying to say "orphan"; in a roundabout way I was hoping to get to nepotism. "How do you say it if a child doesn't have parents?" I asked.

"Sishengzi?" she said.

"Right," I said. "I read that Li Peng was a *sishengzi*, and Zhou Enlai took care of him."

Her reaction was immediate.

"Budui!" she said angrily. "That's foreign *luanshou!* That's *waiguoren* talking noise! It's not true! I know you read that in your foreign newspapers, but it's completely false!"

It was the first time I'd seen her openly angry, and I had never imagined that Li Peng's adoption was such a touchy subject. I asked her to write that word, *sishengzi,* and she scratched it hard on my notebook, her face red. The three characters translated literally as "personal child." I grabbed my dictionary and looked it up: "illegitimate child; bastard." I had been saying that Li Peng was Zhou Enlai's bastard son.

"Uhm," I said, "that's not the right word. Sorry."

I picked up the dictionary again and fumbled through it until I found the correct term: *gu'er*. I apologized again for the mistake and she seemed relieved; yes, she said, Li Peng had been adopted by Zhou Enlai. I left it at that—I was embarrassed to have pushed her so far, even if it had been partly unintentional. The next class she asked me pointedly why the American government helped its athletes take performance-enhancing drugs, and we went around again, this time with me on the defensive. And so it went every other week, our Opium Wars raging as the countdown to Hong Kong's return drew closer and closer.

ONE DAY IN LATE MARCH, I was studying Chinese at my desk when I saw a lizard skittering across the ceiling. He was dull green with bulging black eyes, and he moved in jerks and starts, like a film missing every third frame.

He was the first one I'd seen since October. On warm autumn nights the apartment had been full of them, slipping across the ceiling in search of mosquitoes. Light startled them; often I'd walk into a room, flip the switch, and three or four would fall off the ceiling. They always landed flatly, their webbed feet slapping against the concrete floor. The March lizard was a small one, and he crept slowly around the doorway and disappeared.

The peach trees on Raise the Flag Mountain showed tiny white buds. Flowers on campus were beginning to bloom, and every few days we had rain. The sand banks and rocky islands in the rivers were steadily shrinking. The White Crane Ridge disappeared.

For two days the winter fog faded and the sun shone more brightly than it had in months. I went running in a short-sleeved shirt. Peasants in the fields were wading behind oxen, plowing the mud. Rice-planting season was here.

And then the cold returned as suddenly as it had left. The fog came back and settled thick above the rivers. Some of the flowers died. The buds on Raise the Flag Mountain paused. The peasants kept plowing. In the stairway outside of my apartment, I found a dead lizard, his dusty eyes gray and dull.

A FEW DAYS LATER I took a long hike up the Wu River. I packed my tent and sleeping bag, along with my camping stove. I put a compass in my pocket. Recently my younger sister Angela had sent me an old paperback copy of Ted Williams's baseball autobiography, which I brought as well. I hoisted the pack onto my shoulders and walked out the side gate of the college.

I headed south past the mouth of Mo Pan Valley and up the street through the Taiji medicine factory district. Everybody stopped to stare as I walked past; I heard laughter behind me. An old man paused on the side of the road, smiling. "Are you going home?" he asked.

"Yes," I said, and I waved to him and kept walking.

It was a gray, misty morning, with a cold wind blowing down the Wu River valley, but it felt good to have a full pack on my shoulders, and it felt good to be walking. I came to the Wu River Great Bridge, where the East River road swung west across the water, and I crossed the street, taking the footpath that ran above the river. All winter I had looked out my window at the steep green hills and the far bend of the Wu, hazy in the distance, and all winter I had been thinking: Someday in the spring I'll see what's beyond that bend.

The water was a chalky green and I followed the paths along the Wu's western bank. I passed the first side valley with its broken Buddhist shrine tucked underneath low trees, and I walked through some small farms and came to the Fuling Liangtang ore factory, where they dug gravel out of the hills. A pale dust covered everything—the docks, the workers' dormitories, the massive steel chutes that carried the rocks down from the hills. In the center of the complex was a sign:

Happy Happy Go to Work,
Safe Safe Return Home

In Chinese you can double adjectives for emphasis, and that was a common propaganda message in factories and construction sites. It was always a pretty good indication that you should keep moving. There were lots of those signs across the Yangtze River, where they were blasting the hell out of the mountains with dynamite to make a new highway to Chongqing.

The air in the ore factory tasted like dirt and jackhammers roared steadily. Workers—curious curious, surprised surprised—stared at me as I passed. I climbed the torn hillside above the factory, the dust settling dry in my throat, and then the path swung west into another cross valley and I had entered the countryside.

The Wu was bordered by high white cliffs of limestone, and crops in the lower valley were terraced atop walls of rock. Wheat stood in neat rows, nearly ready for harvest, and the hills were sprinkled with the yellow of rapeseed coming into season. I walked alongside vegetable plots—radishes, onions, purple-flowered broad beans. Down along the valley floor were farmhouses, mud-walled with tile roofs, and a cow grazed beside a stand of bamboo. The noise of the factory was gone; I heard birds chirping, and occasionally a rooster crowed. Banana trees stood in the lowlands, their dead leaves rustling in the slight breeze.

I kept the river to my right and followed the paths that looked good as I made my way south. In the wider valleys, the peasants were plowing their paddies behind placid water buffalo, and they always stopped in astonishment when I walked past. The water buffalo stood thoughtfully while the peasants asked me where I had come from and where I was going. I had no clear destination in mind, which bothered them; their shouts echoed up through the valley: "*Butong! Butong!* That path doesn't go through! Come back!" I always heard the same thing but I kept walking, because one path always led to the next peasant home and from there another trail set off through the hills.

Here the water of the Wu looked even cleaner than in Fuling, a deep dull green that was torn into white strips by the rapids. The river traffic was light—the occasional ferry, a barge every half hour or so, some small sampans flitting along the banks. The little boats bumped over the rapids and then settled calm in the deep water.

By noon I could feel a rhythm developing—the steady footsteps, the even swing of my pack—and I wondered what it would be like to keep going, to walk south into Guizhou and beyond, watching the hills change and listening to the accents become less and less intelligible. Even here it was difficult to communicate with the people; their dialect was much stronger than in the city and usually they were overcome with the shock of seeing a *waiguoren.* It was hard to ask them for directions, because they always believed that I was hopelessly lost and they wanted to help me catch a boat back to Fuling. But I smiled and thanked them, heading off southward while their warnings rang in my ears.

Sometimes the white cliffs rose too steeply and I detoured away from the river, and then I used my compass and kept an eye on the deep airspace above the Wu. You could see it from miles away, because the hills fell away suddenly at the edge of the river valley, leaving an emptiness that hung like a shadow across the sky. And so even when the water was out of sight I followed the Wu's reflection along the horizon as it twisted south.

In late afternoon the sun shined weakly through the fog as I made my way down a steep path toward the banks of the river. I had no idea how far I'd gone—perhaps twelve miles, maybe fourteen. I met four people who had just returned on the last boat from Fuling, and they warned me that there wouldn't be another one until early tomorrow morning. I said that was fine. They asked where I had come from, and I told them I was an American teacher who worked in the city.

"How much money do you make?" asked a young man. He was dressed in a new sweater and he had just done some shopping in the city. His was a common question and I answered it truthfully, as I always did. I made one thousand yuan a month, which was almost 120 American dollars.

"Wah!" he said. "That's not enough! A *waiguoren* should make more than that! Why don't you find another job?"

Everybody told me that wherever I went. One of the difficult aspects of being a Peace Corps volunteer was that the locals often thought you were a fool for accepting such low wages. The man shook his head and then his girlfriend stepped forward shyly, asking why I had come to this part of the country.

"It's spring and I like walking," I said. "And in Fuling I have no work to do."

This was even more ridiculous than my salary and they shook their heads. "You carry too many things," the woman said, tugging at my bag. That was also true and I was happy to see that the people in this remote place were as sensible as the ones I knew in Fuling. They waved goodbye and headed up the path, and I walked down through a narrow gorge to the Wu.

Nobody else was down by the water. It was rocky along the bank, with a big slab of limestone where the docking ferries had worn a deep square groove. Higher up there was a grassy spot overlooking the river. I pitched my tent there and it was a good place for sleeping. There were no houses nearby and the cliffs rose sheer into the mist.

I sat on a rock at the water's edge, watching the river. I took out Ted Williams's book and started reading:

> I wanted to be the greatest hitter who ever lived. A man has to have his goals—for a day, for a lifetime—and that was mine, to have people say, "There goes Ted Williams, the greatest hitter who ever lived." Certainly nobody ever worked harder at it. It was the center of my heart, hitting a baseball.

It was a good book to read at the end of March on the banks of the Wu River. I finished half of it there on the rock, and then the mist grew heavier and the temperature dropped. A sampan drifted past and I sat motionless, so the passengers couldn't see me in the growing darkness. They were husband and wife, like so many of the pairs that worked the small fishing boats. The woman stood sculling in the stern with the long oar while her husband worked the nets at the prow. They did not speak to each other. I wondered what that would be like, to be married to somebody and spend all day working together on a boat that was fifteen feet long. The couple on the sampan seemed to be handling it all right. They worked skillfully and all I could hear was the soft slipping sound of the oar and the quiet splashing as the man pulled the nets on board. It was too dark to see if they had had any luck. They drifted out of sight around the bend, heading downstream.

The rain started softly and I found a rock overhang that kept my stove dry. I arranged everything carefully and boiled the rest of the water I had been carrying. I cooked oatmeal and then noodles, and after eating I turned off the stove so the water would cool. Some of it I poured into my bottle and the rest I left to clean the bowls.

The rain was falling harder now and I made sure that the tent was satisfactory. I laid out my sleeping bag, and I put all of my gear inside the tent, checking the lines and stakes. Everything was fine. In Switzerland I had once camped in that tent for two months, and ever since that summer there was a specific way in which everything had to be done.

The water on the stove cooled and I used it to clean up. I thought about Ted Williams and wondered how he would like Sichuan. Probably not very well; he had fought on the wrong side in the War of Resistance Against the Americans and in Support of the Koreans, and during that war his plane had been shot down. But he was a hell of a good fisherman and maybe the Wu River would appeal to that. It wasn't a bad place to be a *waiguoren* once you were accustomed to things.

The rain came down hard after I got in the tent. I could hear the river running fast over the rocks. In the morning a rusted boat pulled up to the bank and for three yuan I rode it back to the East River dock. That was my first spring in Fuling.

白山坪

WHITE FLAT MOUNTAIN

PAULOWNIA TREES BLOOM PURPLE AND WHITE along the lower slopes of White Flat Mountain. The trees' flowers are short-lived—next week they will begin to wither and fade—and the soft yellow of the rapeseed will soon be cut down from the hills. After that, the bright green ricebeds will disappear, moved and dispersed into the waiting muck of the paddies. Spring in Fuling does not arrive so much as it rushes through, a blur of changing colors.

Today is April 5, Qing Ming, the Day of Pure Brightness. He Zhonggui and his family are taking the ferry across the Yangtze to White Flat Mountain. They are well dressed: the children in new clothes, the women in high heels, He Zhonggui in a checkered sports coat and a red paisley tie. They stand out from the other passengers, most of whom are peasants returning from market with empty rattan baskets and blue pockets full of money.

He Zhonggui's parents were from peasant families on the mountain, and as a child he spent much time there, but now he rarely returns. He is the owner of a Fuling construction company, and there is little building to be done on the steep slopes of White Flat Mountain. But his parents are buried there, and the Day of Pure Brightness is a Chinese holiday of remembrance, of visits to rural graves in places like White Flat Mountain, where stone tombs stare silent and unblinking at the river valley and its breathless spring.

He Zhonggui is accompanied by a clan of fifteen people—aunts and uncles, cousins and nieces and nephews, ranging from old women in their sixties to a baby of fifteen months. The group disembarks on the northern bank and makes its way eastward along the Yangtze's rocky shore. Somewhere in the middle of the clan is Dai Mei, He Zhonggui's fourteen-year-old niece. She is a talker—a bundle of energy in brown corduroy overalls and short bobbed hair, chatting constantly as she bounces from stone to stone.

A few miles downstream, a slender white pagoda rises above the horizon, its distant shape shadowy and bright like a mirage in the late-morning mist. "Do you know why they built those?" Dai Mei asks. "They believed that a dragon was there, under the earth, and they believed that if they built the pagoda he would stay there. But if it ever falls down, the dragon will come out."

She pauses, looks up the hill, flicks her glossy black hair, and, like fourteen-year-old girls the world over, changes the topic with mind-numbing fluency. "My grandparents' tombs are up there. Some of the peasants are buried down here on the lower part, but most are up high. They wanted a place with good *fengshui*, and they thought it was better higher up. They chose the spots themselves. Often they asked a Daoist priest to help, and the priest told them whether a place had good *fengshui* or not. In fact, the priest only cheated them—it's just superstition. But even today many of the peasants still believe in *fengshui*, just like everybody used to. Our generation, though, doesn't believe in this kind of thing. We know it's *jiade*, fake—it's only superstition. We believe in science, and we say things like that are feudal ideas."

Like many young Chinese, whose instinctive rejection of all things traditional has been more than amply complemented by school lessons, she uses "feudal" the way an American child would use "backward." One of her common refrains is that China is "too feudal," and on another occasion she complains vehemently about the older generation: "People in our China, especially people in their sixties and seventies, are very, very, very feudal! If you want to wear a short skirt, or a blouse that's like this on your shoulders, they'll say it's not proper. My mother isn't feudal—she wears short skirts, too, because she looks very young. But my father is very, very, very feudal! We call people like that *Lao Fengjian*—Old Feudal."

Today she keeps such ideas to herself. She says that she has no faith in *fengshui* or Buddhism, but she shrugs. "On a day like the Day of Pure Brightness," she says, "we'll do things the way our parents and the older people want us to do them. We'll go to our grandparents' tombs and pray and burn incense, and we'll act like we believe in all of it. But in our hearts we don't believe."

FIREWORKS EXPLODE ON THE SUMMIT, the sound echoing back and forth across the river valley, and the family slowly climbs the slope of White Flat Mountain. They follow narrow switchbacks of rough stone steps; the pace slows; their breath comes in gasps. This is by far the steepest mountain in the Fuling area, and the only one that is actually something more than a hill—even Raise the Flag Mountain, with its staircases of rice paddies and crop terraces, is too gradual to be considered a true mountain.

Most of the south face of White Flat Mountain is too steep for terracing, and pines grow thick along its summit, above a rocky wall that falls away sheer for more than a hundred feet. This limestone cliff is possibly the origin of the mountain's name—although, like so many other names in this part of Sichuan, the truth has been lost in the past. Indeed, many locals say that the name is actually North Flat Mountain. In the local dialect both "white" and "north" are pronounced the same way—*bei*—and the confusion is heightened by some Fuling maps using "North Flat Mountain" while others refer to "White Flat Mountain." In a region where literacy has only recently become common, names were spoken long before they were written down, and in the end the spoken word is still all that matters. You pronounce it *bei.*

The family climbs to the east of the cliff wall, where the slope is more gradual, and after thirty minutes they come to the home of He Zhonggui's cousin. He is a peasant who lives above the mountain's initial rise, and everybody stops to rest here on the edge of his threshing platform, in the shade of the farmhouse's tiled eaves. For peasants, the threshing platform is the center of home life—this is where grain is threshed, spices are dried, vegetables are cut, grandchildren are raised, visitors are served tea. And this particular platform, perched high above the river, has a view whose magnificence quiets today's guests.

Below them is spread all the mountain's layered scenery, with all its textures and colors: the green terraced fields of wheat, split into neat rows; the plots of rapeseed, their buds a wild tangle of yellow glory; the soft-flowered paulownias, rising above gray-roofed houses; the great Yangtze glinting silver in the sun; and, across the river, the hazy pagoda shimmering slender and white in the distance. A light breeze brushes the nearby rows of young wheat. The temperature in the shade is perfect.

The peasant and his wife serve tea. The guests chat; the breeze blows. The tea cools. After a polite amount of time has been spent, the clan files out behind the house to the back fields, past a massive old tomb.

Nobody knows the name of the family that is buried here. "Qing Dynasty," the locals say, when asked when the tomb was built. But in Fuling this is the standard response to almost any question about old tombs, ancient houses, or other relics whose origins have been lost in the rush of the last century. "Qing Dynasty," the people always say knowingly. They realize it's a safe guess—the Qing ruled for nearly three centuries, from 1644 to 1911. *Paradise Lost* is Qing Dynasty, and the American Revolution is Qing Dynasty, and the most recent Chicago Cubs World Championship is Qing Dynasty. When people in Fuling say Qing Dynasty, often what they seem to mean is: It's very old, but not as old as many other things.

They know that this is a landlord's tomb, because it is easily five times the size of the other graves in the area. The tomb is fifteen feet high, set into the side of the mountain, and nine rows of corn have been planted on its earth-covered back. Nearby, a dark stand of bamboo rustles and creaks in the wind. Stone carvings decorate the tomb's face, and several figures have had their heads knocked off—vandalism, perhaps from the Cultural Revolution. And maybe this was also when the family name was removed. But most of the stone face is remarkably intact, and an inscription reads, in part:

> May the orchids and laurels give sweetness to your heart
> May your descendants find success
> And may your soul be at peace.

Looking at such a tomb, one can only imagine the typical fate of a landlord's descendants: the post-Liberation executions, exiles, struggle sessions, reeducation camps. Probably the scions of this landlord did not find the success he imagined—but this is only a guess. All that is certain is that the tomb has no name, and here in the bamboo's shade there are no orchids, and today on the Day of Pure Brightness there are no descendants paying their respects. Nearby, the family chatter as they offer paper money at the graves of He Zhonggui's father and uncle. But this massive tomb has no offerings other than the young corn along its back, and all is silent except for the mysterious devotion of the wind among the creaking stalks of bamboo.

HE ZHONGGUI'S FATHER AND UNCLE are buried side by side, a pair of solid limestone tombs facing south and east toward the Yangtze and the world beyond. The visitors have walked single-file through wheat fields to the graves, careful not to trample the young green stalks, and now they light fat red candles and burn piles of paper money.

The bills, which are in denominations of $800 million, say "Bank of Heaven" on the front. They are legal tender in the next world. The money crumples into black balls of ash as the fire flickers and gasps. The candles dance in the Yangtze wind. Waves of heat come and go as the flames rise and fall.

The old women kowtow and pray before the burning money. After they finish, the children take their turns, urged on by their elders. They giggle and sloppily kowtow three times, kneeling on strips of paper so their trousers and dresses won't get dirty, and then they close their eyes and pray, sometimes aloud. "Please help me do well on my examinations," murmurs Dai Mei's cousin, a sixteen-year-old boy in glasses.

Afterward, the group files back through the wheat, but three young men stay behind. For most of the ritual they have hung back, tolerant but cool and uninterested; they are in their twenties, and the Day of Pure Brightness is not a young man's holiday. But now they clamber up and stand on the graves, holding cigarettes and long strands of fireworks, and then they light the fuses.

Ghosts and evil spirits scatter as the fireworks explode. The children clap and scream; the old people hold their ears and turn away. The young men remain calm—the fireworks erupt in a deafening roar, but each man holds the exploding string in hand until the flame leaps nearly to his fingers, and then, nonchalantly, he drops the strand and lights another. They do not plug their ears. They do not laugh or grimace. They make no expression at all; outwardly they are completely cool. But something in their eyes cannot be controlled, flashing with the sheer exhilaration of standing on the tomb while all the scenes and sounds of the holiday suddenly converge on this spot: the throbbing explosions, the heavy smell of gunpowder, the swirling dust and smoke and sunshine, the long streak of the Yangtze far below like a dragon basking in the sudden roar of the valley.

THE PROCESSION CONTINUES UP THE MOUNTAIN, past green rows of broad beans, past waist-high wheat, past another steep ridge of short terraces and winding stone paths. The Yangtze is still visible to the south. Fireworks echo in the distance. The family continues to the tomb of He Zhonggui's mother, who is buried farther up White Flat Mountain, in a plot a few minutes away from the grave of her husband. She died thirty years after him, and perhaps she had different ideas about the *fengshui* of the mountain. In those days it was not uncommon for a couple to be buried separately.

A tablet on the front of her tomb is engraved with five large characters: Li Chengyu, Mother of He. Below this title are two neat columns of names.

"See, those are her descendants," Dai Mei says, when she comes close to pay her respects. "The women are on the left and the men on the right. And there's my name!"

She reaches out and touches the very last name on the list. Between Dai Mei's name and the name of her grandmother are more than a dozen others. Some of them have also come today to pay their respects, while others live too far away. Still others have died themselves. But everybody has been accounted for on the tablet. Dai Mei runs her finger over the engraved strokes of her name, and then she says, simply, "That's me."

IN LATE AFTERNOON the family returns down the mountain. They have eaten lunch on another cousin's threshing platform, and now they take their time going home, stopping occasionally to enjoy the scenery.

But He Zhonggui has no great love for the land. To most outsiders, the fields seem beautiful and romantic, but his parents lived here, and the mountain represents a hard life that he is happy and proud to have left behind. He stops to rest halfway down the hillside, and staring out at the Yangtze he speaks softly. "I grew up in the city," he says. "Not here in the countryside. But we were still poor; my father worked on the docks. At fifteen, I went to work, too. I went all alone, and I worked in construction. I was just a common worker. I was the same age as her."

He points at Dai Mei, and for a moment it seems that he will continue the story, but he falls silent. He is not a great talker, and perhaps the tale has already been told too many times.

In any case, its trajectory is clear. It can be seen in everything about him—his clothes, his confidence, his cellular phone, which has rung several times during today's rituals. And the tale can also be seen in his home, a three-story building that he has constructed in the heart of downtown Fuling. All of the residents are his relatives—a daughter on this floor, a brother on that landing, another brother in between. The apartments are ranged around an open-air courtyard, and the family members can easily call out to each other across floors. The apartments themselves are spacious and equipped with top-of-the-line VCD players and karaoke machines. The ceilings are decorated with faux-jeweled light fixtures, baroque patterns of plaster detail, and velvet tapestries of deep red and purple. From the roof, which has a green fish pond and an orange tree, one can look over Fuling's tiled roofs to the Yangtze River and the fields of White Flat Mountain.

There are very few private cars in Fuling, but He Zhonggui owns a brand-new Red Flag sedan. He likes to point out that this is the same type of car that transported Mao Zedong and Deng Xiaoping. He Zhonggui drives the car himself, and later today he will drive it slowly and lovingly across town to the East River district. He will drive past an apartment building that he recently constructed, which he will point out with quiet pride. It is a massive uptown building of white tile and blue glass, the same kind of structure that is springing up without distinction all over China. The car will slow as it passes the building, and He Zhonggui will turn on the air-conditioning and ask, "Is it cool enough back there?"

But this is later. First he leads his clan back down the twisted stone path of White Flat Mountain, and at its foot he buys ice cream for everybody as they wait for the ferry. They eat their ice cream on the pebbled shore of the Yangtze. Above them, the mountain grows quiet; today's fireworks are finished. A breeze runs east through the valley. The pagoda is clear now in the afternoon sun. The family finishes their ice cream, and, laughing, they wash their hands in the spring river.

CHAPTER SIX

Storm

IN THE BEGINNING OF MAY there was a fire high in the mountains east of Fuling. For weeks it had been hot—hot and hazy, bright blurry days with temperatures in the nineties. Ribbons of dust hung above the unpaved roads behind campus, and the air was heavy with the heat. Everybody told me that the spring rains had been too infrequent, and then the fire broke out on Two Views Mountain.

The mountain was the highest in the area; from its summit on a clear day you could see both Fuling and Fengdu. There were forests up there, as well as small farms, and the fire burned out of control. Nobody knew how it had started. There was a hot dry wind coming off the Yangtze and it swept the flames across the mountain.

On the first night of the fire they took fifty student volunteers from the college to fight it, and the following morning another two hundred went. From my balcony I watched the second group gather in the front plaza. All of them were boys, dressed in their military training uniforms, and they laughed and chattered excitedly as they waited to leave. Buses took the volunteers away and the campus was quiet again.

That day the sun was a hot dull disk in the sky and smoke filtered down from the mountains. I could smell it from my balcony. Many of the boys were gone from my classes, and as the day passed I wondered how they were doing up on Two Views Mountain. The girls were distracted and classes did not go well.

Later I was studying in my bedroom when I saw black clouds fill the western sky across the Wu River. A sudden wind began to blow papers off my desk. I closed the window and took my laundry off the line, and then I went through my apartment and fastened all the windows and doors. The storm was close now, swelling dark behind the city, and I could hardly shut my living-room windows against the force of the wind.

I turned off the lights and put new batteries in my flashlight. I went out to my glassed-in kitchen balcony just as the rain was starting. It fell in sharp diagonal streaks, the wind growing even stronger, and the branches of the trees bent angrily. Across the courtyard, the windows of the teaching building shattered as they blew shut, and the students shouted and screamed. They always yelled in excitement whenever the big storms came, and sometimes they forgot to fasten the windows. In spring the landings were often full of broken glass from the storms.

I heard more glass shattering down in the East River district, where people scurried across the streets. On the western flank of Raise the Flag Mountain there was a sudden blue flash, followed by an explosion, and then all the lights in Fuling went out.

I watched the storm from my balcony. Clouds rolled in low over the mountains and the rain fell harder. The sky darkened and then suddenly flared white, as if somebody had scratched an enormous match against the quick-moving clouds. A tangle of lightning illuminated the peak of White Flat Mountain. For an instant the summit loomed high above the Yangtze, frozen in the electric flash, but then the mountain disappeared as thunder rang through the angry sky. Soon the rain brought a mist over the rivers, until at last the Yangtze was invisible and the Wu was only a flat streak of gray that blended smoothly into the unknown horizon.

After half an hour the heavy storm was finished. The hills looked green again; the dust and smoke had been rinsed from the air. It rained lightly throughout the evening. The next day my students returned from the hills, and it turned out that the storm had put out the fire before they even made it to the mountain. But the trip had been a break from the routine, and they were just as excited to return as they had been to leave.

TWO WEEKS LATER, the college had a three-day track meet in the new stadium that had been constructed in the shadow of Raise the Flag Mountain. Most Chinese schools had sports days in the spring, but ours was especially big that year because of the new athletic complex, and because Hong Kong would return in a month and a half.

Everything that semester had to do with Hong Kong, just as everything in the fall had been related to the Long March. There was a spring examination contest about Hong Kong's economics, and the Party Members wore special Hong Kong pins that distinguished them from the other students. A "Welcome Back Hong Kong" sign decorated the entrance to the library, and every day they changed the numbers to show how many days it was until the colony returned to the Motherland. Sometimes I asked my students how many days were left, and they always knew the exact number.

They spent weeks preparing for the track meet. The serious athletes trained on the old athletic grounds beside the cafeteria, and everybody practiced for the parade that would precede the event. The boys worked on their goose-step military marches while the girls prepared elaborate flag dances, and during their Sunday-night political meetings they sang songs about Hong Kong.

The opening ceremonies for the competition were held in a downpour. The Hong Kong banners drooped sadly, and the brightly colored helium balloons refused to rise. But the celebration continued: the students, more than a thousand of them, slogged grimly along the muddy track, and they wore tight faces as they did their dances in the pouring rain. Nearly all of the spectators left, and the cadres, who huddled under the overhang in the center of the stands, shivered as they reviewed the marching. Next week all of my classes were full of coughs and sniffles.

The athletic competitions were postponed for two days, and then the weather improved and the meet went off without a hitch. Classes were canceled, and the students were seated around the stadium according to department. It was a serious competition. All of the girls' events over four hundred meters in length ended in every single competitor collapsing at the finish, and before their races the runners carefully recruited groups of friends to carry them away after it was over. In a way it was touching, like a soldier writing a farewell note home before going into battle. A girl would give her friends clear instructions, and then after the race she would collapse in their arms and be carried out of the stadium gates, gasping and crying—exit stage right, a curious form of Sichuan opera. In the boys' races it was less common, but still about a quarter of the runners collapsed at the finish. Friends helped the boys to the department aid tables, where they were given hot tea and Magnificent Sound cigarettes. After five minutes they were fine.

I was scheduled to run the 1500 meters, the 5000 meters, and the 4x100-meter relay. Faculty members had their own teams, and there were special races for the retired teachers, who ran hard but never collapsed at the finish. Because I had won the Fuling road race, I was entered in the student competition, and this spectacle—the foreign teacher going head to head against the students—was enough to work the crowd into a frenzy. They pressed close along the finish area, until only the first two lanes were open, and my own students lined the backstretch. Huang Xiaoqiang, the owner of the noodle restaurant where I usually ate lunch, came onto campus with his son to cheer for me.

The other runners were excited about competing against the *waiguoren* and they started too fast, the roar of the spectators in their ears. But from the beginning I could tell that it was a different crowd from the January road race; I heard voices calling my own name, both in English and Chinese, and the English department students cheered as I steadily came from behind. I won both races easily, and at the end of the 1500, when my students gathered to greet me at the finish, I felt more like a member of the department than a *waiguoren.* It was the same way in the sprint relay, in which the distance was too short to give me an advantage and I ran the second leg without distinction. Party Secretary Zhang anchored our faculty team, sprinting past the Chinese department in the homestretch, and all of the English students cheered madly. Afterward the four of us posed for pictures with Raise the Flag Mountain in the background, and Party Secretary Zheng beamed and lit a cigarette.

But during the 5000 meters the physical education students in the crowd started taunting me, shouting "Hahllooo!" and *"Yangguizi!"* as I went by. *Yangguizi* meant "foreign devil," and they quieted down after some of my students scolded them, but I still heard their mocking cries, and in response I put my head down and ran hard for the last mile. It was unnecessary to do that—I was already winning and I could feel a cold coming on. But I couldn't help it: in a race that was the only way I would ever react to being taunted.

I returned home to discover that I had a fever of 102 degrees. I realized how foolish it had been to run the 5000 meters hard, and I saw that there was nothing much good about competing in events like that. I was too competitive and the locals were even worse; no matter how much things improved, inevitably it seemed to come down to me against everybody else. I decided that it was more enjoyable to watch than to run, and after that I never raced again.

ALL THROUGH THE COURSE OF THAT SEMESTER, my health grew steadily worse. A few times I ran a fever, but mostly I was developing chronic sinus problems from the pollution, and I was always on antibiotics. It was a strange time, because despite the health problems I had never been so satisfied with life in Fuling. I was growing comfortable in the city, and I was starting to make friends who spoke no English. My Chinese life was developing and now I sensed that in the second year everything would be better.

Even my classes with Teacher Liao had become markedly less tense. It was as if our Opium Wars had allowed each of us to see the other clearly, albeit in very brief flashes of contrary opinions, but the honesty of these viewpoints seemed to matter more than their substance. To some degree I knew where she stood—she had definite suspicions about *waiguoren* and their views on China, but she was open enough to make these suspicions clear. Increasingly I was inclined to see this as a welcome change from the English department cadres, who smiled and treated me kindly but never dropped their guard. Teacher Liao at least respected me enough to provide glimpses of her viewpoints, and I sensed that she saw me in a similar light—a *waiguoren* who didn't always respect China but was at least willing to talk about it. Our Opium Wars didn't end in victory or loss; rather they quietly slipped away, and increasingly I enjoyed my classes.

But at the same time part of me was starting to wear thin, both physically and psychologically, and I knew that I needed time away from the pressures of living in a small place like Fuling. Adam was the same way, and as the semester wound down there was something grim about the way we pushed onward. The term was scheduled to end just after Hong Kong returned to China, on midnight of June 30, and after that we would be free to travel and study Chinese.

I had first sensed the magnitude of Hong Kong's return during the first term, when I asked one of my third-year classes to write about the happiest day of their lives. Most of them responded as I had expected—they described the day when they received their admission notice to the college. Don, who was from a particularly poor part of the Fengdu countryside, wrote:

> On that day, I got up very early. As soon as I had breakfast, I went to the post office very quickly. I was very eager to see my score of entering college. The postman saw me coming toward him, so he shouted at me, "congratulations! This is your admission book." I caught it from his hand. I lifted it above my head. I shouted without consciousness, "I have succeeded at last!" At that time my happy tears came out of my eyes. This is the result that I worked hard for fifteen years. During fifteen years, I had studied very hard all the time. As a son of farmer, I wanted to go out of the countryside. It is the only way that I study harder than the people in city or town. I didn't disappoint the heavy expectation my parents and relatives had given. It was a turning point in my life. I can enter college to study a lot of knowledge. Thirty-first August 1994, I will never forget you. You are my happiest day of my life. You are what I got with my sweat and blood.

Probably three-quarters of the responses were of this sort, and they made for pleasant reading: I saw the way that education was making a difference in my students' lives, and I was a small part of that process. But I was less inspired by the two students who wrote that the happiest day of their lives hadn't happened yet, because it would be when Hong Kong returned to China. One of them, whose English name was Peace, wrote:

> I'm sure that the day of July 1st, 1997 is my happiest day. On that day all of us Chinese will be cheerful and happy. Because the day of July 1st 1997 is very especial day for us. Hong Kong will be restored to China on that day, this shows accomplishment of the great cause of reunification

in China. All of us know that the return of Hong Kong to the motherland and China's resumption of the exercise of sovereignity are a firm position and are not negotiable. Of course, I am happiest on that day.

As the semester progressed, I was struck by how all of the political classes and special events had made the return of Hong Kong a personal event in the lives of my students. Ostensibly, of course, my subject matter had nothing to do with Chinese politics, but it was inevitable that occasionally we drifted in that direction. For literature class we studied Kate Chopin's short story "Désirée's Baby," which led us into discussions about racism. We talked about the situation of blacks in America, and the issue of interracial marriage, and the students asked me if there were any prejudices and stereotypes about Chinese people in America. I told them that current stereotypes often had to do with Chinese-Americans being overserious students, but I mentioned that in the nineteenth century many Westerners had believed that the Chinese were weak and incompetent.

"Why was that?" one of the students asked.

"Well, I guess it was because of the Opium Wars," I said.

"What do you mean?"

"You know what happened in the Opium Wars," I said. "At that time, China wasn't a very powerful nation, and it wasn't difficult for the foreign countries to defeat the Chinese armies. As a result, many of the foreigners believed that the Chinese people were weak. This idea changed later, of course, but at that time it was a common prejudice."

After I spoke there was silence and the students stared at their desks. That was always what happened when you broke a taboo—there was an instant hush and you found yourself looking at forty-five circles of black hair as the students dropped their heads. They had done the same thing a week earlier, during another discussion on racism, when I had said gently that I thought racism and xenophobia were problems everywhere, even in China.

"There is no prejudice or racism in China," Wendy said quickly, and I could see that she was offended. She was one of the best students, as well as one of the most patriotic.

"I don't think it's that simple," I said. "Why is it that people often shout at Mr. Meier and me when we go to Fuling City?"

"They are being friendly," Wendy said. "They just want to talk with you, but they aren't educated. They aren't trying to be rude."

"Sometimes I've had children throw things at me," I said. "That doesn't seem very friendly."

"They are only children!"

"But their parents just laughed and did nothing to stop them," I said. "I'm not saying that this is such a terrible thing, but I don't think racism and bad behavior toward foreigners are issues only in America. These problems could be improved in China as well."

The students dropped their heads and there was an uncomfortable silence. I realized that this was something we couldn't talk about, and quickly I changed the subject back to "Désirée's Baby" and American racism. As a foreign teacher you learned to respond to the moments when the heads bowed, and mostly you learned that it was impossible to criticize China in any way. But I was still surprised to see that a week later my reference to the Opium Wars touched this same sensitivity.

It was especially odd considering that earlier in the semester, during our unit on "Rip Van Winkle," they had shown no sensitivity whatsoever with regard to more recent periods in Chinese history. My assignment had been to perform skits about a Chinese Rip Van Winkle; each group had to write and perform a story from a different period. One of them was about a Chinese man who had gone to sleep in 1930 and woken up in 1950, and another spanned 1948 to 1968, and so on. Among the seven groups it was a capsule of twentieth-century Chinese history, and I was especially curious to see how the group assigned to the Cultural Revolution would depict such a painful period.

In their skit, Rip was played by Aumur, an owlish boy with thick glasses and short black hair. He woke up confused, and soon the other students in the group, who were Red Guards, put a dunce cap on his head. They wrapped a CAPITALIST ROADER sign around his neck, and they tied his hands behind his back. Roughly they forced him to his knees before the class. The Red Guards crowded around and then the struggle session began.

"Why aren't you a Red Guard?" one of the girls shouted at him.

"What's a Red Guard?" Aumur asked, confused.

"You know what a Red Guard is! Why are you a Capitalist Roader?"

"I don't know what you are talking about. What's a Capitalist Roader? My name is Rip Van Winkle and I'm a loyal soldier in the Kuomintang army."

"What did you say?"

"I'm a loyal soldier in Chiang Kai-shek's Kuomintang army. I'm just a poor man—"

"A Counter-Revolutionary! He's a Counter-Revolutionary!"

"My name is Rip Van Winkle and I'm just a—"

"Shut your mouth!" the girl screamed. "Now you will do the airplane!"

Two of them forced him to a standing position, pulling his arms back. The other students beat spoons against metal bowls and shouted as they marched back and forth. I watched from the back of the room, hoping desperately that Dean Fu wouldn't happen to walk past my class and poke his head inside. I didn't want to explain how "Rip Van Winkle" had taken us to this point.

The strangest part was that the class loved it—by far it was the most popular of all the skits, and the audience cheered and laughed. This wasn't at all what I had expected; I had thought that they would find a way to perform a tactful skit that avoided the uglier aspects of that period, because I knew that many of the students had parents who had suffered during the Cultural Revolution. But I never would have guessed it from watching them; nobody seemed upset, and the skit was as hilarious as *A Midsummer Night's Dream* or any other comedy. It was similar to what the Chinese writer Lu Xun once remarked: "People with good memories are liable to be crushed by the weight of suffering. Only those with bad memories, the fittest to survive, can live on."

But my students' memories weren't uniformly bad. Although they joked about the Cultural Revolution, they were incredibly sensitive about the Opium Wars. I knew that part of this sensitivity stemmed from my being a foreigner, but there was also a degree to which time had been turned around in their eyes, until events of the mid-1800s were more immediate and unresolved than the struggles of their parents' generation. Chinese history books deemphasized the Cultural Revolution, and the issue of Mao Zedong's excesses was neatly handled by Deng Xiaoping's judgment that the Chairman had been 70 percent correct and 30 percent wrong. These were numbers that everybody seemed to know, and they had an almost talismanic ability to simplify the past. During conversations, I sometimes nonchalantly mentioned that Mao had been 67 percent correct, just to see what sort of reaction I would get. Invariably the listener corrected me immediately. It made the Cultural Revolution seem incredibly distant, a question of statistics: the lifetime batting average of Mao Zedong.

In contrast, nothing was simple about the Opium Wars, which seemed far heavier in the minds of my students. All year long they had been drilled on the shamefulness of that history, and the return of Hong Kong was portrayed as a redemption that would have a real impact on their lives. In contrast, the student protests of 1989 were the most distant event of all, because as far as my students were concerned the violence had never happened. They had been forced to undergo tedious military training as a direct result of the Tiananmen Square crackdown, and yet some of these Sichuanese students were so patriotic that the return of Hong Kong would be the happiest day of their lives.

This was how the changeover looked on campus, but as I spent more time in the city I began to realize that everything was different for the average Chinese worker, the sort of person who was described as *laobaixing*, "Old Hundred Names." Two or three times a week I stopped to chat with Ke Xianlong, the forty-seven-year-old photographer in South Mountain Gate Park, and the more I got to know him the more I was surprised at his political views. He was completely uneducated but he had interesting ideas; sometimes he talked about the need for more democracy and other political parties, and these were views I never heard on campus. Once I mentioned Hong Kong, but he simply looked bored—it meant nothing to him.

"If Hong Kong hadn't been British for so many years," he said, "it wouldn't be as rich as it is today. If it had been Chinese, it would have had the Great Leap Forward and the Cultural Revolution and all the other problems, and those would have affected its development. We would have ruined it like everything else."

I had never heard another person in Fuling say anything remotely like that, and I told him that none of my students would agree with him.

"Of course they have different ideas than me!" he said scornfully. "What do they know? They're too young! They don't understand the real world; they have no experience."

"But even the older teachers I know don't have ideas like that."

"Of course! They have those political classes every week—they have to believe whatever the Communist Party says. We Old Hundred Names can have our own ideas. I don't have to study that stuff they study in the college."

I realized that as a thinking person his advantage lay precisely in his lack of formal education. Nobody told him what to think, and thus he was free to think clearly.

It wasn't the sort of revelation that inspires a teacher. The more I thought about this, the more pessimistic I was about the education that my students were receiving, and I began to feel increasingly ambivalent about teaching in a place like that. In particular it bothered me that very little in my relationship with the third-year students had changed since the fall. They had always been obedient and respectful, and they were incredibly enthusiastic about literature. I had a great deal of faith in poetry, but nevertheless this faith had its limits; I believed that my job was not only to teach literature but also to develop a mutual respect and understanding that would allow us to exchange ideas comfortably. I could see this happening with my Chinese tutors, despite the enormous language and cultural barriers that had made things so difficult in the beginning, and this change was impressive because it had required a great deal of patience and effort from everybody involved. Mostly, it had required honesty, even if these moments of candor were occasionally unpleasant.

But my relationship with the students was still miles away from making this transition. I could not mention Chinese xenophobia without their becoming defensive, which told me that they identified more with the random Chinese harasser on the street than they did with their *waiguoren* teacher. And there were still far too many moments when they dropped their heads in discomfort. This was something I came to loathe—the great head bow. Whenever that happened, I realized that I was not teaching forty-five individual students with forty-five individual ideas. I was teaching a group, and these were moments when the group thought as one, and a group like that was a mob, even if it was silent and passive. And always I was a *waiguoren* standing alone at the front of the class.

Other aspects of local life were starting to disturb me as well.

Increasingly I realized that I was being monitored in Fuling, although it was hard to tell what the point was. My letters home often showed signs of tampering, and occasionally I received something that had been opened. That spring my parents mailed me a copy of the *New York Times* travel section, in which I had written a story, but somewhere along the way my article had been carefully cut out. The strangest part was that the story had been about the Mississippi River, and the only reference to China was the brief biographical note at the end of the article, which said I lived in Fuling. Not long after that, I sent my parents a long letter on computer disk, and by the time they received it one section of the text had been erased and replaced with a string of x's. It was the only sensitive part of the letter, a description of an incident in which I had been harrassed by three drunk college students. The rest of the story was intact, and out of curiosity my father took it to a computer expert at the University of Missouri, who said that the change could only be the result of deliberate tampering. It was impossible for a disk error to produce an alteration like that.

These incidents were mildly disturbing, but mostly they were pathetic. What was the point of censoring an article about the Mississippi River? Who took the time to read letters sent by foreign teachers in places like Fuling? Couldn't this effort be put to some more useful application? I figured that the purpose must be intimidation—it was so clumsily done that they obviously wanted me to know it was happening. But in fact the tampering was far more effective in giving me examples of the kind of pointless paranoia that composed Communist China.

College life also showed signs of well-organized monitoring. In January, another Peace Corps volunteer near Chengdu had been taken to the local police station after an altercation with a cab driver. The volunteer was clearly in the wrong, and eventually he was sent back to America; but during questioning he learned that the police station had a record of everything controversial that he had ever said in class. All of it was there—his remarks about Capitalism, and Mao Zedong, and everything else that was sensitive in any way. He had been particularly disrespectful of the Chinese political restrictions, but I knew that all of us had stumbled across those lines in one way or another. And I knew that in the Fuling police station there was probably a file with my remarks about Chinese xenophobia and the Opium Wars, along with many other things that I had said in class.

There were students whose job was to report on the material I covered—political informers, more or less. Most likely they were the best students; probably they were some of the ones I liked the most. But still they kept track of what I said, and it was hard not to think about that when I taught.

ONE OF THE MOST DIFFICULT THINGS to do in class was to have a debate, because usually the students' opinions were exactly the same. You had to think of something foreign like Robin Hood, because in those cases they couldn't turn to what they had been told to think. The point was, more or less, to trick them into coming up with their own opinions. In the fall it had worked well with Robin Hood, and in the spring it was the same way with Adam's planned-birth-policy debate.

He was doing a unit on population problems in his culture class, and we thought of the debate topic one night while we were sitting on my balcony drinking local beer. There was no way you could ever debate openly about China's planned-birth policy—nobody would dare to oppose it—but you could speak freely about America. So that was the topic: Should America also have a law that limits most couples to one child?

Adam did it with four classes, and it always divided them evenly. There was a pattern to these divisions—the Party Members and the other students in positions of authority were always in favor of instituting the policy, while the opposing side included more of a fringe element. They wouldn't have been considered a fringe element in an American class, of course, but in Fuling they stood out—some of the quieter students, the ones who seemed slightly removed and had nothing to do with the political organization of the class.

In every case they ended up debating about China without realizing it, which of course was exactly what Adam had wanted. During the last debate, as the arguments grew heated, a student named Rebecca stood up.

He was one of the third-year students who had chosen his English name poorly. He had bristly crew-cut hair and tired eyes, and it was clear that he was intelligent, but he was hopelessly lazy and often failed examinations. I never saw him associating with other students. In the debate he was opposed to America's adopting the one-child policy, and he quickly made his point.

"In America," he said, speaking clearly, "the people are used to having more freedom than we have in China. They are very concerned with human rights. Americans would never support the one-child policy, because they would see this as going against their freedom."

He sat down. An angry murmur ran through the class; for an instant it felt like one of those times when they bowed their heads awkwardly. But then somebody rebutted Rebecca and the moment passed, and the debate concluded without any more comments of the sort.

The next day I finished literature class and Rebecca followed me into the hall. He asked if he could borrow a magazine, and I told him to come with me to my office, where we had stacks of old *Newsweek*s that the Peace Corps had sent us.

We were walking up the stairs when Rebecca spoke again. "I think you must notice that in China there is not as much freedom as in America," he said. There were students all around us and many of them could speak English. Adam had told me about yesterday's debate, and I knew that must be what was on the young man's mind.

"Let's go into my office," I said. "I have lots of magazines there."

I left the door partly open. In the hallway it was too loud for people to hear us, and I assumed that Rebecca must already have a reputation; a closed door would only seem suspicious. But he didn't seem worried about that—he sat down and looked me straight in the eye.

"I often think that our China has many problems," he said. "There is not enough freedom in China. I think in America you have more freedom."

It was the first time I had heard a student speak this way, and I wasn't sure how to respond. "I guess I would agree with you," I said slowly.

His English was not very good and he had to think for the words. After a pause he said, "I very much admire your American freedom."

"But some people think Americans have too much freedom," I said. "That is one of the reasons why there is so much crime in America. People have the freedom to own guns, and they can have any strange ideas they want."

"I think that is not so important," he said. "The life for most people in America is very good, and the economy is very good, because there is so much freedom."

"I think that most of your classmates would not agree with you."

"No!" he nearly shouted. "They are all different. But they say that *I* am not the same—sometimes they say that I am a 'New Man.' They don't understand why I think this way."

"Well," I said. "I guess I agree with your ideas. But I think you probably should be careful."

"Sometimes I have fear," he said. "Often I am afraid I can't say what I think." The crowds in the hall were diminishing, and it was growing quieter, and I was thinking: Why are you still talking so loudly? But it was clear that he had steeled himself for a long time to have this conversation, and he ignored everything else as he stared at me and spoke evenly.

"I don't like this college," he said. "I don't like the rules, and I don't agree with the ideas of the other students. And I don't like the rules in China."

"Probably things will be different in the future," I said. "And already I think they are a little different in places like Beijing and Shanghai."

"Everything changes too slowly in China," he said. "I wish I could live in a place like America where you have freedom."

I knew that this was unlikely but I didn't say it. "Many people think China is changing quickly," I said. "You might find that it's very different in a few years. I read something about it a week ago." I picked out a magazine that had an article suggesting the government might reevaluate the Tiananmen protests in the near future. It wasn't much, but I had nothing else to offer Rebecca.

"You might think this is interesting," I said, handing him the magazine. He took it and thanked me, and then he stared me in the eye again.

"Do you like living in China?" he asked.

"Yes," I said. "But probably I don't have the same problems that you have. Sometimes I don't like the political system, but it doesn't affect me very much. There are many other things I like."

"If I were you," he said, "I would not like it here at all. I would stay in America."

That was all he had to say. He stood up, nodded goodbye, and left. On the way out he closed the door to my office.

I sat there alone for a while, thinking about what he had said. He was the only student who was anything like a dissident, and I remembered how I had imagined those figures before coming to Fuling. I had always assumed that they were noble characters—charismatic, intelligent, farsighted, brave. Perhaps that was the way it had been in 1989, and perhaps it was still like that in the bigger cities; but here in Fuling things were very different. My best students—Soddy, Linda, Armstrong, Aumur; the ones who were charismatic, intelligent, farsighted, and brave—those were the ones who had been recruited long ago as Party Members. If you had any talent you played by the rules; being a Party Member was good for your career, and in any case all of the students seemed to think that it was good to be patriotic in the narrow way that they were told to be. The image I had once had of the Chinese dissident had no reality in Fuling.

All I had was Rebecca—he was the only one, and he was a loser. He was a bad student, and he was socially awkward. He had no friends. He had a girl's name. Some of these characteristics had conspired to set him apart, and in his bitterness his ideas had undoubtedly swung even further from the Party line. If there were big changes in China's future, it was hard to imagine them coming from people like Rebecca, or, for that matter, from any of my other students. I realized again that any major developments would happen first in Beijing or Shanghai, and then at some point they would reverberate down to places like Fuling, just as they always had.

Never again did Rebecca speak openly about the subject, but a couple of times I gave him magazines and he always thanked me. On the final exam I graded him higher than I should have. Partly I admired his bravery, but mostly I just felt sorry for him.

IN THE MIDDLE OF JUNE, the sinus infection moved into my right ear and broke the eardrum. It happened quickly—one afternoon I began to feel pressure building in my ear, and by dinner it was painful and soon it was unbearable. The entire right side of my head throbbed with the pain, but there was nothing to do except wait for the pressure to break the eardrum.

It was impossible to sleep, and the pain was too distracting for reading. Painkillers did nothing; finally all I could do was sit on my couch and watch television. There was a music program with elaborate floor shows and I watched that for a while, and then there was a show where small children wearing lots of makeup danced and did tumbling routines. There were always programs like that on television—the Chinese love children intensely, and at almost any hour of the day you could find a channel where a pack of them were grinning and bouncing across a stage.

When it got late there was only one station left, and in preparation for the return of Hong Kong they showed a movie about the Opium Wars. The pain in my ear was growing even more intense, and in my bitterness I consciously made things worse by watching the movie closely and scribbling quotes onto a pad of paper. The movie had English subtitles, which made it easier to take notes from the dialogue: "These foreigners are really avaricious"; "These treaties are not only humiliating but unequal"; "But the foreigners have evil designs"; "Foreigners invade us only for gains"; "Foreigners have insatiable lusts"; "Frankly, we can bluff to foreigners"; "Why? Why are they so arrogant?"

The foreigners were British and at the end of the film they looted the Summer Palace. There was an auction and an ugly red-bearded Brit held up a scroll and said, "This is the oldest Chinese painting." He asked for one pound, but nobody responded. After the auction they burned down the palace.

The movie finished just after one o'clock in the morning and there was nothing else on television. I went outside and walked around campus for a while. The walking was a better distraction than watching a movie about the Opium Wars. The temperature was perfect, and everything was quiet, and stars flickered above the dark profile of White Flat Mountain. I knew that this was not a high point of my experience in China, but it was a pleasant evening and that was worth something.

Finally after another hour I was able to fall asleep. In the morning I awoke with my eardrum broken and my pillow covered with blood. But my head didn't hurt anymore, and I was able to take the long trip back to the Peace Corps headquarters in Chengdu—three hours by fast boat, four hours by bus. I visited the staff medical officer, who cleaned out my ear, and then I rested for five days, sitting in the teahouse at Chengdu's

People's Park. When my health improved, I went back to Fuling for the end of the term. The main consequence was that for a month I couldn't hear anything out of my right ear, except for a constant ringing sound. For a while the ringing was annoying, but soon I realized that it was better than listening to all the honking. If you have to be half-deaf somewhere, you might as well be half-deaf in Fuling.

ON JUNE 30, all classes were canceled for Hong Kong's return. The countdown sign was moved to a prominent spot along the college road, and red banners were hung from the dormitories. Colored lights and lanterns decorated the hallways of the teaching building.

My classes were finished. Adam had left early; I would go in two days, after grading my final exams.

At four o'clock, the students filed into their classrooms to watch television. There were special programs until two o'clock the next morning, and the students were scheduled to watch ten consecutive hours of television. They were excited and the teaching building was full of laughter.

At nine o'clock, fireworks exploded above the city and the students ran shouting onto the breezeway to watch. The Wu River pulsed with streaks of red and yellow, the sound booming across the valley. Everything in Fuling was illuminated—the shops, the apartment windows, the long riverside road—and it seemed that the city was burning on the hills beside the rivers.

There were groups of children wandering around campus, the way they always did on holidays, and some boys came up to see me in my office. I was grading papers and they were led by Wang Xuesong, the eight-year-old who lived in the apartment across from mine. One of my more memorable conversations in Fuling was on another occasion when I asked Wang Xuesong who China's enemies were.

"England," he responded quickly.

"Why?"

"Because of the Opium Wars. They stole Hong Kong from our China."

I asked him if there were any enemies besides England, and again he answered immediately.

"Japan. Because of the Nanjing Massacre."

"Are there any others?"

"Portugal."

I asked him why, and this time he had to think for a moment.

"Because they took Guangzhou."

I let the mistake slide, assuming that he meant Macau. I asked him one more question.

"Who are China's friends?"

He furrowed his brow and cocked his head to one side. "I don't know," he said at last, shrugging.

On the night of Hong Kong's return, Wang Xuesong and the other boys bounced on the furniture in my office, chattering excitedly. I gave them some foreign stamps I had lying around, and we talked about Hong Kong. I told them I had lived in England for two years, which seemed to impress them—somehow I had survived.

At half past eleven, a few of my first-year students stopped by my office to chat. They had become my favorites—at the beginning of the year they were painfully shy, but they were enthusiastic and the classes were always enjoyable. I didn't feel quite as much distance as I did with the third-year students, probably because the first-years were at a much lower level and my expectations weren't so high. When students studied Shakespeare, and studied it well, it was difficult to understand why they couldn't seem to overcome the simple fact that their teacher was a foreigner.

I had named the first-year students, which made them especially appealing. Some of them had been named after friends and family; often I put relatives together when I assigned group work, so that my sister Angela could work with my grandmother Doria, while my other sister Amy could be with Connor and Heidi, who were her children. The rest had names I simply liked: Puck, Anfernee, Miranda, Latoya, Ariel, Mike D, Ophelia, MCA. In that sense they were a very diverse group—much different from your standard class in Fuling, in which so many of them had similar backgrounds and similar ideas. It seemed inevitable that students named Latoya and Ophelia would have vastly different opinions about virtually everything; or at least that was my fantasy, because diversity was something about America that I missed. In particular, it was strange to live in a place where everybody was the same race. For a year I hadn't seen a black person. But in my first-year class I had Latoya and Anfernee, who were better than nothing. And mostly I liked calling role at the start of class, saying names that were both exotic and familiar.

Tonight they were exhausted—they were like children who had been given permission to stay up all night, and in their excitement they had worn themselves out by dinnertime. Ariel's eyes were heavy with fatigue, and she told me that she had tried to go back to the dormitory but the doors were locked. Nobody was allowed to go to sleep until Hong Kong returned.

Ten minutes before midnight, I stepped into one of the TV rooms. All of the lights were off and almost one hundred students were watching the tiny screen. I looked for Rebecca and saw him sitting alone in a corner. The light of the television flickered blue off his glasses.

For days there had been torrential rains in Hong Kong. The ceremony continued, as steady as the clock that counted down in the corner of our television screen, and the students cheered when President Jiang Zemin appeared. They applauded when they first caught sight of the Chinese flag. They laughed at Prince Charles, and at the kilted Scottish flag-bearers who marched across the podium. At the stroke of midnight the students screamed when the red flag rose and the Chinese national anthem began to play, and the teaching building rang with the roar of the celebration.

After midnight there were speeches, with Jiang Zemin promising that there would be no changes in the economy and the human rights of the Special Autonomous Region. In Hong Kong it was still raining hard. I listened for a few minutes and then left. On the way back to my apartment, I cut through the croquet court, where a few student couples were celebrating in their own way. They were making out in the shadows, taking advantage of the night.

PART · II

CHAPTER SEVEN

Summer

YAN'AN LOOKED AS IF A HARD RAIN would wash it away. A fine yellow dust covered the small city, and the crumbling hills above town were pockmarked by the oval mouths of caves. People still lived in caves in the suburbs of Yan'an, and many of the troglodytes were making a good show of it. There were caves with televisions, refrigerators, karaoke machines. North of Yan'an were villages whose school buildings and government offices had been carved into the dry loess hillsides. It was, in a land of blazing summers and cold winters, a sensible way to live.

The countryside in this part of northern China was forbidding and desolate, but it was also eerily beautiful. And it was exactly what I needed after a year in Sichuan; nothing could be more different from Fuling's green rice terraces and misty rivers. The air in Yan'an was dry and there was a hard blue sky above the dusty hills.

I was free that summer. The Peace Corps was going to fund my Chinese study for a month in Xi'an, but that wouldn't start for two weeks and now I was wandering into northern Shaanxi province. In some ways this region was the heart of modern China, at least politically, because the Long March had ended here in 1935. Ever since my arrival in Fuling, I had heard about the Long March and the Yan'an years, and I knew that northern Shaanxi province had been crucial to the Communist resistance against both the Japanese and the Kuomintang. And from history I also knew that the fragility of the landscape was an illusion; these hills had seen far worse than hard rains, but they were still here.

A sign near the entrance to the Yan'an Revolution Museum said: "Celebrate Hong Kong's Return, Wish Prosperity to the Motherland." I paid ten yuan and saw the museum's exhibits. Mao Zedong's horse was stuffed and on display, along with Mao's machete and saddle. There was a war poem written in Mao's distinctive flowing calligraphy. There were maps of major battles, and photographs of the revolutionaries who had lived in Yan'an. There weren't many tourists. The glass-eyed horse's name was Xiao Qing and it stood slightly off-kilter.

Looking at the horse's name I thought about Jiang Qing, the woman who married Mao in Yan'an, and I realized that I hadn't seen any photographs of her. I walked back to the entrance, where the ticket-taker was knitting a sweater.

"Didn't Chairman Mao meet Jiang Qing here?" I asked.

"Yes," the worker said.

"Do you have any pictures of her?"

"No photos of the Gang of Four," she said curtly, and then she went back to her knitting.

It was the same at Zaoyuan Park, where they had the cave homes of Mao and the other Red Army leaders. Liu Shaoqi's cave had photos of him and his wife, Wang Guangmei; and Zhu De was pictured with his wife; but in Mao's cave all traces of Jiang Qing were gone. She was a complication of history, and so her memory had been removed, leaving the cave with only its simple furnishings: a bed, a bathtub, a bookshelf, a stone floor. Out in front, tourists could dress up in the gray uniforms of the wartime Communists and have their photos taken. Teenage girls giggled as they mounted horses and brandished pistols.

I met a Xi'an railway mechanic in his forties, who said that he had come to teach his daughter about the Revolution. She was eight years old, with pigtails and plastic Hong Kong Returns slippers. "The younger people in China don't know about the Revolution," her father said. "Our generation does, so I've taken her here to study our Chinese history."

He asked me what Americans thought about the Revolution, and I said that most people didn't understand it, which was the safest response. It always made the Chinese happy when *waiguoren* said they didn't understand China. The mechanic and I talked for a while and then, as a polite way to show that the conversation was ending, he said solemnly, "Our two countries have taken different roads. But now we are friends."

"Yes," I said. "We can forget about the problems of the past." Many of my random discussions in small places like Fuling and Yan'an ended like that; the people seemed to feel a need to summarize the relations between China and America, as if this had great bearing on the conversation at hand. Often it was the first time they had spoken with an American, which made our interaction seem like a momentous occasion. I liked that aspect of spending time in remote parts of China—every casual conversation was a major diplomatic event.

I was in the mood to talk, and so I sat on a bench near the park entrance. Within minutes an old man caught sight of me and hurried over. He told me that he was a veteran of Yan'an's Red Army, and he smiled when I said I was American.

"Thank you for helping us in the War of Resistance Against the Japanese," he said. It wasn't the first time I had been thanked for my country's role in World War II. Chongqing cab drivers were particularly fond of expressing their gratitude, and I gave the old man the same response I always gave the cabbies.

"Mei guanxi," I said. "No problem."

By now a small crowd had gathered, curious to see the *waiguoren.* I began to talk with a student from Xi'an's Communications University, who explained that she had come because she was interested in the early years of Chinese Communism. I asked her what would have happened if the revolutionaries had failed.

"Today there would be no Communist Party," she said.

"What if there were no Communist Party?"

"China would be different?"

"How?"

"It would be like Taiwan," she said. "Like America."

"What are those places like?"

"The economy is developed, but—" and now she shifted from Chinese into faltering English, because it was a phrase she remembered from her studies—"but the rich get richer and the poor get poorer."

"What about the new economic policies—do you agree with Reform and Opening?"

"Of course. All of us agree with that."

"But what about the gap between the rich and the poor? Doesn't it get bigger?"

"Some people will get rich," she said, "like scientists and businessmen. But this is necessary to develop the economy, and although others will improve more slowly, they will improve."

We talked for a few minutes longer. She asked if it was true that most Americans didn't understand China, and I agreed. I said nothing about the challenge of understanding a country in which one heard theories of trickle-down Capitalist economics in front of the enshrined cave homes of Marxist revolutionaries. On my way out of the museum, I passed rows of souvenir stands, where they sold Mao pendants, Communist Party history books, fake jade, cloth hangings, necklaces, statues, bracelets, stamps, cymbals, drums, gourmet rice. A commemorative Hong Kong Returns coin set was 320 yuan. The hawkers shouted out to me as I left.

THAT EVENING policemen burst into my hotel room after midnight. It was a cheap hotel near the train station, and I was fast asleep when the cops came in.

There was no warning. I had locked the door but the policemen got a key from one of the workers, and they entered and turned on the light. By the time I sat up, five officers were crowding around my bed, and I was terrified.

"What's the problem? What's the problem?" I asked the question again and again, but they simply stared at me. "What's the problem? What's the problem?" They listened and stared, and finally one of them spoke.

"We want to see your passport," he said.

Trembling, I took out my money belt and gave him the passport. He opened it and looked at the photograph on the first page. Then slowly he gazed at the second page. There was nothing on that page except the colorful designs of the passport paper, and the other policemen crowded around to look. The cop turned to the third page, also emptily full of color, and they stared at that as well.

My head was starting to clear and now I saw how young-looking they were—little more than scrawny boys in baggy uniforms. They gazed at me shyly. I showed them the passport page with the Chinese visa and they liked that, because they could read it. They flipped through the rest of the pages and then handed it back, smiling.

"Is everything okay?" I asked.

"Yes," said one of them. But still they stood there staring at me in bed. There was a long silence.

"Well," I said, "I'm tired. I think I will go to sleep now. Thank you very much."

"Thank you," all of them said at once. They took a long last look at me before they walked out. I locked the door behind them and went back to sleep.

THERE WAS NO GOOD REASON TO GO to Yulin and it took ten hours to get there. None of the guidebooks said much about it, except that *waiguoren* were restricted to staying in two expensive hotels. Yulin was a small town at the very northern tip of Shaanxi province, right near the border of Inner Mongolia, which was why I decided to go.

North of Yan'an the countryside grew even more desolate, rising through narrow canyons filled with cave dwellings. The river alongside the road died to a trickle, and in the burning heat all life was centered around that frail stream of water: peasants toting buckets, women washing clothes, boys swimming naked in shallow green pools. There were crop terraces high above the river, decorated with dusty signs: Control the Population, Improve the Population Quality. Having people here at all said a great deal about China, and it said far more that even in this godforsaken place their population was controlled.

After five hours I had seen enough. It was a brutally hot, dusty day, and the road was under construction, and the broken-down bus was crowded. But there was nothing to do except stick it out. Virtually every bus trip I took in China seemed to reach that point—all of them were exactly twice as long as I was willing to bear. And I knew that I would have to come back the same way, and that in Yulin I would undoubtedly pay a ridiculous price to stay in a three-star *waiguoren* hotel, and I wished I hadn't come.

I arrived just after sunset and saw a cheap hotel next to the bus station. My guidebook said that it was restricted to Chinese, but I figured there was nothing to lose by trying. The worker stared at me in surprise when I walked in. Frantically she waved and gestured me back toward the door, her eyes wide and silent as if she had been struck dumb.

"I can speak Chinese," I said, and the shock of hearing this made her eyes widen even further. Finally she recovered enough to ask what I wanted.

"I want to stay at this hotel."

"*Waiguoren* can't stay here," she said. "You have to go to a different hotel." But she was still too shocked to be rude, the way most workers were when they were set against giving you something. This gave me an idea.

"They've changed that rule," I said. "*Waiguoren* can stay in the same places as Chinese now."

Her eyes narrowed but she was still listening. I took some of my Chinese textbook's vocabulary and ran with it. "The National People's Congress changed the law," I said. "In Beijing they just changed it. Haven't you heard? At least it's changed if you're a teacher. Foreign teachers can stay in Chinese hotels, because we live in China and our salaries are the same as Chinese. See—here's my *danwei* card."

I gave her my red work unit card, my light green foreign resident card, my dark green foreign expert card, and my blue passport. The cards made a colorful pile and the worker leafed through them slowly, awed and overwhelmed. The Chinese have a weakness for official documents, and they often liked staring at the black-and-white foreign devil pictures on my identification cards. She gazed at them carefully, one by one, and then she gave me a registration slip for a two-dollar room. For the rest of the summer, I always referred to the National People's Congress when all else failed, and this turned out to be a remarkably effective tactic. Finally I saw the point of all the political jargon that I had memorized in class.

The next morning I caught a taxi north of Yulin, where the Great Wall ran through the desert. Tourists rarely came to see the wall here, because it was unrestored and the northern Shaanxi roads were so bad. There was no mention of the wall in my guidebook, but I had a Chinese map of the province which marked the ruins clearly.

The cabbie took me to a big Ming Dynasty fort that stood five miles outside of town, where Yulin's irrigated fields ended and the desert began. From the fort's highest tower the view stretched northward for miles. Occasionally the barrenness was punctuated by a slice of green where water had found its way—a stand of trees, a lonely field—but mostly it was just sand and low brown hills and a vast thoughtless sky. At nine in the morning the sun was already hot. I looked out at the empty landscape, at the hard low line of the horizon, and I realized why they had built the wall here. Even if there had been no Mongol threat, the terror of the land's monotony would be enough to make you build something.

The wall ran east and west from the fort. Westward it continued to its final stopping point at Jiayu Pass, in the mountains of northern Gansu province. Eastward the ruins ran to Zhonghai Pass, at the shore of the Yellow Sea. All told the distance between these two endpoints was probably more than fifteen hundred miles, and Yulin was somewhere roughly in the middle; but the wall had never been fully surveyed and nobody knew the exact length. I stood there at the desert fort, looking out at the heat waves shimmering above the sandy hills, and I decided to go toward the ocean. I tightened my boots and walked east along the ruins.

Most of the wall was just a three-foot-high ridge of packed earth that had been worn down by the wind and sand. Every two hundred yards or so I passed the ruins of a signal tower—a crumbling twenty-foot-high pile of dirt standing uselessly under the burning sun. I followed the wall through a brick factory, and then it swung across an irrigation canal and through a cornfield. A mound of sand swallowed the ridge, and I skirted the dune until I saw the next tower rising in the distance. A field of poplars had been planted nearby, the trees thin and brittle-looking under the Shaanxi sun. The Great Wall sank to a foot-high mound, and beyond that the lone and level sands stretched far away.

It was a ragged, patchwork landscape, and the green swaths of corn and clusters of poplars spoke of hard work that, in the face of the dunes and the dead brown horizon, appeared likely to be wasted. Likewise the ruined wall was a testimony to another sort of wastefulness, because the Ming rulers had built the fortification against outsiders who would have been better handled through diplomacy. And the size of the thing—both its pathetic smallness and its amazing bigness; the fact that I could step across it easily and the fact that it stretched for fifteen hundred miles—all of that showed how far the Chinese could go with a bad idea.

But it also seemed very Chinese that despite its original failure the wall now had great value. It had become perhaps the most powerful symbol of national pride, and nobody connected it with negative qualities like isolationism and stubbornness. Television stations often showed a music video that had been filmed on the Great Wall; the song was called "Love My China," and it celebrated the nation's fifty-five minorities and the happiness they enjoyed in the People's Republic. "Love My China" was a miserable, cloying song, but like so many of the bad music programs on television it had a sort of fatal attraction—I always watched it to the bitter end. The song's conclusion featured representative minorities dancing on the Great Wall, dressed in traditional costumes as they sang about how much they loved their China. Every time I watched it, I thought: Your China built that wall to keep you people out.

It seemed there was always something of this sort on television—at virtually any hour of the day you could find a channel that was focusing on some happy minority, usually the Tibetans. This kind of entertainment struck me as uniquely hypocritical, at least until the next year when I returned home from China and tutored at a public elementary school in Missouri, where the children celebrated Thanksgiving with traditional stories about the wonderful friendship between the Pilgrims and the Indians. I realized that these myths were a sort of link between America and China—both countries were arrogant enough to twist some of their greatest failures into sources of pride. And now that I thought about it, I remembered seeing Indians dance more than a few times on American television.

But just like Thanksgiving, the Great Wall had outgrown its original significance and now it simply meant greatness. Much of what was commonly written about it was false—that it was two thousand years old, that it could be seen from space—but the facts didn't matter. Even as a metaphor for Chinese isolationism it had lost its force, because every foreign dignitary was taken to view the Great Wall near Beijing, and every *waiguoren* tourist visited it. It was a major attraction of the new open China, a bridge rather than a wall, and it allowed the Chinese to introduce outsiders to the glories of their country in a single awe-inspiring vista. Rather than keeping the barbarians out, it ensured that after arrival they viewed China with a certain respect, and thus its construction hadn't really been a waste. It had taken an extra five hundred years, but finally the Chinese had made something useful out of the Great Wall. And in the same way I knew that the hard-fought patches of corn among these sand dunes weren't wasted; somehow they would survive.

I followed the wall east for nearly an hour. Sometimes I walked on top and the dirt crumbled beneath my feet. I passed another group of poplars, startling a pheasant that crashed away through the underbrush. Lizards skittered across the sand. I ran out of water and then I walked back to the fort.

IT WAS IN YULIN that I first realized my Chinese life had turned a corner. It had never been easy to live as a *waiguoren* in a place like Fuling, where the pressures could be exhausting—the stifling attention, the constant mocking shouts, the ongoing struggle of establishing what a foreigner could and couldn't do. But there was also another side to these hassles, because the Chinese were fascinated by *waiguoren* and once a conversation started they tended to treat me much better than the average person. It was very different from America, where you wouldn't shout at somebody just because he looked strange, but at the same time you probably wouldn't go out of your way to talk with him or show him kindness.

In the spring I had sensed that the benefits were starting to outweigh the difficulties, and mostly it was a matter of developing patience and trust. I had to allow things to happen—if somebody approached me, I talked with him, and I accepted virtually any invitation. I couldn't expect to control every situation, and I couldn't be constantly suspicious of people's intentions, which were almost invariably good. To live as a *waiguoren* required a certain passivity, but I had never been a passive person, and it took most of the spring to become comfortable with this role. In Yulin, it finally felt right—at last I accepted that things happened best when I simply let them happen.

One of the keys was time, which was something I always had in China. Even during busy teaching periods in Fuling, I always had plenty of spare time, because so much of what usually occupied me in America had been stripped away: family, friends, familiar routines. I had no access to the Internet and I couldn't afford to call people. I could write letters, but the post was so slow that communication was barely possible. When my older sister gave birth to a daughter in the fall of my first year, I didn't find out for three weeks.

It could be overwhelming to have so much free time, but it was also enormously liberating, and there were countless afternoons when I did nothing but sit in a teahouse with a newspaper, talking with whoever showed up. This became my traveling routine as well; in a new city I'd find a park or someplace where I could sit and read until a local stopped to chat.

After walking along the wall, I sat in the shade of the Ming fort, writing in my journal. A few minutes later, three young women paused to ask where I was from, and we talked for a while. They were former middle school classmates who were back in town for a reunion. Another old classmate and her husband had opened a restaurant just down the road, and they invited me to join them for lunch. The local specialty was something that involved pig stomach, so we ate that and drank Yulin beer.

None of them could understand why a *waiguoren* would travel all the way to Yulin, until I told them that I had been living in Sichuan. In their eyes this explained a great deal.

"The people in Sichuan are very *jiaohua*—sneaky. And their women have a bad reputation."

"They don't have culture in Sichuan like we do in Shaanxi. Did you know that this is the cradle of Chinese culture?"

"Have you been to Xi'an? That's the capital of our Shaanxi and the ancient capital of China. And that's why it's easier to understand us than the Sichuanese, because our dialect used to be the country's standard speech. The Mandarin in Beijing is similar to the way we speak here. In Sichuan the way they talk sounds terrible."

They were right about the dialect—traveling in Shaanxi was like having an enormous linguistic weight lifted off my chest. I took the rest of their opinions with a grain of salt, because I knew that the

Chinese always had strong prejudices about people from other parts of the country. Before I had left Fuling, Teacher Liao had given me a careful introduction to Shaanxi province.

"I wish I could visit Xi'an," she sighed. "You'll be able to see the terra-cotta warriors, the tomb of Emperor Qin Shihuang, and the Forest of Steles. You are very fortunate. But the people from the north are different from us here in the south. They're bigger, you know, because they eat wheat instead of rice, and the women aren't as pretty as the women here in Sichuan. That's because the sun's so terrible, and there's too much wind and sand. All of the women in the north have bad skin."

Listening to the Shaanxi women criticize Sichuan made me remember what Teacher Liao had said, and I figured that as a faithful student it was only right that I bring up the drawbacks of the north.

"In Sichuan," I told the women, "some of my friends say the south is better than the north, because of the climate. They say many people in the north have bad skin because of the sun. I don't know if this is true, but that's what they told me."

This took nobody by surprise; obviously they had heard these theories before and there was a ready defense. "That's true in most parts of the north," agreed Wang Yumei, who was the most talkative of the women. "But Yulin is different, because of our water. Our water here is very, very good! It comes from very deep in the ground, and people say that because of our water the women here are beautiful. So even though the sun is terrible our skin is still good. Look—my skin isn't black."

I had to admit it was true—there was nothing wrong with Wang Yumei's skin. And I thought that if you could somehow pipe Yulin's water down to Fuling you would without a doubt have the most beautiful women in China, and perhaps in the entire world, because of the mountains and the rivers and the deep well water of the desert town.

After lunch we went across the street to a Buddhist temple so that Guo Xiaoqin, who was the only unmarried woman in the group, could have her fortune told. As we entered, the priest and a young man were screaming at each other. The priest had given the young man a bad fortune, after which he had refused to make a donation, and in the resulting argument the young man had knocked over some things in the temple and the priest had hit him. The priest, who was in his sixties, stood in the center of the courtyard, shaking his fist. The young man was with a friend who held him back while he screamed obscenities. It was very hot now, and the women and I sat in the shade of a side temple, waiting for the argument to end.

As far as public disputes went, it was average, consisting of two acts. The young man was dragged out of the courtyard by his friend, but then he fought his way free and stormed back into the temple, where he and the priest screamed at each other for another five minutes. It was clear that the young man had no interest in hurting the priest, and certainly it was too late to change his fortune; he was simply saving face, and his friend laughed as he pushed him back toward the exit. After they were gone, we waited until his shouts trailed off into the distance and it was clear that there would not be a third act. Some of the public disputes I had seen in Fuling had so many acts that even the stick-stick soldiers got bored and wandered off.

The argument wasn't a particularly auspicious omen for fortune-telling in this temple, but Guo Xiaoqin, who was twenty-six years old and clearly felt that time was an issue, decided to continue. The priest collected himself, prayed, and told the woman to kowtow three times before the altar. He struck a gong as she bowed, and then he gave her a tube filled with wooden sticks. She shook the tube until one of the sticks rattled free, and the priest looked at the number and interpreted the fortune. He said that she would be married soon, perhaps within the year, and everybody sighed with relief. Wang Yumei gave the priest ten yuan. He smiled as we left.

We walked down the road to the Red Cliff Gorge, where Daoist and Buddhist temples, some of them more than thirteen centuries old, had been carved into the sandstone cliffs. In the center of the gorge a river flowed clear between sandy banks. We took off our shoes and waded through the shallows, and then we sat in the shade. Across the river a group of six young peasants had come to have a picnic. They were men and women in their early twenties, and after lunch they splashed in the river, the women screaming as the men chased them up and down the sandy gorge.

"Do you have places like this in your country?" Wang Yumei asked. I tried to imagine having a reunion with my friends in America and picking up a random foreigner and spending the day with him, simply out of curiosity and kindness.

"No," I said. "It's not quite the same as this in my country."

I DIDN'T WANT TO LEAVE YULIN. The hotel was fine and, despite the heat of the days, the nights were desert-cool and there was never any problem sleeping. The mornings were pleasant, and every day I woke up early and watched the traffic on the main street. Old men swept their shopfronts, and women dragged milk carts along the main street, and the night soil collectors headed past on their way out to the countryside. Junkmen pulled wagons, thumping little hand drums to attract sales. Horse-drawn carts delivered coal to the small restaurants, and the sun rose bright above the tiled roofs of the buildings, and slowly the dusty city grew hot.

The main street passed beneath three Ming Dynasty towers, and nearly all of the other buildings on the street dated to at least the Qing Dynasty. Yulin's ancient city wall was still intact, rising twenty feet above the buildings. I had never seen such a well-preserved old town in China, and yet there weren't any other foreign tourists in the city.

Every day I watched the morning street until it started to become hot, and then I'd buy some yogurt and find a shaded restaurant where I could eat steamed rolls and try to read a newspaper. One morning I bought my yogurt from an old man who became very excited, gesturing for me to wait while he ran back home. He returned with an old Chinese book, which he handed to me without a word.

I opened it and tried to read the first page. Some of it was unclear but I could get the general idea—something about the start, earth and water, light and dark. The man waited patiently while I read. I made my way through the rest of the page, and then I realized what I was reading. I looked up at the old man.

"Are you Christian?" I asked.

"Yes!" He beamed and shook my hand.

"Where is this Bible from?"

"Our friends from Sweden gave it to us," he said, and I figured they must have been Lutheran missionaries. I told him that I had lived in Sweden as a child, which pleased him. He asked if I was also Christian.

"I'm Catholic."

"Chabuduo," he said. "That's almost the same as our Christianity. Most of it is the same but you believe more in *Mali."*

He was right about Mary being a sticking point, but nevertheless he seemed happy to meet me. His name was Luo and he invited me to come back later, so I could meet his son and grandchildren.

The Luos lived on the main street, in a traditional *siheyuanr,* an old brick complex organized around a central courtyard. Now there were seven branches of the family living there, all of them named Luo, and the buildings had not changed much in centuries. In the old man's home they still slept on a traditional *kang,* an old-fashioned brick bed that was heated by coal in the winter.

He told me that his ancestors had been Qing Dynasty soldiers sent north from Xi'an in the 1700s to fight the Mongols beyond the wall. They were posted here to keep the foreigners at bay, but their descendants came under foreign influence anyway—missionaries had converted the old man's parents before Liberation. A simple cross hung above his old *kang,* a curious conjunction of relics.

The old man's son was named Luo Xiaolei; he was in his mid-forties and he edited a local literary magazine. His daughter had just graduated from the Chinese department of Yulin Teachers College. They were friendly, well-educated people, and during the week I spent in Yulin I went to their home every day. Often they served me a late breakfast, and after eating we would sit with tea and watermelon in the shade of their living room.

Luo Xiaolei had spent five years in prison during the Cultural Revolution, because he was an intellectual and a Christian, and his father had been exiled to ten years of labor in a remote part of the desert. The old man didn't say much about that experience, except that the work was difficult and served no purpose. That was often the way people described their exiles—the wasted time was the worst part.

I found it easy to speak openly with the Luos, because their experiences had made them skeptical, and because soon I would leave this place. That was the best part of traveling—I wasn't really accountable for things I did and said; I could wander off with anybody and talk about anything I wanted. It wasn't like living in Fuling, where people kept track of me and there was always the knowledge that I still had another year left in the river town. There were many good things about having a home in China, but that was one of the drawbacks.

One afternoon, Luo Xiaolei asked me what I thought about teaching in China, and I realized that it was a difficult question.

"Mostly I like it very much," I said, "and especially I like the students. I think they respect teachers more than we do in America. I teach literature, and that's also good; my Chinese students like poetry more than most American students do. But I don't like the political system in the college. It's hard to explain—sometimes this system affects the students. Many of their ideas are very *xia'aide*—narrow."

Teacher Kong had taught me that word near the end of the semester, and it summarized the difficult aspects of Fuling. Luo Xiaolei nodded. "Probably they aren't used to *waiguoren* yet," he said. "In remote parts of China you know that we have not had very many."

"I know, but there are other problems, too. Their books are bad, and sometimes what they study isn't true."

I asked his daughter, who was sitting with us, if they studied Confucius in the Chinese department of her college.

"No," she said.

"But you study Marx?"

"Yes."

"It's the same way in Fuling. My students read Shakespeare and Marx, but they don't read Confucius. Those are foreign ideas, and Confucius is part of your culture, but nobody studies him anymore."

"Did you study Marx in college in America?" she asked.

"Yes, but only a little. Many college students do in America, because he's a philosopher."

"What do they think of Marxism in your America?"

"Most people think it is interesting, but it's not very . . . " I was groping for the word and she knew what I was thinking.

"Shiyong," she said. "Useful."

"Right. It's not very useful."

"I agree," she said. "I think it's a waste of time. Most of the politics we study are a waste of time." She flipped her hair away from her face and looked across the room at her father. He was thinking of something else, and then he smiled when he realized that his daughter expected him to respond. He was a gray-haired man with round glasses and his eyes were bright with memory.

"No," he said. "Marxism is not very useful." And his own father, who was sitting in the shadows eating watermelon, said nothing at all.

I FOLLOWED A REGULAR ROUTINE IN YULIN, visiting the Luos during the morning and eating at a small restaurant in the afternoon. The restaurant had good dumplings, along with cheap local beer, and the owner was the sort of tough no-nonsense woman who could often be found in places where men went drinking after work. She teased me about my accent, which she said was half foreign and half Sichuanese, and whenever other customers came into the restaurant she announced my vital information: nationality, age, Chinese name, *danwei,* and salary. Usually the customers remarked the lowness of my salary and bought me a beer. To maintain my dignity, I explained the nature of the Peace Corps, and how we had come to build friendship between America and China rather than make money, which invariably inspired the customers to buy me another beer. I tried to cover the third round, usually without success. After that we would shake hands warmly and say something about the improving relations between our nations, and I would return to my hotel and sleep until it cooled to evening.

On my last day in Yulin, two men in their late twenties came into the restaurant and began buying me drinks. One of them was named Wang and the other was Zhao. They said I could call them Comrade. It was Friday and they had just finished working the morning shift in a nearby factory.

Each of us finished two beers quickly, and during the next beer the two men began to turn red and tell stories about Chinese history. Comrade Wang told me about Emperor Yu, who had been the first to control the floods of the Yellow River. This was a story I had studied in my textbook, which was fortunate because Comrade Wang's version frequently became entangled in the local dialect. I kept nodding and acting as if I understood, and periodically Comrade Zhao would interrupt him:

"Speak Mandarin! He's not going to understand if you speak the dialect!"

Comrade Wang would nod and speak a few sentences in Mandarin, and then he would drift back toward the dialect as Emperor Yu made more heroic efforts to build dikes and levees along the Yellow River. The gist of the tale was that Emperor Yu had worked so hard that although he often passed the doorway of his family home, he never had time to stop and visit. It was a hell of a project, controlling the Yellow River.

Finally the river was under control and Comrade Wang sat back and drained his beer. They were buying bottles and our table was full of empties. One of the many good things about small Chinese restaurants was that they never cleared the bottles until you left, which meant that passersby could glance over and see how much damage you had done by two in the afternoon. There was big face in that and today we were doing fine.

"Did you understand the story?" Comrade Zhao asked. "You didn't understand, did you? He kept speaking our dialect!"

I said that everything was clear, reciting the version from my textbook.

"You see?" Comrade Wang was triumphant. "He understood all of it!"

There was a sudden need to show me Comrade Wang's investment down the street, and the owner agreed to hold our table until we returned. They were both big men, and I walked between them, the three of us stumbling unsteadily over the cobblestones. We passed Mr. Luo's stand and I waved. I had no idea where we were going, or what the investment was—that was all they said, that we were going to see Comrade Wang's investment. It was a hot afternoon and after the beer we were sweating as we walked down the street.

We entered a doorway and climbed a narrow flight of stairs. On the second floor there was a big room and a single girl in roller skates was spinning around the hardwood floor.

"This," said Comrade Wang, "is my investment."

Proudly he looked out over the roller rink, and then he went over to the concessions area and talked with the worker.

"The investment was too much," Comrade Zhao whispered mournfully, once Comrade Wang was out of earshot. "He had to borrow too much money. He'll never pay it back!"

I could see that Comrade Wang was telling the worker something about me and I strained to hear.

"They don't have enough people coming," Comrade Zhao whispered. "And last night there was a fight and some glass was broken. He's going to lose so much money!"

Comrade Wang returned with roller skates and presented them to me. "Here," he said. "You skate. Now. For free."

I stuttered, explaining that I didn't know how to roller-skate. "Of course you know how!" said Comrade Wang. "It comes from your country!"

I told them that I had a hurt leg, and they offered to take me to a doctor. There was one down the street, Comrade Zhao said, and Chinese medicine was very effective. I explained that I knew the benefits of Chinese medicine, because a Chinese doctor had told me to sit down as much as possible and avoid activities like roller-skating. After many polite offers and protests, we solved the problem by going back to the restaurant, sitting down, and having another beer. They didn't seem offended; Comrade Wang was pleased that he had been able to show me his investment. The empties were still on the table.

We finished another round and Comrade Wang looked me in the eye.

"He Wei," he said, using my Chinese name. "The only other time I saw an American was on Mount Emei, and I didn't have a good impression. He was very fat, and he was telling people to do things for him. "Do this! Do that!" He had workers carry him up the mountain, like he was a great landlord. But you're different—before I met you, I thought that all Americans are bad, but now I know that's not the truth."

I was touched, and I felt guilty that I had lied about seeing the doctor. But it was a Chinese type of white lie and probably that made it all right. I thanked Comrade Wang and we toasted each other.

"Also, that American on Mount Emei was very white," he said. "His skin was so white and bad-looking! But you're actually a little yellow—you look more Chinese. Your skin is much better than his!"

EVERYTHING WENT WELL that summer. I studied at a college in Xi'an, where the classes were not too difficult, and the city had plenty of good parks where you could buy a cup of tea and chat with the locals. Every day it was thirty-five degrees Celsius (ninety-five degrees Fahrenheit). Supposedly the government had a policy that if the temperature reached thirty-seven degrees everybody was given the rest of the day off, and so they always announced the official temperature as thirty-five. Often I rode a friend's bicycle over to Xingqing Palace Park, where I'd get a cup of tea and ask the workers what the temperature was.

"Thirty-five degrees," they'd say, fanning themselves with newspapers.

"What was the temperature yesterday?"

"Thirty-five degrees."

"How hot do you think it'll be tomorrow?"

They'd roll their eyes and tell me to go drink my tea; it wasn't much of a joke to them. China was perhaps the only country in the world where the government controlled the temperature, although two years later the Beijing weather stations finally started announcing the temperature as it actually was. Local newspapers hailed this development as an important step toward telling citizens the truth, and perhaps it was: today the temperature, tomorrow the full report on the Tiananmen Square massacre. But the government also made it clear that the policy of giving a day off was merely a myth, so the new temperatures didn't result in any vacations. It just meant that you knew exactly how hot it really was.

Xi'an was the hottest thirty-five degrees imaginable and at night I had trouble sleeping, but even with the heat everything went well that summer. My sister Angela, who was a graduate student in geology at Stanford, had been sent out to a summer project in Xinjiang, the province in the far west of China. She spent a week with me in Xi'an and together we saw the historical sights of the city. I always told people that she was helping China find oil in Xinjiang, while I was a volunteer English teacher in Sichuan; this pleased everyone and they gave us special treatment. The worker at the terra-cotta warriors museum was so inspired that he let us in for the Chinese price, waiving the *waiguoren* surcharge, because of the good work we were doing for China.

Angela flew out to her project, and a week later I finished my studies and caught a train to Xinjiang. It was a forty-eight-hour trip along the old Silk Road, through the deserts of Gansu and Xinjiang provinces, and I had always liked long train trips and big empty landscapes.

I traveled hard sleeper, which I considered to be the most enjoyable class on a Chinese train. Hard seat was a nightmare, a crush of peasants and migrant workers; soft sleeper was too much in the other direction, cadres and overfed businessmen and *waiguoren* tourists. Hard sleeper cars weren't uncomfortable—everybody had a berth—but the tickets were cheap enough for travelers who considered themselves Old Hundred Names, the common people. Old Hundred Names were always easy to talk with, especially on trains, where they chatted lightly, drinking their tea and eating instant noodles.

On the first day, a young man from Hebei province came and sat across from me, watching the Gansu hills slip past. He was twenty-five years old, and he had worked in Xinjiang for two years, and he did not like it. Xinjiang was too extreme, he said—too hot in the summer, too cold in the winter. He had just finished four months of vacation, and it was not pleasant to take a forty-eight-hour train trip and know that at its conclusion you had to start work again in a place like Xinjiang. His job involved safety management for an oil company.

"Every year, two or three workers are killed," he said. "Especially on the roads in the desert. The transportation is terrible in Xinjiang, and that's why workers die every year. There's not much we can do about it."

I told him that my younger sister was looking for oil near Turpan. He shrugged, as if to say: She can have it. Outside there was a dusty streak of low hills and the land was getting steadily drier as the train rocked west.

He was bright and it wasn't the sort of rote conversation that I often had in China. There was something quietly sharp about his eyes—he had a heavy-lidded gaze but I could see that he took careful notice of everything around him. He saw that I was jotting in my notebook, but unlike most people he didn't ask what I was writing, probably because he guessed the truth. Usually I told people that it was my diary, or sometimes I simply said, "I'm writing my foreign language." That was enough to satisfy nearly everyone—if you knew a foreign language, it was obvious that you would spend a great deal of time writing it. Nobody seemed to realize that in fact I was writing about them and everything else around me, but the man from Hebei watched my pen skim impulsively over the pages and I sensed that he knew that he was being described. But he still spoke freely; we talked lightly about politics, and the Communist Party, and I asked him if he was a member.

"No," he said. "I don't want to be."

"Why not?"

"Too much trouble. My friends—and most young people—all of us are the same. We're not interested in that. It's not the same as your America. We only have one party in our China."

The differences between these countries interested him. "All Chinese like Americans," he said, a while later. "But many Americans think there are problems with human rights here. In fact, Old Hundred Names doesn't care about that. Old Hundred Names worries about eating, about having enough clothes. Look out there."

He pointed out the window—a dusty village, garbage beside the tracks, a skinny donkey followed by a peasant in blue. Old Hundred Names.

"Do you think people like that worry about democracy?" he said. "They need to improve their living standard and then they can start thinking about other things. That's the problem with America and China—you can't compare them in the same breath."

We slipped away from politics; he talked of marriage and how after three more years he would find a wife. There were often schedules like this for the young Chinese I knew; they were pragmatists about love as well as politics and nearly everything else. The young man explained his reasons—in three years he would be twenty-eight years old, which was neither too old nor too young, and by then he should have enough money to get married. It took a great deal of money to marry, he said, and it wasn't something you wanted to do in a place like Xinjiang. In three years he hoped to live in Hebei, or perhaps Qingdao, the former German concession on the east coast. He spoke lovingly of Qingdao, of the beautiful red roofs and the clean streets, the friendly people and the calm sea; and meanwhile our train rocked steadily west into the desert.

It was a long, empty day—nothing to see out the window, nothing to do on the train. I sat and talked with people for a couple of hours, and then I climbed up to my bunk. We passed through Lanzhou, the capital of Gansu province, where the smog hung limp above the sullen stain of the Yellow River, and I fell asleep. When I awoke everything had changed—we were in a bright landscape of green grass and yellow rapeseed, and dune-shaped hills rolled off toward the horizon.

A fertilizer salesman materialized and began to ask me questions about money. How much is a new car in America? A used car? What about the license fee? Taxes? Insurance? In a notebook he scrawled my responses—guesses, all of them—and I was glad to see that somebody else on this train was writing. But what were they growing in this desolate place that required fertilizer?

"Wheat and corn," he said. "Of course, there are grapes as well, and other fruit, but there are grain crops near Urumqi. But the fertilizer we make is shipped back into the interior." He returned to the money questions: How much is a house in America? What are the unemployment benefits? What kind of insurance does the government give you?

After that was finished we sat in silence, looking out the window. I felt I should continue the conversation, but there were only so many questions you could ask about fertilizer. I asked him when he had come to Xinjiang.

"I was born here," he said.

"When did your parents come?"

"My parents came to Xinjiang in the 1950s, after Liberation. They came to help build the country. It was like America."

We stared at the scene outside: a shepherd with his flock in a green field, a man in blue riding a bicycle along a dusty road, a row of mud houses surrounded by earth-colored walls, a range of craggy white peaks to the south, and, westward, a broad empty horizon of the sort I had rarely seen in China. There were no trees for miles.

"Go west, young man," said the fertilizer salesman, remembering a phrase from history class long ago.

SOMETIME DURING THE SECOND NIGHT our train passed Jiayu Pass, the westernmost fort of the Great Wall. I didn't see that barrier, but in the morning it was clear that a line had been crossed. There were no villages or walls, only rocks and dust and low rugged hills that were sharply shadowed by the desert sun.

We had come to the edge of China—or rather, a figurative edge of China, because you could continue westward for another thousand miles and still be within the country's borders. But this was the end of where the Han, or ethnic Chinese, traditionally lived, and now we were reaching the uncertain regions of the Silk Road. The Chinese called this province the Xinjiang Uighur Autonomous Region; the Uighurs were the indigenous people, and they called this land Turkistan or Uighurstan, and they wanted it for themselves.

Xinjiang means New Frontier, and for more than two thousand years it had slipped in and out of China, until at last the Communists took firm control of the region in 1949. But it was a difficult place to govern—it bordered Tibet, India, Pakistan, Tajikstan, Kyrgyzstan, Kazakhstan, Mongolia; it composed one-sixth of China's total land area, containing a wealth of oil and minerals; and the majority of its residents, the Uighurs, were Muslims who spoke a Turkish tongue and had nothing in common with the Han Chinese. All of these factors made Xinjiang a complex place, and in February of that year there had been violence in the northern reaches of the province. For them the most immediate issue was keeping the Han out—four decades ago, only 15 percent of the region's population had been Chinese, but now that figure had swelled to nearly 50 percent. The Han came to do many jobs—to work as soldiers, as government cadres, as fertilizer salesmen—and they kept coming, arriving on trains like this. In my car there was not a single Uighur, but there were plenty of Han who were heading west to work.

The tension was something that nobody on the train wanted to talk about—a few times I asked about the problems of the spring, but everybody was evasive. A woman in her forties told me that she didn't understand the issue, because she was simply Old Hundred Names. That was the best part of being Old Hundred Names—they were never responsible for anything. It was the same way in any country where the citizens spoke of themselves as the "common people," but in China there was a much higher percentage of Old Hundred Names than in most places. Virtually everybody you met described himself as such, and none of them claimed to have anything to do with the way things worked.

After establishing herself as Old Hundred Names, the woman

started asking me Da Shan questions. Da Shan was a Canadian who spoke Chinese fluently and appeared frequently on television, and he was without a doubt the most famous *waiguoren* in China. He was what people called a *Zhongguotong*—a foreigner who "knew about China," or, essentially, a China hand. On good language days people referred to me as a *Zhongguotong*, but I knew it was only flattery. I had a long way to go before I could be accepted a China hand, and from what I had seen of Da Shan, this wasn't a particularly appealing goal. Probably he was a nice enough person, but in his "cross-talk" comedy routines and opera singing there was more than a touch of the trained monkey.

People everywhere asked me about Da Shan, and his fame testified to how badly foreigners did with the Chinese language. It was the equivalent of Americans becoming fascinated with a Chinese person simply because he spoke idiomatic English.

"Do you know Da Shan?" the woman asked. "You speak our Chinese well, but you're not as good as Da Shan."

"Yes, he speaks much better than me." This was why most *waiguoren* in China hated Da Shan: the more your Chinese improved, and the more you chatted with Old Hundred Names, the more you heard about Da Shan and how much better than you he was.

"Do you know him?" the woman asked. This was another common assumption—that all *waiguoren* who studied Chinese knew each other, maintaining contact through an intricate nationwide system, like the Freemasons.

"No," I said. "I have never met Da Shan."

"He's very good at the cross-talk—he's very funny."

"*Dui.* I've seen him do it. Indeed he is very good."

"Da Shan speaks Mandarin better than most Chinese," the woman said.

"Yes. That is what many people tell me."

"And he can sing our traditional Chinese songs. Is he from your America?"

"No. He's from their Canada."

"What do people in your America think of Da Shan?"

"We don't have Da Shan on television in our America. Nobody in our America knows who he is."

"So he's only on television in their Canada?"

"He's not on television in their Canada, either. The only place where he is on television is China."

For the woman, like many of the Chinese that I met, this was a great disappointment. It was tragic for a nation to produce somebody as gifted as Da Shan and allow a foreign country to monopolize his skills. But in fact, as I explained to the woman, this is a common pattern in Canada, where all talent leaves the country as soon as possible, just like NHL franchises. She thought about this for a while and then continued talking about Da Shan.

"He has a Chinese wife," she said. "Have you heard that?"

"Yes," I said. I had heard every theory there was about Da Shan. Occasionally people said that his grandmother was Chinese, which seemed unlikely given that he was blond. His Chinese teacher had also become famous, and sometimes people recommended that I move to the east of China and seek out this pedagogue, the way itinerant scholars had done more than two thousand years ago during the Spring and Autumn Period. I had a good start in Chinese, they said, and it was a shame to waste that in a place like Sichuan, where even the locals couldn't speak the language.

"Do you know what Da Shan's salary is?" I asked. I wanted to talk about anything else, and money sounded promising.

"He makes thousands of yuan every month," the woman said with certainty. "He has a very good salary. How much do you make?"

"One thousand yuan."

"That's not as much as Da Shan."

"No," I said. "It's not as much as Da Shan."

"But it's enough," she said. "For a young man who is single, one thousand yuan is enough."

"Yes. It's a better salary than most people in Fuling, where I live. Have you heard of Fuling? It's in Sichuan."

She thought hard and shook her head.

"I'm sure you've heard of Fuling hot pickled mustard tuber," I said. "It's very famous in China. Have you seen the advertisements on television?" And I sang the jingle:

Wu River brand,
Fuling hot pickled mustard tuber!

It sounded much better in Chinese than it does in English, and the woman recognized it immediately. All of the Chinese were familiar with Fuling hot pickled mustard tuber and that was the easiest way to tell people where I was from. The woman and I talked for a while longer, and then she said something tactful about our China becoming more open to foreign countries. I thanked her and she returned to her part of the car.

The train grew hotter as we passed into the Turpan-Hami Basin, where the earth beside the tracks was cracked by the sun. The hills in the distance dropped steadily, and with them the horizon fell lower and lower, until at last the land was perfectly flat and the clear sky sat like a great dome of blue stretched taut above the black earth.

We stopped for an hour in the oasis city of Hami, where the station signs were in Arabic script as well as Chinese. It was the first place on this journey where I saw Uighurs; they were standing on the station platform, selling grapes and melons. The Uighurs had long sunbrowned noses, and their features would have been at home in Saudi Arabia, or Turkey, or even Italy. Centuries ago many of them were caravan people, nomads who bought and sold along the Silk Road, and even today some spark of that same spirit inspires them to travel across China in search of business. Uighurs often work as black-market moneychangers in big cities, where they also sell raisins and fruitcake. Even in Fuling it is common for a couple of them to set up a fruitcake and raisin stand on a downtown street. They follow the Yangtze with their bushel baskets, drifting east, stopping in a city for a few weeks and then moving on. Of all the small entrepreneurs I saw in China, the Uighurs were the most remarkable—you'd find them two thousand miles away from home, and yet all they had was a basket of raisins and a tray of fruitcake. I had no idea how they made money.

At Hami the safety management worker and I stood there watching the fruit salesmen, and I asked him about relations between the Han and the Uighurs.

"We have problems," he said. "Sometimes the *guanxi* is bad. Now our government helps their education, agriculture, economy, but still there are problems. It's because of the history, not today's policy. Every country has this kind of trouble—you have the same kind of problems with blacks in your America."

It was a good point, and I told him that I didn't think Xinjiang's troubles were America's affair. But I said that if it was a Chinese affair, it seemed strange that the violence in the spring hadn't been discussed in the newspapers in Chongqing and Fuling.

"Sichuan is too remote. Bigger cities heard about what happened here."

"What happened?"

"There were bombs," he said, shrugging. "It was like Israel."

"Does your company have any Uighur workers?"

"No. Their education level isn't high enough, and if it's not high enough, it's not safe. If their level was appropriate, we'd hire them."

"Do you speak Uighur?"

"No. You don't need it here. You always use Chinese at work and when you go shopping."

"Do you know any words?"

"I know a few. *Salaam aleikum* is 'hello.' And 'thank you' is. . ."

He paused, thinking hard. He had lived in the Uighur Autonomous Region for two years. "I forget," he said at last. "But I know 'goodbye.'"

And he said it, but he spoke softly and the word was lost in the hot desert wind that swept through the station.

THE OASIS TOWNS appeared every hour or two, rising suddenly alongside the tracks and then disappearing just as quickly into the rock and dirt and sand. They weren't oases in the romantic sense: no palms or shining pools of water; just concrete and dust and glass. It was as if the oases and the desert had been reversed; we would roll out of town and I would breathe a sigh of relief, unable to imagine that once these places had been inviting to travellers. The land was barren but it was also mesmerizing, and the towns had no charm.

I would have been happy to continue like that for days, passing from oasis to oasis, watching the great nothingness beside the tracks. The train was comfortable and the people friendly; I was the only *waiguoren* of our car and often the other passengers brought me food and drink—tomatoes, cucumbers, flavored ices, dried fish, beer. Occasionally somebody stopped by to talk about prices or Sino-American relations, but at last it was as if the wasteland had swallowed all conversation. Nearly everybody sat silent, staring out at the scenery.

The Flaming Mountains rose to the south, red and scarred by countless ridges, and then the Heavenly Mountains came into view. Snow was streaked bright in the high peaks. It grew dark; a full moon hung heavy in the eastern sky. The train rocked westward. It seemed we'd never get to Urumqi, but I didn't care.

THERE WERE CHECKPOINTS on the Xinjiang highways where policemen with machine guns inspected all vehicles. It was unusual for Chinese policemen to handle weapons like that, and in Xinjiang they were very proud of the responsibility, fiddling constantly with the clip and the handle. They couldn't simply carry the guns on their straps—the point of having a weapon was to keep it constantly in their hands, aimed at something. It was like giving an automatic rifle to a child. I took a bus from Urumqi to Turpan, and the policeman at the checkpoint used the barrel of his machine gun to motion bluntly at the passengers as he inspected our identification.

The tension in the big cities was palpable; conversations with Uighurs didn't last very long before they started complaining. They complained about the number of Han migrants, and they complained about how all the good government jobs went to the Han, and they complained about the planned-birth policy, even though for Uighurs the limit was extended to two children and was imposed only in urban areas. I wasn't particularly surprised to see that the problems of the spring hadn't blown over; everything I had learned about the Chinese suggested that they would be particularly bad colonists. They tended to have strong ideas about race, they rarely respected religion, and they had trouble considering a non-Chinese point of view. One of the best characteristics of the people I knew in Fuling was that they had a powerful pride in their own culture—I had never lived in a place where the people had such a strong sense of their unique cultural identity. Despite the self-destruction of the Cultural Revolution and the subsequent rush to open to the outside world, there was still a definite sense of what was Chinese, and I believed that this would help them survive modernization. But there was also a narrowness to this concept, and it seemed nearly impossible for a Chinese to go to a place like Xinjiang, learn the language, and make friends with the locals. In the five thousand years of their history it was striking how little interest the Chinese had had in exploration, and today that same characteristic limited them, even within their own borders. They seemed completely content in being Chinese, and they assumed that this feeling was shared by everybody else.

When the Han went to western places like Xinjiang or Tibet, their initial reaction was that the people needed to become more like the country's interior, particularly with regard to modernization, even if it came at the expense of culture. I had trouble understanding this perspective; to me it seemed that already too many beautiful places had been modernized too quickly, and I felt that the relatively untouched corners of China should be left that way. But I had never been poor, which made a great difference in the way you saw a place like Xinjiang.

Everything looked different to the average Chinese, and I had gained some sense of their perspective when my writing class studied the American West in the fall. We discussed Western expansion, and I presented my students with a dilemma of the late nineteenth century: the Plains Indians, their culture in jeopardy, were being pressed by white settlers. I asked my class to imagine that they were American citizens proposing a solution, and nearly all responded like the following two students:

> The Indians should become a part of American society like everyone else. Even though they are poor and savage, we can help them found reservations to make them civilized, and give them advanced knowledges and experiences to change their lifestyle and develop their economy. By this way, we can make them become rich and be suited for modern life. At last, the Indians can get along well with us and advance together.

> The world is changing and developing. We should make the Indians suit our modern life. The Indians are used to living all over the plains and moving frequently, without a fixed home, but it is very impractical in our modern life. . . . We need our country to be a powerful country; we must make the Indians adapt to our modern life and keep pace with the society. Only in this way can we strengthen the country.

That was the first time I realized how different our perspectives were on progress and modernization. If anything, I had presented them with an idealized version of the Plains Indians, and yet the lifestyle and culture had no appeal to my students. But like most Chinese, the majority were but one generation removed from serious poverty. What I saw as freedom and culture, they saw as misery and ignorance.

And Xinjiang, as well as Tibet, looked much the same. The Han that I met in Xinjiang couldn't understand why the Uighurs didn't appreciate China's efforts; they pointed out how backward the region had been before Liberation, emphasizing the work that had been done by the government. There was no question that this was true—the government had built roads, railways, schools. But the Chinese had failed to take the logical first step; they had never made a serious effort to understand and respect the Uighur culture, and settlers rarely learned the local language. The result was that tremendous amounts of money and work had been sunk into the desert, but with regard to improving relations much of it had been completely wasted.

I found myself oddly situated in the middle of this tension. The Uighurs disliked speaking the language of the Han, and in tourist areas some of them spoke better Japanese or English than Chinese. There was a certain distrust of foreigners who spoke Chinese; it was better if you used English. This was hard for me to do—all summer I had enjoyed the benefits of becoming conversational in Chinese, but now my use of the language established me as an outsider, and a politically charged outsider at that.

In addition to the language, there was a host of new cultural rules that complicated my interactions with the Uighurs. They were very different people from the Chinese I knew in Fuling—the Uighurs showed emotion, angering easily, and I found bargaining unpleasant because sometimes the routine involved a mock show of anger or disgust. I missed the even predictability of the Chinese; I was accustomed to their social rules, and I knew how they would react to the things I did and said. There was something comforting about all of those rote dialogues—the conversations about my salary, U.S.-China relations, and Da Shan. In Xinjiang I found myself gravitating to Chinese restaurants and shops, and especially I liked talking with the Sichuanese, who had migrated to Xinjiang in large numbers. After a summer on the road it was good to hear their slurred tones again—much more soothing than the Turkic trills of the Uighur tongue. And I realized that I had picked up some of that distinctly Chinese narrowness: I was also content in being Chinese, even here in Xinjiang.

But things were different if I didn't say anything. I have some Italian ancestry and don't look too much different from the Uighurs, and I could walk down the street and not attract attention. Occasionally I was mistaken for a native—the Chinese sometimes asked if I was a Uighur, and the Uighurs sometimes asked if I was a Kazakh. In Fuling I was always extremely conscious of my appearance, because every day I was confronted by the ways in which I looked different from the locals, but now in these desert towns I saw people with noses and hair and eyes like mine. For the first time I realized the full importance of race, not just in the way it divided people, but also in the sense of feeling a link to those who looked like you. For a year I hadn't felt that connection, but here in Xinjiang, although the link was tenuous, it was better than nothing.

My vacation was winding down, but I had no eagerness to leave. I liked the lazy freedom of traveling, and I liked the uncertainty of my position here in Xinjiang, where I had no job and even my race was in question. It was a vague place—even time was uncertain here. All of China is on one time zone, which meant that in Xinjiang the sun didn't rise until eight or nine o'clock and it set after ten at night. Most of the people followed a more practical schedule, based on a mythical local time zone that was two hours later than the one in Beijing, but all of the government offices and state-run transportation followed the official standard time. It was the perfect symbol of the divide between the government and the governed, both of them living in the same place but going about their separate routines a full two hours apart.

Mostly in Xinjiang I liked the brutal landscapes. For three days I camped at altitudes of more than ten thousand feet in the Heavenly Mountains, and a day later I was in Turpan, where the desert basin dipped to five hundred feet below sea level and the Flaming Mountains rose north of town. Turpan was so hot that even the government couldn't control the temperature. Every day I was there, it reached forty-two degrees, 107 Fahrenheit, and it was reported as such. Shops closed during midday, so everybody could rest inside until the worst of the heat had passed.

It was almost as hot in Hami, where my sister Angela was looking at rocks. Along with another Stanford geologist, she was employed by a Chinese state-owned oil company that had built an entire city outside of Hami. It was literally a city—schools, hospitals, shops, apartment buildings; everything was neatly laid out on well-planned streets that had been desert wasteland but four years ago. There were fifty thousand employees who worked there, all of them Han Chinese who had been shipped in from Gansu province. When I went to the market, people mistook me for a Uighur, because they had seen so few of the locals. The Chinese rarely left the complex; everything they needed was provided by their oil-built oasis in the desert.

And yet the city was a mirage. There wasn't much oil in Hami, at least according to Angela and her colleague, who knew the region's geology. All of it was a mystery—why had they built the city here in the desert? Why had all of these people been transferred out to this desolate place? What were they looking for? In five hundred years, would it be like the Great Wall, money and work buried in the sand? What was it about the Chinese that made them come slightly unhinged in the border regions—what inspired them to build walls, forts, cities; why did they construct Ozymandian monstrosities in the far reaches of their country? And what prevented them from actually talking with the people who lived there?

But these were mysteries that I didn't have time to untangle. I was in Hami for three short days—I stayed in Angela's hotel, along with Adam Weiss, another Peace Corps volunteer, who had met me in Turpan. And then our time was up, and Weiss and I left the city in the desert, catching a train back to Chengdu.

THE TRAIN TO CHENGDU TOOK FIFTY HOURS and I had a bad feeling about it from the moment Weiss and I tried to buy tickets. They wouldn't sell us sleeper berths at the Hami station, and all they said was that we could try to upgrade our hard seat tickets once we boarded.

School was about to start, and the train was full of college students who were returning to Sichuan. There weren't any sleeping berths left, and there weren't any open spots in the hard seat cars. People were stuffed in the aisles, sitting on their luggage, leaning against each other. The walkways between cars were packed with passengers squatting on the floor. People sat in the sinks. It was the most crowded train I had ever seen in China.

Fifty hours is a long time to ride on a train without seats. For the first night Weiss and I did the best we could in the aisle, sitting on our bags, but it was impossible to sleep and always there were people coming through and bumping us. The worker in charge of our car was annoyed by the crowd, and out of spite she mopped the entire carriage three times during the first evening. In order for her to do this, all of us had to stand up and hold our luggage over our heads while she pushed at our feet with the dirty mop. She mopped at eight o'clock, ten o'clock, and midnight. Everybody grumbled but nobody resisted; in China you tolerated the bad behavior of the people who were employed to serve you, the same way you tolerated bullies and all other hassles of that sort. Or you tried to leave, which is what Weiss and I finally did, scouting out a different car where the worker seemed more reasonable. It was an improvement, but we were still standing in the aisle as the train plodded east through the desert.

It wasn't the sort of trip that inspires positive thoughts. Weiss and I discussed other Peace Corps volunteers in our group, and things they did that annoyed us, and we talked about the new volunteers who had recently arrived and how badly they would do this year. We complained about the various *waiguoren* we had seen over the course of the summer. We watched the other passengers in the car, criticizing their flaws. We discussed things we would do and eat whenever we returned to America. We reviewed the most offensive rap lyrics from the Notorious B.I.G.'s recent album, and we talked about what the Notorious B.I.G. would do on a train like this, and how his reaction would be distinct from that of Snoop Doggy Dogg. Neither of the rappers would like the train very much, we decided. At least ten times an hour I looked at my watch.

I rarely glanced out the windows, and I couldn't read. Sometimes I listened to my Walkman, but I hadn't brought enough tapes. Mostly I was too exhausted to speak Chinese, although in the afternoon I had a long conversation with a group of students who were on their way to Chengdu. But that was a very calculated effort; I figured that if they realized we were teachers they might share their seats, out of respect. Sure enough, after thirty minutes' conversation they kindly offered us a spot on the end of their bench. For the second night Weiss and I shared the seat in shifts, one standing while the other sat, but the seat wasn't comfortable and neither of us slept for more than ten minutes at a stretch.

Time crept, especially when I was standing, and to pass the evening I did something that I often did in China when things got rough. I remembered other places I had visited, thinking about what I had liked the most about them—a comfortable hotel, or a good restaurant, or the way a river wound through a green valley. I spent some time thinking about which part of the world was the perfect opposite of this particular Chinese train, and at last I decided that it was Switzerland. To distract myself I recalled some of the long hikes I had taken there, and in my mind I walked them over again. I remembered a certain stretch of the Swiss Valais where I had hiked up hard from the Val d'Anniviers, because night had been falling, and I remembered camping high above St. Luc. My clothes were damp with the effort of the climb, and I put the tent up quickly, because it was growing cold; and then I went to sleep.

The next morning I climbed the Bella Tola. It was early summer and the mountain was still snow-covered, and the ice was streaked red with Sahara sand that had been blown across the Mediterranean by the *föhn* winds. After the Bella Tola, I continued over the Meidpass into the Turtmanntal, which is the first German-speaking valley as you head east across the southern Valais. The Turtmanntal is a steep empty valley with a blue glacier trembling at its southern end, and I made camp in a meadow midway up the slope to the next pass. I arranged everything carefully, checking my tent and sleeping bag, and then I went to sleep. Always I went to sleep.

The train rocked east and south. By the last day it was as if something inside of me had snapped and I was too tired to do any more walks in my mind, not even short ones around my home in Missouri.

Passengers started getting off after we reached Sichuan, and for the last five hours Weiss and I had seats. But it was too late to do us much good and we stared ahead without speaking. We reached Chengdu in early evening, and I realized that I had just spent two days of my life standing on a train. My summer vacation was over. During the rest of my time in the Peace Corps, I never rode another train.

神甫

THE PRIEST

IN THE OLD SECTION of Fuling City is a Catholic church, and in the courtyard of the church is a propaganda sign, which consists of four lines of four characters each:

Love the Country, Love the Religion
Respect God, Love the People
Throw Your Body into the Four Modernizations
Serve the Masses

The Four Modernizations are Industry, Agriculture, Defense, and Science; and it is difficult to see their connection to Fuling's Catholic church, which was constructed by French missionaries in 1861, and whose Masses are served by Father Li Hairou, who at eighty-three years of age is more than four times as old as the Four Modernizations.

Father Li stands well under five feet tall. Usually he wears a soft black beret atop his white-haired head. He has a long, proud nose—an Italian nose for a Chinese Roman Catholic priest. His eyes are black, and sometimes they flicker and flash and show emotion when his voice, which is low and raspy, does not. Visitors occasionally remark on his brilliant white teeth, and Father Li responds by saying that they are a species of Modernization that cost him two hundred yuan and two months of eating nothing but rice gruel. He smiles easily. He walks with a dragon-headed cane. His kidneys often hurt, as does his knee, and when these problems flare up he says the Mass in Latin, because it is quicker that way. If the pain is serious he does not say the Mass at all, but that rarely happens. He is strong, although he moves slowly, and there is a pronounced dignity in his carriage. Most elderly people in China have this dignity, because they live in a culture where age commands unquestioned respect; and many of them, like Father Li, have an extra sense of pride that comes from not only the years but the bitter way so many of them passed. Those bitter years are what lie behind the flash in his eyes.

For more than half a century, Father Li has been a priest in Fuling. Anywhere in the world that is a long time to be a priest. In Fuling, fifty years of priesthood is an eternity.

LI HAIROU'S GREAT-GRANDFATHER was converted to Catholicism by French missionaries in the early 1800s. The Li family lived in Dazu, not far from Chongqing, and Li Hairou was the second son of a shopkeeper. At eleven he was sent to a French-run parochial school in Chongqing, and then in Chengdu he studied to be a priest. He learned French and Latin, and, like the other young seminary students, he dreamed of studying in Rome. Others were sent to Italy, but Li Hairou stayed, becoming a priest in 1944, at the age of twenty-nine. Three years later, he was sent to Fuling—remote, undeveloped, a distant backwater of a poor province. Perhaps in another age it would have been a quiet post. But the midcentury was a time when nothing in China was quiet, when the War of Resistance Against the Japanese was followed by the Civil War and Communist Liberation, and these were struggles that touched almost everybody in the Chongqing region. Li Hairou's older brother died during the wars, and his younger brother, having found himself on the wrong side of Liberation, fled to Singapore, where he married and became a teacher. But Father Li stayed in Fuling, serving the three thousand parishioners, working with the two French priests who lived in the area, waiting for the ripples of revolution to make their way down the Yangtze Valley. And then the French were gone, and the ripples came to shore, and Father Li had to wait no more.

"In the 1950s," he says, "first there was trouble because Catholicism was considered Foreign Teaching. Later, during the Great Cultural Revolution, there was more trouble because they were Destroying Superstition—but that was later. At first they were trying to stop Foreign Teaching, and so after Liberation I was sent out to the countryside. That was in 1953. I was sent to the north of Fuling, about seventy miles away. The conditions were terrible. Often there wasn't enough to eat, and many people in China starved. That was the time of the *dagongfan*—the communal meal. They had one pot, and one person would put in some radishes, another person put in some rice, another person put in some other vegetables. But there wasn't enough for everybody to eat. It was the same with the Great Leap Forward—that was a huge mistake. Those were both Chairman Mao's ideas. He didn't understand economics the way Deng Xiaoping did. What Chairman Mao liked was revolution; he liked struggle. People became poorer, and the poorer you were, the more you were controlled."

Father Li is sitting in his office, a small dark room next to the church. As in so many Chinese sitting rooms, the decorations are a mystery of quirkiness: an empty aquarium, a plastic Donald Duck, a small statue of Mary, a slightly smaller figure of Santa Claus, a talking digital clock that announces the hour in Mandarin. But by far the strangest decoration, hanging on the wall across from Father Li, is a large photograph of Mao Zedong and Deng Xiaoping.

The black-and-white picture features the two men smiling over cups of tea. The chairs of both men are reclined, and the scene would not be out of place in a Sichuan teahouse. But the photograph is from near the end of Mao's life, when Deng Xiaoping had already suffered more than his share of troubles from the old man's policies, and undoubtedly there were emotions in this meeting that the camera missed. And there are certainly feelings in Father Li's heart that are not reflected in the simple and careful way that he speaks about the past. But there is a spark in his eyes as he glances up at the photograph, and then he shakes his head and continues his story.

"In the countryside I didn't have my vestments. I didn't have a Bible. I had nothing—all I had was a rosary, so I said the rosary three times a day. I returned to Fuling in 1955, but I didn't come back to the church, because it was closed down. I couldn't be a priest anymore, so I was sent down to work on the docks. My job was cleaning—mopping, sweeping, cleaning the docks. I made twenty-four yuan a month. It wasn't enough, you know.

"Often I said Mass for myself. We weren't allowed to have a church, but I could say Mass alone. But once the Great Cultural Revolution started, I couldn't even do that. The Red Guards turned the church into a sock factory, and they always watched me. I wasn't in jail, but I was constantly guarded, and the Red Guards made me do many things. Often I wore the High Hat while they criticized me, and they'd force me to kneel down and bow like this"—he dips his white head and gives a short laugh, the way he often chuckles when he remembers the Cultural Revolution. "They'd march me through the streets with a sign that said: 'Down with Imperialism's Faithful Running Dogs!' I'd wear the sign like this, in front and in back, with big characters on it."

He traces the ten characters on the surface of the low table in front of him, stroke by stroke, dipping a finger into his tea. This is a common Chinese habit when speaking with foreigners—because many characters have the same sound, a conversation will sometimes pause as the speaker writes a word in order to clarify the meaning for the *waiguoren* listener. They write them in the air, on the palm of their hand, in tea water on a table; and to watch a Chinese person do this is to realize how unique the written language is, and how its words are truly shapes—not just sounds, or collections of letters, but tangible things that are handled and touched. And in this case the words are so tangible that they were once worn in public. But Father Li says nothing more about that; he merely traces his ten characters on the table, and the hot water steams and evaporates, and the words disappear.

"For three years it was particularly bad," he says. "Especially for three months. During those three months, I had four Red Guards watching me all day, and five times each day they took me out on the street for demonstrations."

His visitor asks what year that was, and Father Li pauses, muttering softly as he stares into space. But the date will not come to him, and at last he shakes his head. "I can't remember for certain," he says. "But that was the worst time. During the struggle sessions, the Red Guards used to throw things at me—fruit, or other hard things. All of them were students—they were children. They thought it was fun."

He is not smiling now. Something in his eyes has hardened, and he points up at the picture of Mao. "It was his idea," Father Li says. "His mistake. When Deng Xiaoping came to power it was different, but during the Great Cultural Revolution it was terrible. I was never injured very badly—that wasn't the problem. The problem was that I didn't get much to eat. Every day they gave me only two bowls of rice gruel. Many priests in China died during that time. Most of them died because they got sick; we didn't have enough to eat, and all day long we couldn't rest. In Chongqing there were many who died."

Again he pauses to count, but this time the number comes to mind easily. He is thinking of old friends, men he studied with, prayed with, and suffered with, and because of that his memory is clear. But still there is a long pause before he responds. Perhaps in his mind he sees their faces, the way they died and the way he nearly died. His eyes are distant as he remembers, and then he speaks again.

"Six," he says. "In Chongqing there were six priests who died."

BUT FATHER LI is not a bitter man, which is probably why he has lived so long. He does not complain about today's Communist Party, and he seems sincere when he says that its policies are fine; indeed, things are infinitely better than they once were. The church is in reasonably good repair, and it is granted tax-free status by the government, which also provides Father Li with a living stipend of two hundred yuan a month. The priest is allowed to say Mass again, and his parishioners can attend without harassment. Weekday services are in Latin while Sunday Mass is in the dialect.

On the average Sunday there are about fifty worshipers, mostly women, all elderly. Rarely is there anybody under forty years of age. There are no weddings or baptisms in the church—only funerals.

There are, of course, plenty of rules. Missionary work is illegal in China, and official connections to Rome are not allowed—a point of contention that, having strained relations between China and the Vatican for five centuries, is unlikely to be resolved easily.

"We can recognize the Pope personally," explains Father Li. "In our minds, in our faith, we can recognize him. If we didn't recognize him, how could you call us Catholic? Every day we pray to him. But there's no economic *guanxi* with Rome—they don't give us money. And also there's no political connection with them, and the Pope can't come to China. He would like to come but he can't, because right now he recognizes Taiwan. If he recognized China instead, then he could come. But even now there are priests in China who have visited Rome to see him. This year the Pope went to Cuba, and it had been many years since he had last been there. That visit went very well, too. So maybe in the future he'll also make it to China."

These are distant issues, and Father Li seems far more concerned about the problems he faces here in Fuling. He worries about his aging parishioners, and he worries about the serious shortage of clergy in Sichuan, which has but seventy priests for 120 churches. He also worries about money, because his parishioners are too poor to give much support, and foreign assistance has diminished since his younger brother died in Singapore five years ago.

But he doesn't worry too much, because such concerns seem minor compared to everything that he has seen in the past. He has seen the War of Resistance Against the Japanese, the Civil War, and Liberation. He has seen, personally, the campaign against Foreign Teaching and the campaign to Destroy Superstition. He has seen the old French-built church turned into a sock factory. He has seen ugly words draped over his shoulders. He has seen the church reopen back in 1981, and on the first Sunday he saw fewer than twenty nervous people come to Mass. Now the Fuling area has more than a thousand Catholics, even if rarely there are more than fifty at a given service, and for an old priest like Father Li there is a great deal of satisfaction in seeing that much. Others weren't so fortunate.

But still it seems strange that in his office he can look up and see the photograph of Mao Zedong, who made a three-decade hole in Father Li's life as a priest. It is not uncommon for Sichuanese victims of the Cultural Revolution to have a poster of Deng Xiaoping on their walls, because he suffered as they did, but very few of them display pictures of Mao. Perhaps for Father Li there is a political reason—maybe he does it to appease cadres, the way somebody is appeased by the Four Modernizations sign in the courtyard. In China, many officials see religion as subversive, particularly the Catholic Church, and perhaps the photograph is intended to put their minds at rest.

Father Li often looks at the picture. While talking about the trials of the past, he glances at it repeatedly, and every time there is the sudden flash in his eyes, as if something about the photograph holds his memories together. At the end of his story, he looks at it once more. Again he points a steady finger at Mao.

"All of that was his idea," he says. He pauses, still staring at the picture, whose smiling figures give no sense of what "all of that" entails: the broken church, the cruel and violent children with their red armbands, the lost years and the lost friends. Then the priest says, simply, "Because of that, we don't respect him."

CHAPTER EIGHT

Chinese Life

ON SUNDAY MORNINGS in Fuling I went to eight-o'clock Mass. I had gone to Mass alone during the spring of my first year, but now in the fall I went with Noreen Finnegan, who was one of the new Peace Corps volunteers sent to Fuling. There were two of them—Noreen and Sunni Fass. It felt strange to have suddenly doubled the population of *waiguoren,* and neither Adam nor I knew exactly what to think about the change. We were comfortable with our routines of the first year, and our relationship had always been easy—we were very close, but at the same time we had always been able to spend time apart. There were sections of the city and the college that each of us had carved out for himself, and we didn't interfere with each other's routines.

In a small place like Fuling it doesn't take long to feel possessive about the city. Neither Adam nor I had ever seen another *waiguoren* there, apart from friends who had come to visit us, and our contact with the Peace Corps was minimal. Two administrators had made visits during our first month of service, but after that we were left alone. Fuling was far from the Peace Corps headquarters in Chengdu, and none of the administrators liked taking the Yangtze boats, which were slow and dangerous. Back in the spring, two of the Fuling boats had collided near Chongqing in a particularly bad accident, killing more than a dozen people, and several times on the river I saw abandoned boats that were in various stages of sinking. I was always careful to pass these stories along to the Peace Corps, so they'd be less inclined to visit. It was simplest if we were left alone, and for the most part we were.

But now there were four of us, and for a while I worried about the change. In the end, though, it didn't have much of an effect. Life was slightly different in the college, but the city was big enough to swallow four *waiguoren* without any trouble. And for the first semester Noreen and Sunni were very similar to Adam and me at the beginning; they were shell-shocked by the pressures of downtown Fuling, and neither of them spent much time away from campus.

Noreen's parents had immigrated to New York City from Ireland, which was one reason she went to Mass on Sundays. When she first mentioned that her father had been an Irish potato farmer, Mr. Wang, who was the *waiban* representative, became very excited. "So your father was a peasant!" he said.

Noreen didn't know what to think about that. "Well," she said, "he was a farmer in Ireland."

"But you said he was poor, right?"

"Well, yes."

"So he was a peasant!"

"Uhm, I guess."

"My parents were also peasants! Most of your students in this college are peasants!"

Noreen knew little about class background in China, and she asked me how one should react when people said your father was a peasant. But in Chinese there isn't really a word for farmer—people who worked the land are *nongmin,* literally "agricultural people," and in English it is usually translated as "peasant." In some ways this is an inaccurate translation, calling to mind feudal Europe, but also a term like "farmer" fails to convey the negative connotations that are associated with working the land in China. Roughly 75 percent of the population is involved in agriculture, and the divide between these people and the urban Chinese is one of the most striking gaps in the country. City dwellers in a place like Fuling can recognize a peasant at a single glance, and often they are victims of prejudice and condescension. Even the world for soil—*tu*—can be applied to people as a derogatory adjective, meaning unrefined and uncouth.

But so many of our students were from rural families that these prejudices weren't strong on campus. In a class of forty-five there were usually fewer than ten who had grown up in any sort of small city, and these cities tended to be even more remote than Fuling. Very few of the students had much money, which meant that it was rare to see either the snobbishness of privilege or the sensitivity of coming from a lower-class background. When I asked my students what their parents did for a living, almost always they responded, in English, "My mother and father are peasants."

At the beginning these responses embarrassed me, because the students used this feudal word in such a matter-of-fact way. Once I asked a freshman about his family, and he said, "My father is a peasant, and my mother is a sweeper."

"I'm sorry, I didn't understand. What does your mother do?"

"She is a sweeper."

"A sweeper?"

"Yes. She sweeps the streets."

He said it without any self-consciousness, the same way that all of them described their backgrounds. I told Noreen that she should be proud to be the daughter of an Irish peasant—of all the Fuling *waiguoren,* she had the most revolutionary class origins.

Noreen and I went to church on Sundays, which was one of my favorite routines in Fuling, because I liked watching the priest and the old women who went there every week. They were survivors—there was a quiet strength to the congregation, and they had none of the well-dressed smugness of American churchgoers. All of them had paid for their faith, in ways that money could not measure, and Father Li had paid the most of all.

Watching the priest also made me remember my mother's father, who had been a Benedictine monk. He had grown up in Arkansas, where his parish sometimes awarded promising students with scholarships to Italy, and in 1929 my grandfather was sent to San Anselmo Abbey in Rome. He was eighteen years old, and his plan was to become a priest and perhaps a missionary.

I had read his diary from those years and it was full of homesickness, but it was also full of the beauty and wonder of Rome, the stunning churches and the history that caught the young man's eyes everywhere he turned in the city. He was in the middle of that history, too;

often his diary mentioned nationalistic rallies in the streets, and a few times he caught sight of Mussolini at parades.

In the spring of 1931, a group of priests returned to the abbey from Catholic University in Beijing. On March 1 of 1931, my grandfather's diary reads, in neat black script:

> A bunch of us Americans visit Fr. Sylvester Healy in his room this morning, and have a long talk about China in general and the Catholic University of Peking in particular. Fr. Healy made his Solemn Profession this morning in the College Church. He seems very optimistic about the future of the Catholic University and to have given himself wholeheartedly to the work.

After that day, the diary changes. There is less of Rome and more of China; the fascination grows quickly, until "China" is capitalized and underlined, a sacred word:

> March, 18, 1931: Fr. Francis Clougherty, Chancellor of the Catholic University of Peking, arrives here to-day on his way back to China. A big strapping Irishman.

> March 22, 1931: Fr. Clougherty holds an informal "at home" this morning and about 15 of us troop up to his room. Of course there are smokes and a general spirit of congeniality. Fr. Clougherty is very interesting to listen to. According to him the University is now on a perfectly solid foundation and he has received promises to come out to China from a considerable [number] of very capable teachers, both Benedictine and otherwise.

> March 23, 1931: All small talk among Americans is about China now.

> March 25, 1931: Talk to Raph and Donald about China upon my return. Fr. Clougherty had a big day to-day but comes down to Donald's room and gives Donald, Hugh, Edward and me an inspiring talk. We are so wrought up that when Clougherty leaves at 12 o'clock Donald, H., and I stay up and talk it over till almost 3 A.M. I believe that this is the turning point in my life and I am going to sign up for China. God be with us!

March 26, 1931: CHINA! Get up rather late this morning after last night. Spend most of the morning in Donald's room discussing China. Fr. Clougherty comes down and brings pictures of the statues about which he spoke last night. It seems there will be quite a little colony of Americans emigrating from San Anselmo, Rome, to Catholic University, Peking. *Deo Volente,* I am one of them.

March 27, 1931: Everything is China at present. I breathe, eat and sleep China and I think that is about the case with all of our "China group."

As my grandfather came closer to taking his vows of priesthood, his superior informed him that he would be sent back to Arkansas. My grandfather responded with a long letter explaining that deep in his soul he had a call from God to serve in China. But his superior countered by saying that sometimes this is how God works—occasionally He gives a young man a false call, simply to test his loyalty to his earthly superior, and sometimes you feel truly that you are meant to go to China when in fact you are intended to go to Arkansas.

And so passed the turning point of my grandfather's life. He did not want to be a priest in Arkansas, and the Benedictines did not want him to be a priest in China; and thus he left the order and returned to America. He sold insurance. He married. He had children, grandchildren. He retired, played golf, traveled. On Sundays he always went to Mass. He never did go to China. He didn't talk much about his time as a monk, and I never knew about his interest in China until I came across his diaries as a graduate student. But by then it had been seven years since he had died in 1987, when I was seventeen years old—nearly the same age as the young monk in Rome and, like him, too young to have any sense of time, of what the future might hold and how the past might reappear.

I CONTINUED WITH MY CHINESE TUTORIALS in Fuling, alternating between Teacher Kong and Teacher Liao. We always started classes with small talk, and often Teacher Liao told me about what she had watched on television the night before. Like most of my friends in

Fuling, she watched an enormous amount of television, and one day she came to class particularly interested in what she had seen.

"Last night there was a *waiguoren* on television," she said, "He was speaking Chinese."

"Was it Da Shan?"

"No, it wasn't Da Shan; his Chinese wasn't nearly as good as Da Shan's. His Chinese wasn't as good as *yours.*"

"That can't be true."

"Actually, his grammar was better than yours, but his pronunciation was worse. His tones were bad."

"I don't believe it."

"I'm not kidding," she said. "I think your Chinese is better than that of the *waiguoren* who was on television. And if you improved your grammar, it would be much better."

"Where was he from?"

"Australia. He was very ugly—he had bad skin and very long hair. He was extremely hard to look at."

For a moment we sat there, silent in our shared distaste for the long-haired *waiguoren* with bad tones on television. Then we started class, and Teacher Liao paid particularly close attention to my grammar.

After that she kept me updated on the *waiguoren* who appeared on television. For the most part it was a small and select group, with Da Shan as the mainstay, and all of the regulars were very good at Chinese—it was clear that I still had years to go before I could enter that league. But Teacher Liao apparently felt that there was hope, and occasionally a *waiguoren* with tone problems would appear and she would criticize him mercilessly. Always she was careful to point out any physical defects or shortcomings, especially if the *waiguoren* was fat. Teacher Liao was an extremely slender woman and she did not like fat *waiguoren.*

There was still a certain formality to our relationship, but it had become a comfortable formality—the Chinese relationship between a teacher and a student. She took pride in my progress, and now that I was starting to read newspapers she carefully reviewed the *Chongqing Evening Times* and clipped articles that we could use in class. She liked clipping stories about the Japanese atrocities of World War II, and she also liked stories about Hong Kong's improvements since its return to the Motherland (great things had happened in those three months). Occasionally she could not help but select articles that criticized America's imperialist tendencies. In late September, when France complained about American sanctions of Iran, our tutorials consisted of a slew of stories condemning America's role as "the policeman of the world." But even in those classes there was no tension; our Opium Wars were long finished, and we had learned how to deal with each other. Both of us had changed, but probably I had changed the most: I was no longer strictly a *waiguoren,* neither in her eyes nor in my own.

I liked Teacher Liao because now I could see that she was a very traditional Chinese woman—in my mind, she was the most Chinese person I ever came to know in Fuling. She refused to allow a *waiguoren* to condescend to her, because she was a fiercely proud woman, but at the same time she was capable of extending this pride to me after months of work. Along with her pride, she had a strong sense of propriety and tradition. She didn't dress in revealing clothes like many other young women did, and she didn't Westernize her hair by dyeing. Unlike Teacher Kong, she refused to have our classes in my apartment. Teacher Liao was a married woman and I was a single man, and people might talk if she spent six hours a week in my home. We always met in my office.

I also liked studying with Teacher Liao because I could get some sense of the prevailing Chinese attitude to nearly any issue by simply asking her, because she was so Chinese, and often I used our classes to untangle things that I had seen or heard in my encounters with other people. For a while I was intrigued by the Chinese fascination with Hitler—if you ever talked with Old Hundred Names about the Führer, they generally gave good reviews. The summer before in Xi'an, I had known a German student who was disturbed by the way many Chinese became excited when they discovered her nationality.

"Oh, you're from Germany!" they would say. "*Xitele*—Hitler! Very good!"

Out of curiosity I often asked the Chinese about him, and many people said the same thing—that he had made some mistakes, but he had been a great leader who did some fine things for his country. It seemed natural enough that Chairman Mao had left the Chinese with a certain appetite for dictators, but I was still curious, and I asked

Teacher Liao why the Chinese were so positive about Hitler. As usual, she was extremely helpful. She said that for years Charlie Chaplin's *The Great Dictator* had been seen in theaters and on television; everybody in China had watched it.

"Have you seen it?" I asked.

"Certainly!"

"How many times?"

She paused and counted in her head. "Four, I think," she said. "Maybe more."

"What's it like?"

"It's very wonderful! I always liked the way Hitler talks in the movie, like a crazy man. He's like this"— and she imitated Charlie Chaplin imitating Hitler; she raised her shoulders and shook her fist, chin in the air.

"Wah wah wah wah wah!" she shouted, as if giving a speech in a foreign language, and then she collapsed into giggles.

"But doesn't that movie make fun of Hitler?" I asked.

"Of course!"

"So why is it that so many Chinese people tell me that there are some good things about him?"

"Most of us have two contrary ideas—that Hitler was a great leader, and that he was a crazy man who did terrible things. We have both of these ideas at once, you see. And I think people believe that he is an interesting character, and that also makes them like him. He's very interesting to watch."

Perhaps the strangest part of the Chinese fascination with Hitler was that simultaneously they had a deep respect for the Jewish people. Jews were the next best thing to the Chinese—they were an extremely intelligent race, as one could tell from the examples of Einstein and Marx. In Xi'an, I had studied with an Israeli student, and the teachers and workers had made an enormous fuss over him. Everybody was very impressed by his intelligence, despite the fact that he was not particularly bright and a horrible student of Chinese. But he was Jewish, and all Jews were intelligent; everybody knew that and so they overlooked the reality of his particular case. It was the same as my blue eyes.

Ideas of this sort were standard and completely predictable, and the longer I lived in China the more I realized that in this sense the country wasn't as complicated as outsiders often said. Foreigners always talked about how difficult it was to understand China, and often this was true, but there were also many ways in which the people's ideas were remarkably uniform and predictable. There were buttons that you could push—Hitler, Jews, the Japanese, the Opium Wars, Tibetans, Taiwan—and 90 percent of the time you could predict the precise reaction, including specific phrases that people would use. It was natural enough, given China's conditions: virtually everybody was the same race, the country had been isolated for centuries, and the current education system was strictly standardized and politically controlled.

And it was also natural that these conditions resulted in some particularly bizarre notions, like the admiration of Hitler or the fascination with Thai transvestites. This was something else I had realized over the summer: if you asked random Chinese people about Thailand, virtually all of them would say the exact same thing, that the Thais are famous for their *renyao,* or transvestites.

It was interesting to figure out these common beliefs, and occasionally you could work them to your advantage. During the summer, my sister Angela and Todd, her Stanford colleague, had been bored by eating meals with their Chinese interpreter, so I gave them a list of subjects that would surely make things more entertaining. Todd was Jewish, and I told him that this was a trump card that should not be wasted. After I left, he broke the monotony of a meal by announcing his ethnic background.

"You are Jewish?" the interpreter said, eyes wide.

"Yes."

"You must be very clever!"

After that, he treated Todd with new respect. It had been the same way with a teacher in the second Peace Corps group; everything changed once the people discovered that she was Jewish. One of her Chinese friends apologized to her, because before the revelation the friend had not treated her with the appropriate respect that should be accorded a Jew.

Once during the summer I had studied my Chinese textbook while riding a train, which impressed the other passengers. As a *waiguoren* it was never hard to impress—even the most pathetic command of the

Chinese language made the people respect you. But on that train there was one woman who studied me with particular interest.

"You are a *Zhongguotong*," she said. "A China hand. I can see that you study very diligently."

"That's not true," I said. "If I studied diligently my Chinese would be better."

She peered at me, and it was clear that she was thinking hard about something. "Are you Jewish?" she finally asked.

"No," I said, and something in her expression made me want to apologize. But I suppressed the urge, and we talked for a while longer. I sensed her disappointment as she returned to her berth, but there was nothing to do about that: I was just another *waiguoren,* and not a Jew at all.

EVERYTHING IN FULING was new that second year. I had new students—all of last year's seniors had graduated, and most of them were teaching in the countryside. My own Chinese tutors were as good as new; they were real people now, and we could talk comfortably about anything. The city didn't seem as dirty and loud as last year, and the people were friendlier. When they spoke, it made sense. The only thing that hadn't changed was my job; I still taught literature, but now it was easier because I had last year's notes. I spent most of my spare time in the city, wandering around and talking to people.

I had city routines for every day of the week, every time of the day. Sometimes in the mornings I went down to South Mountain Gate and sat in the park, watching the city come to life. Tuesday afternoons I talked to the photographer and went to Wangzhou Park. Monday evenings I walked along the busy streets of Mid-Mountain Road. On Sundays, I went to church, and afterward I sat and talked with Father Li, who served me bad coffee. I did not like good coffee but I drank the priest's coffee out of respect, just as he served it to me out of respect for the *waiguoren* tendency to prefer coffee to tea.

After talking with Father Li, I would wander through the old city and watch the blacksmiths at work near the river. Then I would walk up to the teahouse in the middle of town, because on Sundays a group of middle-aged and older men brought their pet birds there, hanging the cages from the rafters. They were always happy to see me, especially Zhang Xiaolong, who was the Luckiest Man in All of Fuling. Ten years ago he had been injured in a motorcycle accident, shortening one leg, and now he walked with a limp. It was a wonderful injury because it meant that he was officially classified as disabled, and thus he could never be fired from his job at the Hailing factory. It was a state-owned enterprise, and reforms were leading to layoffs, but none of this concerned Zhang Xiaolong, whose job was completely secure. It was more luck than one could expect from a motorcycle accident, but Zhang Xiaolong had beaten the odds again when his wife became pregnant and gave birth—not to a daughter, or to a son, but to *twin* sons. To be slightly but certifiably disabled, and to have twin sons—that was fantasy; it didn't happen in real life; people wrote books about good fortune of that sort.

Every Sunday, Zhang Xiaolong limped proudly to the teahouse, carrying his birdcage, and he sat beaming in the sunshine as he drank his tea. He was the Happiest Man in All of Fuling, as well as the Luckiest, and I liked talking with him—not because he was particularly interesting, but simply because he was always pleasant. And he reminded me that my own life in Fuling was also charmed. Almost everywhere I went, people knew who I was, and I could follow my routines and be assured that the regulars would be happy to see me. There were still plenty of young men who shouted a mocking "Hah-loooo!" when I walked down the street, but it was less of a problem than last year, and in any case the harassment was drowned out by the kindness of most people. It was the same paradox that I had realized during the summer—the Chinese could be hard on foreigners, but at the same time they could be incredibly patient, generous, and curious about where you had come from. I felt I had spent my first year coping with the hard part of being a *waiguoren,* and now I enjoyed all the benefits.

In many ways the city had turned full circle for me, but of course I was the one who had really changed. I was a new person, He Wei, or, as the Sichuanese pronounced it, Ho Wei. That was the name I had been given during Peace Corps training, and it was common in China: the given name, Wei, meant "great" and was as run-of-the-mill as John in America. The family name was also prevalent; there were plenty of Hos wherever I went in Sichuan, and when I introduced myself they always said that we were *jiamenr*, family. There was even another Ho Wei at the college, who taught in the physical education department.

It was different from living in most countries, where you could use your real name or something similar to it, which was a clear link to who you had originally been. My Chinese name had no connection to my American name, and the person who became Ho Wei had no real connection to my American self. There was an enormous freedom in that—at the age of twenty-eight, I suddenly had a completely new identity.

And you could tinker with that identity, starting with changing your name itself. Adam had done this at the end of our first year, because his original name, Mei Erkang, sounded too much like a foreigner's name (it also sounded a lot like a popular Sichuanese brand of pig feed). Looking for something that was more authentically Chinese and less agricultural, Adam asked his students to propose new names, complete with explanations, and after several rounds they came up with Mei Zhiyuan. The given name, Zhiyuan, meant "Motivated by Lofty Goals," and it was shared by Ma Zhiyuan, a Yuan Dynasty poet who seven centuries ago had written a famous verse on homesickness. Virtually all educated Chinese recognized the allusion, and there were subsequent writers who had used the two characters in other poems. Suddenly, Adam went from pig feed to a noble-sounding classical allusion—that was how easily a *waiguoren* could redefine himself in China.

I never changed my Chinese name, but I sensed the ease with which my Chinese identity became distinct from my American self. Eventually, I came to think of myself as two people, Ho Wei and Peter Hessler. Ho Wei wasn't really a person until my second year in Fuling, but as time passed I realized that he was becoming most of my identity: apart from my students, colleagues, and the other foreigners, everybody knew me strictly as Ho Wei, and they knew me strictly in Chinese. Ho Wei was completely different from my American self: he was friendlier, he was eager to talk with anybody, and he took great pleasure in even the most inane conversations. In a simple way he was funny; by saying a few words in the local dialect he could be endlessly entertaining to the people in Fuling. Also Ho Wei was stupid, which was what I liked the most about him. He spoke with an accent; he had lousy grammar; and he laughed at the simple mistakes that he made. People were comfortable with somebody that stupid, and they found it easy to talk with Ho Wei, even though they often had to say things twice or write new words in his notebook. Ho Wei always carried his notebook in his pocket, using it to study the new words, as well as to jot down notes from conversations. And when Ho Wei returned home he left the notebook on the desk of Peter Hessler, who typed everything into his computer.

I had two desks in my apartment. One was for studying Chinese, and the other was for writing; one desk was Ho Wei's and the other belonged to Peter Hessler. Sometimes this relationship unnerved me—it seemed wrong that behind Ho Wei's stupidity there was another person watching everything intently and taking notes. But I could think of no easy resolution to this divide; I had my Chinese life and my American life, and even if they occupied similar territory, they were completely different. My apartment was big and I kept the desks in separate rooms. Ho Wei and Peter Hessler never met each other. The notebook was the only thing they truly shared.

ONE SUNDAY there was a funeral at the church. Noreen was sick that day and I sat alone, trying to follow the service in my missal. I always liked doing that, because it was good Chinese practice and it reminded me of boyhood, when some of my earliest reading had been done during Mass.

People milled around the courtyard after the service and I could see that it was a special event. Father Li and I sat in the rectory, where he called for coffee and cookies, and one of the old women who lived there brought them on a tray. The coffee was even worse than usual. I thanked the woman and drank as much as I could bear, eating cookies to dull the taste. Father Li and I asked about each other's health, and then he mentioned that today's service had been a funeral.

"Oh, I'm very sorry," I said. "Who was it for?"

He said a woman's name that I didn't recognize. "How old was she?" I asked.

"Eighty years old."

"She had a very long life."

"Yes," the priest said. "And she was very good for our church. She was here every Sunday."

"What was her job?"

"She was retired, of course. But before that she worked at the Hailing factory."

There was a small number of parishioners who went to Mass every week, and I asked some more questions to see if I could remember the woman. Father Li answered patiently, and then finally he pointed behind me and said, "She's right there."

I turned around and saw the woman laid out ten feet behind me, on a table at the back of the room. The place was dimly lit and I hadn't noticed her when we came in. A white sheet was pulled up to her chin. She was a small woman with gray hair and her mouth was pinched shut. I remembered seeing her in church. I was in the middle of eating a cookie and now I put it down on the tray.

"Oh," I said. "There she is."

"Yes," said Father Li. "That's her."

"Well," I said. "I think I'll go outside now."

It was sunny in the courtyard and the parishioners were writing memorials on long strips of white paper. A number of big funeral wreaths, made of white tissue and bamboo, were set against the wall of the church. In the sunshine I recovered quickly from the shock of seeing the body on the table, and I watched the people as they went about the business of mourning. All of the old ladies had been waiting patiently for me to finish my coffee, and now they entered the room to pay their respects to the body.

The woman's son was there, a man in his fifties, and he was thrilled that a *waiguoren* had come to his mother's funeral. I told him that his mother had always been very kind to me, which made him even happier. It was a tradition for the family to give small gifts at a funeral, and the son gave me some fruit and a box of Magnificent Sound cigarettes. I thanked him and accepted the cigarettes. It was hard to imagine a more appropriate funeral gift.

Later I went to the teahouse, where Zhang Xiaolong, the Luckiest Man in Fuling, grinned and waved. He was with some of the other old men and I took an empty table nearby. The waitress came over, smiling, and asked me what I wanted.

"The *yangguizi* wants a cup of tea," I said. Calling myself *yangguizi,* "foreign devil," was one of the easiest and most disarming jokes in Fuling.

I had started using that word to describe myself during the summer, and people often didn't know how to react; sometimes they were embarrassed and tried to persuade me to call myself something different. But I always responded by proudly saying something like "We foreign devils have a long history" or "We foreign devils have a great culture."

At the teahouse it was an old joke between me and the *xiaojie,* the young woman who worked there. She covered her mouth and laughed, and then she poured me a cup of tea. I had bought a newspaper on the street and now I read it while the tea cooled.

It was a typical day at the teahouse and a few people came up and talked with me. At the end of the morning, a young woman whom I had never met came and sat at my table. We talked for perhaps ten minutes. It was slightly unusual for a woman to approach me, but not so unusual that I thought anything of it. Her name was Li Jiali, and she asked for my phone number. This was also common—I always gave my number to people in Fuling. The only problem was that some of them had a tendency to call between the hours of five and seven o'clock in the morning, so I often took my phone off the hook when I was sleeping. I gave my number to Li Jiali and thought no more about it.

A week later I returned to the teahouse, and once again she sat at my table. She was dressed in a very short skirt and tights and she wore a great deal of makeup. She was not pretty, but she had successfully adopted a number of the habits that you saw in a certain type of *xiaojie,* who smiled too much and talked in a cutesy way, drawing out her words at the end of sentences. The woman who worked at the teahouse was not like this, and I saw her shaking her head as Li Jiali sat posing at my table. The old men were staring; even their birds seemed stunned into silence. I could see that something was happening that I didn't understand, and so I excused myself, paid for the tea, and left.

Li Jiali followed me out of the teahouse. "Where are you going?" she asked.

"I have to go now," I said. "I'm going to eat and then I'm going home."

We passed a noodle restaurant where I often ate. Suddenly I had a great fear of this woman following me home and being seen with me on campus. "I'm leaving now," I said. "I must eat at this restaurant. Goodbye."

"Oh, I'll eat with you," said Li Jiali.

The owner of the restaurant cleared a table and I found myself sitting there with the woman. That was how everything always went in Fuling—things happened to me. Usually I liked the passive unpredictability but today I was suspicious of her intentions, and yet I had no idea what to do. She sat there chattering about something and I asked her where she worked.

"That's not important," she said, and suddenly it became very important.

"Do you work here in Fuling?"

"It's not a good job," she said, shrugging. "But my uncle is getting me a better job in Chongqing. He owns a big restaurant—he's very rich! He's giving me a job there as a *xiaojie.* The *xiaojie* at my uncle's restaurant wear fine clothes—I'll have to wear a *qipao* like this"—she showed me how it would look: no shoulders, tight around the neck, slit high up her thigh.

"Oh," I said.

"But it's very expensive," she said. "I'll have to buy the *qipao* myself."

"That's too bad," I said.

"Do you like to sing karaoke?"

"No," I said. "I do not like to sing karaoke. Most Americans do not like to sing."

"We should go to a karaoke bar sometime. I'll teach you how to sing."

"Sorry, but I'm not interested in karaoke."

"That's okay," she said, smiling. "I'm very interested in your America."

"What about my America interests you?"

"Everything. I would like to go there."

I did not like the way this conversation was going. "It's very difficult to do that," I said.

"I would like to live in your America," she said. "People there have more money than here."

"There are many poor people in my America."

"Not as many as there are here in Fuling."

She had a point and I tried a different tack. I talked about how difficult visas were to obtain, and then our noodles arrived. I ate quickly and tried to think of what to do next.

"Ho Wei," she said. "You are very *ke'aide*"—adorable. She said it in the best *xiaojie* manner and I was certain that the others in the restaurant were listening now.

"Your eyes are very pretty," she said. "I think you *waiguoren* have prettier eyes than us Chinese."

"It's not true," I said dumbly. "Chinese are much prettier than *waiguoren. Waiguoren* are very hard to look at." She took this as a compliment, smiling and trying to blush. I thought: Ho Wei, you are a jackass.

"I like to hear you speak our Chinese language, Ho Wei," she said. "It sounds very funny!"

I remembered how guys in college used to hit on the local au pair girls from Sweden with their accents and cluelessness. It was not a pleasant comparison, and I tried not to think about it.

We were leaving the restaurant now and the owner grinned knowingly as I paid. On the street Li Jiali took my arm and I stood there in passive disbelief. A Fuling woman was touching me and we were right near the intersection of South Mountain Gate; everybody was honking at us, or so it seemed.

"I have to go now," I stammered. "You can't come with me. I am very busy today."

"Next week is my birthday," Li Jiali said.

"That's nice," I said.

"I'll see you next week," she said.

A cab swung by, horn blaring, and I smelled the hot breath of its exhaust. The sun was warm and now I was sweating. "Goodbye," I said, and at last she let me go.

TWO DAYS LATER, Li Jiali called and Ho Wei answered the phone. She asked if he would be at the teahouse on Sunday and he replied that he would. He was there every Sunday and there was no reason to lie about that.

After the phone call, I began to think once more about the possible complications of this particular aspect of my Chinese life, as well as the many ways in which Ho Wei was not capable of dealing with them. The simplest solution was to avoid going to the teahouse, but she knew I worked at the college and I did not want her to track me down there.

I knew that Li Jiali was trouble—she was far too forward for a Chinese woman, and either she wanted money or she was crazy. Adam and I had both had experiences with this in the first year. A freshman girl student had spent a couple of weeks lurking outside of Adam's apartment, and there was a middle-aged woman named Miss Ou who had pursued me more or less throughout my time in Fuling. Both of these women were clearly unbalanced, and undoubtedly they turned to us because we were outside the loop, just like them. That was at once the most interesting and most disturbing aspect of living in Fuling—as a *waiguoren* you tended to attract a certain fringe element. It was possible to have a Chinese life, but that didn't mean it was a normal Chinese life.

Last year those complications had at least been in English, which gave us a certain degree of control over the interactions. But now it was strictly in Chinese—I met the people on their terms. And I knew that Li Jiali's terms would be difficult to deal with; somehow I would have to convince her that she would not get whatever it was that she wanted. It was all Ho Wei's show and I didn't have much confidence in his ability to handle the problem.

The next Sunday, I delayed my trip to the teahouse as long as possible. I spent a long time chatting with Father Li, and then I wandered down to the blacksmith's shop and watched them make chisels. It was nearly noon by the time I made it to the teahouse.

The *xiaojie* brought me tea; I was too nervous to make any foreign-devil jokes. She smiled and said that Li Jiali had been looking for me. I asked her if she knew the woman.

"I know her, but she's not my friend."

"Where does she work?"

"She works across the street, at the *meifating.*" It meant "beauty parlor," but it also meant something else, and the *xiaojie,* like everybody in Fuling, spoke the word with distinct scorn. Most of the city's prostitutes worked in beauty parlors and now I knew for certain what Li Jiali did for a living.

I sat there and waited for her. One of the teahouse regulars came over and talked with me. Usually he was annoying, because he was a fanatical disciple of Falun Gong, which was a mixture of Buddhism, Taoism, and *qigong*-style deep-breathing exercises. At first I had been interested in hearing him talk about Falun Gong, simply because I had never heard of it and the local followers seemed to believe with religious intensity, which was a rare passion in Fuling. But soon the man came to see me as a potential convert, and he often telephoned and gave me long lectures on the benefits of Falun Gong. He especially liked to call at five o'clock in the morning, because it showed how little sleep he needed now that Falun Gong had entered his life.

It was another mess of Ho Wei's. I had no interest in any sort of *qigong*—I was a runner and I disliked the idea of an exercise regimen that involved moving as slowly as possible. Of course, I might have been more interested in talking with the man if I had known that in 1999 the Communist Party would ban Falun Gong as a cult, persecuting its followers. But in Fuling I had no idea that the practice would someday become such a political issue, and I never would have imagined that the government would consider it to be a threat. As far as I was concerned, the main problem with Falun Gong was that it woke me up at five o'clock in the morning.

But today I was happy for any distraction and I listened to the man's lecture. A major sticking point between us was alcohol—his personal interpretation of Falun Gong stressed no smoking or drinking, and in a moment of desperation I had latched onto this as a way of discouraging him, explaining that there was no way I could ever give up beer. Like so many of Ho Wei's solutions, this was a serious miscalculation. It resulted in the man's making a full-fledged assault on the dangers of alcohol, week after week, in mind-numbing detail. His lectures began with the way alcohol settles in your cells, whereas Falun Gong seeks to bring everything into balance at the cellular level. There was more to this explanation, but I always lost the thread and sat there nodding as if I understood.

Li Jiali arrived while the man was lecturing. She smiled and sat down at our table. I didn't acknowledge her, and the man continued lecturing about alcohol and Falun Gong. All of the old bird men were watching.

She was dressed brightly again and she put on her makeup at our table. She dabbed rouge onto her cheeks, looking into a tiny mirror, and then she put on eyeshadow. In Fuling, few women wore much makeup, and even fewer painted their faces in public, which was a sign of loose morals. There were many signs like that—the clearest was for a *xiaojie* to smoke a cigarette in public, because when a Fuling woman did that you could be almost certain that she was a prostitute. Li Jiali was not smoking but the show of painting her face was bad enough.

She tried several times to get my attention until at last I looked over.

"Ho Wei," she said, "your American name is Pete, isn't it?"

"Yes." She had asked me this the first time we met, and now I regretted telling her.

"Pete," she said. She pronounced it "Bee-do" and I didn't like hearing her say it; I saw no reason to bring that name into Ho Wei's mess. "Bee-do," she said again, "did you bring me a gift?"

"No."

"I told you it was my birthday!" Again this was the flirty *xiaojie* voice and I felt my anger rise.

"In America we don't have that tradition," I said.

"You don't give presents on birthdays?"

"We don't ask people to give us presents."

It was one of the sharpest things Ho Wei had ever said, but it didn't faze her. I could bring her a present next week, she said. She asked if I would take her to lunch today, and I decided that I had had enough.

"I already have a girlfriend," I lied. "At the college I have a *waiguoren* girlfriend—the tall one with red hair." I figured that Noreen was the best choice, because she was tall and her height sometimes intimidated the Chinese. The Falun Gong man was listening carefully now.

"That's okay," Li Jiali said. "It doesn't matter if you have a girlfriend."

"I have to go now," I said. "I don't want to eat lunch."

"I'll go with you," the man said.

We stood up and Li Jiali said something to him. They were talking quickly in the dialect, and I walked out of the teahouse. On the street they caught up with me. The Falun Gong man was on my left, and Li Jiali started tugging at my right arm. "Bee-do," she said, "where are you going?"

"Please leave me alone," I said.

I pulled away, slipping into the crowd, and the Falun Gong man whispered in my ear, "What's your *guanxi* with her?"

"There's no *guanxi.* I don't know who she is. She bothers me."

"You don't have any interest in her?"

"No, not at all."

Li Jiali had caught us again, and she came between me and the man. He said something to her and she responded sharply, and now he turned and faced her. He shouted at the woman and she shouted back, calling him a *gui'erzi,* a Sichuanese obscenity meaning "son of a turtle." All of the *xiaojie* cuteness was gone, and it was as if a mask had been stripped away; she spat at him and shouted obscenely like a whore. People stopped to watch. The man stood his ground, shouting back, and in a minute it was over. Li Jiali tossed her head and stormed down the street.

The crowd dispersed and I walked to the bus stop with the Falun Gong man. I looked back over my shoulder and I could feel my heart beating. For once I was glad that I had tolerated so many of the man's phone calls and lectures about alcohol. I promised myself that I would always be polite with him, and that at least once I would try his exercises.

"She was asking me to leave you alone with her," he said.

"Is she a prostitute?"

"Perhaps," he said, but it was the Chinese perhaps that meant: Certainly.

We came to the bus and I thanked him.

"You need to be more careful," he said. "Often people like that will want you for your money, or because you're a *waiguoren.* You shouldn't give your phone number to everybody. And remember that I don't want your money—I only want to teach you Falun Gong. I'm different from her."

I nodded and got on the bus. For the next three weeks I shifted my routines to avoid the teahouse. Li Jiali moved to Chongqing, and later that fall she sent me a series of love letters, which I ignored. I never saw her again. I never tried Falun Gong. In the early mornings I kept my phone off the hook. I realized that complications were an inevitable result of my Chinese life, but I also realized that even at his worst Ho Wei could find a way to bumble out of problems. I had allowed him this much freedom, and in the end it was like an adult watching a child grow up—there was only so much control that I could take over that part of my life, and its unpredictability, although risky, was much of its charm. All I could do was let Ho Wei go his own way and hope for the best.

老板

THE RESTAURANT OWNER

HUANG XIAOQIANG WANTS A VIDEODISC PLAYER. He wants a cellular phone. He wants a car so he can work as a cab driver. He wants to invest more money in the stock market, and he wants to increase his earnings so all of the people he lives with, his parents and wife and two-year-old son, can have a better apartment and more security. He wants all of these things, but all he has right now is a small noodle restaurant called the Students' Home, and so he does the best he can with that.

What the noodle restaurant has is good location. It is more or less at the center of the East River district, across the street from the college gate, where women sell fruit and snacks from makeshift stands. There are almost always students sitting at the restaurant's six tables, and things are especially busy on Sunday evenings, when the students finish their political meetings and head out for dinner. Above the Students' Home there is a karaoke bar of suspicious purpose, and in the evening the karaoke *xiaojies* come downstairs for meals. The *xiaojies* wear beepers and too much makeup, and they talk too loudly, eating noodles alongside the fresh-faced students who have just finished their discussions of Socialism with Chinese Characteristics.

Huang Xiaoqiang knows all of the locals—the bus drivers and the fruit vendors, the ceramics factory workers and the shop owners, the students and the karaoke *xiaojies*. He knows their routines, the bus schedules and the factory work shifts and the college political meetings, and his own routine is intertwined with the rest of the East River lives. The restaurant's schedule is simple: it opens at six o'clock in the morning and closes at eleven at night. *"Hen xinku,"* Huang often says. "Very difficult."

But he is only half in earnest, because he has so much help: his parents and his wife, a pretty twenty-five-year-old woman named Feng Xiaoqin. Often his older sister, who works down the street at the ceramics factory, stops by to help. And usually there are other workers, relatives and friends from the Huangs' home village of Baitao, south of Fuling. In fact, of all the workers Huang Xiaoqiang is probably the least diligent. His wife and mother are the backbone of the restaurant, because Huang spends much of his time smoking Magnificent Sound cigarettes and cultivating *guanxi* with the local men.

He is twenty-six years old, and five years ago he took the long train ride from Chengdu to the western desert province of Xinjiang in order to look for work. "Too cold," he says. "There were jobs, and the jobs were fine, but the weather was no good. Too cold in the winter, too hot in the summer." The following year he went south to Guangzhou, where the weather was better but the jobs not to his taste.

This is a common pattern for young people in Sichuan, which in the past was the most populous province in China, home to more than 120 million people. In March of 1997, the province was split in two, with Fuling and the other river towns falling under the jurisdiction of the newly created Chongqing Municipality. This change was made to improve administration of the overcrowded region, as well as help prepare for the Three Gorges Project, but the split is still too recent to have affected the common notion of what composes Sichuan. Fuling residents still refer to themselves as Sichuanese, and there is still no shortage of men and women from this part of the world. One of every fifty people on earth comes from Sichuan.

And often they go somewhere else. The region's mountains and river valleys have long been home to the sort of hardships that send young people away, and in every Chinese city it is possible to find Sichuanese migrants. They can be found with particular frequency working in restaurants, or laboring on construction sites, or staffing beauty parlors. The urban Chinese often do not like the Sichuanese migrants, describing them as hardworking but uncultured, clever but untrustworthy. Some people say the Sichuanese women are tramps; the men are *jiaohua,* sly. These are, of course, familiar stereotypes to anybody who is an industrious and determined migrant in any part of the world, and they deter the Sichuanese exactly as much as they deter others who have left difficult conditions—in short, not at all. This is something else that the Sichuanese are famous for, their ability to *chiku,* to eat bitter. They don't care what people think, and they don't care what work they find, as long as it is work. And in hordes they continue to leave the region.

But Huang Xiaoqiang came home. He married, bought his restaurant, settled into the routine. In the mornings, he and the other workers make *chaoshou,* the local version of wonton, and at midday they hustle to handle the lunch rush, and late at night, when the next day's rice noodles arrive, they tie the soft strands into five-ounce bundles so they will be ready for tomorrow. Day after day it is exactly the same.

RARELY DOES Huang Xiaoqiang talk about politics in the restaurant. One evening, when asked about the government, he shrugs his shoulders and says that with regard to China's policies he has no *guanxi.* "Jiang Zemin is very big," he says. "And I am very small."

He notices a picture of Mao Zedong on the cover of an English book, Edgar Snow's *Red Star over China,* and he studies the title. *"Kanbudong,"* he says, laughing. "I don't understand." But he comprehends the picture; he has a poster of Mao on the wall of his home. "Mao Zedong was our leader," he says. "During the Revolution, he was a great man, but afterward . . ." He shakes his head. And then comes one of those stories that are so common in China, the kind of story that makes the country seem hopelessly foreign to any outsider.

It's a short story, really. Huang's grandfather was a peasant landlord, and in 1958, during the struggle of Communist land reform, he was executed. Huang demonstrates how they shot him—in the back of the neck—and then he laughs. But it is the unsettling Chinese laugh that has nothing to do with humor. It simply takes the place of words that aren't there.

But in the mad rush that is recent Chinese history, 1958 was a very long time ago, which is another reason why such stories are so short. They are told and then they are gone.

"Today everything's better," Huang Xiaoqiang says quickly. "In the past you couldn't speak freely. Everything you said, you always had to worry about whether it was Capitalist or Counter-Revolutionary.

But it's not like that now. Since Deng Xiaoping was the leader, everything has been fine. The living standard is much higher and we can have private business. We're the same as landlords, really."

This causes a brief debate in the restaurant, where the customers begin arguing with Huang. The word "landlord" is still politically charged, and perhaps he used it too lightly. But the debate doesn't last long; the others realize that he is referring to opportunity rather than exploitation, and in any case none of them cares much for politics. Most, like Huang, are independent workers: bus drivers, vendors, shop owners. They don't belong to a *danwei,* which means that profits are defined solely by intelligence, effort, and luck.

The absence of a *danwei* also means that they enjoy significant freedom. Huang Xiaoqiang attends no political meetings. Nobody tells him how many hours to work or what to serve in his restaurant. The income tax he pays is minimal and actually has little *guanxi* to what he makes. A government official comes every year to estimate the monthly earnings of the restaurant, and Huang pays ten percent of that. Currently the estimate is one thousand yuan a month, and accordingly his monthly tax is one hundred. In fact, the restaurant generally clears between two and three thousand yuan each month, but regardless, the tax is the same. One of the Characteristics of Chinese Socialism is that small enterprises can engage in virtually unrestricted capitalism, which works to the advantage of the Huang family.

But another Characteristic is that the government provides no insurance to people without a *danwei,* and so the restaurant follows a long schedule of seventeen-hour days while Huang Xiaoqiang looks for new ways to make money. In the meantime, though, he is content to run his restaurant, and with regard to China's politics he has neither deep complaints nor broad vision. And his non-*danwei* customers are more or less the same. They just want to work and carve out a good living, and if, like him, they can work with their families, their happiness is doubled.

THE WORLD of the Students' Home is small. It doesn't extend much beyond the East River district, and it is centered on Huang's family. His two-year-old son, Huang Kai, took his first steps in the restaurant.

He read his first simple characters from the menu board, and his first favorite food was *chaoshou.* During lulls in the day, the boy sits on his grandparents' laps and looks at children's books. His grandmother, Wang Chaosu, is illiterate, but she knows the books by heart and she recites them to Huang Kai.

They have no desire to go elsewhere. "We're here for *yibeizi,*" Huang Xiaoqiang says. "A lifetime." Sometimes they express interest in the outside world—Huang's father, Huang Neng, often asks how much a plane ticket to America costs, and how long it takes. "Fifteen hours!" he says once, amazed. "Do they have bathrooms on the plane?"

"Of course they do," laughs his daughter-in-law, Feng Xiaoqin. Another customer at the restaurant, a local shop owner, speaks up. "There are big buses between Chongqing and Chengdu that have bathrooms," he says knowingly. "Telephones, too. On the high-speed expressway they take just four hours."

But this is only talk; they have no wish to travel. "It's too expensive," says Feng Xiaoqin. And if she had the money? "If I had ten thousand yuan, then I'd want forty thousand," she laughs. "That's the way I am, just like everybody else—it's never enough. You Americans like traveling so much. It's too much trouble: you have to carry your bag here, carry your bag there. I wouldn't want to go to America and have to learn English. It's too much hassle."

Any changes are made within the world of the restaurant. In the fall of 1997, the college, which owns the building, suddenly raises the monthly rent from three hundred yuan to seven hundred, and the Huang family cuts down on spending. They buy a public telephone to increase profits. But the first month they lose three hundred yuan, because they don't understand the long-distance rates. The next month they adjust and turn a profit. Huang Xiaoqiang spends four weeks and three thousand yuan on a training course so he can get his driver's license. This document is his proudest possession; obtaining the privilege to drive is difficult and expensive in China. He begins to look for work. "I have no *guanxi,*" he says. "But that's not the most important thing. Mostly they look at your ability, and you have to be lucky."

And so he has no job, but he has his license, which means opportunity. And of course he has his restaurant and his new phone. He also has a five-room apartment, which is big by Fuling standards. He has a color television and a stereo and a 35mm camera. He has one son. He has his family, and his family has the patronage and respect of the students and the East River people, who see the Huangs as generous and good-hearted. Their world is small, but they take good care of it.

IT IS EARLY MORNING and Huang Xiaoqiang is making *chaoshou.* He sits in front of the ingredients: a bowl of pork filling, a plate of small square dough wrappers, a bowl of water, a pan. He holds a chopstick. He picks up a wrapper in one hand. With the chopstick he draws out a pinch of pork filling and places it in the square of dough. Then he dips the chopstick in the water, and uses it to fold the corners of the wrapper around the meat. The finished dumpling extends in two points, one crossing on top of the other. He drops the dumpling into the pan.

Elsewhere in China this food is called *hundun,* but the Sichuanese have their own way of speaking, and they call it *chaoshou*—"crossed hands"—because of the way the corners of the dumpling overlap. In most parts of Sichuan, you can walk into a restaurant and order *chaoshou* without making a sound. Cross your arms and they will understand exactly what you want.

It takes Huang Xiaoqiang less than five seconds to make the dumpling. He picks up another wrapper, inserts the meat, wets the corners, folds them over, and drops the *chaoshou* into the pan. It looks exactly the same as the first one. He makes another, and then one more. Outside the sun is rising and the minibuses are honking and the fruit women have set up their stands. Oranges are in season. Huang Xiaoqiang makes more *chaoshou.* All of them are well-made and they look exactly alike.

CHAPTER NINE

Money

MONEY MEANT VERY LITTLE TO ME IN FULING. I made one thousand yuan a month, while the average per capita income for a Chinese urban household was 430 yuan—fifty-odd American dollars, at the official exchange rate of slightly more than eight yuan to the dollar. In rural areas the per capita income was only 175 yuan a month, but peasants could stretch money farther because they grew their own food.

My salary was relatively high, and it was comfortable as long as I didn't travel much. A ticket on the hydrofoil to Chongqing cost eighty yuan, although you could save money by taking the overnight slow boat for twenty-four yuan, which was how most of the locals traveled. During my first year I always rode the slow boat upstream, until one evening when a rat ran over my head while I was sleeping.

I woke up and turned on the light. There were rats all over the cabin—fat brown Yangtze rats with long noodle tails. They scampered across the floor, rooting in people's luggage. One of them was climbing over a sleeping woman in a lower berth. The woman shifted under her covers but didn't wake up. I watched the rats for a while. At last I left the cabin.

The rest of the night I sat out on deck, listening to the river slip past. I thought about the money I was saving by taking that boat, which amounted to seven dollars. After that trip I always paid extra for the hydrofoils when I went upriver, but these were rare occasions. I had some friends in Chongqing, but otherwise there wasn't anything interesting about going there. Mostly I didn't travel.

Staying in Fuling made it difficult to spend all of my monthly salary, which was my goal. There was no reason to save it; by living carefully I could put away three hundred yuan a month, which meant that a year of frugality would reward me with a total of four hundred American dollars. That was one of the best aspects of life in the Peace Corps: my salary was so low that it was pointless to save money, but my Fuling routines were so simple and cheap that I didn't have to worry about budgeting my expenses. In a sense it was the richest I could ever be, because it was like toy money and I didn't have to think about it at all.

I wasted a good part of my salary while I wandered around the city, buying anything that caught my eye—books, pictures, trinkets, black-market cassette tapes. Once I picked up a bamboo fishing rod for no reason at all and put it in the corner of my dining room, where it gathered dust. At the military surplus stores I bought People's Liberation Army uniforms and accessories. They sold nearly everything at those stores—clothes, shoes, gear. A nightstick was 30 yuan; handcuffs cost 130. Anybody with 300 yuan could walk in off the street and pick up a high-powered electric stun gun. If you had a permission slip from your *danwei,* you could buy a wicked spiked mace for less than 200. They didn't sell pistols but you could buy the holsters.

From different stores I put my uniform together piece by piece: old-style PLA trousers with a red-and-yellow stripe down the leg, a Public Security vest, a nice military jacket with padded shoulders, a short-brimmed Red Army cap with a star on the front. When I picked up my epaulets for fifteen yuan, the saleswoman told me very seriously that they were the wrong ones—apparently there was something else that a *waiguoren* should wear on his shoulders when he dressed up as a PLA officer. I bought them anyway; they matched the star on my cap and the stripes on my trousers.

On special occasions I wore my uniform for teaching, which always made the students excited; some of them tried to convince me that I should wear it every day. I never wore the entire ensemble into town, but I often wore the trousers, which were comfortable. Many of the peasants and stick-stick soldiers wore those as well, and sometimes people asked if was a Uighur.

Apart from the money I wasted, nearly all of my salary went toward food, because I ate out every meal. The restaurants were among the most pleasant places in the city, with some of my best friends as their owners, and the Sichuanese food was excellent. There was no reason to cook for myself in Fuling.

At least once a day I ate at the Students' Home noodle restaurant. Often I ate alone, but sometimes during the week all four of the volunteers met there for lunch. We showed Feng Xiaoqin how to cook a Sichuanese version of spaghetti, and Adam wrote that foreign word on the menu. Nobody else ever ordered the spaghetti. After they acquired a telephone, Adam and I sometimes called to order our meals in advance. This professional touch pleased the workers, who in turn started telephoning our apartments and inviting us to meals. I'd answer the phone and Huang Xiaoqiang would say: Are you coming for lunch? What do you want to eat? Adam and I would tell him one bowl of noodles and one bowl of spaghetti, and then we'd run down the hill and catch it hot off the wok.

I liked the restaurant best on Sunday nights, when it was crowded with students and the street was full of people enjoying the last of the weekend. But it was also good in the late afternoon, when business was slow and I could sit alone with my newspaper. I'd chat with the family, often about money, which was what everybody talked about in Fuling. I was accustomed to talking about that, even though for me it wasn't real money and I let it slip through my fingers every month.

One afternoon in December, I sat there watching Huang Kai play on the steps of the restaurant. He was, like all Chinese children in winter, a bundle of grubby clothes. His cap and pants had been hand-knit by his mother. His pants were slit at the crotch, because he had not yet been toilet-trained, and his buttocks and inner thighs were pink in the cold. He was nearly two years old. He wore layer upon layer of shirts and sweaters, topped by a fake leather jacket that his mother had bought in town. "It's poor quality," she had said dismissively, when I complimented her on it. "It was only twenty yuan." She always told me the prices of Huang Kai's clothes and toys.

I was eating noodles and drinking water from my clear plastic American-made Nalgene bottle. In China those camping bottles were invaluable; they were made of hard plastic that could hold the boiled water that was always available in hotels, restaurants, trains, and boats. When I first arrived in Sichuan, the bottles had been uncommon, although occasionally in a big city like Chengdu I'd meet a cab driver who had one. Usually it had been purchased by a relative or a friend in one of the well-developed coastal cities like Shenzhen.

In early spring of 1997, a few Chengdu shops started stocking Nalgene-knockoff bottles, and by June everybody had them. Chengdu was a relatively hip city where Western styles tended to spread quickly, often without clear cause or meaning. Most bicycles in the city had rear fenders decorated with "Pentium Intel Inside" stickers, the same kind that accompanied computers in America. Nearly all of the Chengdu bicycles had only one gear, and they most certainly did not have Intel Inside; but the stickers were trendy and you saw them on fenders everywhere.

The demand for Nalgene-knockoff bottles was much more understandable, especially in a tea-drinking city like Chengdu, where the bottles spread quickly throughout the city's social strata. They were first acquired by cab drivers, who tended to be at the forefront of such trends—cabbies had a certain maverick quality, as well as plenty of money. After that, the businessmen followed suit, and then the *xiaojies*, and finally by summer even the old people in the teahouses were sipping their tea out of fake Nalgene bottles. Soon you could buy them for twenty yuan in any Sichuan city or town.

The bottles came with a label that described them as American-developed Taikong Pingzi—Outer Space Bottles. But they were clearly the product of Chinese factories, because they weren't quite standard and often the label was misspelled. In that regard things hadn't changed greatly from the seventeenth century, when a Spanish priest named Domingo Navarrete described business methods in China. "The Chinese are very ingenious at imitation," he wrote. "They have imitated to perfection whatsoever they have seen brought out of Europe. In the Province of Canton they have counterfeited several things so exactly, that they sell them Inland for Goods brought out from Europe."

Even after the bottles became common in Fuling, Huang Kai never got over the fascination he had with the ones that Adam and I carried. It had something to do with the shiny plastic, as well as their association with the *waiguoren*, whom Huang Kai never quite trusted.

On that day in December, I shook my bottle and set it on a stool. The child toddled over, cautious but interested.

"Gupiao," he said. *"Gupiao."*

The word meant "stock," as in stock market. I turned to his mother. "He thinks it looks like the stock market report on television," she said, laughing. She pointed to the side of the bottle, where the volume levels were marked in gradients from one hundred to nine hundred milliliters. My water was at five hundred and falling.

Huang Kai forgot the bottle and returned to the steps. He crouched over, pants gaping, and rolled a toy car along the ground. A moment later I heard him babbling to himself. *"Mao Zhuxi, Mao Zhuxi,"* he said. "Chairman Mao, Chairman Mao." I had no idea what had prompted him to say this; there was a poster of Mao in his living room at home and perhaps he was thinking of that. He was not yet two years old but already plenty was mixed up inside his head.

CHAIRMAN MAO HATED MONEY. His father—a crafty, grasping landlord—had made quite a bit of it, and partly in reaction Mao Zedong despised anything that had to do with money. As a poor revolutionary he was scornful of it, and as the Communist Party's Chairman he refused to touch it.

Mao was the father of New China, and perhaps it was in reaction to him that the Chinese nowadays spent so much time thinking and talking about money. Or maybe it was simply that now they had more than ever before, with more ways to earn and spend it, and yet with all that new money it still wasn't enough. Everywhere in Fuling that was what people talked about.

It was nothing to be ashamed of; there was no reason to be coy when it came to financial matters. Everybody knew everybody else's salary, and if a friend had something new—a shirt, a radio, a pen—you asked him how much it cost, and he told you. Mentioning money was nearly as routine as the traditional greeting people used in Fuling and other parts of China: *Chi fan meiyou?* Have you eaten yet? Until recently most of the country had been poor, and eating was something the people took real pleasure in, just as they took real pleasure in earning whatever money they could.

I liked this openness; it helped me understand people's lives, because I could ask them about their salaries or expenses without offending them. I always told people my own salary—generally it was the second or third question they asked. By the second year this disclosure was hardly necessary; it seemed that everybody in the city already knew. One evening I sat on a bench at South Mountain Gate, talking with the crowd that gathered, and somebody asked how much I made every month. Before I could respond, another voice in the crowd shouted out, "He makes one thousand yuan! All of the foreign teachers at the college make that same salary."

People talked about money all the time, and yet I wouldn't describe them as greedy: the Chinese I knew in Fuling were incredibly and sincerely generous. If I ate a meal with somebody else, he or she paid; that was simply how it worked, and usually there was nothing I could do about it. Our students were the same way—if they happened to be eating in the Students' Home at the same time as Adam and me, they always tried to pay our bill, despite their tight finances. The average student budget was around two hundred yuan a month, or twenty-four dollars, which was a significant expense for many of their families. Because most of the college's students came from poor rural areas, the government gave each one an additional stipend of fifty yuan a month.

At the noodle restaurant we learned to pay in advance when students were around, although the owners didn't approve of this. "You're their teacher," Feng Xiaoqin told me once. "They respect you, and they should pay for your meal. That's our tradition in China." She was generous, too; often at the restaurant I ate for free.

Part of this was simply the "foreign friend" syndrome, but to a lesser degree they were the same way with each other. In particular they were generous with their families—if a close relative needed money, it was given without hesitation and with no expectation of repayment. One of my graduated first-year students, Aumur, had taken a teaching job in Tibet, where the salary was one thousand yuan a month—more than twice what he would have made in the countryside of Sichuan. But Aumur sent half of his Tibet salary home to his parents, who were peasants, and yet there was not the slightest sense of burden or regret that accompanied this generosity. "It's my duty," he said simply, when I asked him about it, and he explained that this was the only way that his younger brother could afford his school tuition fees. Aumur's commitment in Tibet was eight years, and if he left early the fines were as high as twenty thousand yuan, but I never heard him complain about the work he was doing to support his parents and brother.

Everything had a price in Fuling, where fines were a common part of life. Students were fined ten yuan if they failed an exam, two yuan for unsatisfactory cleaning of the classroom, and one and a half yuan for skipping morning exercises. I knew Peace Corps teachers at another Sichuan college where a student was fined five hundred yuan—enough money for two months' expenses—for publicly holding hands with his girlfriend on campus while a government delegation was in town.

All of this was good preparation for adult life, which also had its share of fines. Sometimes you even had to pay to take a new job—a sort of reverse bonus. Teacher Liao had originally worked in a college in her hometown of Zigong, but her husband was on the Fuling faculty and after they married she wanted to move. She applied for and received a job in Fuling, but that was when the complications started. The Zigong *danwei* required a payment of five thousand yuan before it granted her permission to leave, and Fuling Teachers College also could have charged her a similar amount before allowing her to start work. But Fuling waived the fee—a sign that they very much wanted Teacher Liao in their Chinese department. She was proud that Fuling Teachers College had given her a job without charging her a single yuan. You had to be a good teacher to get a job like that for free.

The going rate for a second child was more than ten thousand yuan, at least in the countryside close to the college. In the city it was rare that anybody got to the point where she paid this fine—if a woman was pregnant with her second child, she would be threatened with the loss of her job. If she didn't work for a state-run *danwei,* there were other ways of applying pressure, and having a second child could result in a woman's being forced to undergo sterilization surgery.

Most of the city residents seemed accustomed to the planned-birth policy, accepting its implications without complaint. After all, they spent every day negotiating Fuling's crowded streets and sidewalks, which made the need for population control easy to understand. But attitudes were different in the countryside. Out there you could dodge the authorities, and the Chinese had a phrase for this evasion—*Chaosheng Youjidui,* "Guerrilla Birth Team." A woman might go live with relatives until she had the baby, and then she would return home and pay the fine. It wasn't so common close to the city, where the authorities could control things tightly, but the average family size increased as you went farther into the hills.

Once I was on the bus with a peasant woman who was returning from market, and we had the same simple conversation that I had with so many of the dialect speakers. She asked me how much money I made, and where I was from, and why I had come to such a lousy place as Fuling. This was a common theme in my conversations—people always wondered why a self-respecting *waiguoren* would live in a place like Fuling for one thousand yuan a month. I had no answer for that; I wasn't about to tell them the truth, that Fuling's imperfections were part of why I liked the city so much, and that I felt rich precisely because I made so little money that I didn't have to worry about saving anything.

I told the woman that I had been sent to Fuling by the U.S. government, which was the simplest way to explain my situation—everybody in China understood what it meant when a government decided where you worked. I asked the woman about her family, and she said she had two children, a daughter and a young son.

"But don't you have trouble if you have two children?" I asked.

"Yes, but not too much. We had to pay a fine."

"How much for your son?"

"Four thousand yuan."

"That's not as much as people pay now, is it?"

"No. Nowadays they pay more than ten thousand. For us it wasn't so much."

"That's good," I said.

"It was cheaper back then," she said nostalgically. "In those days the fines weren't so bad."

"Can you save four thousand yuan in a year?"

"Unless it's a bad year."

"So that's not too much at all."

"No," she said. "It wasn't."

The woman sat there smiling, thinking about the four-thousand-yuan son who was waiting for her at home. She arranged the things in her bamboo basket and turned to me again.

"Do you have a planned-birth policy in your country?"

"No."

"So how many children can you have?"

"As many as we want."

"Really?"

"Really," I said. "If you want to have ten children, you can have ten. There's no limit. But most people only have two, because that's all they want."

The woman smiled wistfully, shaking her head. I wondered what amazed her more—that there was a country where birth wasn't limited, or that Americans were so foolish as to want only two children. Many of the peasants I met seemed inclined to go with the second viewpoint, and sometimes they had the same reaction to American farming, which to a Sichuanese peasant seemed to be an incredible combination of luck and incompetence. They found it remarkable that the average farmer in a state like Missouri had 292 acres of land, as well as mechanized equipment and the occasional government subsidy, and yet there were still years when it was difficult to make ends meet. As far as the peasants were concerned, you had to be a particularly bad farmer to ruin a setup like that, just as you had to be particularly foolish to respond to complete procreative freedom by having just two children.

My students were part of the last peasant generation whose fines had been minimal. The second-year speaking class had thirty-five students, of whom only two were single children. Those two were free and the rest had cost very little, if anything at all. Diana cost one hundred yuan. Davy's little brother cost three hundred yuan. Rex had a 650-yuan sister, while Julia's brother was only 190. Jeremy was one hundred yuan. He was the sixth child in his family, and the older five had all been girls. That was a very well spent one hundred yuan if you were a Chinese peasant.

Many of their families were like that—a string of girls punctuated by a boy that marked the end of the children. In those days the fines had been minimal, and the peasants still followed the traditional pattern of having children until there was at least one son. The fines, like everything else regarding money, were not sensitive subjects. Sometimes I teased Jeremy because he had cost only one hundred yuan. I offered to buy Julia's brother for five hundred, so her parents could double their investment, but she only laughed and shook her head.

MOST OF MY GRADUATED STUDENTS were assigned jobs in the countryside, where they made around four hundred yuan a month—less than fifty dollars. It was very little money but the jobs were secure, and they didn't have to search by themselves. Communist China had no tradition of independent job searches, and the thought of relying on themselves terrified most of my students, who generally accepted the assignments. They also took these positions because they were penalized if they refused the government job. If they chose to find work on their own, they had to repay the scholarship they had received, which usually amounted to around five thousand yuan. During my second year, the authorities began to reform these rules, phasing out the automatic assignments, but my first group of graduated students was still in the traditional system.

The more aggressive students often paid the fine or found some other way to avoid the assigned job. Five of the boys took teaching positions in Tibet—all of them were Party Members, and they went for reasons of patriotism as well as money. North, who had been one of the class monitors, took a sales job with the Wu River Hot Pickled Mustard Tuber factory. Two of the best girl students found teaching jobs at a private school in the eastern province of Zhejiang. Anne, the student whose family lived in my building, wandered southward—first she worked as a secretary in Kunming, in Yunnan province, and then she went to Shenzhen, the special economic zone near Hong Kong.

Shenzhen was a sort of promised land for Sichuanese migrants. People made money quickly there, sometimes without *guanxi* or education; all you needed was your wits and some luck. There were Shenzhen legends at all of the Sichuan teachers colleges where my Peace Corps friends taught. Students whispered about classmates who, having been thrown out of school for cheating or failing exams, went south to Shenzhen and were rich within a year, thankful that the college had tossed them. During my first year, an English department student named Don had been kicked out of Fuling for cheating, after which he followed the standard expelled student route and went straight to Shenzhen. But in the booming city he struck out—no money, no job, no *guanxi.* And there was no face for Don the next year, when, after paying a substantial fine, he returned to the college and resumed his studies. That was the other side of Shenzhen—but there weren't so many legends about the people who failed. Sometimes you heard about nice Sichuanese girls who turned into prostitutes after running out of money, but mostly you heard about the ones who had succeeded.

Anne sent Adam and me vivid letters from Shenzhen, describing the "talent markets" where she had to pay ten yuan to talk with prospective employers. It was a stressful and expensive place to look for a job, and soon Anne, who was there with her sister, had spent all of her savings in the markets. At last they pooled resources to send Anne's sister into the talent markets, where she tracked down an interview for a position that called for English fluency. Anne went to the interview and got the job. She asked for twelve hundred yuan a month; the boss countered with nine hundred; and Anne, who had already been rejected enough times, accepted the offer.

She had never left the Fuling area before graduation, and now suddenly she was working on her own in what was perhaps the most exciting city in China. Not long after she started her job, she wrote me a letter describing her early days at the office:

> During the first two days, only one girl in our office showed her hospitality; others acted as if they didn't notice my exist. I felt very lonely. I thought of you—you must have felt lonely in your early stay in Fuling. I encouraged myself to try to show my anxiety to make friends with them. My efforts ended in success; I was took as one of them soon.
>
> In our office there are only eight people. Except the boss (an old man), others are all young girls. They are from three different provinces. Lulu, Luyun, Xuli, Lily are from Jiangxi Province; Yi Xiaoying from Hunan, Linna from Sichuan. Lulu is the most beautiful, able and shortest girl, who is liked by everyone. Luyun is very kind, who reminds me of Airane [a Fuling classmate]. Xuli is a classical beauty, most private telephones from boys are for her. But I don't like

her very much, for her word sometimes hurtful. Lily is the other secretary, who came two days earlier than me. She leaves us an impression of stupid and irresponsible. So she is not very popular in the office. Xiaoying is the fatest girl concerning much about losing weight. She is very good at computer but poor in English. We have an oral contract that she teaches me how to use computer and I teach her English. Linna is the one I can speak Sichuan dialect with. But Sichuan dialect is so understandable by everyone that we don't have a sense of superiority when speaking it.

Oh! Till now, you still don't know what our company does. Our company was just moved from Taiwan several months before. It acts in the field of exporting fashion, costume and shell jewelry. My job is keeping touch with our customers by letters or faxes, receiving purchase orders, giving order to factories and finding the best company to ship products to our customers. Since I'm not familiar with my work, Lulu helps me a lot these days.

IF YOU DIDN'T GO TO SHENZHEN, you could make money quickly in the stock market. The Fuling exchange office was next to South Mountain Gate, a huge room with rows of chairs where people sat and watched the stock listings on an enormous digital screen. For a while I used to go there, hoping to practice Chinese with the people, but none of them ever talked. They simply stared at the money as it raced across the boards.

Many of my friends had invested, despite the expensive registration deposit of thirty thousand yuan. This fee was refundable after a certain period of time, but it was an enormous amount and people usually pooled their resources and registered as a group. Teacher Liao had investments through one of her relatives, and the family at the Students' Home had invested money through Huang Xiaoqiang's sister. One afternoon they took Huang Kai to the exchange, because every night the child became excited and shouted "Stock!" repeatedly when the ticker appeared on television. But when confronted with the market's reality—the crowds of people, the flashing billboard, the noise and lights and energy of the place—he burst into tears and cried inconsolably until they returned home, where the familiar portrait of Chairman Mao decorated the living-room wall.

On January 9 of 1998, which was a Friday, my friend Scott Kramer called from New York and warned me that the Chinese stock market was under serious speculation. He worked in emerging markets on Wall Street, and for my sake he always kept an eye on China.

That day I had class with Teacher Liao, and I told her it might be a good time to take her money out of the market. She shrugged it off—what did I know?

The following Monday, the Shanghai Index fell 9.1 percent and the Shenzhen Index dropped 7.8 percent. It was one of the worst days in the history of the Chinese markets, and Teacher Liao lost a thousand yuan. The family at the Students' Home lost nearly as much. They told me about it while I ate lunch, and Huang Kai picked up one of the words and babbled it over and over again. *"Diele, diele,"* he said. "It fell, it fell." Within a week the family had sold all their stock.

The next time I had class with Teacher Liao, she grinned sheepishly as she walked into my office.

"You were right," she said. "I forgot all about what you said until that Monday, when I got home and watched television. But by then it was too late—they had already closed the market. Afterward I told my husband that you had known it would happen."

"I didn't know anything," I said. "But my friend in America thought it might fall. That's his job and he understands it very well."

"We should have listened."

I asked her how much she had lost, and she told me. She said everybody was losing money; two years ago the stocks went up all the time but now there hadn't been a good month all year. I told her I'd keep her updated on Kramer's tips.

ANNE HAD ACCESS TO THE COMPANY PHONES in Shenzhen, and sometimes at night she called Adam or me. One evening she phoned and reported that she had gotten a raise to one thousand yuan, and I congratulated her. As time passed, I would find this to be one of the most satisfying aspects of teaching, because former students occasionally called to report milestones of adulthood and independence. Often these benchmarks had to do with money: a new raise, a new apartment, a new beeper. Once a student called to tell me that he had acquired a cell phone. He told me about the cell phone for a few minutes and then he mentioned, in an offhand way, that he had also gotten engaged.

I told Anne that now her salary was as high as mine, which made her laugh. But on the phone she sounded a little funny, and finally I asked if something was wrong.

"The company has an agent in Hong Kong," she said slowly. "He often comes here to Shenzhen. He is an old man, and he likes me."

"What do you mean by that?"

Silence. I tried again. "Why does he like you?"

"Because I am fat." She giggled nervously on the phone. She was a pretty girl and I knew that she had gained a little weight since graduation, and in some ways this made her even prettier.

"What do you mean when you say that he likes you because of that?" I asked.

Silence.

"Does he want you to be his girlfriend?"

"Perhaps."

"Is he married?"

"He is divorced. He has small children in Taiwan, where he is from. But he usually works in Hong Kong."

"How often does he come to Shenzhen?"

"Twice a month."

"Is it a big problem?"

"He always finds a way to be with me."

"Will you leave the job?"

"He says he will help me find a job in Hong Kong if I want one. The salaries are much higher there, you know. He says I can make much more money if I go to Hong Kong."

I breathed deeply and thought about how to handle this. "That sounds like a very bad idea," I said slowly. "If you want another job, you should not ask him for help. That will only cause big problems in the future."

"I know. I think I would never do that."

"You should try to avoid him."

"I do," she said. "And I tell my coworkers to always be with me if he is there."

"Do you think it is a big problem?"

"Not now."

"Well, if it becomes a big problem, you should leave the job. That can be a very bad situation."

"I know," she said. "I don't think that will be necessary. But it is not such a good job, and if I have to leave, I will."

ONE OF TEACHER KONG'S DISTANT COUSINS had been kidnapped and sold into marriage in Anhui province. The woman wasn't a close relative of Teacher Kong, but they shared the same family name. We talked about her during a tutorial in which we discussed *fanmai renkou,* people who were bought and sold for money.

I asked if the woman had been able to escape her husband, and Teacher Kong said that they still lived together. She had been sold in the mid-1980s; now they had been married for more than a decade.

"She was relatively satisfied," Teacher Kong said. "Her husband had money."

To a certain degree this struck me as obvious—after all, he had purchased the woman. But apart from finances, wasn't she angry about the violation?

"I'm not sure, because I don't know her well," Teacher Kong said. "But I think she wanted to leave Fengdu. She was from a very poor part of the countryside, and you know that it is difficult for a woman to leave a place like that. Usually they aren't taken by force—they're tricked. Somebody might promise them a job somewhere else, and once they arrive they're sold as a bride. They're far from home and there's nothing they can do. I think that's what happened to my cousin."

"So she never came back?"

"After about five years she did. At first she was very ashamed—too ashamed to write. But after a while she got back in contact, and finally she made a visit home. Now she's been back a few times. She likes her husband. Quite a few of them turn out like that, if the women are from very poor places like my cousin. The only serious problems are with the women who are sold to idiots, or cripples, or old men. They're not happy if they have a husband like that, of course. That's when there's trouble, but as long as there's enough money most of the women aren't too upset."

"Usually they're taken far from home?"

"Yes, and sometimes that's a problem—the husband will live in a very remote area, and the women are watched so they can't get away. Some of them are illiterate and can't write home, or they don't know how to travel back. Does that happen much in America?"

"No," I said. "That doesn't happen very much in America. I've never known anybody who was bought or sold."

"It's not so common anymore in China, either. It was more common in the 1980s, just after the Reform and Opening started. Now it doesn't happen so much, but in the remote areas I've heard that sometimes it's still a problem."

EVERY YEAR AT THE BEGINNING of the American section of my literature course, we read the Declaration of Independence, which was in the textbooks. The Chinese publisher had included the Declaration because it smacked of revolution, which was always an appropriate subject for Chinese students. They never would have included the American Constitution or the Bill of Rights.

I assigned the chapter, and then I asked the students to write their own Declarations, asserting independence from something that limited them. Nearly all of the boys declared independence from the college, although a few responses were different. Marx, who was true to his name, declared independence from Money:

> We are slaves of the money, all of us, this is the case. But we all know clearly that money is only the thing that people create. We want our food, coat, car, and all of the things not controled by the money. We don't want to fight against money, because at least money has given us some convenience. But its harm is much bigger than the remittance. We must get rid of money. Money is the tyrant of our society. We must throw it off.

None of the girls wrote about money, and few of them declared independence from the college. Many wanted to be free from their parents—they wrote about how their mothers read their diaries and prevented them from choosing their friends freely, especially their boyfriends. Quite a few of the girls declared independence from men entirely. One student wrote:

> The laws and God give each man equality. They give us freedom from want, freedom from fear, freedom of speech, freedom of loving, and so on. However, my boyfriend almost abolishes the freedom of my speech and deed, the freedom of my loving.
>
> He is an all-controlling person. He and I are open-minded. He could speak with anyone he would like to. He could play with his "little sisters." He could also laugh and laugh with them. I don't know around him, how many "little sisters" he has. But he hates my doing these. Before our love, I had had many friends. I liked to chat with them, to go for an outing, to have a joke with them, etc. At that time, I don't know what's the meaning of mental pain. I was like a happy bird. Now, when he saws me talk with boys, he must snap at me. Even more, he doesn't show due respect for my feelings. I lost my friends. I am so alone that my characteristic also changes. Sometimes for trifles, I might fly into a rage. I can't find own original image. I can't bear his rudeness. So I decide to leave him forever. When he knows my idea, he threatens me. He says, "If you leave me, I will kill you." My dear! What can I do?
>
> I still believe laws and God give each man equality. Now I'll declare loudly that I must be independent! Freedom and independence are more important than anything else in the world, including love!

NOT LONG AFTER my telephone conversation with Anne, she wrote in a letter that the Hong Kong man had cooled in his pursuit of her. She was satisfied with the job, and now a former classmate from Fuling was coming to Shenzhen to try her luck. They were to live together, along with Anne's older sister.

Anne was always concerned about her sister, who had a tendency to bounce from job to job. The last time Adam had spoken with her, she had described her sister's current job, which sounded more or less like part of a pyramid scheme. Those scams were very common in Shenzhen, as well as many other places in China, and Anne's sister had naturally found a position toward the bottom of the pyramid. Adam and I both suggested as tactfully as possible that Annc should encourage her sister to find a different line of work—pyramids were collapsing all over China, and the government was currently cracking down on them. Anne gave me an update in her letter:

> My sister's situation is getting better now. Frankly, she is more capable than me. What she lacks most is luck. Although these days, she has done very bad in getting money, she is successful making friends and having experience, which we think will be good for whatever job she may have in future. But my parents, especially my mother doesn't think so. They are getting worried about her, because she is already twenty-five years old now, but still has neither a stable job nor a boyfriend. It's a very funny situation—when they got know that I had a boyfriend, they were so upset, even became angry. As I was still a little girl in their eyes—three or four years makes so big a difference!
>
> I have read every letter (two total) from you for many times; it has been a great pleasure to "talk" with an elder man who can always come up with wise ideas. My father may be a wise man, but I'd rather act like a spoiled child before him; we seldom talk seriously.

A couple of weeks later Anne called from work. I asked her about the Hong Kong man, and she laughed.

"He likes all women he sees," she said. "Because of that he is not such a problem."

She told me her job was going well, and I asked how her sister was doing.

"She is fine."

"Does she have a new job?"

"Yes. She answers the telephone."

"What do you mean by that?"

"People call her," Anne explained, "and she talks to them."

"She has conversations with them?"

"Yes."

"Do many people call?"

"Yes."

"What do they talk about?"

"About troubles."

"What kind of troubles?"

"About affections!" She giggled after saying this and there was a pause.

"Does your sister like the job?"

"I think she likes it."

"How is the salary?"

"She makes six hundred a month," said Anne. "But if more people call, she makes more money."

"Who calls—are they men or women?"

"I think half are men, half are women. There are many people who call."

"Why do they call?"

"Everyone here in Shenzhen has many troubles."

"Why is that?"

"There are many troubles about affections. Some people say there is no real love in Shenzhen. People are too busy with earning money to exist."

DURING OUR FIRST YEAR IN FULING, Adam's best freshman student had been a girl named Janelle. She was so far ahead of the others that there was no comparison, and something about this intellectual distance also set her apart socially. She had no friends in the class and spent her time alone, often talking with Adam or me to practice her English. At the end of the school year, she seemed depressed, and then for some unknown reason she went home early, missing her final exams.

At the start of the second year, Adam had class for the first time and called roll. Everybody was there except for Janelle, and Adam asked if she was sick. A few students shook their heads. Nobody said anything.

"Will she be here later?" Adam asked.

"No," said Shannon, who was the class monitor. "She will not come back this year."

"Why not?"

"She is dead," Shannon said, and then he laughed. It was a nervous and humorless sound, the sort of Chinese laugh that was simply a reaction to an uncomfortable situation. It wasn't difficult to distinguish these laughs from normal ones, but nevertheless they always sent shivers down a *waiguoren*'s spine. The students had their heads down and Adam quickly changed the topic. On that day class was a long two hours.

The subject was difficult to broach and we never heard much about it, because none of the students had known Janelle well. All they could tell us was that during the summer she had jumped off a bridge in her hometown. When the Chinese commit suicide, it's common for them to jump off things—bridges, buildings, cliffs. Sometimes in the countryside they eat pesticide. They tend to do a much more thorough job of killing themselves than Americas do, especially American women, who often take pills and are saved by having their stomachs pumped.

Chinese women are more likely to commit suicide than Chinese men. More than half of the female suicides in the world take place in China, where the suicide rate for women is nearly five times the world average. China is the only country on earth in which more women kill themselves than men.

In Fuling there were plenty of signs that things could be difficult for women, and Adam and I had strange experiences with women who seemed unbalanced. During our first year, a freshman girl used to lurk outside Adam's apartment, accusing him of loving her. Adam tried to reason with her, asking why she believed this, and sometimes she said that she had heard it from her body. Other times she invented a story about how Dean Fu had called a meeting and told all of the students about Adam's interest in her. Once she angrily accused Adam of being too timid to pursue her, and she said that, like all Americans, he was a coward and a liar.

I had my own troubles with a woman named Miss Ou, who worked in a downtown department store. She was in her mid-forties, unmarried, and she telephoned at strange hours—at six in the morning she would invite me to come and see her. She gave me gifts: chopsticks, books, hand-knit sweaters. She was a kind, harmless woman, and at the beginning I tried to be friendly, but soon I was overwhelmed by her desperate loneliness. Every two or three weeks she sent me poetry and brief sayings that she copied out of English textbooks or translated herself. "We open up the future dream together!" she once wrote. "Harmonious family condition is the fatal term of the success of career."

Occasionally she sent me longer letters, like the one entitled "Keep the Trees of Love Green Forever":

> You should fully realize that woman is the unexhausted source of the strength of man. She can affect him, give him self confidence, lead him up, make him exciting, she can make timid brave, make weakness strong. It all depends on how the woman excavate the great potential power of her own.
>
> Good woman is a school, she will affect, encourage, and model you (man) with a kind of magical spirit. Benefit you all your life. Man should enter this school to refine himself. The man who has ideal is the most powerful one.

While it seemed that Fuling women were far more likely than men to feel isolated and frustrated, I had trouble untangling the reasons behind this unhappiness. Gender relations were hard to understand very fully, because these were sensitive, private issues and I was an outsider. But even from my distance I sensed an enormous gap between the experiences of local women and men.

In particular, I noticed that they had vastly different relationships to money. In my mind, money was a male quality in Fuling—it was something that I naturally associated with men, and to some degree it was connected to the standard dress code that represented local masculinity. City men almost never wore shorts, regardless of how hot it was, and in cool weather they dressed carefully in Western-style suits with the tailor's label left prominently on the sleeve. In hot weather they wore bright silk shirts and thin polyester slacks. They clipped beepers and cell phones prominently to their belts, which were wrapped one and a half times around their narrow waists. They carried their money in fat black leather purses. They were finicky about shoes—most men wore dark loafers, which they kept well polished. This was part of the routine when I had dinner with a group of well-to-do male friends in town: first we would have our shoes shined, all of us sitting on a row of curbside stools, and then we would go to a restaurant.

Some Fuling men allowed their pinkie nails to grow a full two inches, because this was a sign that they didn't do manual labor. A number of my male students had nails like this, which looked absurdly feminine on hands that clearly had been toughened by work in the fields. But none of the students planned on returning to the peasant life, and their nails were a clear indication that their lives were moving forward. Most of the long-nailed men in Fuling were of this transitional social class; they tended to be former peasants who were finding success as cab drivers, clerks, or small entrepreneurs. The truly rich rarely grew out their nails, because their wealth was already obvious enough from their expensive suits and cell phones.

The pinkie nails, like so many male accouterments, represented money—indeed, men in banks and shops occasionally used their elongated nails to count out bills. Fuling women also had their share of accessories that showed they were from the upper class, but on the whole these indications were less bluntly obvious and materialistic than those of the men. Upper-class males even wielded their leather purses in a far more showy manner than the women ever did. When one of these men paid a bill, he would ostentatiously open his purse, allowing bystanders to see a fat wad of cash.

It was clear that men controlled most of the money—they were quicker to earn it, quicker to spend it, and quicker to talk about it. They had more opportunities than the women, who were less likely to go into business or find lucrative independent jobs like driving a cab. In the end, money simply meant more to the men. I had trouble imagining what Fuling men had been like before Reform and Opening, because money struck me as such a fundamental part of their identity.

And it could be a distinctly tedious part, at least in my eyes. After a year in the city, I found that I least enjoyed associating with one particular socioeconomic group: the young moneyed male. There were exceptions, of course, but when I tried to define the average person from this group, I saw a man driven by a set of goals and aspirations that were so narrow they became a sort of caricature of showy masculinity. He tended to be passionate about acquiring beepers and cell phones, and he worked hard to accumulate increasingly advanced videodisc players and karaoke machines. He smoked Magnificent Sound cigarettes constantly. He tended to be loud, and he was very conscious of face, carrying himself with a certain swagger. On weekends he sometimes engaged in senseless drinking competitions with his male friends, challenging each other to shot after shot of *baijiu.* If he wanted some illicit excitement, he found prostitutes at a karaoke bar or a beauty parlor.

I realized that this was an unfairly narrow prejudice, and during my second year in Fuling I became friends with several wealthy young men who didn't match this stereotype. But nevertheless I found that it was easiest to make friends from the middle and lower classes. I was far more comfortable with somebody like Teacher Kong, who was thoughtful, interesting, and not in the least materialistic, and most of my boy students lacked the swagger of the Fuling rich. Even a small entrepreneur like Huang Xiaoqiang, who clearly spent a lot of time thinking about money, wasn't inclined to present the sort of macho facade that was standard among relatively wealthy men. In fact, this facade was often only skin deep, and it merely took time to penetrate beyond it; but in the end I didn't have the patience. Apart from a few exceptions, I essentially wrote off that entire class of people.

I also developed these prejudices from looking at my own behavior as a man in Fuling, especially when I participated in the macho routines that played such a large role in local upper-class male lives. During our second year, Adam and I both became tired of the banquet routine—the senseless competitive drinking, the constant bullying, the *baijiu* strategy. It had been entertaining during the first year, largely because we had so few social outlets, and some of the banquets were among my most humorous memories. But they were also some of the most embarrassing. For Christmas of my second year, the college held a banquet that coincided with a visiting delegation of cadres from Chongqing. As far as alcohol consumption went, it was hard to imagine a more auspicious coincidence than cadres and Christmas—that was like having nine planets line up at exactly the same time. From the moment I first heard about this event I knew that it would be ugly.

There were more than thirty cadres at the banquet, and by the time the parade of holiday toasts was finished, Adam and I were shouting Sichuanese swear words and firing toy plastic pellet guns at each other from across the restaurant. At least this was what I later heard; I had no memory of the last two hours and only knew what Sunni and Noreen told me (they also handled their share of toasts on that evening, although most of the attention had been focused on Adam and me).

In another culture I would have woken up mortified, but that was the least of my concerns the next morning. I was hungover, and badly bruised, but I knew there was no point in making apologies, because none was expected. Probably every single cadre had made a jackass of himself at some banquet within the past year, and without question their enjoyment of the event had been heightened by Adam and me being out of control. That was where the pellet guns came from, after all—a visiting foreign friend suggested the gift and the cadres instantly recognized their potential as a Christmas present. Somebody bought the guns on the street, loaded them, and put them in our hands.

Alcohol was always a viable excuse for bad male behavior in Fuling. Once in my first year I was eating dinner by myself in the college cafeteria when a group of three drunk physical education students came to my table, taunting and laughing at me. I tried to ignore them, but they just pressed closer, brushing against me while their insults became louder. Finally I stood up, and for a moment a fight seemed likely, but the cafeteria staff stepped in and escorted the students out. But that was all the staff did—they didn't take any names, or alert the college authorities. They made sure the students left, and then they apologized to me and explained that the three young men had been drunk. In their view, that was all that needed to be said—the drunk students weren't responsible for what they did.

While male drinking occasionally led to aggression, I mostly disliked its tediousness. When I looked back at the most vivid banquet of my first year, when the literary magazine had recruited me to write my Dickens essay, I saw it as a humorous incident but also as one that was full of wasted opportunities. The table had been full of intelligent, well-educated people, and yet virtually all of the evening's energy had been focused on making Teacher Sai drink when he did not want to. It reminded me of high school parties, except these men were in their forties and fifties. After the Christmas banquet in our second year, Adam and I finally took the original Peace Corps advice and refused to participate anymore in the competitive drinking.

But this was a decision that we had to make ourselves, because nobody expected us to behave responsibly and not act like drunken fools. In the end, this was probably my strongest prejudice toward men in Fuling, and especially upper-class men—on the average, I didn't see their lives being shaped by particularly high expectations. It was like any extremely male-dominated culture in which men are given more leeway than is healthy, and in Fuling it became even more pronounced when male pride was swollen with financial success.

While I typically avoided associating with wealthy men, there were moments when I was tempted to extend this prejudice to all young men. Again, this was an attitude that I tried to resist, but to a large degree it was a natural reaction to all of Fuling's anti-foreigner harassment, which invariably came from young males. Every single day that I spent in the city, people shouted at me, and probably less than 5 percent of these catcalls came from women. Generally it was the result of men trying to be macho: if I saw three young men walking toward me, I could be almost certain that one of them would shout something at me to impress his friends. In that sense it was similar to any sort of harassment in America, which typically comes from young men, but in Fuling it was far more routine.

It didn't take me very long to come to the conclusion that men were far more likely to give me trouble than women, and I shaped my routines accordingly. If I went shopping and saw two people selling the same thing, I invariably went to the woman first, because there was a much lower chance that she would cheat me or mock me. I knew other Peace Corps volunteers who followed the same pattern; it was a prejudice, but one that stemmed from experience.

All of these reactions and prejudices made it even more difficult for me to sort out gender relations in Fuling. My own life was contradictory: while I instinctively learned to be more wary of males, I nevertheless found that my closest friends were men, and I was far less comfortable associating with women on a one-to-one basis. If you were a male *waiguoren* in a small Sichuan city like Fuling, there were tacit barriers that stood between you and the women, and I avoided crossing these divides because I didn't want to find myself in trouble. The Peace Corps staff had all but formally recommended that we avoid dating in these small towns, because people were so skittish about *waiguoren.* But even if there hadn't been such a recommendation, I would have seen at a glance that such matters would be complicated, and it was something that all of the male Peace Corps volunteers in my group took seriously. There were seven single men, and over the course of two years not one of us had a romantic relationship with a Chinese woman.

As a result, local women were always somewhat mysterious and foreign, which was probably why *xiaojie* was one of the first Chinese words that Adam and I incorporated into our everyday English speech. It meant "miss" or "young woman," but it also conveyed the foreignness of the women in Fuling, as well as the barrier that we felt because we were *waiguoren.* In fact this is a term adopted by virtually every foreigner living in China, partly because young women workers are ubiquitous in certain jobs—as waitresses, shop assistants, train attendants—where they are addressed simply as *xiaojie.* But at the same time there's a complicated vagueness to this term, because it can also refer to the sort of young women who can be found in karaoke halls or suspicious beauty parlors. People in Fuling spoke of *san pei xiaojie*—"three-with girls," who worked in karaoke halls. Men could drink with them, sing karaoke with them, and dance with them. And for enough money some of the three-with girls would perform a fourth "with," sleeping with the customer.

It was impossible to define exactly what *xiaojie* meant, because it stretched across a broad range of implication. Anne was a *xiaojie* and so was Li Jiali, the prostitute who had pursued me at the teahouse. *Xiaojie* was a vague term, which was appropriate because it was difficult to define exactly what was expected of young women in a place like Fuling. They weren't like young upper-class men, whose aspirations could be neatly summarized, and I found that I had no equivalently simple definition for the average young woman in Fuling. She was expected to marry young and promptly have her child, and yet her childbearing was strictly and legally limited. She was expected to have a job and earn money of her own, but job discrimination was even more severe than in America. Traditional morality was breaking down, but this happened unevenly and in unhealthy ways; prostitution was becoming increasingly common and so were love affairs. I was amazed at how many of my young married friends in the city were cheating on their spouses, but divorce still came with a definite stigma for the women involved.

When a woman had an affair with a married man, people said that she *tou ren,* or *tou hanzi*— "stole men." There was no equivalent phrase that meant to steal women. If a single man had a romantic relationship with a married woman, people described her as *shuixing yanghua*—"as fickle as the way the water flows and the willow seed blows." Again, this phrase couldn't be applied to men; even the language did its part to protect them from being blamed for their indiscretions. Other aspects of Chinese were even more bluntly sexist. If you wanted to call a woman a bitch, you could say that she "stunk three-eight," because March 8 is International Women's Day.

Fuling women lived under complicated expectations, and the economic pressures of Reform and Opening seemed to weigh particularly heavily on them. In the countryside, many of the men had left to work in urban areas, and for every stick-stick soldier or construction worker in the city, there was a peasant wife back at home, tending the farm alone. A total of 66 percent of China's agricultural workers are female. Social scientists believe that this imbalance is partly responsible for the high female suicide rate, which occurs predominantly in the countryside. Rarely do these rural deaths seem to be the result of poverty; in fact, most happen within a relatively affluent and well-educated class of peasants. Adam's student Janelle was a textbook example of this trend: she wasn't poor, and she had academic opportunities that were unusual for peasant girls. But Janelle's career path most likely would have involved returning to her hometown to teach, which probably had been a depressing prospect for somebody so bright. I suspected that she had recognized clearly her own potential, as well as the bleakness of her future: to become a rural schoolteacher, marry young, raise a child. In the end it was more—or less—than she could bear.

Of course, things were worse in other parts of the world. Women in China could go much further than in most developing countries; there was no comparison with the Middle East. Also, there had been clear improvements in China, where post-Liberation reforms had made it easier for women to work, and the Communists had always campaigned hard against wife-selling while supporting women's right to divorce. Chinese women were also much better educated than ever before—but in a sense this only served to make them more aware of their plight. Like so many aspects of Chinese life, the issue of women's independence had reached a transitional stage, and it seemed to be a particularly painful one.

Everything was further complicated by the influence of traditional collective thinking. The longer I lived in Fuling, the more I was struck by the view of the individual—in my opinion, this was the biggest difference between what I had known in the West and what I saw in Sichuan. For people in Fuling, the sense of self seemed largely external; you were identified by the way that others viewed you. That had always been the goal of Confucianism, which defined the individual's place strictly in relation to the people around her: she was somebody's daughter, somebody else's wife, somebody else's mother; and each role had its specific obligations. This was an excellent way to preserve social harmony, but once that harmony was broken the lack of self-identity made it difficult to put things back together again. I sensed this whenever I read personal accounts of victimization during the Cultural Revolution, because these stories were surprisingly full of shame—one day a person was a good Communist, and the next day the winds changed and he was a mortified Counter-Revolutionary forced into the "airplane" stance at a rally, his arms outstretched and bent painfully back. The shift in itself was not so remarkable—irrational political purges happened the world over—but the strange part was that so many of these victims were racked by shame, clearly believing that they were somehow flawed. It was like a target of McCarthyism immediately breaking down and admitting that he was wrong, or a Holocaust victim hating herself because she was indeed a "dirty Jew." Often it seemed that in China there was no internal compass that was able to withstand these events.

Group thought could be a vicious circle—your self-identity came from the group, which was respected even if it became deranged, and thus your sense of self could fall apart instantly. There wasn't a tradition of anchoring one's identity to a fixed set of values regardless of what others thought, and in certain periods this had contributed to the country's disasters. The Cultural Revolution showed how Chinese society could become completely unhinged, but to a lesser extent there were bound to be problems during any sort of transitional period. And in recent decades nothing had been more disruptive to social roles and expectations than Reform and Opening

Group mentality seemed particularly troublesome for women, who lived under a strange combination of strictness and uncertainty. When compared to men, their traditional role in Chinese society was much more narrow, but the new economy resulted in frighteningly vague expectations and demands. On the whole these changes were undoubtedly positive, but they were happening so quickly that freedom could easily look overwhelming to somebody who was caught in the middle.

And often there wasn't anywhere to turn for help. Time and time again I saw this with my classes; for the most part they were incredibly close and supportive, but they could be cruelly isolating when a member was somehow different. Nobody had ever shown any interest in Janelle, and every class had at least one student who seemed alone; more often than not it was a girl. Being different wasn't liberating, as it sometimes is in America, and this was especially true for women from a peasant background, who were unlikely to feel comfortable ignoring the opinions of others and blazing new ground. The result was that they became outsiders not so much by choice as by helpless inclination, which naturally made them feel that they were the ones at fault.

To some degree, Anne had been like this. She had never quite fit in with the others, but she was also very bright, socially gifted, and attractive. In the end, these qualities gave her enough confidence to ignore certain aspects of the group. But Janelle was only extremely intelligent, which probably served to sharpen her sense of isolation.

Often money lay at the heart of these stresses. Peasant women saw their husbands go off in search of work, gaining financial security but leaving their spouses isolated, and sometimes this loneliness destroyed them. Women could earn money themselves; this was a way of becoming independent, but a career could also result in the frustration of sexism and the criticism of people who felt that a woman shouldn't strive in this way. A woman like Anne could go south to Shenzhen, where there was money; but Shenzhen money could be earned in many ways. There were *xiaojies* who worked as secretaries and there were three-with *xiaojies*: *xiaojies* like Li Jiali and *xiaojies* like Anne. All of them were doing whatever they could to earn money. And they were surrounded by plenty of men who had sold their souls long ago, and often the women had to negotiate this uncertain world alone.

AT THE END OF THE SEMESTER, before the Chinese New Year, Miss Ou slipped an envelope under my door. Inside the envelope was a letter, a copy of her health certificate, and five hundred yuan. The letter was in broken English:

Dear Pete,

How long have to see you, where you has gone recently?

Please remember: "First thing first." Can you tell me. May I help you?

"Make every-thing risk must rise early."

"Take a chance! All life is a chance the man who goes furthest is generally the one who is willing to do and dare."

"Although language isn't complete interlinked, it isn't misunderstood to express love."

"The best relationships are these which we create at our own expense with our own honesty and understanding."

Because not easy, so we should double cherish.

"Miracles sometimes occur, but one has to work terribly hard for them."

"Bold and mighty forces will come to your aid."

"A good wife and health is a man's best wealth." "Happiness is being married to your best friend."

"Think more and become wiser." Your own are wonderful!

May I ask a favor of? I sure you able to do something. I'm sorry to trouble you, I do appreciate your kindly help. Please to my home have food, spend Spring Festival together, shall we? The best of luck to you!

Sincerely,

Ou Xiaomei

P.S. This is my health certificate.

The health certificate noted that she was 1.70 meters tall and weighed sixty-seven kilograms. There weren't any problems with her heart, chest, or lungs. Her teeth, nose, and ears were also good. She was listed at thirty years of age, which was not true; the certificate was a photocopy of the original and obviously this detail had been doctored. But everything else looked accurate.

On the upper right corner of the health certificate was a photograph of Miss Ou. The picture was at least twenty years old. It was a small black-and-white snapshot of a much younger Miss Ou wearing heavy-rimmed glasses and neatly curled hair. She was smiling in the photograph, a pretty young woman who looked at the camera with confidence.

The one-hundred-yuan notes were folded neatly in half. It was more than half of what Miss Ou made in a month. Even in America it was a good sum, sixty bucks, but in Fuling you could eat for two months on five hundred yuan. If you had that much money twenty times over, you could buy yourself a second child.

I WAS AFRAID OF MISS OU and rarely dealt with her directly. During the first year I had learned that directness only encouraged her; once I asked her firmly to stop coming to my apartment at night, and she became very excited and showed up every evening for the next week. Like all of my Miss Ou stories, it seemed funny when told out of context, but when it happened I was only annoyed and depressed by how desperately unhappy she seemed.

I took the money to Fei Xiaoyun, who worked in a different section of the same department store as Miss Ou. Fei Xiaoyun was possibly the prettiest *xiaojie* I knew in town, as well as one of the kindest; she had been one of the first to talk with Adam and me when our Chinese was still bad. I often stopped to chat with her when I went into town, and I knew that she would understand the problem with Miss Ou. I gave her the money and explained the situation.

"You know that soon it's the Spring Festival," Fei Xiaoyun said. "There are many Chinese traditions at this time of year, and one of them is to give people money. So that's probably why she gave it to you—she just wants to show her kindness."

Years ago, Fei Xiaoyun had been a student at the college, and because of that the sound of her Mandarin was very pleasant. I listened to her clear tones and then I shook my head.

"During the Spring Festival people give money to children," I said. "I understand that tradition. But I'm not a child and you don't give this kind of money to an adult. Would it be appropriate if I gave you five hundred yuan because you're my friend?"

"No," she said. "That wouldn't be appropriate."

"It's the same way with this money. I think it's very strange and it embarrasses me."

"Yes," she said, sighing. "It is a little strange."

That was what I liked the most about Fei Xiaoyun—she didn't feel the need to lie to me just because I was a *waiguoren.* She had enough sympathy for Miss Ou to try to defend her, but at the same time she understood where I was coming from. Sadly she looked at the bills in the envelope.

"Will you please help me and give that back to Miss Ou?" I asked.

"Yes. I'll be sure to do that."

"You can tell her that I'm sorry I can't accept it. But please don't encourage her—I don't want her to bother me anymore. I don't want to be rude, but I don't want her to call me or come to my apartment again."

"I understand. I'll try to tell her that." But I could see that Fei Xiaoyun knew it was hopeless. Miss Ou was one of those who had slipped beyond the pale, and there wasn't much that you could do about people like that. I assumed that whenever I left Fuling for good there would be some kind of minor hassle with Miss Ou, which was precisely the way it would happen. But standing there in the department store I didn't worry too much about the future. In Fuling I always dealt with problems one at a time, and right now the most important issue was to give the money back.

I thanked Fei Xiaoyun and wished her a happy Spring Festival. She smiled, placing the envelope in her desk, and a couple weeks later she reported that she had returned it successfully. I put Miss Ou's health certificate in a folder where it could be forgotten. But sometimes I found myself thinking about the old photograph, and I wondered why the young woman had never married, and what had happened to make her the way she was today. For some reason I never threw the photograph away.

老师

THE TEACHER

"EVERYBODY NEEDS SOME KIND OF FAITH," says Kong Ming. "Whether it's religion, or Capitalist Democracy, or Communism—regardless of what the faith is, everybody needs something. My faith is the Communist Party. I first wanted to join when I was a college student, but at that time I wasn't accepted."

Teacher Kong is a Party Member and a former peasant and a current instructor of Ancient Chinese Literature in the Chinese department of Fuling Teachers College. He is thirty-three years old, and there are a few streaks of silver in his black hair. He has a soft smile that is shadowed by the barest hint of a mustache on his upper lip. He knows a great deal about Han Dynasty poetry, and his three-year-old son has the given name Songtao, which means "waves of pines": the sound a pine forest makes when the wind blows.

"It's a common phrase in Chinese poetry," Teacher Kong explains. "It was also used once by Shelley—I read it in translation. There's a poem he wrote about a forest, where he describes the trees making that same sound. I think the forest was in Italy but I'm not certain."

There are only 58 million Party Members in all of China—less than 5 percent of the population. For more than a decade, Teacher Kong was interested in joining, but it wasn't until last year that he was finally accepted, after a formal application and a series of interviews and evaluations that took months to complete. "In the past they used to look more carefully at your home and your family," he says. "Your background was very important. But that's not the way it is now—they look at your ideas instead, which is better.

"I think the basic goals of Communism—to help the poor, to make things equal—I think those are good goals. The Party certainly has problems, of course, and some people join for selfish reasons. They want more power, and after they become Party Members they only care about themselves. That's not good—that's why we have corruption, because a few people only care about themselves. And if the Communist Party gets worse and worse, of course the common people won't believe in it. This is the biggest problem right now. But I believe that most people still support the Party, and I certainly agree with its ideas. There always will be some problems, but the fundamental goals are good."

ONE OF THE FUNDAMENTAL GOALS of the Chinese Communist Party has always been stability for the average citizen, which traditionally has been maintained through the system of state-run work units. Teacher Kong's *danwei* is the college, and as a result his life has none of the scramble and uncertainty of the entrepreneur. His three-room apartment is owned and maintained by the college, which rents it for roughly thirty yuan a month—a sum so small that its payment is essentially a formality. The college also provides Teacher Kong with health insurance, as well as a retirement pension. At less than eight hundred yuan, his monthly salary isn't high, but the big perk is security, because it's unheard-of for the college to fire an employee. Teacher Kong has what Americans would call tenure, except that traditionally in Communist China such tenure has been given the moment you start your job, and it has been given to everybody who works for a state *danwei:* teachers, government officials, post office employees, train attendants, dock laborers, factory workers. Under Chinese Communism, all of them have job security—"the iron rice bowl."

But already this term is slipping into the past tense, and people in Fuling tend to use it in one of two ways. Usually it is heavy with irony, as locals emphasize a wasteful system that needs further reform; but there are still those who use it nostalgically as they describe something comfortable that is steadily disappearing. The way this term is used depends on where one stands in the *danwei* system, and increasingly the government is adopting the more critical viewpoint of the iron rice bowl. As a result, no rice bowl is entirely iron, and no *danwei* is without reform, and never is Socialism without those Chinese Characteristics that are developing into a strange marriage of Communism and Capitalism, constantly shifting and redefining the parameters of lives like Teacher Kong's.

The first major change will hit him later this year, in June of 1998, when his apartment will be privatized. No longer will he enjoy the formality of a thirty-yuan rent payment; instead, the apartment's fifty-four square meters will be sold to him for a little more than ten thousand yuan. It's a good price—but nevertheless a lot of money for a man who makes eight hundred yuan a month, and whose wife makes even less as a freelance photographer. There is, of course, the possibility that the apartment's value will rise, providing Teacher Kong with a profit in the long run—but nothing in the past has taught him to see an apartment as an investment. Nobody in Fuling speaks of mortgages and refinancing, and it's unheard of for a common citizen to get a loan from a bank. To make a big purchase, you pay from your own savings, or you borrow from family and friends—or, if the money can't be found, you don't buy at all.

Other cracks are spreading across the iron bowl. Already the government has decided that the *danwei* insurance system will be reformed. The details of this change have yet to be determined, but probably Fuling's teachers will have to buy their own policies from China's fledgling insurance companies. And soon Teacher Kong and his wife, Xu Lijia, will have to deal with the issue of schooling. Elementary schools in the East River district charge the standard fees—more than one hundred yuan per semester in tuition, along with book and uniform charges. Such expenses are not difficult to bear, but the quality of public education in Fuling has started to vary widely, because schools with good reputations can charge higher tuition fees, thus paying higher salaries to keep top-rate teachers. The East River institutions are slipping in this competitive environment, and most teachers at the college choose to send their children to downtown schools. But such transfers are increasingly expensive—a few years ago it cost eight thousand yuan to change districts, and now the one-time fee has leaped to twelve thousand. How much higher will it be in three years, when Kong Songtao is ready for school? And is it worth the money? Are there other Characteristics that will crop up in the once-stable world of the Socialist *danwei,* leading to more difficult decisions for the family? And will these changes ever reach the point where Teacher Kong no longer speaks of Communism as a *xinyang,* a faith?

BUT EVEN AMID THESE CHANGES, Teacher Kong is not particularly worried. Decisions will be made when necessary; in the meantime, he teaches ancient Chinese literature and watches his son grow up. This equanimity has nothing to do with Teacher Kong's status as a Party Member, committed to the government's policies. Instead, he is calm for the same reason that so many other Chinese are strangely placid in the midst of changes that seem overwhelming to outsiders. Quite simply, he has seen far worse.

"When I was a boy we didn't have enough to eat," says Teacher Kong. "Especially in 1972 and 1973—those were very bad years. Part of it was that we lived in a remote place where the land wasn't very good, but also there were some problems associated with the Cultural Revolution—problems with production and agricultural methods. It was a little better later in the 1970s, but still it wasn't too good. We never ate meat; I was always hungry. Every day we ate rice gruel, and we only had a little bit of that. Rarely did we have salt. We ate weeds, wildflowers, pine needles—I've eaten all those things.

"My mother died when I was five, after she gave birth to my sister. Of course, we didn't have milk or anything like that to help the baby, who died as well. I don't remember that. But at the age of ten my father died, which I do remember. He got sick suddenly, a very bad cold, and in three days he was dead.

"After that, things were even worse. My grandfather wasn't strong enough to work, and I was too young to do much, so my uncle had to support all of us. At that time the Production Team in that village was very bad, and they weren't of any help. Later, things improved and they were able to assist us, but for many years it was terrible."

All of Kong Ming's early life took place in the mountains outside Fengdu, a town that nowadays has about thirty thousand residents. From his childhood home it took an hour by foot to reach the nearest road, which was three hours by rough bus ride from Fengdu, and as a result Kong Ming never saw the town until he was fourteen years old. He helped his uncle farm the land, where they grew wheat and corn on the slopes, rice in the paddies, and vegetables where they could. "The work didn't seem hard back then," he says, "but it would be hard now, because I'm not used to it anymore." He looks at his hands and smiles, for now they are the hands of a teacher—ink-stained and soft, the dirt and calluses long gone.

"I go to the countryside now," he says, "and I can't believe how hard the work looks, even around the suburbs of Fuling, where the peasants are relatively well off. I can't believe I used to live in a place like that. And I see the students here at the college, most of whom are from peasant families, and I want to tell them that they shouldn't waste their parents' money. So many of our students are from backgrounds like mine, but they've already forgotten how hard the work is. On weekends they go out and waste so much money."

Only a few of his middle-school classmates made it to high school, and none of the others tested well enough to go to college. He was admitted to Sichuan Teachers College, a four-year institution in Chengdu that is the top teachers college in the province. After graduating in 1988, he taught in a Fengdu trade school for six years, and then he was offered a job in Fuling.

Almost anybody in America who has made a rise like Teacher Kong's would be full of the confidence—and perhaps the arrogance—of the self-made man, but it is characteristically Chinese that such pride is completely absent. He rarely talks about his background, and he never emphasizes its difficulty, because he knows that things easily could have been worse.

"My family never had any trouble during the Cultural Revolution," he says, when asked about political problems. "We were too poor. After Landlords, there were three types of peasants: Rich Peasants, Middle Peasants, and Poor Peasants. We were very poor—when you were as poor as we were, you didn't have anything to worry about during the Cultural Revolution. As long as you didn't steal something, or kill somebody, or commit another crime, there wasn't anything to worry about. Nobody in my family was persecuted.

"I can remember some of the village meetings at the end of the Cultural Revolution, in 1974 and 1975. I didn't really understand, of course, because I was only in elementary school, but I remember them clearly. They would take a Landlord, or maybe a Capitalist Roader—usually somebody who had been trying to sell firewood or vegetables—and they would have a meeting to criticize him. He'd stand like this."

Teacher Kong demonstrates: feet together, waist bent slightly, head bowed so that his chin is tucked against his chest. For a few seconds he stands completely still, and then he laughs and continues the story.

"They didn't do the airplane so much. Mostly they had to stand like this, and if they didn't bow their head far enough, the people would force them down. I remember one older man in the village who had been a Landlord. At all the meetings they made him stand for hours like that, with his head bowed. He would shift his head to the side, because it was more comfortable that way, and finally after all the meetings his head was like that all the time. Even after the Cultural Revolution was finished, he would walk around the village with his head bent to the side."

Teacher Kong is still standing, and now he tilts his head to the left and walks across the room. He laughs again and shakes his head.

"When you're a child, all of that seems very exciting. Of course it has some influence on a child—you see something like that when you're small, and it affects your thoughts. At the time we thought it was fun. During a meeting they might criticize the father of a classmate, and then afterward we'd make fun of the child: 'Your father's a Counter-Revolutionary! Counter-Revolutionary! Counter-Revolutionary!' It wasn't something we understood, but we used to say it."

He imitates a child, pointing and laughing and covering his mouth as he says the words, *Fan Geming, Fan Geming, Fan Geming.* Counter-Revolutionary, Counter-Revolutionary, Counter-Revolutionary. And then suddenly he is serious again.

"Nowadays people look back at that time and say it was absurd. It's almost funny, because the things people did were so *huangtong,* so ridiculous. But back then, all of that was serious—it was real life. It wasn't funny. It's impossible to understand that today.

"And perhaps in the future it will be the same with what's happening now. Ever since Deng Xiaoping's Reform and Opening, everything has been much better, and we know that those problems of the Cultural Revolution will never happen again. But still it might look different in the future. Today we look back at the Cultural Revolution and say it's so ridiculous, but perhaps in the future people will look back at today, and maybe they'll say the same thing."

CHAPTER TEN

Chinese New Year

AT THE END OF THE FALL SEMESTER, our third-year students went off to do their practice teaching. In December, Adam and I made a trip south to watch a couple of our favorite students teach; they were training at middle schools in Wulong, a town up the Wu River near the border with Guizhou province. It was a very remote area and the schools were honored to receive foreign guests; for two days we gave speeches and attended banquets, and we played in an exhibition basketball game.

Adam and I had spent so much time together that we could give a good joint speech without a bit of planning; we knew how to play off each other and everything always went smoothly. We gave the Wulong speeches half in English and half in Chinese, and mostly we tried to get the students excited, which wasn't difficult. After every speech hundreds of them crowded around, asking for autographs, and we signed until finally the cadres dragged us off to some other event. We were scheduled to give speeches and attend meetings for virtually every hour that we were in Wulong.

After two days of that we were completely exhausted. Often my days in Sichuan ended like that, in absolute and total exhaustion. Part of it was that I was usually sick—I had chronic sinus infections from the pollution, which finally made me stop running, and my health was bad enough that I was infected with tuberculosis during that year. By the time I left Fuling, my Peace Corps medical folder would be swollen with the illnesses and injuries of those two years: tuberculosis, amebic dysentery, chronic sinusitis, a broken ear drum, a broken nose (from basketball), one eye with dramatically reduced eyesight (a mystery).

The climate wasn't healthy, but mostly I was run down by the pressures of daily life as a *waiguoren.* It was tiring always to be the center of attention, and being a foreigner meant that you were more likely to attract complications. Often there was some minor crisis or issue that demanded my attention—a Miss Ou incident, or somebody from the teahouse calling me every day for a week, or something of that sort. I didn't really mind, because this was the life I had chosen; the teaching itself was rarely stressful, and I pushed myself in the city simply because I found my Chinese life fascinating.

Traveling usually added more stress, and there was nothing harder than spending time in a tiny river town like Wulong, where the pressures of Fuling were intensified. It was also rewarding, because the people were thrilled to see outsiders, but in the end it was impossible to maintain any control over your life in a place like that. The hardest thing for me to imagine was that someday foreigners might live in towns like Wulong. It was bound to happen as Reform and Opening accelerated, but I couldn't envision it, because it seemed to me that if a *waiguoren* lived there he wouldn't last three months. The intentions of the community would be nothing but the best, but they would kill you with kindness—an endless parade of banquets and special events. After two days in Wulong, Adam and I became sick, and it took us half a week to recover.

We had five weeks' vacation for the Spring Festival, or Chinese New Year, starting in mid-January. Sunni went to Thailand; Noreen headed off to southern China and Vietnam. Adam decided to take the boat to Shanghai and then swing south to visit Anne in Shenzhen. I planned to do some hiking alone in the Guizhou mountains, but the more I thought about travel in China the more clearly I remembered the last train ride I had taken in Xinjiang. I also thought about the exhaustion of Wulong, and my comfortable Fuling routines started to look better and better.

In six months I would leave the city. As the vacation started, I realized that my time in Fuling was limited, and I knew that there was no other place in China where I wanted to spend the Spring Festival. It was the biggest Chinese holiday, a time for family reunions; Fuling was my home, and so I stayed.

I WOKE UP EARLY IN THE MORNINGS and wrote for three or four hours. That was the English part of my day; usually it was over by ten or eleven in the morning. To clear the language from my head, I studied Chinese in my apartment for another hour, reading a newspaper or listening to tapes, and after that I went to lunch at the Students' Home. In the afternoons and evenings I walked around the city, and often I ate dinner with friends. Teacher Liao and her husband had me over a couple of times, as did Teacher Kong, and there were several people in the city who often invited me to eat. If nobody had me to dinner I ate in town or went back to the Students' Home, which was the same as eating with friends.

English became a language strictly for writing; during that month I spoke nothing but Chinese. Later I would look back on that holiday as my favorite time in China, because at last my Chinese life was settled, and I saw precisely how I fit into the local routines. All of it had to do with Ho Wei—not a single English department colleague invited me over or had anything to do with me during the vacation. Later that spring, I would discover that this was the result of explicit instructions, because from the moment Adam and I had arrived in Fuling, the department authorities had told the English faculty not to associate closely with the foreign teachers. Like so many of the cadres' policies, it stemmed from a vague and pointless paranoia, and perhaps the saddest part was that it was extremely effective: I was much closer to the uneducated family at the local noodle restaurant than I was to the English-speaking teachers in the college. But by isolating me, the department authorities had simply pushed me to become something else, and now even if they changed their minds I would never trade the life I had for English-speaking friendships. During the holiday I was the only *waiguoren* in the city, but for the first time I no longer thought of myself as being alone.

Groups of local children often came up to my apartment, because I had strings of holiday lights on my balcony and it was beautiful out there at night, high above the Wu River. Sometimes there were girls led by Ho Li, an eleven-year-old who shared my family name and called me *gege*, older brother. Other times I was visited by packs of wild boys who followed Wang Xuesong, the nine-year-old across the hall. He lived with his grandparents and his mother, who was divorced, and the adults in his apartment had strictly told him never to bother the *waiguoren* neighbor.

But Little Wang and I learned how to trick them; either he'd come with a group of other kids, or he would leave his apartment and walk loudly down the steps before turning around, sneaking back, and knocking softly on my door. I enjoyed talking with him; he would tell me about incidents on campus, life at school, and the fat kid in his class, who was so thoroughly despised that he had been nicknamed Chiang Kai-shek. Little Wang liked to watch my television, look at my photographs, and shout at people from my balcony; I let him do whatever he wished. I missed my niece and nephew at home in Missouri and it was good to have a child around the apartment.

Together Little Wang and I strung nearly one hundred holiday lights across my balcony, and now at night you could see them from the Yangtze. It took us two hours to put all of them up, and afterward, as a reward, I let Little Wang throw all of the burned-out bulbs down to the sidewalk six floors below, where they popped and shattered nicely. I didn't feel particularly guilty about encouraging his delinquency; whenever the college workmen came to replace a light in my apartment they did exactly the same thing. And they seemed to enjoy it nearly as much as Little Wang, the workmen giggling as the glass exploded on the sidewalk.

Downtown Fuling glowed bright across the river in the evenings. The city streets were strung with red lanterns and strands of electric lights, and all of the trees were decorated. The small park at South Mountain Gate had been turned into a riot of color—its coal-stained shrubs and trees were covered with lights, dazzling in the heart of the city. Crowds gathered to look at the park and take photographs. As the holiday approached, it seemed that everybody in the city came out in the evenings, families and young couples and packs of children, all of them strolling aimlessly up and down the streets: buying snacks, gazing at shopfronts, watching the crowds. Soldiers had returned home on leave, and they marched proudly in their uniforms, keeping an eye out for *xiaojies.* Food stands sprouted along the streets and stairways—barbecue grills, potato vendors, tofu men, hot pot stands—and it seemed that everybody ate out on the sidewalk. I did, too; I had always liked Fuling at night, but now everything had intensified, and I had never seen a place with so much energy. Even the pathetic trees along the main road finally seemed alive, glowing with bright white lights. These lights had been wired carelessly and sometimes they exploded and caught fire, the tree shining proudly with a sudden burst of flame and smoke. The pedestrians would stop to watch, chattering and laughing, and after the flame died—the tree hissing softly, the smoke drifting upward—they kept walking through the brilliant city.

ON THE NIGHT BEFORE THE CHINESE NEW YEAR, the family at the Students' Home invited me to dinner. It was the most important meal of the year, a traditional time for family reunions—the equivalent of Christmas dinner in America. Huang Xiaoqiang closed the restaurant early, and together we walked up to his apartment at the foot of Raise the Flag Mountain.

Huang Kai was now two years old, and he had reached a stage where he was frightened by *waiguoren*. From the beginning he had gone through cycles; he was a skittish child and sometimes he played with me and other times he was terrified by the sight of my face. It was a strange, mixed reaction—part fear and part fascination. Whenever a *waiguoren* appeared on television, Huang Kai became excited and called out "Ho Wei!" His parents said that he often talked about me at home, but for some reason that winter he had become terrified of seeing me in person.

The child started crying when I arrived at their apartment for the New Year's dinner. "He's been doing that off and on for an hour," his mother said. "I told him you were coming and he started to cry; I don't know why."

"I'm sorry," I said. "I wouldn't have come if I had known he'd be unhappy."

"No, that doesn't matter! He'll be fine—I'll just take him into another room for a while."

I sat on the couch with Huang Xiaoqiang and his father, Huang Neng, and together we watched television. That seemed to be what most Chinese people did for the Spring Festival—for two days they watched as much television as possible. The first year I taught in Fuling, I had given my students a vacation assignment to write about what they did on the day of the holiday, because I was interested in learning about Chinese traditions. The second year I did not repeat that assignment. It was depressing to read about a holiday older than Christmas whose celebration seemed to have been refined to gazing at televised floor shows.

The Huang men sat smoking. Neat formations of PLA soldiers marched across the television screen. I could hear Huang Kai crying from the back room, but he was starting to calm down. His mother talked to him softly, and occasionally I heard my name as she spoke to the child.

"Your soldiers in America don't march the same way ours do in China, do they?" asked Huang Xiaoqiang.

"No, they don't."

"When Hong Kong returned," asked Huang Neng, "were those soldiers American?"

His son corrected him: "Those were English soldiers!"

"Well, they marched differently from us Chinese—they marched like this." Huang Neng stood up and stomped his feet. He was a small man of forty-nine years and he had the wiry build of a peasant. He marched across the living-room floor, bringing his knees up high. "Is that how you march in America, too?"

"More or less."

"We think it looks strange—it certainly looked funny when Hong Kong returned!"

"In Western countries we don't march like you do in China, and we think the way you march looks strange. It reminds us of *Xitele* and *Nacui*—Hitler and the Nazis."

"Oh, I see—you don't like them because of the war, right?"

"That's right. It's the same as the way you Chinese see the Japanese."

"We Chinese don't like the Japanese at all."

"I know."

"They killed many Chinese people in Nanjing. And they bombed your America, too."

"Yes, they did. In Hawaii."

"In China we call them 'small devils,' or 'Japanese devils.' What do you call the Japanese in America?"

"During the war, people called them Japs."

Huang Neng liked the sound of the word and he said it a few times: Jia-pahs, Jia-pahs, Jia-pahs.

"Is it an insult?" he asked.

"Yes. It's like saying 'small devil' here in China."

"So you Americans also don't like the Japanese?"

"I think that now most people like them, or at least they don't hate them; we don't call them Japs anymore. But during the war Americans didn't like them."

"That's because they bombed your America."

"That's right."

"But then you dropped the atomic bomb on Japan."

"Yes. We did that twice."

"America was the first country to have the atomic bomb."

"That's true."

"In science your America is number one in the world. That's why you are a *chaoji guojia*—a supercountry!" Huang Neng gave me the thumbs-up and returned to watching television. It had been a satisfactory conversation, which pleased him; he was the oldest man of the household and it was his duty to make me feel at home. On television the soldiers were finished, and now there was a floor show involving colored hoops and *xiaojies* in tight costumes. Feng Xiaoqin returned with Huang Kai. He looked at me uncertainly and started to play with a toy car in the far corner of the room. I ignored him until he accidentally rolled the car close to me. I picked it up, watching the child shrink in fear. I pushed the toy back to him and he turned away, shyly.

Wang Chaosu, Huang Neng's wife, finished preparing dinner and all of us sat down. There were several pork dishes, all very spicy, and tofu and bean sprouts, and a fish from the downtown market. We could have eaten for three days and still there would have been food left over. There was rice, too, and Wang Chaosu spooned some into my bowl.

"I know you like to eat your rice with your meal!" she shouted. "That's different from us Chinese! We like to eat it afterward!"

Wang Chaosu shouted everything at me, the way many Americans do when they meet foreigners with bad English. She was my favorite character in the whole family, an earthy, illiterate woman who spoke only the dialect, and she had a wonderful sense of humor. She loved the way that I always referred to myself as "the foreign devil," and she also thought it was funny that Adam and I lied constantly about each other and the new volunteers. Back in the fall we had told Wang Chaosu that she could charge Sunni and Noreen five times the normal price for noodles, and in return for half of that we wouldn't tell them they were being cheated.

"That's not polite," she said, shocked. "They just arrived and we shouldn't cheat them."

"Who cares?" I said. "They're just foreign devils! And they have so much money—both of them are very rich."

"You're lying! I know you're lying! Next time I'll cheat you!" That was a constant joke between us—every time we came to the restaurant she talked about how badly she was going to cheat the foreign devils.

She was a very good cook and the Spring Festival meal was excellent. Periodically Wang Chaosu would shout out, "It's very bad!" and I would reassure her that in fact it was perfect, and then she would spoon some more into my bowl. *"Man man chi!"* she'd shout. "Eat slowly!"

After dinner we returned to the couch and I played with Huang Kai. He was over his fear now and we rolled a car back and forth, the child laughing. His father was watching television while the grandfather sat in a chair nearby, carefully cutting white and red tissue paper into strips to make *fenpiao,* or tomb decorations. The *fenpiao* were long narrow tubes made of white paper, with a band of red in the middle and thin white strands hanging down from the bottom. Tomorrow for New Year's Day the family were going to Baitao, their home village, where they would use the *fenpiao* to decorate their ancestors' tombs.

"We'll go to my father's tomb," Huang Neng said. "I usually go there at least twice a year. He died after Liberation."

It always seemed to me that this word should stick in the mouths of people like Huang Neng, who had been Liberated from having a father when the Communists shot him. But like everybody else I knew in Fuling, he used the term without a trace of irony. I asked him how old he had been when his father died.

"I was ten years old."

"That's very young."

"At that time I didn't understand death," he said. "At ten years you don't understand anything."

He was smiling as he worked, cutting the paper. I rolled the car past his grandson, who chased after it, laughing and shrieking.

"Your Christmas is the same as our Spring Festival, isn't it?" Huang Neng asked.

"More or less. It's our most important holiday."

"Do you go to your ancestors' tombs at Christmas?"

"No, we don't have that tradition. Most Americans don't know where their ancestors' tombs are. It's an immigrant country and people often move. You see, my grandparents' tombs aren't in my hometown; they're in California, which is like going from here to Shanghai. I don't know for certain where my other ancestors are—some are in Italy, others are in Germany, and a few are in Ireland and England."

"So many countries!"

"Most Americans are like that."

"You couldn't visit tombs in all of those places for Christmas. Imagine how much money it would cost!"

"Certainly it would cost too much. Europe is very far from my home."

"Well," he said, "tomorrow we just have to go to Baitao. On the bus it's only four yuan."

All of us sat together, watching television. An electric coil heater kept us warm and the men used it to light their cigarettes. The floor shows were better than usual. The holiday wasn't depressing at all now that I was sitting with the family rather than reading about it in my students' papers. We chatted and joked for a while, and suddenly Feng Xiaoqin became serious.

"When you first came here," she said, "were you sometimes disgusted by the Chinese people?"

I was taken aback by the question and I didn't see where it had come from. I asked her what she meant.

"Do you think that some people are very rude, because they laugh at you?"

Again I didn't know how to respond—it was very kind of them to have me in their home, and we seemed far away from anything unpleasant. Everybody else was intent on the television, and I thought it was better to talk about something else.

"No," I said, "I think people are very friendly here."

"No, no, no," she said, impatiently. "Like the time you and Mei

Zhiyuan were eating in the restaurant, and that woman was laughing at the two of you."

Mei Zhiyuan was Adam's Chinese name. I remembered the incident, which had been minor—a month before, one of the karaoke *xiaojies* had been laughing at us, mocking our Chinese and the way we ate. She made a few remarks and we told her to shut up and mind her own business. Usually we did nothing about the laughter, but we considered the restaurant to be our turf; people had no right to mock us there, especially not karaoke *xiaojies.*

I could see that Feng Xiaoqin wanted me to answer honestly. In some ways I felt that she understood me as well as any of the people in Fuling—she was always at the restaurant, where she had seen me react to many things. Like everybody, she watched me carefully, but unlike many others she also seemed to watch with a sense of empathy.

"Yes," I said. "I thought that woman was rude. She was making fun of us and that's why I told her to stop laughing. But it didn't bother me very much; after that she didn't say anything else."

"She has no culture," said Feng Xiaoqin. It was a common way of saying that a person was uneducated. Feng Xiaoqin shook her head and continued: "That's why she treated you like that, because she has no culture. Too many people in Fuling are that way."

"No, most people aren't like that. And it's much better now than it was when we first arrived."

"Still they should not laugh at you. It's very rude, I think."

She was looking at me steadily, and something in her black eyes made me glance away. I gazed at the child, babbling to himself as he played.

"It's not important," I said. "It's very kind of you to have me for dinner tonight—that's much more important. Huang Kai is a very polite host."

She smiled at the child, and we talked about how much he had grown and how many words he could say. We didn't mention that earlier in the evening he had been afraid of me, because now the fear was gone and he was comfortable with me in their apartment. And I said nothing about how in the child's fear I had seen a reflection of all the difficulties that I had ever encountered in Fuling, the people's uncertainty about things new and strange. It was a natural, helpless, human response—an instinct as blameless as a child's. It took time and effort to deal with that, as well as patience, and now I realized how much work had been done on the other side.

There was a great deal of generosity in their having me over for dinner. They had known that the child would cry and possibly offend me, but they had invited me anyway. I thought about Christmas dinner in America, and I wondered if I would invite a foreigner or a black to eat with my family if I knew that my child was afraid of such people. Probably I would—but there would be a point to what I did. I would realize that this was an important lesson for my child, as well as an important gesture toward the guest, and this would make me feel good about it. I would do it for myself as well as for the others involved.

But tonight there wasn't any point. Feng Xiaoqin understood me, but not to the degree that she knew exactly what I saw in Huang Kai and so many others in Fuling. She and her family hadn't invited me in order to make a point about xenophobia, or anything like that. They knew that I was alone on the holiday, and I was their friend; nothing else mattered. They were simply big-hearted people and that was the best meal I ever had in China.

FIREWORKS AT MIDNIGHT CALLED IN THE NEW YEAR. I had left the Huang home early, because I was a little tired, and I was getting ready for bed when the sound started, low and steady like thunder rolling over the hills. The noise grew louder, echoing across the river valley, and I went out on my back balcony to watch.

The Wu River looked sullen in the night. The city was also dark, but as midnight approached the fireworks increased; I could see them flaring and flashing among the streets and stairways. The intensity of the sound doubled, tripled; explosions joined in from Raise the Flag Mountain, and in the distance, across the Yangtze, there were flashes on White Flat Mountain. At the stroke of midnight the entire city gathered itself and roared, its voice reverberating back and forth across the Wu, the windows of the buildings flickering in reflections of sparks and bursts of fire. The old year died; evil spirits fled; deep in the valley's heart the Wu trembled, its water colored by the bright shadow of the blazing city. And finally midnight passed, and the fireworks faded, and we were left with a new year as empty and mysterious as the river that flowed silently through the valley.

THE NEXT MORNING I WENT INTO TOWN, where the streets were full of people wearing their new clothes. Traditionally, on New Year's Day you didn't wear anything old, and especially the children were dressed brightly. Many of the little girls wore makeup; all of the boys carried guns. That seemed to be another holiday tradition: plastic pellet guns were for sale everywhere on special streetside stands, and every male child had a rifle or a pistol, or both. The guns were accurate and powerful, and in America you could sell perhaps two of them before you were sued. In America there was also a chance that a child would use the guns to shoot at birds, dogs, or cats; in Fuling there were very few animals but plenty of people. All around town boys chased after each other, shouting and firing their weapons.

Another New Year's trend was the appearance of student-beggars. There were always beggars around South Mountain Gate; usually they were handicapped, and sometimes there were minority women with filthy children who pulled at your sleeves. But now every time I went to town I saw two or three students, dressed in their uniforms, hanging their heads in shame before message boards that featured long stories under the title "Tuition Needed." The tales were roughly the same—they couldn't afford their high school or college fees, often because of a death in the family, and they asked for donations from passersby. Usually the beggars displayed their school acceptance letters and student identification cards. None of them came from Fuling; they were passing through on the Yangtze boats.

They made good money—piles of five- and ten-yuan notes. It said a great deal about the Chinese respect for education that you could make money that way; I couldn't imagine getting any response in America to such a scam. At least it seemed to be a scam; over the last couple of weeks I had noticed that two of the boys were obviously working together, sharing a uniform and identification. They alternated days, and I could always spot the other one watching while his friend begged. My impression was that in the heart of the holiday they easily pulled in more than one hundred yuan a day. It was a hell of a lot more productive than staying home and watching television.

I took a bus out to the Buddhist temple above the Yangtze and watched the monk tell fortunes. That was Fuling's only real temple—people told me that before the Cultural Revolution there had been more than three hundred temples and shrines in the area, but now there were only three, and one with monks. Usually the temple had but a handful of visitors, but today on the first day of the New Year there were hundreds of people having their fortunes told. On the street below, vendors sold balloons to children, and other children shot the balloons with pellet guns. Everywhere I went, children were crying and throwing fits, and everywhere their parents were buying them whatever they wanted. Like other Chinese holidays, the Spring Festival at moments seemed to be a celebration of the social effects of the one-child policy.

It was a sunny, cold day, and I walked in the hills above the river, where a few people were lighting fireworks and decorating the old tombs. On the path back down to the street I passed a boy sitting on a rock. He was about seven years old and he had a rifle in his lap. As I passed I gave him a long look that said: Don't even think about it. I kept walking down the trail.

The pellet hit me square in the back. I had been listening for the click of the barrel, but the gun was already cocked and he caught me by surprise. He had been ready just in case somebody happened to walk past.

I turned around and walked back slowly. Had he cocked the gun and shot me again in the chest, I might have let him keep it, out of a perverse respect for his gall. But he froze, watching me come closer. I had had enough of this particular New Year's tradition and I grabbed the gun before he could react. He was stunned into silence for a moment and then he started to wail. I turned and walked away. At the bottom of the mountain I could still hear him crying, his voice rising above the fireworks that echoed in the distance.

A few days later some of the neighborhood kids came over and I let them use the rifle to shoot things in my apartment. They compared how much money each had received for the Spring Festival—that was another tradition, as relatives and friends gave children *hongbao,* "red bags" full of cash.

Little Wang had received 1,250 yuan, which was roughly three times the per capita monthly income for an urban Chinese household. All of the other children had cleared between eight hundred and one thousand yuan, except for Fang Siyang, who had made less than seven hundred. She was an adorable girl with pigtails, and I could see that she was embarrassed to have received so little money for the holiday. Once, when I had asked what Fang Siyang was like, Little Wang described her social class succinctly. "Her family," he said, "owns chickens and roosters."

I gave Fang Siyang and the others some American coins and postcards, and they left. Little Wang hung behind, playing with the gun.

"Can I borrow this?" he finally asked.

The last time I had seen Little Wang, he had been particularly well armed, and I asked him what had happened.

"I lost all my guns," he said. "I don't know where they are."

I looked carefully at the boy and saw that he was lying. "Did your family take them away? Tell me the truth."

He stood there staring at his feet, silent.

"Did you hurt somebody else?"

"No," he said. But it wasn't a very firm reply and he hung his head. He fingered the plastic barrel of the gun.

"If I give you this gun," I said, "will you promise not to shoot anybody?"

"I promise."

I gave him the gun, knowing that I was a hopeless hypocrite. He was a cute kid, and when it came to children I was just as weak as Chinese parents. Also, to be honest, I didn't have much affection for the adults in his apartment. They seemed pleasant enough, but they never invited me over, and whenever they saw me in the stairway they spoke very slowly and simply, as if I were a simpleton or a dog. Their intentions weren't bad, I knew, and in any case it didn't justify arming their child. But one of my pet peeves in Fuling was when locals didn't treat me as a person. Ho Wei was stupid, but he wasn't that stupid.

Little Wang slipped the gun into his coat and I let him out the door. He grinned at me and tiptoed down the stairs. I shut the door, quietly. A few seconds later I heard him come charging loudly up the steps, pounding on his door as if he had just returned from playing outside.

IN THE FIRST WEEK OF FEBRUARY I went down river to Fengdu, where I met Teacher Kong and his wife's family. His own parents had died when he was a child, so he always spent New Year's with his in-laws, who lived in the city.

Together we climbed the stone steps up Double Laurel Mountain to get a view of the area, and after a few minutes we passed the 175-meter watermark. We stopped and looked down on the city. It was a gray morning and all of Fengdu lay below us, stretched across the northern bank of the Yangtze. All of it would be flooded by the new reservoir, and I asked Teacher Kong where his wife's family would go after the dam was finished.

"They're moving across the river, to the New Immigrant City," he said. "We can go over there after lunch, if you want to see what it's like."

"When will they move?"

"They don't know yet. Maybe in two years, or longer. Many of the details are still uncertain."

"Will they have to pay anything?"

"The government gives a lot of support, but it's not free. They'll have to pay some money for the apartment, but I don't think it's too much. Probably two thousand yuan or more."

"Are they opposed to it?"

"No," he said. "They want to move. You'll see their current apartment—it's too small. Their new apartment will be nicer, and anyway Fengdu City is so dirty. It's small and crowded. The new city will have more space, and it won't have the same problems with traffic that Fengdu has. Very few people around here oppose the dam."

This was another benefit of the Three Gorges Project, which was a boon to civil engineers and urban planners, who could finally create cities with efficient roads and good sewage systems. And I could see why The Xus didn't mind moving; their apartment was cramped and it was located on a filthy alley. But at the same time I liked Fengdu, although I liked it with a foreigner's eye—I liked the coal-stained gray of its old-fashioned houses, and the narrow cobbled streets that bustled with traffic. It was an old river town and there was a certain charm in its dirtiness and inconvenience.

Xu Lijia was Teacher Kong's wife, and today was her thirtieth birthday. Both of her sisters had come to their parents' apartment to celebrate. The youngest sister was in her early twenties and worked in Fengdu, while the middle sister, whose name was Xu Hua, worked for an insurance company in Xiamen, one of the booming cities on the east coast of China. Neither of the younger sisters was married.

Xu Hua carried a cell phone and contributed three bottles of French wine to the birthday party. We drank a bottle with the dumplings that Mrs. Guo had made, toasting each other. The dumplings were very good. The wine was not so good and Mr. Xu, who was fifty-three years old and worked at the local electric plant, made a face as he drank. But the wine was imported, and Xu Hua was proud to have brought it in honor of her sister's birthday.

I had always liked Teacher Kong's wife; she seemed more comfortable with me than most people on campus were, probably because she was an independent photographer and not a formal part of the college *danwei.* Many entrepreneurs were like that—they dealt much better with *waiguoren* than the average person. The same was true with Xu Hua, the middle sister, who had a certain east-coast sophistication. She told me that I should move to Xiamen, where there were plenty of *waiguoren* and the people were not as backward as those here in Fengdu and Fuling. There were several McDonald's restaurants in Xiamen, she said—a sign of development that struck me as impressive, since I hadn't seen a McDonald's in a year and a half. Xu Hua's hair was cut short, and she wore tight white pants and a bright yellow jacket with padded shoulders. I asked her if she had any interest in living in Sichuan again.

"Why should I come back?" she said, laughing. "Fengdu, Fuling—they're too small and remote; the jobs aren't good. I can return for the Spring Festival every year. That's enough."

As we ate, Mr. Xu told me that he had a younger brother who lived in America. This surprised me, especially when he said that his brother had a doctorate from Columbia University and was now teaching at New York University. It seemed unbelievable that a boy could come from a place like Fengdu and have an American academic career, and I asked Mr. Xu if his brother had gone to school here.

"No, no, no," he said. "My brother grew up in Taiwan, along with my three sisters. My family was split."

He said no more about this until after lunch, when he went into another room and returned with a stack of letters.

"These are from my brother in America," he said. "He usually writes me twice a year."

The stack was tied with string. Mr. Xu undid it carefully, then handed me the letters. All of them had been kept in their original envelopes, although most of the stamps had been steamed off for Mr. Xu's collection. Slowly I leafed through them. Some of the envelopes were from Taiwan and others had been sent from America. Mr. Xu's brother used the complex Chinese script of Taiwan and Hong Kong, and I would have had trouble reading the letters even if I had felt bold enough to take them out of their envelopes. But I had just met Mr. Xu, and so I merely looked at the envelopes and the bare places where the stamps had been.

In some ways it wasn't necessary to read the letters, just as it wasn't necessary to know the full details of Mr. Xu's story. That stack of envelopes was poignant enough—they had been preserved with such reverence that they were heavy with the intimation of a story that I knew could only be sad. And mostly it was clear that this brother in Taiwan had had a very different life than had Mr. Xu in Fengdu.

He handed me a photograph of a Chinese man in his graduation gown, standing before the red brick buildings of Columbia University. The man in the photograph was much younger than Mr. Xu and he was smiling. He had his arm around a pretty Chinese woman. It was a sunny day and the campus looked bright and clean.

"That's when he graduated with his doctorate," Mr. Xu said proudly. "And that's his wife—she's Chinese, too, but she grew up in America."

"Have they ever come here to visit you?"

"No," he said. "I have never met my brother."

After he said that, the envelopes seemed even heavier. I was about to ask how they had been split, but his daughter interrupted and asked how much money I thought the young man made as a teacher at New York University.

"I don't know," I said. "But that's a very good university. Probably he makes at least fifty thousand dollars a year."

"He has a car, too," said Mr. Xu.

"Most people in America do," I said.

"How much does a car cost?"

"It depends. Usually more than ten thousand dollars."

"So he must have a lot of extra money from his salary, especially since she works, too. In his letters he doesn't say very much about money."

"Well, I think they probably have expensive rent, you know. The living expenses in America are very high, especially in New York."

"His wife's father bought them a house. So probably they can save a lot of money, right?"

I wasn't exactly sure what they were getting at, but it seemed they were just curious to find out what the man's life was like in America. They asked how one acquired American citizenship, and they asked what it was like to teach in America. We talked a little about politics, and Mr. Xu asked me what I thought about the Taiwan issue.

Sitting there with the stack of envelopes, I couldn't have been thrown a more loaded question. I replied that I had never been to Taiwan and thus I didn't understand it.

"What do most Americans think about it?" he pressed.

"Most Americans also don't understand the problem very well. I think mostly they want things to be peaceful."

"They think Taiwan is a separate country from China, don't they?"

I was glad to see that at least we had shifted the pronouns—whenever I was on uncertain ground I tried to make it "their America" rather than "my America." That was a small but crucial distinction, but still I found it difficult to respond to his question.

"Most Americans think Taiwan is like a separate country," I said. "It has its own government and economy. But Americans know the history and culture are the same as the mainland's. So maybe they think it should return to China, but only when the people in Taiwan are ready. Most Americans think this problem is much more complicated than Hong Kong."

My response seemed to satisfy him. I considered asking him about his brother, but I decided that it was safest to talk about it with

Teacher Kong some other time. Instead I asked Mr. Xu what Fengdu had been like in the past.

"When Mao Zedong was the leader," he said, "everything was bad. We couldn't talk to a *waiguoren* like you. In those times there wasn't any freedom and there were no rights at all. But after Deng Xiaoping started the Reform and Opening, then everything started to improve. Things are better now."

It was similar to what I heard so often from people in Sichuan, although Mr. Xu's opinions on Mao were much more blunt. He had a poster of Deng Xiaoping in his apartment, hanging prominently above his television.

ON THE WAY ACROSS THE YANGTZE, Xu Hua told me that she knew how to drive an automobile. We were riding an old battered ferry to the southern bank, where they were constructing Fengdu's New Immigrant City. The conversation had been about some other topic when suddenly Xu Hua told me that she knew how to drive.

I had lived in Sichuan long enough to be impressed. "Is that for your job?"

"No," she said. "I studied it in my spare time."

"Just for fun?"

"Yes. It's my hobby."

"That must be very expensive. I know it's expensive in Fuling."

"It's much more expensive in Xiamen—it costs six thousand for the training course. But I think that someday I'll be able to buy a car, so I wanted to learn how to drive now. It's like your America—don't most people in America have cars?"

"Yes. Even students do—I bought one when I was in high school."

"You see? Here in our China the living standard is rising so quickly, and eventually the people will be able to have their own cars just like you do in your America."

The ferry wallowed slowly across the heart of the Yangtze. I had a brief but terrifying vision of Fuling's traffic in twenty years. Xu Hua kept talking.

"I want to go to your America," she said. "New York, especially. Maybe someday I'll go there on business for my company."

We were close to the shore now and I could see an enormous sign that had been erected for investors:

The Great River Will Be Diverted
What Are You Waiting For?
The New City Open District Welcomes You

Three months earlier, the river had been diverted into a man-made channel beside the construction site of the future dam at Yichang. The diversion was the first tangible sign of progress on the dam, and it had been televised live all across China. I had watched part of the coverage, which turned the newly bent river into a celebration of nationalism: construction workers waved their hard hats and cheered while a military band played "Ode to the Motherland." President Jiang Zemin and other politicians gave speeches about the glories of modernization and the success of Socialism with Chinese Characteristics. It was a foggy day and fireworks echoed through the misty hills.

But here in Fengdu the November celebration seemed far away. We disembarked and headed up the sandy bank, walking beside mustard tuber fields and piles of trash. We climbed to a row of peasant homes. The homes were poor and there was a heavy smell of night soil as we passed. The path climbed steeply, winding between more flimsy huts. Xu Hua and the other women were dressed nicely, in high heels and bright clothes, and they moved slowly through the mud. At last we crested the hill, passing through a final cluster of peasant homes, and spread before us was the entire new city of Fengdu, sprawling half-constructed in the mist.

Ever since I first arrived in China, this was what I had been expecting to find someday. All of the cities I had seen were to a large extent construction projects—even Yulin, the ancient city in northern Shaanxi province, had its share of scaffolding and building crews. Fuling changed every month: new buildings sprouted like a forest of fresh white tile and blue glass, and then a month later the buildings aged prematurely as coal stains started creeping down from the roofs. Everywhere in China, people were building; the cities were growing, changing entities, more alive than the countryside; and I always imagined an entire nation rising at once, a China locked by scaffolding rather than the Great Wall.

And now in Fengdu that image had finally become reality: an entire city was being constructed literally before my eyes. There were streets, sidewalks, apartment buildings, businesses—all started; none finished. You could guess only vaguely where the new Fengdu was going, but mostly you could tell that it was going very quickly, and nothing would stop it. Indeed, if it was stopped at this moment, it would be completely worthless. Here in the forgotten heart of China I had found the perfect metaphor of the entire country's development.

Today there was little work being done and the construction site was quiet. But it wasn't empty—crowds of people had come across the river from Fengdu to see their new city. Most of them were well-dressed, the way Chinese looked when they went to spend a day at the park. The men wore neat suits and the high-heeled women stumbled over the rough dirt streets, giggling and splashing mud onto their stockings. They stared at the scaffolding and the enormous piles of dirt that bordered the intersections. The half-built streets bristled with propaganda signs:

The Development Relies on the Immigrants,
the Immigrants Rely on the Development!

The People Build the People's City; If It Is Built Well,
the City Will Serve the People!

We stopped on what would someday be the main street—Pingdu Road—and Xu Hua used her cell phone to call a friend in Xiamen and wish her a happy birthday. Among the new buildings there were still a half-dozen peasant homes, small and resolute in the shadow of their towering neighbors. Chickens wandered down side alleys. Potato fields were squeezed between the construction sites. A few graves still remained, their white tomb decorations hanging limp in the mist, paying homage to the ancestors who lay in the earth below this rising city.

The majority of the peasant homes had been removed and now the people lived in a couple of apartment buildings that had been nearly finished. The ex-peasants sat at tables in the middle of the construction site, drinking tea and playing mah-jongg. I asked Teacher

Kong what the peasants would do now, and he said that most of them helped with construction work and waited for the factory jobs that would be given to them once the city was built. In the meantime, like the ex-peasants whom I had seen in the resettlement area behind Fuling Teachers College, they seemed perfectly content to drink tea and play mah-jongg while the city rose around them.

We took photographs in front of an enormous sign that showed the street plan for the new city. The two younger women liked my baseball cap, and they took turns wearing it for the pictures. Xu Lijia spent a roll of film there, mostly for photos of her sisters in classic *xiaojie* poses: shoulders pushed back, head angled seductively, a soft smile and flirty eyes. For all of the pictures they wore my dirty old Princeton cap. In the background was the sign and the scaffolding and the piles of dirt. We hiked back down to the ferry, through the potato fields and the thick river mist, and Teacher Kong asked, "So, what do you think of the New Immigrant City?"

In truth I had never before seen anything even remotely like it: an entire new city, dozens of dislocated peasants playing mah-jongg, future flood refugees strolling through the construction site as if it were a park. The question was unanswerable, and so I answered in the same way that I did to all questions of that sort.

"I think it's very good," I said.

BACK IN FENGDU we caught a cab on the docks. I was heading to the bus station, and we would drop off the women along the way.

A Yangtze boat had just docked and there was a long line of cabs waiting to go to town. It had started to rain softly, which made the road slippery with mud. Cabs were honking madly. People scurried along the street, holding newspapers over their heads.

The road climbed steeply to the city, and the last stretch was too slick for the cabs. Four of them tried to accelerate up the rise, but their tires spun uselessly. One by one the cars drifted backward. Our driver gunned his engine and made it halfway up the hill before sliding back. He tried again.

After our third attempt, the women got out of the cab and walked up the hill into town. This time our driver started from farther back, working up a great deal of speed, but still his tires spun near the top and we didn't quite make it. The hill was very steep and smooth, and I found myself looking at the situation analytically and thinking of all the simple ways in which it could be improved. This was a very bad habit that nearly all foreigners fell into when they lived in China, and even after a year and a half I couldn't quite shake it.

I thought about how it wouldn't be difficult to regrade the hill, making it less steep, or they could wind the road across the slope of the bank. Probably the simplest solution would be to cut lateral grooves into the pavement, so tires would have something to grip when it rained. I considered all of these options and was engaged in choosing the best solution when suddenly I thought: Screw it. This entire city will be underwater in a few years. Who gives a damn? They can build a new road in the new city across the new river.

On the fifth try we finally made it. I could smell the tires as the driver raced through town. At the station I shook Teacher Kong's hand, thanking him for his hospitality, and then I caught a bus back to Fuling. The road ran low alongside the river. It rained harder. All of the villages I passed through were waiting patiently for the flood.

A COUPLE OF WEEKS LATER I had class with Teacher Kong and asked about his father-in-law, Mr. Xu. He explained that Mr. Xu's father had graduated from university in Wuhan, after which the Kuomintang had sent him to do radio work in Chengdu. That was in the 1940s, and eventually he was transferred to Taipei, the capital of Taiwan. His wife and two young children stayed behind with relatives in Fengdu. The move wasn't permanent, and always Mr. Xu's father thought he would return to his family in Sichuan.

But after 1949, when the Kuomintang fled to Taiwan, the family was divided for good. They couldn't even exchange letters, and Mr. Xu, who was a young child in Fengdu, started a long lifetime of helpless bad luck.

"After Liberation their life was very hard," Teacher Kong explained. "His mother starved to death in the early years, because things were so bad in the countryside. The children barely survived, and once they started school they had many problems with persecution, because their father was in Taiwan. During the Cultural Revolution they were labeled

Pantu, 'Traitors,' and *Tewu,* 'Special Agents'—spies, really. At that time there were the Nine Black Categories—do you know about those? There were Landlords, Rich Peasants, Counter-Revolutionaries, Bad Elements, Rightists, Traitors, Special Agents, Capitalist Roaders, and the Old Stinking Ninth, who were intellectuals. You and I would be the Old Stinking Ninth—sometimes even now teachers like us will call each other that, as a joke.

"The two children didn't suffer much violence, but they were persecuted. Mostly it meant they didn't have opportunities. If they wanted to study past middle school, or get a good job in a factory, they had no chance. And during the political meetings everybody criticized them, even though they had hardly known their father.

"After Reform and Opening, Mr. Xu started sending letters to Taiwan to see if his father was still alive. Sometime after 1980, he found him—until then he didn't even know if his father was dead or not. They started corresponding, and in 1988 his father returned to the mainland to visit for the first time. He had a good job in Taipei with the telegraph company—he was basically the same rank as a high cadre is here on the mainland. He had remarried after Taiwan was split, and he had other children, including the son who is now in America.

"After China-Taiwan relations started to improve, the government began to give jobs to people like my wife's father, because they had been persecuted. This was a way to improve relations. So in 1988, Mr. Xu was given a job in the electric plant. But of course by that time he had already had a very hard life. Even today he doesn't like to talk about the Cultural Revolution."

I thought of the old man in Fengdu with his stack of envelopes. So often my experiences in Sichuan were like that—I brushed against people just long enough to gain the slightest sense of the dizzying past that had made them what they were today. It was impossible to grasp all of the varied forces that had affected Mr. Xu's life and would continue to affect him in the future—the war, the Taiwan split, the Cultural Revolution; the dammed river and the new city; his pretty daughter in Xiamen with her cell phone and driving lessons. How could one person experience all of that, helpless from start to finish, and remain sane?

But I remembered the poster of Deng Xiaoping above his television, and I remembered the way he had grimaced while drinking the bad

French wine that his daughter had brought from Xiamen. It was clear that he didn't like the taste of the wine, but he knew that it was an expensive and prestigious part of the celebration, and thus he drank it dutifully until his glass was empty. Afterward his daughter refilled the glass. He drank that, too.

NEAR THE END OF VACATION I was involved in a public argument on Gaosuntang, the main uptown intersection in Fuling. It happened out of the blue, and it was by far the most serious dispute I had ever been involved in.

Often in the evenings I ate there during the holiday, because I had gotten to know a few of the regulars who worked the sidewalk. Zhang Longhua was my main friend; during the day he sold cigarettes and ran a pay phone, and at night he peddled kebabs from a barbecue stand. He was a friendly, even-tempered man, and I had noticed that the regulars tended to defer to him. Occasionally there were disputes out there at night—sometimes between customers and salesmen, but more commonly between the vendors, who had staked out certain spheres of influence on the busy sidewalk. At night the walk was crowded and a barbecue man like Mr. Zhang could clear fifty yuan on a good night. Last year he had sold kebabs down in Shenzhen, but he returned to Fuling because the overhead was lower.

Once I saw two barbecue *xiaojies* engage in a vicious turf fight, the kind that started with cursing and graduated to hair-pulling, growing increasingly violent until finally they were screaming and tearing at each other's clothes while a crowd gathered. The strange thing was that both of the women worked barbecue stands with men whom I assumed were their husbands or boyfriends, and yet these men stood by passively during the fight. They seemed embarrassed, or stunned; one of them kept his attention on the grill and fiddled with the coals as if nothing was happening. The other man simply watched dumbly. At last Mr. Zhang stepped in and stopped the fight, but by then the shirt of one of the women had been badly torn and she stood there in her bra, cursing and spitting, until finally somebody led her home. After she was gone her husband stayed behind, quietly working his grill.

That sort of fight was unusual; most nights the regulars got along well and supported each other if there were difficulties. I liked this aspect of Gaosuntang—there was a sense of community, with Mr. Zhang at the center, and by knowing him I came to meet the other vendors. One of them was a ten-year-old shoeshine girl who had dropped out of elementary school because her family couldn't afford the fees. I never knew how to react to that; often I had my shoes shined in town, and sometimes I figured that I might as well give the girl my business. Other nights I decided that it was horrible to have your shoes shined by a ten-year-old elementary school dropout, so I went to somebody else instead. Like many aspects of my life in Fuling, it was inconsistent and I never could figure out what was the right thing to do.

One night near the end of the holiday I ordered five kebabs from Mr. Zhang, who invited me to sit on his stool, as he always did. A few of the other vendors came over to chat, as well as a number of passersby who stopped to stare at the *waiguoren.*

After a while the attention died down. I finished the kebabs and sat there reading the *Chongqing Evening Times.* I felt somebody come close, and then he leaned forward and shouted "Hahh-lloooo!" in my face. He shouted as loudly as he could, and after that he laughed. I didn't look up—there was no reason to acknowledge people like that.

I felt him move away and I assumed that he had left; usually the people who harassed me were best handled by being ignored. But a moment later he returned, grabbing one of the sausages from Mr. Zhang's barbecue stand. He shoved the sausage past my newspaper and into my face. *"Chi! Chi! Chi!"* he shouted. "Eat! Eat! Eat!"

There were two things in particular that could anger me quickly in Fuling. One was any sort of physical violation—somebody shoving, or grabbing at me, or pushing past rudely. The other was when people treated me like an animal, grunting or gesturing bluntly because they assumed that the *waiguoren* was very slow and couldn't speak Chinese. The man with the sausage had successfully touched both of these sensitivities at once, and my customary passivity disappeared immediately.

I stood up quickly and knocked the sausage out of his hand. He was a small man in his late thirties, and he moved back, surprised. I stepped forward. "Why are you bothering me?" I asked. He stuttered, fumbling for words. I took my hand and placed it even with the top of his head, and then I drew it back, level. It came to my chin.

"You are much smaller than me," I said. "You should not bother people who are bigger. Next time I'll fix you."

He took another step backward and I sat down again. The people around us had become quiet. For the first time I looked carefully at the man and saw that he was trouble. There was a mean look in his eyes and clearly he was poor. He gathered himself to speak.

"I have friends who are bigger than you," he said.

"I'd like to meet them," I said.

"They're just up the street."

"Go get your friends," I said. "I'll stay here and wait for you. Go—blow away." It was a common insult and a few of the people laughed. The little man didn't move.

He said something else, angrily, which I didn't understand. Mr. Zhang came over, and I asked him if the man was his friend.

"No," said Mr. Zhang. "He shines shoes. He has no culture. You do not want to bother with him."

"I wonder what kind of little thing he is," I said. It was another common insult in Sichuan, to ask a person what kind of thing he was. I should not have been baiting him further but for some reason I couldn't stop. Logically I knew that the scene was absurd—as the big man of the dialogue I weighed in at all of 135 pounds, and the five-footer was threatening to go get his big friends.

But nevertheless there was a serious air to the confrontation, and already I was sensing that to both of us it meant more than a simple exchange of insults. The man was poor, and in my leisure he undoubtedly saw money and the scorn that comes with it. For a year and a half I had been different, and in his small-mindedness I recognized the worst of the hate and fear that I had dealt with in Fuling. It was an unfortunate conjunction of sensitivities, but now the trouble had already started and I was unwilling to back down. "Go, small friend," I said. "Go find your big friends."

The people laughed, which made him angrier. Mr. Zhang looked worried and told the man to leave, but he refused. He stood there ten feet from me, staring furiously.

I turned back to Mr. Zhang and talked with him as if nothing had happened. A few minutes passed, and the people went back to their routines. Still the little man was there, glaring. One of the regular hot pot women chatted with me while I held her baby son. The ten-year-old shoeshine girl came over to see the baby, and on the way back to her stand she insulted the man.

"Shenjingbing!" she shouted. "Crazy man! You're a crazy man! Don't give trouble to the *waiguoren*!"

I looked at the little man and saw that he was growing angrier. Partly it was the girl taunting him, but mostly he was galled by the way that the people were making such a fuss over me—giving me their stools, handing me their babies. I tried to sympathize with him; he worked his shoeshine stand alone, hustling for everything he got, and then the *waiguoren* with the big salary sat there comfortably, eating barbecue and chatting with the people.

He spoke again. Behind his eyes whatever he was thinking had hardened into a little bead of hatred.

"We Chinese don't need this kind of *waiguoren*," he said, loudly. "Why do we let *waiguoren* like this come to our country? Look at how rude he is, insulting me like that. We don't need this kind of *waiguoren* in our home."

I knew then that I was capable of matching almost any hatred that he could find. I would not start a fight, but if he struck me I would retaliate. The person that he had angered was somebody I myself didn't really know, because that person had never existed at home. Part of what Sichuan had changed about me was that in many ways I was more patient and tolerant than before, but there was also another part that had neither tolerance nor patience for more abuse of this sort. I spoke to the crowd.

"You Chinese don't need that kind of Chinese," I said. "This kind of person gives you a bad reputation. When I go home I'll tell people that nearly all Chinese are very friendly, like all of you here, but I'll say that sometimes there is a man like this who hates *waiguoren*. He's the one who is rude, and he bothered me for no reason at all. He started the trouble."

Everything had gone quiet except for my voice; the silence made me shiver. I was angry but I held the emotion down so I could speak clearly. "You came and bothered me, small friend," I said. "I told you to stop. Now if you want a problem, I'll give you a problem. Come on, small friend. Come here."

The man took a step forward and Mr. Zhang moved between us. The hot pot woman was yelling at him: "That *waiguoren* is a teacher! He has culture—you shouldn't treat him like that." It was clear that nobody was backing the little man, and without help he wasn't going to start anything. His big friends had not materialized. He sat back down at his shoeshine stand, glaring at me from a distance.

I wanted to leave but I knew that I should wait until it was obvious that I wasn't frightened. I talked with the people and read my paper. Tension was still in the air, and I could see that everybody was waiting to see if the little man would make a move.

I was ashamed of what I had done. I was glad that the people on Gaosuntang liked me enough to come to my defense, but I knew that I had been needlessly cruel and petty. The incident left me embarrassed; I had been educated at Princeton and Oxford, and yet for some reason I felt the need to face off with a Sichuanese shoeshine man until the locals said he had no culture. I knew that his harassment had nothing to do with me personally, and I knew that I should have sympathy for him, because his bitterness was the result of other pressures.

But after a year and a half in Fuling I couldn't push away the wave of hatred that I felt. I could remind myself who I was, and I could think about the advantages that I had received my whole life; but out on the street all of that slipped away. The strangeness and the pressures of life in a place like that were bound to change you, and something inside of me had stiffened long ago. Indeed, I wasn't certain that the man was entirely wrong: perhaps the people in Fuling didn't need this kind of *waiguoren*. But to some extent they had helped create him, and for better or worse we were stuck together.

I wondered what the little man was thinking. He sat at his stand, staring at me. Nobody stopped to have his shoes shined. After a while it started to rain.

"I have to go now," I said to Mr. Zhang.

"You should watch your money," he said, nodding toward the little man.

"That's not a problem," I said. I thanked him and left. Deliberately I passed in front of the little man's stand. He did nothing. Without looking back I walked away.

土地

THE LAND

April 15

THERE IS A NEW METHOD OF TRANSPLANTING RICE, and about half of the peasants on Raise the Flag Mountain are using it. In the past, seedlings have always been transplanted by hand, row by row, but now many peasants are trying *paoyang*—literally, "throwing the seedlings."

The seeds are first planted in plastic trays, each of which holds five hundred plants in individual pockets. When they are ready to be transplanted, the seedlings have a round clump of earth formed around the root; when thrown, the weight of this earth carries the seedling and sinks it into the muck. *Paoyang* saves time—the peasants can throw the shoots from the edge of the paddy rather than transplanting each one by hand.

Halfway up the mountain is a man who has been using this method for two years. Yesterday he threw his seedlings; today he wades in the paddy, straightening any plants that have slipped out of the mud. He is thirty-five years old, with a black mustache and hard muddy calves. He wears a fake beeper on the belt of his blue trousers. He has one and a half *mu* of land, or roughly a quarter of an acre, which is more land than the average peasant works in these hills.

Numbers are important here, as they are for farmers anywhere in the world. This particular paddy, one of four that compose his land, is two hundred square meters. The peasant estimates that this paddy will use twelve pans of rice seedlings, which is a total of six thousand plants. These stalks will produce approximately 330 pounds of rice, which will sell for three hundred yuan.

On the threshing platform of a nearby house a small girl sits at a desk, doing her homework. Beyond the girl is the backdrop of the city with the setting sun falling orange behind the gray buildings. Next to the house, two young men throw seedlings into a newly plowed paddy. They are laughing and tossing the rice carelessly in every possible direction. They complain about life in the countryside, although they say that at least in the city they can find construction work, which is better than becoming shoeshine men or stick-stick soldiers. "The peasants from the very remote countryside do those jobs," says one of the men. "Those of us who live here in the suburbs won't do that kind of work."

He is asked to compare his life to that of a factory worker, and he thinks it over.

"Peasants, workers," he says. "It doesn't matter. They're all bad jobs."

April 28

THE SUN IS UNBEARABLY HOT. It has rained once in the last two weeks; a drought is building. The corn plants are now about two feet tall. The earth around the stalks is dry and powdery, scorched by the sun.

In other parts of the world this strange weather is blamed on El Niño. But the peasants, who never speak of El Niño, have their own reasons for the heat. The traditional Chinese lunar calendar follows a system in which a month must be made up every fourth year—sometimes there is an extra ninth month, or an extra second month, and so on. This year the extra month is the fifth one. Whenever there are two fifth months in one year, you can count on a hot dry spring followed by an extremely wet summer. This is the way it has always been in the past, and thus the peasants are not surprised by the current heat and dryness. Everywhere in the countryside they complain quietly about the problems of having two fifth months in one year.

May 5

MOST OF THE WHEAT IS GONE. Over the weekend it rained, and after it dried the peasants harvested almost all of the crop on Raise the Flag Mountain. It was harvested by hand, with short scythes. The wheat stalks were cut close to the ground, leaving rows of stubble, which will be plowed into the earth when the time comes to sow another crop.

The loss of the wheat has subtly changed the mountain's texture. Last week the crop stood soft and yellow along the terraces, but now those fields are bare. The cornfields are beginning to fill out, and the transplanted rice has started to thicken in the muck of the paddies. Soon the lower mountain will be covered by lush carpets of green.

Peasants are using sticks to beat piles of wheat on the threshing platforms. The sound of their work—a steady *swish swish swish*—echoes throughout the countryside. There is also the sound of frogs croaking in the paddies, and ducks calling out in the small ponds, and the soft rustling of the breeze in the growing corn.

Along the southern shoulder of the mountain a long thin field is being harvested; workers are piling the wheat stalks into bundles and tying them with reeds. The bundles weigh more than fifty pounds each, and they must be carried to shelters where they will be kept dry. A young man takes a long sturdy stick and stabs it into the heart of a bundle, lifting it onto his shoulder. He uses its weight to help him stick the other end deep into another bundle, and then he lifts both bales, adjusts the load, and carries them balanced across his back. He walks quickly, moving with a loose-kneed bouncing gait, heading toward home.

May 11

AFTER SIX DAYS the harvested wheat field is unrecognizable. It has been flooded and half filled with rice shoots, their green tips poking above the water like drowning blades of grass. In less than a week, the wheat field has been turned into a rice paddy.

A man wades in the paddy, transplanting the stalks by hand. His sleeves and trousers are rolled up. He bends low and moves backward as he works. The rice shoots stretch in neat rows across the water. This peasant does not believe in *paoyang,* and so he transplants his rice completely by hand.

Rice is being tended all over the mountain, in all its early stages. Most of the crop has already been transplanted, but the post-wheat paddies are running later; farther down the slopes a few peasants are still plowing the muck. On the steeper parts of the mountain, where it's impossible to grow rice, the peasants have not quite finished harvesting the wheat. Simultaneously they are weeding the corn, which will be ready in a little more than a month. The corn stalks are still headless but now they are nearly chest-high.

Today is cool and overcast, the late-afternoon sun breaking through the clouds. Westward the Yangtze runs silver between the hills. The level of the river is still low, because the last month has been dry, but spring is always like that in a year with two fifth months. Even as they transplant the rice, and harvest the wheat, and weed their corn, the peasants are waiting for the heavy summer rains that they know will eventually arrive.

June 10

RAIN IS COMING. The air hangs still and thick above the river valleys. Clouds have gathered and faint rumblings echo from beyond White Flat Mountain.

Tonight it won't rain much, but at the end of the month it will pour for a week, and then the rains will continue hard throughout July. In August the downpour will not stop. The rivers will swell and rage. In the east, where the Yangtze leaves the Gorges and enters the flats of central China, the country will suffer its worst floods in decades. Over 64 million acres of farmland will be inundated, and the death count will reach 3,656. All of this will happen because of the two fifth months, and the peasants on Raise the Flag Mountain will not be surprised to see such a bad summer.

But now—in these humid fields, with those clouds dark overhead—now it is still spring. The texture of the growing mountain has shifted once more; the corn stands six feet tall and it is at the point where it has just begun to ripen. The stalks are still a fresh spring green but the tassels are turning pink, a soft feathery color that sits lightly atop the deep green of the close-planted plots.

The rice is thigh-high and long-leafed like swamp grass. The water in the paddies has dropped to about an inch and now it cannot be seen through the lush green. From a distance the rice fields look smooth, like a lawn freshly cut.

All seasons are beautiful in the countryside of Raise the Flag Mountain, but the long Sichuan spring is the most beautiful of all. And this particular moment—today's ripening corn and growing rice—this may very well be the most beautiful day of the most beautiful season. Next month the corn will be harvested, and after that the rice will turn a drab pale yellow; but today any change seems far away. Everything is perfect: the mountain's texture is balanced like sections of a good painting—the long, even brush strokes of the rice plots; the choppy mixed colors of the corn. Standing here in the countryside it is easy to forget that everything is growing, shifting, changing; and it is easy to forget that this moment won't last. It's like waiting for rain without worrying.

CHAPTER ELEVEN

Spring Again

MY FATHER VISITED ME at the start of the spring semester. Since coming to China, I had seen nobody in my family except for my sister Angela, who prodded my father until at last he worked up enough courage to make the trip. My mother decided to stay at home.

I met my father at the Chongqing airport. We stayed in a Chinese hotel near the docks; I figured there was no reason to go to a *waiguoren* hotel and spend four times as much money. During the night the hotel workers called twice on the phone and burst into the room once; it always had something to do with checking our passports. Each interruption terrified my father, who was already badly jet-lagged, and I tried to explain that the workers were probably just curious.

In the morning we caught the nine-o'clock slow boat downriver to Fuling. This, like the hotel, proved to be a serious miscalculation on my part; we could have taken a hydrofoil and cut the travel time in half. I thought that my father would like to get a taste of typical river life, but five and a half hours is a lot to taste, and the nine-o'clock slow boat was always full of Sichuanese unemployed who were heading down to Wuhan to look for work. They sprawled like casualties in the hallways, sleeping, smoking, spitting. It was too crowded to wander around the boat, and the mist was so thick that you couldn't watch the scenery. My father shivered in his bunk until at last we reached Fuling.

On the docks I dickered with the cabbies until I found one who would take us to the college for fifteen yuan. The taxi billowed with Magnificent Sound smoke, and, as usual, the cabby was inspired by the unexpected responsibility of carrying *waiguoren*. He flew through the center of town. Pedestrians scurried in our wake. We swung hard onto the Wu River Great Bridge and the deep green water flowed far below us. My father clung to the passenger grip. The guardrails of the bridge flashed past. The engine roared.

"Why," my father asked, "does he keep honking?"

FOR TWO DAYS IN FULING my father couldn't sleep. The noise, the dirt, the language, the endless swarms of people, the constant bustle of life on the streets—all of that was too much. At night he lay awake in bed, listening to the horns out on the river. It had taken me half a year to come to grips with the city, and now he was trying to deal with it in ten days.

He had always found comfort in hard exercise—at fifty-six years of age he still ran ten miles a day—and I decided that this was the best solution to his insomnia. After all, the simple activity of running had been soothing to me when I first arrived in Fuling. So for two days I led him on long runs past the summit of Raise the Flag Mountain, into the rugged hills of the high countryside, where the peasants stopped to stare as we charged past. We went twelve miles a day; I made sure the pace was fast.

It worked—two days of that and he slept perfectly. But now his nose ran like a faucet and his throat burned; he hacked up coal dust into my sink. He was sick for the rest of his time in Fuling. My sinuses flared up and I was sick, too. My father suggested that we skip the running.

THAT WAS PERHAPS the longest week and a half I spent in China. It was like seeing a reflection of my entire first year, cut and spliced and crammed into ten days—all of the fear, the annoyances, the fascination, the wonder of the city; everything hit my father in the space of little more than a week. And I found that it was difficult to predict what would bother him, because I had been in Fuling for so long that I no longer saw it with a true outsider's eye. A slow boat that might seem perfectly fine to me was terrifying to him, while other things that I had worried about, like the spiciness of the food, didn't pose the slightest problem. Like many Peace Corps volunteers all over the world, I found that the parent visit was a kind of revelation: suddenly I saw how much I had learned and how much I had forgotten.

By the third day he was more accustomed to the noise and the air, and after that we spent hours walking through the city. We watched the streetside doctor perform surgery on a peasant's foot; we watched the blacksmiths pound out chisels on their anvils; we watched the stick-stick soldiers as they watched us. We watched the man at the Lanzhou pulled noodle shop make noodles by hand. We wandered through the markets and watched the workers gut eels that had been harvested from the peasant ponds. One morning we stumbled onto a small shop in the old town where a man was scrubbing syringes with a dirty brush, and we watched that too.

"They're for the hospital," the man said brightly, when I asked why he was doing that.

"The main hospital?"

"Yes, the big hospital!"

That was where I'd go if there was a medical emergency. "They use these needles again?" I asked.

"Of course!"

I translated everything for my father. I told him what the propaganda signs said, and I introduced him to the regulars all over town. He met Huang Xiaoqiang and the folks at the Students' Home; he met the workers at the park; he met the barbecue vendors and the ten-year-old shoeshine girl. I introduced him to my friends at the teahouse, and as we left three *xiaojies* came out of the beauty parlor across the street and started shouting at me: "Ho Wei! Ho Wei! Ho Wei!"

"What does that mean?" my father asked.

"That's my Chinese name."

The *xiaojies* were giggling and yelling my name across the street. They wore lots of makeup and their hair was dyed. One was smoking a cigarette.

"Why are you shouting?" I asked, in Chinese.

"We're calling you," one of them said.

"Why?"

"We want you to come here."

"How do you know my name?"

"From Li Jiali—she's our friend." All of them giggled after the *xiaojie* said that.

"I have to go now," I said.

They laughed as we walked down the street. My father glanced back and asked, "Who are those people?"

I figured it was a good idea to balance that out with a visit to the church. We met Father Li and chatted in his sitting room. Politely he spoke to my father, with me serving as the translator, and I mentioned that the priest still used Latin during weekday Masses.

"Tell him that I used to be an altar boy for Latin Mass," my father said. Father Li nodded and said that nobody else in Fuling still understood the language. I asked my father if he still remembered the traditional service, and he nodded.

"In nomine Patris," he said, *"et Filii, et Spiritus Sancti. Amen."*

"Introibo ad altare Dei," responded the priest. "I will go in to the altar of God."

"Ad Deum qui laetificat juventutem meam," my father said. "To God, Who giveth joy to my youth."

For a few minutes they went through the beginning of the service. I had been translating for nearly a week, and now it was strange to sit silent, listening and not understanding a word between these two men that I knew so well. The priest's Latin was tinged with Sichuanese; my father spoke with an American accent. Theirs was a rote, formal dialogue in a rusty old language, but it was clear that something about the conversation changed the way the two men saw each other. After they were finished, Father Li kept forgetting himself, addressing my father directly in Sichuanese, as if he would understand. But as we left he used Latin once more. *"Dominus vobiscum,"* he said. "The Lord be with you."

"Et cum spiritu tuo," my father said.

We went camping in the high peaks south of Fuling, where Gold Buddha Mountain rose to an altitude of more than seven thousand feet. Adam and I had been there before and it was a beautiful area, completely undeveloped except for old military factories and bases that had been placed there during the height of the Third Line Project, when Mao had restructured China's defense industry to protect against the American nuclear threat. Since Deng Xiaoping began dismantling the project in 1980, the bigger factories in places like Fuling had been converted to civilian use, but many of the smaller ones in remote areas were simply abandoned. The transportation was too bad to justify conversion, and in any case many of the remote plants had been badly built. Even in the boom years of the project, some of the factories had been constructed so quickly and haphazardly that they lasted only a few years before they had to be built again.

On the way to Gold Buddha Mountain, my father and I hiked through a high valley that was full of empty warehouses and factories, crumbling and decrepit, their walls covered with fading propaganda from twenty years ago:

Prepare for War! Prepare for Famine! Serve the People!

The broken walls proclaimed their urgency throughout the silent valley. But there was nobody here to read them anymore; the workers had been moved back to Chongqing, or Fuling, or wherever they had originally come from. It was just my father and me, hiking alone through the ruins of a valley that had been settled hastily in response to the American atomic bomb.

For two nights we camped, hiking up to a cave that led deep into the limestone face of the mountain. The cave mouth was natural, but it had been expanded for some unknown military use—perhaps it had been a munitions factory, or maybe a stockpile—and now there was a long tunnel that led clear through the heart of Gold Buddha Mountain. We made our way through with flashlights, hiking for more than a quarter mile in darkness and finally coming out on the other side, where the northern valley descended to rice terraces and the road back to Fuling.

We returned to campus and discovered that an English department student named Belinda had died while we were camping. On Friday afternoon she got a headache; on Friday evening she was taken to the hospital; by Saturday she was dead. None of the doctors knew why it had happened. She was the second English department student to die in the past year. In addition, one of Dean Fu's sisters had recently died suddenly, and Party Secretary Zhang's daughter, who was an adorable elementary-school student, had died during class in the fall. In some ways that child's death had been anticipated, if not expected—she had had brain surgery the year before, after which her name was changed. Because of the medical problem, Party Secretary Zhang's wife was given permission to have a second baby. The name-changing was a Chinese custom—a changed name in hopes of a change of health.

People died in Fuling. It happened everywhere, of course, but it seemed to happen with particular frequency and suddenness in the river town. And often it happened in strange ways; later that year a woman would be killed at the Catholic church when part of the rectory's roof suddenly caved in. The year after I left, in what was without question the most pointless and pathetic of all the Fuling deaths, another English department student died after slipping in the squat toilet and striking his head. Small accidents sometimes had disastrous results in a place like Fuling, where the medical care was uneven, and the deaths didn't shock my students as much as I would have expected. They mourned, and then they moved on.

And my father witnessed that as well; along with the rest of us, he helped console the students as they dealt with the loss of Belinda. But their grief was quiet and resolute, as it always seemed to be; and I felt overwhelmed by the poignancy of that combination of helplessness and strength.

AND THEN THE WHIRLWIND of those ten days was over. On my father's final afternoon in Fuling, we hiked halfway up Raise the Flag Mountain. It was a warm day; the sun glowed bright above the city. In the hills there was a soft breeze. A farmer was preparing his rice paddies, and he invited us into his home to rest. We sat on rough stools in the inner courtyard. Nobody was shouting; there weren't any cars or crowds; no propaganda was in sight. We simply sat there, breathing the clean fresh air of the countryside.

The farmer's mother came out to speak with us. The old woman was eighty-one years old, and she laughed when I asked if she had grown up in the house. "This used to be the landlord's home!" she said. "I was too poor to live in a place like this."

It was a huge, sprawling complex, and the woman told me that it had been built 150 years ago. Several families lived there now. The roof was tiled and there were old-fashioned carved figures along the eaves. There were very few buildings like that in the Fuling countryside, and I asked what had happened to the landlord and his family.

"They were kicked out in the 1950s, after Liberation," the women said. "They were sent north, to the countryside past White Flat Mountain. I don't know what happened to them."

Her daughter-in-law was listening and she turned to me. "Do you have landlords in your country?"

"No," I said.

I was translating everything for my father and he disagreed with that. "Of course we have landlords in America," he said. I thought it over and realized that he was right. After two years it almost seemed exotic, a country whose landlords hadn't been killed or exiled.

"I made a mistake," I said to the woman. "We do have landlords in my country."

"That's what I've heard," she said. "But all of our landlords in China are gone."

For nearly an hour we sat there in the former landlord's house, chatting with the people. Somebody led a water buffalo through the courtyard. The children returned from school. There was a teenage girl whom my father thought looked like my sister Angela—something in the way she carried herself. The sun dropped orange behind the city. We thanked the family and left, walking back through the fields.

"I never would have imagined that I could do that," my father said. "Just go into a Chinese peasant's home and talk with them like that. If I were you, I'd go up to that place every week."

I looked at my father; he was smiling and walking easily through the fields. For the first time I realized that he wasn't nearly as tired as me. All of Fuling had blazed past him in a bright blur, two years in ten days, and now he was going home. I envied him that—but at the same time I was thankful that he was right; I could go back to the peasant home anytime I wished.

SHORTLY AFTER MY FATHER LEFT, Adam's parents arrived, and he learned from some of my mistakes while repeating others. They stayed in Chongqing's Holiday Inn, but they caught the same kind of slow boat and had the same taxi adventures. And at the beginning his parents had the same frazzled look that I had seen in my father.

After a few days, Adam planned an evening lecture for the students. His parents, who used to live in the countryside of Wisconsin, would show some slides and talk about American farming. Adam went to the *waiban* office and told Mr. Wang, who was the foreign affairs officer. This was something I hadn't done when my father lectured—my personal policy was to clear nothing with the *waiban,* because that only left you open to unpredictable complications. But Adam thought Mr. Wang might want to hear the lecture, and so he told him. Mr. Wang said that unfortunately the students would be busy on Wednesday night.

"They have class?" Adam asked.

"They already have something planned. I'm sorry."

"That's no problem," Adam said. "We can do it on Thursday."

Mr. Wang laughed lightly. He always laughed lightly at everything. It was the sort of laugh that made you distrust Mr. Wang until you got to know him better, and then you trusted him even less.

"I'm afraid that won't be possible," he said. "The students will be busy on Thursday, too."

"In the evening?"

"Yes."

"Well, I'll talk with them and find a time that works, and I'll tell you. I thought you might want to hear the lecture, too."

"Actually," said Mr. Wang brightly, "it won't be possible for your parents to talk with the students."

"Why not?"

"People in the college have decided that it is not appropriate." He laughed again.

"How can it not be appropriate? They're studying English, aren't they? This is a good opportunity for them to practice, and it's only about farming—there's nothing political. They're just going to talk about the countryside where we used to live."

"Yes, but you must teach your own courses."

"My parents have taught for many years at an American college. They are better teachers than me, but if that's the problem, we can have an extra class. I just think it's a good chance for the students to listen to different English speakers."

"Believe me, *I* understand," said Mr. Wang, "I would very much like to hear their lecture, but Mr. Tan is opposed. I'm sorry about that."

This was one of Mr. Wang's favorite routines—Good Cadre/Bad Cadre. Mr. Tan was an upper-level administrator who was in charge of the *waiban,* and usually he was Mr. Wang's Bad Cadre. In fact, we thought that Mr. Tan was the most likable administrator in the college, a friendly man who was far more honest with us. Things would have been simpler if we had been allowed to deal with him directly, but it was more useful to keep Mr. Tan at a safe distance, where he could be the Bad Cadre.

"How about this?" Adam said. "I'll teach the class, and then afterward the students can ask my parents questions. Is that okay?"

"I'm afraid not."

"So my parents can't talk with the students?"

"Oh, certainly they can talk with the students!"

"But if I have class they can't say anything?"

"That's correct."

The next day Adam called role and canceled class. The students were free to leave, he said, but if they wanted to stay and listen to Mr. and Mrs. Meier, they were welcome to do so. Nobody left. His parents showed slides and lectured on American agriculture. The students asked questions. The questions were answered. No cadres were there, but undoubtedly they heard about it later.

By that semester we were growing less tolerant of the mindless political restrictions. Generally I avoided the cadres, which fortunately wasn't hard to do. I never went to the *waiban* unless it was absolutely necessary, and I tried not to talk with any of the administrators. In my apartment I had two telephones: one for outside calls and a campus line. It worked nicely because only the cadres used the campus line, which I never answered.

Mr. Wang was the only one whom I really disliked—time and time again he had proven to be particularly oily and dishonest. I didn't feel the same way about any of the others, but something about them depressed me. Dean Fu was perhaps the saddest case, because I knew that he genuinely liked us and cared about our welfare, and yet he seemed to be under immense pressure from above, and a few times this had prevented him from being open with us. Invariably it was like that—there was always some pressure coming from above, the Bad Cadres pushing the Good Cadres. There were lots of Good Cadres and you never met the Bad ones, but somehow they seemed to decide how everything worked.

Back in December, Sunni, Adam, and I had written a short version of *A Christmas Carol,* so our speaking classes could perform the Dickens play. During our preparations, I was called into Dean Fu's office, where he told me nervously that under no circumstances could we teach Christmas carols to the students.

"You know that the Communist Party is very sensitive about spreading religion," he said. "I'm sorry, but the students are not allowed to sing Christmas songs in class."

"Can we talk about Christmas at all? They're studying American culture."

"Yes. That is fine. But they can't sing songs."

"What about songs that aren't religious? There's a part in the play where they're supposed to be singing Christmas songs, and I could have them sing one that isn't about religion at all. You know, in America for many people Christmas isn't a religious holiday. For example, there's a song that goes, 'We wish you a Merry Christmas, we wish you a Merry Christmas, we wish you a Merry Christmas, and a Happy New Year!' "

"No," said Dean Fu, still smiling tightly. "I'm afraid that we can have no songs about Christmas. I'm sorry, but you know it is not my decision."

I could have pointed out that even in spring the campus propaganda speakers, as part of their noon entertainment program, often played a Muzak version of "What Child Is This?" But I knew the argument was hopeless; there was no logic to any of it. And in the same spirit I instructed my classes to replace the Christmas carols with patriotic Communist songs, which if anything improved Dickens. My favorite scene was when a furious Scrooge swung his cane at a band of merry carolers who were belting out "The East Is Red," singing the praises of Mao Zedong while the old man shouted, "Humbug!"

Most of our problems with the administration were more absurd than anything else, and rarely were they significant: I couldn't care less about teaching Christmas carols. But it seemed that after a year and a half some of this awkwardness should have passed; we should have become good enough friends to speak comfortably about something so insignificant.

But other restrictions weren't so minor. Sunni and Noreen's Chinese tutors were two young women who worked in the English department, and over the course of the year they became good friends. During a holiday that spring, one of the teachers invited Sunni and Noreen to her home, and then, at the last moment, revoked the invitation, explaining that there was a problem with the road. It seemed strange—the spring rains hadn't yet arrived and there was no reason for a road to be washed out. And later we learned that department officials had instructed the young teacher not to invite the two *waiguoren* to her home. Ostensibly the reason was that they were afraid something would happen to Sunni and Noreen, and the teacher would be responsible. But more likely the command stemmed from the same shapeless paranoia that had shadowed us from the start—the sense that *waiguoren* were politically risky and should be kept at a distance.

These commands always took place behind our backs, which was the worst part. It served to transfer the paranoia, until we overanalyzed every minor conversation and every small change of plans, looking for signs of manipulation. When Sunni and Noreen told me about the canceled invitation, the first thing I did was go to the local bus station, where the drivers said exactly what I expected—the road wasn't washed out, which meant that somebody in the college had lied to Sunni and Noreen. It was a classic pattern in any Communist system, where fear and paranoia pass from one level to the next, creating a network of perfect distrust.

But increasingly we realized that this distrust was well earned; our paranoia wasn't unfounded. We had friends who told us the way things worked, and it was startling to see the degree to which we were managed. When the movie *Titanic* came out that spring, one of our colleagues invited us to his home to watch the film on videodisc, but again the invitation was revoked at the last moment. Later, he explained candidly that the cadres had been afraid that the *waiguoren* would realize that the movie was pirated—a laughable cover-up considering that it was impossible to go anywhere in Fuling without having a vendor shove a bootleg copy of *Titanic* in your face. The movie was so popular that they hung an enormous promotional sign above the local theater, a curious marriage of propaganda and advertising:

The Futong Jewelry Store is the Sole Sponsor of *Titanic,* Which Has Been Recommended by President and Party Secretary Jiang Zemin.

By now the department commands were often doubly self-defeating: not only did we realize that the movie was pirated, but we saw clearly the degree to which the college hoped to manipulate the world around us. At the same time, we recognized how inconsistent this control was, because in many other ways the college gave us impressive leeway. This was particularly true with regard to our teaching, which logically should have been where we were restricted the most. Apart from the occasional petty incident like Adam's lecture or the Dickens play, our teaching freedom was arguably greater than it would have been in America. Nobody checked our syllabi or hassled us about course content, and we structured our classes exactly as we wished. I was especially impressed that they even let us teach classes like literature and culture, which often had strong political overtones.

For the most part they treated us well, and, considering Fuling's remoteness and lack of foreigners, they trusted us quite a bit. But that final small step hadn't yet been taken, and it was all the more frustrating because so many of the more important barriers were already gone. By the spring I realized that these last obstacles would not be removed during my time in Fuling, and I tried not to worry about it. Other aspects of life had gone much better.

In particular, our relations with the students had improved a great deal during the second year. Much of this was because of Adam, who had always been a more dedicated teacher, spending extra time with the students and helping them set up a library in our office. He was the first *waiguoren* teacher to really win their trust, and, since in their minds the two of us were virtually indistinguishable, it was natural that they extended this trust to me.

But also time made a difference—they had known us for two years. This wasn't simply a matter of their coming to accept the *waiguoren;* we had changed a great deal, and now we had a much better understanding of how to approach them. They could still count on our informality, which from the beginning had distinguished us from other teachers on campus. But they also knew that we could be serious, and in those moments we weren't propagandists; in particular, we tended to be blunt when it came to discussing America. That semester I taught "Désirée's Baby" and Langston Hughes, while Adam's American Culture class focused on the civil rights movement. He pulled no punches with that unit, which included videos of James Meredith lying beside a Mississippi highway, shot by a racist sniper. The students knew that nobody had forced Adam to show those films—he could have given positive lectures about American success in technology, or economics, or education—and it made the students more willing to be honest about things that they felt were important.

Another critical difference was that now we spoke Chinese. In the fall I had first started talking with some of the students in Chinese when I met them outside of class, because they liked to hear what I was learning. But as time passed, I realized that this wasn't simply a novelty; like me, they were completely different people when they spoke the language. They were much more at ease, and this wasn't just a linguistic issue; it was political as well.

One evening after Adam's parents left, I was eating in the Students' Home when Jimmy, Mo, and George stopped by. They were three of my favorite third-year students and we chatted lightly in English. They asked if Adam's parents had enjoyed Fuling, and I said that they had, except that they weren't particularly impressed by the cadres.

The three of them leaned close around the table. *"Weishenme?"* Jimmy asked softly. I answered in English: "Because they thought the *waiban* was rude to them, and they didn't understand why."

"Women waiban gan shenme?"

Now I responded in Chinese, telling them the story. In China it was seriously disrespectful to make somebody's parents feel unwelcome, and there was disappointment in the students' eyes. I told them frankly about the way I saw the department, and how small incidents like this added up over time. Mo and George were both Party Members; a year ago I would never have spoken honestly to them in this way. But using Chinese made everybody more comfortable, including me.

As I began to meet the students more frequently outside of class, I noticed how strong this pattern was: whenever something sensitive came up, we handled it in Chinese. It amazed me, because English should have been our secret language—virtually nobody else could understand it off campus, and it was the safest way to discuss such topics without anybody hearing. But even in a crowded restaurant like the Students' Home we switched to Chinese at key points, when we talked about politics, or sex, or our *guanxi* with the college. Even the best students often made that shift, despite their English being better than my Chinese.

At last I realized that the fear wasn't of somebody else hearing. It was a question of comfort, because uncertain topics were more easily handled in their native language. But also I sensed that the true fear was of themselves: virtually all of the limits had been established in their own minds. English had been learned at school, and thus it was indistinguishable from the educational system and its political regulations. When they spoke the language, warning bells automatically went off in their heads—it was a school language, as well as a *waiguoren* language, and in both of those contexts they had been trained to think and speak carefully. Once I realized that these limits were internal, I began to wonder if it was the same way with the Bad Cadres. Perhaps they existed only in a small corner of the Good Cadres' minds, a nagging fear that got the best of everybody's good intentions.

THAT SPRING A NUMBER OF THE BOY STUDENTS decided that they needed English surnames. The foreign teachers had Chinese family names; why should the students be different?

I first noticed this trend when I was grading papers one day and thought: Who the hell is George Baker Frost? I had never heard of him before, but there was his assignment with the name written proudly in enormous letters across the top of the page.

I read the paper and realized it had been written by George—the cockiest student in the class, a handsome boy who was also one of the best athletes. He was a trend-setter, too, and soon I began to get assignments from William Foster, who had formerly been Willie, and who subsequently promoted himself to William Jefferson Foster. It wasn't long before William Jefferson Foster persuaded his girlfriend to become Nancy Drew (that was Adam's recommendation), and then Mo, who was the class monitor and couldn't allow his authority to be undermined by any perceived shortcoming, started shopping for surnames. He asked me for suggestions, and soon he was signing his papers Mo Money.

Some of the boys undertook to improve Adam's and my command of thc dialect, and the people at the Students' Home were very pleased when we began using the new words and phrases in daily conversation. "Now you are a real *Zhongguotong!*" Huang Neng said proudly. "A China hand!"

It was only a matter of time before the department caught wind of this development, and one day George Baker Frost pulled me aside during a break in class. As a Party Member he had some of the clearest connections to the top.

"The English department wants us to stop teaching you those words," he said.

"Those sons of turtles," I said in Chinese. "They are very toothbrush."

George grinned and glanced behind him. To say that somebody was toothbrush was a particularly biting insult in the Chongqing dialect. In other parts of Sichuan it was completely meaningless, but for some unknown reason it carried heavy connotations along the eastern river valleys, where it was used as an adjective. It meant, more or less, that you were useless.

"We must be careful," George said.

I wanted to say: The walls have ears. But I smiled and nodded in agreement.

"Maybe you should not say those words too close to the college," he said. "Otherwise they will give us trouble."

We agreed to a no-fire zone around the teaching building, but inevitably such limits failed. This was risky ground—calling people toothbrush was even more treacherous than singing Christmas carols—and soon our shared dissidence brought us even closer to the students. And by now the flow of language, which went both ways, was out of control. Ever since we had studied Jonathan Swift in the first semester, the students had been infatuated with the word "yahoo." It sounded like a Chinese word; in fact, it even had some similarity with "toothbrush," which was *yashua.* For whatever reason, the students said "yahoo" constantly, and it was all the more charming because many of them, with their Sichuanese tendency to confuse the *f* and *h* sounds, pronounced it "yafoo." That was also how Huang Kai said the word, which represented his first English lesson. Often when I came for lunch at the Students Home he looked up at me and shouted, solemnly, "Yafoo!" As a literature teacher I considered that to be perhaps my proudest achievement; I knew that Swift would have been thrilled to see this Chinese two-year-old stumbling around in his split-bottomed pants, calling foreigners yahoos.

In the fall Adam had started a Spanish class, which further complicated matters. Soon *tonto,* or "stupid," also became ubiquitous; along with *yashua* and "yahoo" it seemed to be everywhere, from the top floor of the teaching building down to the Students' Home. I almost felt sorry for the department officials—I could only imagine how confused they were by all of this nonsense, and how the Bad Cadres were working overtime as they tried to assess the political risks of Jonathan Swift and Spanish stupidity. Probably they were eager for us to leave and take all of these words with us; but there were still several months to go, and three languages and one dialect provided enormous potential for abuse.

As a teacher I no longer felt the discomfort of my first spring—that sense of a *waiguoren* standing alone in front of the class—and this year's students never bowed their heads in shared shame. I was pleased to see that finally it was possible to talk with them outside of class, and our relationship had a combination of humor and seriousness that seemed perfect for China. For the first time, college life seemed human, and the students, who had so often struck me as talented but unfortunate pawns, became much fuller figures in my eyes.

One of my favorites was Linda, who felt no need for a last name. She was possibly the brightest of the third-year students, and the year before she had been nominated for a transfer to the Sichuan Foreign Language Institute in Chongqing. That was a big step up from Fuling; every year a handful of elite students were selected to transfer, which meant that they were no longer locked into the track of becoming peasant schoolteachers. But the selection process was both heavily political and prone to favoritism, and Linda had failed the perfunctory physical exam because one of the physical education teachers held a grudge against her from freshman year. Actually, Linda was one of the better athletes among the girl students, and this injustice caused quite a bit of anger in the English department, but there was nothing anybody could do—the PE teacher had the final say. It was a typical example of the mindlessly cruel bullying that was routinely tolerated on campus, especially from the PE department.

Linda handled it as well as one could expect. She was accustomed to that combination of helplessness and strength—her mother had died not long before, and now in the spring her father was struggling with cancer. Both Linda and her sister had been to palm readers that spring, and in both cases the fortune was the same: Your father will die soon. Adam and I saw that as an indication that one should avoid fortune-tellers, and we told Linda as much; but she knew that she was stuck with her fate, and so she bore it quietly. A few times that semester she traveled home for the weekend, but always she kept up a front of normalcy. Even when her father became very ill she remained the best student in class.

One evening in the library she showed me her photo albums. Looking at a student's album was always a strange experience, because the Chinese saw no purpose in pictures that did not feature themselves. For a people known for modesty it always struck me as an odd chink in their armor, a sudden burst of narcissism—a photo album might have more than fifty face shots of the owner. I never knew quite how to react: what do you say after looking at fifty photographs of a young woman's face?

Adam's policy was to pause at every single picture and ask, "Who's this?"

"That's me!" the owner of the book would say.

Adam would turn the page. "Who's this?"

"That's me!"

Adam found that routine endlessly entertaining; sometimes I had to leave the office when he started it, so I wouldn't hit him after hearing him ask the question for the twentieth time. I never had the patience, and so I flipped through Linda's albums as quickly as I could without being rude. The photos consisted of all the standard *xiaojie* poses—often in parks, rarely smiling; sometimes with hats, heavy makeup, a soft filter on the lens; holding a flower, chin turned up dreamily, back slightly arched. There were two albums and it took five minutes. After I was finished I gave them back and said, "Very beautiful!"

"No, not very beautiful," she said, and then she smiled. "But beautiful enough."

I realized that she was precisely correct—she was a pretty girl, but not so pretty that it became a distraction or eclipsed her other talents. That was another example of the sort of pragmatism that I often saw in Fuling, where people seemed much more capable of viewing themselves with cold judgment than Americans. And mostly the people in Fuling tended to know exactly the hand they had been dealt. Linda had had more than her share of bad luck, but she also had her gifts, and she would do what she could with those.

On another evening Adam and I ate dinner with her and Mo Money, and we had a couple of beers and began to speak seriously in Chinese. The conversation turned to the pro-democracy demonstrations in Tiananmen Square, which was a rare topic in Fuling. Most people had very little sense of what had happened in 1989; there had been some small protests in Fuling, with students marching down to South Mountain Gate, and people had heard vague rumors of violence in Chengdu and Beijing. But almost nobody had any sense of the massacre's scale. One of the few exceptions was my photographer friend Ke Xianlong, who listened carefully to the Voice of America and knew that foreign reports estimated the death count to be at least in the hundreds.

He was one of the least patriotic Chinese I knew in Fuling. During my first year he had expressed his disdain for the students' excitement about Hong Kong's return, which he attributed to their ignorance and immaturity. To my surprise, he saw the pro-democracy movement in similar terms.

"All of that was so stupid," he told me once, when we talked about the 1989 student movement. "Many of the problems the students criticized were accurate, of course, but what did they know about it? How could they lead the country? Students are students. They don't know anything about real life, because they're too young. They're not yet mature, and they haven't ever worked like Old Hundred Names, which means that often they complain about things they don't understand."

When I thought about it, I could see his point, at least in the sense that it was never a good sign when a nation turned to twenty-one-year-olds as its moral voice. But it seemed horrible that China's current crop of twenty-one-year-olds had no clear idea of what had happened less than a decade earlier. I said this to Linda and Mo Money during our dinner, partly because I was interested in seeing how they would react.

Mo Money was a Party Member, but the topic didn't make him defensive, and he didn't deny what had happened, which was the government's stance. He knew that my information was probably more accurate than what the official sources said, and there was no point in arguing about the extent of the crackdown.

"But you have to understand," he said, "there isn't much I can do about what happened at that time. It's not because I don't care—I wish there was something that could be done about it. But that's just not possible, so all I can do is try to be a good student and then become a good teacher after graduation. I think that's all I can do."

In many ways he reminded me of Teacher Kong, who was also a Party Member with an idealistic streak. Both men still had faith that the system would work itself out eventually, and they believed that it required a certain amount of forgiveness, patience, and loyalty from people like themselves. Their faith wasn't so much specifically in Party theory as in the notion that people like them could—and should—contribute to society, despite its flaws. It was in some ways a democratic line of thought, or at least a hopeful longing to find democracy buried somewhere within the corruption of the current system. They simply couldn't bear the thought of entirely refusing to participate.

Linda wasn't a Party Member, although I was certain that somebody so talented could have joined if she had wished. I asked her why she had never applied.

"I have no interest in joining the Party," she said. "I've never wanted to do that, and I don't want to do it now. I think that these are important topics that we are talking about, and perhaps someday there will be something I can do. But right now it is too complicated."

She spoke evenly and I saw that her response was as honest as Mo Money's. Both of them were disengaged from the problem, like virtually everybody I knew in Fuling, although Linda's and Mo Money's reasons were different. Mo Money had decided that by being politically involved at the smallest level he could somehow overcome his powerlessness with regard to bigger issues, while Linda simply had other things to worry about. She had already been dealt enough cards; everything else could wait. Many people in Fuling were like that, and after two years I finally understood why.

IT WAS A DRY, DUSTY MARCH, and on the final weekend I went for a long hike up the Wu River. It was the same weekend as last year's walk, the same route. I had always liked the cycles of the countryside and that was my personal ritual, to camp beside the green springtime river at the end of March.

I crossed the first two side valleys and came to the Fuling Liangtang ore factory. Nothing here had changed in the past year, although now I could read two of the propaganda signs whose characters had been unrecognizable last year:

Diligence—Friendliness—Obedience

Respect the Rules and All Will Be Glorious;
Break the Rules and the Operation of Machinery Can Cause Shame

Three carts of gravel came hurtling down the hillside, the workers grinning and hooting as they rode atop the piles of white rock. I passed last year's sign:

Happy Happy Go to Work, Safe Safe Return Home.

I decided that that would be my mantra for the day: happy happy, safe safe. I repeated the words to myself as I hiked across the scarred hillside, and then I descended into the deep green valleys whose streams washed westward toward the Wu.

Spring was everywhere in those valleys—the blooming paulownia trees, the golden fields of rapeseed that shivered in the breeze, the eager plots of radish and lettuce and onions and broad beans. The rice seedlings were bright and green beneath sheets of plastic stretched taut over bamboo frames.

I came to the fourth cross valley where a peasant was guiding a plow behind a water buffalo. The man's trousers were rolled up past his knees as he waded in the muck. The air was sweet with the heavy scent of a nearby rapeseed plot. The old man's wife and grandson were sitting beside the field, and I stopped to say hello.

The woman looked at me intently. "I saw you last year, didn't I?" she asked.

"Yes, I came through last year. I live in Fuling."

The man stopped plowing and smiled. "I remember," he said. "You had a map and you were asking which way to go. But you didn't understand what we said, and you went the wrong way. We were trying to help!"

I promised that this year I would get it straight. They asked what I did in Fuling, and I told them I was a teacher.

"He's a teacher, too!" the woman said, gesturing at her husband. "He teaches in the elementary school, Monday to Friday, but on Saturday and Sunday he works out here."

He untied the buffalo, sending it off to graze in the rapeseed. The man was fifty-four years old, small and thin and as strong as the ox he followed. He had black hair in a neat crew cut, and I could see that he would look like a teacher if he cleaned up. But today was a peasant weekend; his legs were covered with mud, and brown flecks ran up his clothes all the way to his hair.

He offered me a cigarette, lit one for himself, and sat on a rock. I dropped my pack and rested in the sunshine. The man asked if I was German.

"No," I said. "I'm American."

"There was a German who came through here recently."

"Really? What was he doing?"

"I'm not certain. He was studying something here. And he was walking very fast—in the hills he walked even faster than the local people! He had a translator, and he was a rich man who had paid his way to China. What's your salary?"

I told him, and he nodded. "That's better than most. Teachers' salaries here in the countryside are much lower than that. But I think that German made a lot more than you."

His grandson was five years old and he darted behind me, laughing and grabbing at my shirt. The man grinned and scolded him softly. "He's very naughty," he said proudly. I nodded and rubbed the boy's black head. I was thinking about the German—it amazed me that another *waiguoren* had come to this remote place. To be honest, it annoyed me; I had always liked to think that I was the only one who had ever passed through this part of the countryside.

Back in the fall I had thought I saw another foreigner in Fuling, although I wasn't certain—it was only a fleeting glance of a man entering a restaurant, and I couldn't tell if he was actually a foreigner. The only confirmed *waiguoren* sighting for my entire two years had been back in January, when two Danish tourists got stranded when their boat to Chongqing docked for repairs. I ran into them at California Beef Noodle King USA, which was Fuling's closest approximation to a fast-food joint. The restaurant had spicy noodles and I ate there once or twice a week, and often the owner asked me if she was doing a good job of serving the proper California style. I always assured her that indeed it was precisely the same as what I would expect if I ordered Beef Noodle King back in California, which always pleased her. They even had the sign in English above the restaurant, and this was probably why the Danish women had gone inside.

They glanced sharply at me when I entered the restaurant, and then they looked away, as if they hadn't noticed. From my own trips in the past I knew that this was a traveler's routine—you came to a remote place and resented the presence of any other tourists. But in Fuling I wasn't a tourist, and to have other *waiguoren* treat me as if I had violated their solitude did not please me. I said nothing and sat at a table not far from the Danes.

They spoke no Chinese and hadn't been in the country long. They ordered by pointing at pictures on the wall, and the waitress asked them if they wanted hot pepper on their noodles. The Danes did not understand, but they could tell from the waitress's tone that this was an important choice, and they thumbed madly through a phrase book. I was resolved not to help until they acknowledged my presence.

They kept working at the phrase book until finally the waitress, who knew me, asked if I would translate. The Danes acted very surprised that I was there, and they said that they did not want hot pepper. I was tempted to tell the waitress that the Danes not only wanted hot pepper but seemed scornful of Sichuanese *lajiao,* scoffing that in the great country of Denmark such a mild spice would be considered candy for babies. But I told her the truth; I realized that they were simply acting the way any traveler would, just as I had done myself in other places at other times.

We talked for a while and they couldn't believe that I lived in a town like this, because the attention in Fuling overwhelmed them.

"These people," one of the Danes said, "all they do is stare. Everywhere we go, they stare at us. Do they stare at you, too?"

"Yes," I said, "but not as much as they stare at you."

I hadn't intended it as an insult, but the women seemed to take it as such. I didn't care enough to explain that I simply meant that the people were more accustomed to me. But I gave the Danes my phone number out of courtesy, in case something went wrong, and then I left them to the stick-stick soldiers.

Here in the countryside of the Wu River I thought about the German and wondered if this area would ever get to the point where *waiguoren* were common. The old woman saw me looking out at the scenery, and she asked if my home had hills like these.

"Some places do," I said. "But my home is flatter than Fuling."

"What's the farming like?"

"There aren't very many farmers, and they have more land. One farmer might have hundreds of *mu.* In my country the farms use machines."

The man nodded. "It's like Xinjiang," he said, "and in the north of China, where there's more land and it's flat. They use machines there as well. But here we can't."

We talked about farming and he asked me if it was true that peasants in America used airplanes to plant rice. Quite a few people in the countryside around Fuling seemed to have heard about this; it was a common question when I walked in the fields. I always said that indeed Californian rice was sometimes sowed by plane, and often I could see the wheels turning in their heads as the Sichuanese peasants looked at the scene around them—the plow, the ox, the primal muck—and tried to factor an airplane into the arrangement.

Today the peasant shook his head and grinned, looking down at his legs, where the mud had dried yellow-brown. Beneath the layer of dirt his sinews were taut and strong along his calves.

"You came the same time last year, didn't you?" he asked.

"Yes, last year I also came in March."

"Did you notice that it's different this year? Last year you saw that we had so many more paddies with water, but this year the rains haven't come yet, and everything is later than usual. It's too dry."

For a while he complained softly about the lack of rain, explaining that it would set back the whole spring schedule. But all the peasants could do was wait, hoping to survive the dryness of a spring that had two fifth months.

IT WAS WARM and I sweated under my pack. I stopped for lunch at the same place as last year, on the bluffs high above the Wu. I looked down on the river far below and thought: Happy happy, safe safe. The mist had faded and the sunlight flashed in streaks of gold along the river.

People all through the hills remembered me from the year before. They also talked about the German, who had left a deep impression. I stopped to rest at one peasant home and the people told me that he had worn boots like mine.

"He was a *zhuanjia*—an expert," an old man said. "He was studying the trees here, I think. He came because this is such a poor area."

The old man's name was Yang. He gave me boiled water with sugar and I sat with him on his family's threshing platform. There was the old man and his son, the son's wife, and a four-month-old baby. They were doing quite well; for a decade they had had electricity. Their rice was growing thick under plastic coverings. They had six pigs. They had a cat on a leash with a plastic Pepsi bottle tied to the other end. The bottle was partly filled with water and it kept the cat from going very far. I had never much liked cats and the Pepsi bottle struck me as a good idea.

The old man's wife came out of the house. She was seventy-three years old and complained vehemently about their farm, which was in the most beautiful valley I had passed through today. "It hasn't rained for months!" she said. "Last year at this time our fields were already flooded—look at this! It's horrible! This place is so poor!"

They were like farmers anywhere—pessimistic and angry at the weather. I often heard similar comments in the relatively affluent rural suburbs of Fuling, where I sensed that these complaints were a form of humility that masked contentment. And perhaps it was a sort of superstition, a way of guarding against the dangers of pride. Traditionally the Chinese did the same thing with children, trying not to lavish too much praise on a child because the attention could draw bad luck.

The woman invited me to dinner, just as the teacher-peasant had done at my first stop, and I explained that I had to continue hiking. In the countryside it was a common invitation—virtually every time I went for a long walk in the fields somebody offered me a meal. It seemed that you could travel indefinitely in rural Sichuan without any money at all, because the people were so generous that they considered it rude not to offer a meal or a place to stay.

A while later I met a young man in his early twenties who was with his younger brother, a twelve-year-old boy. The boy wore his school sweat suit and he recognized me immediately.

"Are you the *waiguoren* who won the long race last year in Fuling?" he asked.

"Yes."

"I've seen you near the college. I go to the East River Middle School."

There were no middle schools in this part of the countryside and the children boarded in Fuling if they wanted to continue their education. The boy paid 170 yuan a month for room and board, and his older brother estimated that probably 90 percent of the children in this region continued their education to middle school. They took the boat downstream to Fuling and usually came home every other weekend.

A group of children gathered around, staring. The twelve-year-old boy told them that I was the *waiguoren* who had won the Fuling long race, which he described in vivid detail, emphasizing the great distance by which I had triumphed. I was embarrassed to hear the story, although by now I was used to it; even after more than a year it was the reason many people in Fuling knew who I was.

It impressed me that so many of the students in this remote area traveled all the way to Fuling for school, and I realized that these were the sort of children that my own students would teach after graduation. Here I could see the point of my job—not just the literature I taught, but also the simple fact that for nearly two years I had had a role in an education system that included children like this.

I felt the same way whenever I hiked into the fields behind college and saw the students doing their homework on their families' threshing platforms. On sunny afternoons there was a child on virtually every platform—Fuling schools assigned an enormous amount of homework, and the students did it with remarkable diligence, even if they were from uneducated peasant families. I had come to recognize this as perhaps the characteristic that I admired the most about the local people: they had an enormous respect for education, and it was easy to feel good about teaching in a place like that.

In this respect my views had changed quite a bit from the spring of my first year, when I had been so pessimistic about the education system's constant propaganda. In some ways, it helped to get outside of the classroom—when I walked through the hills and saw the children doing their schoolwork, it reminded me of my own students, and the places where they had come from and the places where they would someday return to teach. I came to realize that, although much of the propaganda still disgusted me, it wasn't necessarily the most important issue. The slogans wouldn't last forever—nothing in China did—but the children who were educated would stay that way, regardless of the country's changes.

WHENEVER I WAS UNCERTAIN about which way to walk, I simply asked the people where I had gone last year. Everybody knew—it seemed there wasn't a single person who didn't remember me. And they all talked about the German, too; I wished I could have met him, because now I was curious about what he had been studying. It was like following Kurtz up the Congo: I kept hearing snatches of information, details about the way he walked and how much money he had and the boots he wore. And then I realized that he must have heard about me as well, and that probably he had felt he was following some unknown *waiguoren* through the rugged hills of the Wu River valley.

In late afternoon I began to make my way down toward the river. I came through a sunny valley that opened onto a broad square field with houses in the corners. I stopped to rest and a group of peasant women gathered around. Most of them were in their sixties, dressed in blue, and I told them that this was a beautiful area.

"This place isn't any good," one of them said. "This is a *qiong shanqu*—a poor mountainous region. The economy here is terrible."

I always complimented peasants so I could hear them run down the places where they lived. They never seemed happier than when they stood there in the sunshine, next to the flourishing rapeseed and wheat and young rice, and talked about what a miserable home they had.

A young girl came up to me. "Are you the *waiguoren* in Fuling who does long runs?"

"Yes."

She turned to the old women. "They had a long race in Fuling and he was the best."

"That's why he can walk out here," one of the women said. "He's very healthy. Look how few clothes he's wearing!"

"Look how big his bag is!" said another. "How heavy!"

"His feet are so big—look at those enormous shoes!"

They studied me for a while and I waited for somebody to ask about my salary. But one of the women turned to me and asked instead, "In your country, do you have planned-birth policy?"

"No. You can have as many children as you want."

They shook their heads, amazed. I told them that in America there wasn't a population problem, and so the rules were different from those in China.

"How many children are in your family?" one of the women asked.

"Four. Three sisters and me."

"Here you can't do that," she said. "Only one—if you have another, you have to pay a fine."

"More than ten thousand yuan!" another woman interjected.

Some children had come over to look at me, and I noticed two small boys standing together.

"What about them?" I asked. "They look like brothers."

"That's right," the old woman said. "Their parents had to pay a fine."

One of the boys was about four years old; his brother was six or seven. They were filthy, and they stood tentatively on a wheat terrace above us, afraid of the *waiguoren.* A little girl of about five came over—a tiny thing with wild black hair and dirt-smudged cheeks. Wide-eyed, the child stared at me. She had enormous coal-black eyes, like my youngest sister, Birgitta, when she was little. I smiled, and the girl smiled back.

"She's the third in her family!" one of the women said.

"Oh," I said. "They must have paid a big fine."

"No," the woman said. "Their house was *tuile!*"

"What?"

"Their house was *tuile!*"

"Tuile?"

"Right!"

I couldn't believe it, so I quickly sketched the character on my notebook. "This *tui?*"

"That's right."

It meant any number of things: to push, turn, cut, infer, shift, postpone, elect. But when you *tui*'ed a house it meant simply that you knocked it over. The local planned-birth officials had pushed over the girl's house because she had been the third child.

I had read of such things in the foreign press, but I had always assumed that they only happened in very remote areas. But then I realized that I had been walking all day, and this small beautiful valley was nothing if not remote.

The old women were shaking their heads and looking at the little girl. She wasn't comfortable hearing this conversation and something in her expression said: Sorry. Undoubtedly there were complications to growing up when you knew that your birth had caused your family's home to be knocked over. But there was also something else in her eyes; it was vague and undefined and meant, essentially: Some things are worth more than money and houses. The old women saw it, too. One of them tousled the girl's hair, and then she ran off to play with the other children in the unplowed fields.

I DIDN'T MAKE IT TO LAST YEAR'S CAMPSITE. I spent too much time talking with people, and finally I pulled up short. But I found a good spot in the hills high above the Wu River, where I ate dinner and read Ted Williams's autobiography. I decided that I would read that book every spring for the rest of my life. He wasn't particularly happy happy whenever he went to work for the Red Sox, and I respected that. Also there was something distinctly American about his voice—the cockiness and the earthy slang and the rhythms of his prose. And especially I liked the way the book began:

"I wanted to be the greatest hitter who ever lived. . . ."

In the morning I broke camp early and caught a boat downriver. The water level was low and the limestone cliffs along the bank were white and clean-looking, streaked by diagonal grooves and cuts jutting up from the chalky green Wu. Fifteen feet above the waterline I could see the dark smudge on the rocks where the summer river would rise. It was Sunday and the boat was crowded with peasant children heading back to school. I stood at the stern and watched the white cliffs slip past in the mist, knowing that I would never see this part of the river again. That was my last spring in Fuling.

长江

THE RIVER

THE RIVER IS THE QUICKEST WAY out of Chongqing. The city has a new airport and a new expressway, and the railroad, although now aging, was a technological breakthrough when it was completed in 1952—the first great postwar achievement of Deng Xiaoping, acting as Mao's lieutenant in the southwest. But none of them has improved on the Yangtze. The trains are slow, and road traffic is bad, and, because of pollution and the river-valley fog, planes are often delayed. The convenience of the river has always been here, and in one form or another it always will be.

Today the *Zhonghua,* the six-o'clock slow boat, is preparing to leave Chongqing, and its passengers are more than ready to go. It has been a stifling June day, the sunshine filtered hot and humid through the city's coal-tinted haze, and the travelers are tired and grumpy. Many of them are tourists; they have come from all across China, arriving on crowded trains and heartbroken old buses. Tempers have melted in the Sichuan heat. Ten minutes before departure, an argument breaks out between a passenger and a worker on the top deck.

The passenger is big, with a bull neck and short bristly hair and heavy useful hands. His eyes are tight black beads of anger in a round face that glistens with sweat. He is moneyed—this is obvious from his clothes, from his slick-shined shoes and his silk shirt, and mostly it is obvious from his status as a tourist. Domestic tourism in China has boomed in the last decade, but still the average Chinese does not travel far simply for pleasure. Tourists like this man are part of a new class, and often their money is tangible in the way it literally surrounds their persons: in the fine clothes that they wear, in the beepers and cell phones that are clipped to their belts, and, often, in the simple well-fed bulk of their bodies.

Money is the problem today; the passenger is not satisfied with the quality of his third-class cabin. He purchased his ticket from a broker at Chongqing's Chaotianmen Docks, where he was promised a fine boat, and the *Zhonghua*—serviceable but worn, its decks grimy with river filth—is not a fine boat. The passenger has come a long way to see the Three Gorges, he says, and his ticket was not cheap. His slurred words are angry and in one meaty fist he grabs the worker's shoulder epaulet, holding the man close while speaking loudly in his face.

The worker is smaller, a young man in his late twenties who is too weak to pull himself free. He wears a dirty blue-and-white-striped uniform shirt, and speaking rapidly he tries to defend himself: he did not sell the tickets, he has no connection to the broker at Chaotianmen, and the passenger should not be so pushy. But by now a crowd has gathered, and their voices begin to rise in shared complaint, until at last the worker's superior arrives to rescue him.

The passenger keeps his hold on the worker while directing his complaints to the superior, who makes the same excuses that have already been made, but he makes them with more confidence. For a few minutes the confrontation is at a standstill, but the crowd shifts restlessly, sensing a conclusion.

Finally the big man says, "Do you have any second-class cabins?" And as simply as that the dispute is resolved. Money is exchanged; the tourist and the supervisor shake hands. The big man passes out cigarettes to everybody involved. The crowd disperses. The little man, his pride wounded, smoothes his crumpled epaulets and retreats to the rail of the deck with his ill-bought cigarette. Nobody notices him—and then the *Zhonghua* sounds its horn and pushes away from the dock, and the argument is forgotten as the passengers watch the city slip past, the boat floating out into the heart of the great wide Yangtze.

THREE MILES NORTH OF CHONGQING, the river abruptly turns east, the bend marked by a shrine to Buddha and an old weather-stained pagoda perched high above the water. The hills begin to rise—green rugged hills, falling away to blanched sheets of limestone stained by last year's high-water marks. Many of these slopes are too steep for factories or apartment buildings, and small farms become more common as the boat cruises east. The peasants' homes are simple: mud or brick walls topped by a gray tiled roof. Often they are shaded by clusters of banana trees. And all along the river are crop terraces, carved into the sloping hills where factories can find no foothold.

The scenery is quietly beautiful—not breathtaking, but mesmerizing in the gentle roughness of the hills and the broken regularity of the terraced fields. And just as quietly Chongqing has been left behind, and suddenly it is clear that everything in this landscape has been shaped by the steady power of the Yangtze.

For the river here has strength. Sometimes it widens to several hundred feet, and sometimes it is pinched close between steep hills, but always the current is powerful. The Yangtze carries snowmelt from the western mountains, and it has already been joined by most of its seven hundred tributaries, and so it slips quickly through the hills. Of the world's great rivers, only the Amazon pushes more water to the sea.

The sun is dropping now and a soft cooling breeze sweeps across the river. Most of the travelers stand on the *Zhonghua*'s deck, watching the hills slip past. A cluster of Guangdong businessmen hold cell phones to their ears, chattering loudly in Cantonese. A young woman stands alone against the rail, her long black hair and short pink skirt flowing in the wind.

The air is clean now, with only a few wispy clouds scratched across the fading blue dome of the sky. The small fishing sampans are starting to dock for the evening, and the *Zhonghua* passes a group of children playing barefoot in the shallows. Corn stands high in the hills. The crop is two months old and it has just begun to ripen; the stalks are a fresh spring green but the tips are starting to fade toward gold.

There is no rice growing on the riverbanks; the hills are too steep for that. Some of the slopes are too rocky for corn, but even in the roughest land there is always some sign of cultivation—at the least, a single patch of corn tucked into a break in the rock. The crop rows are vertical, running down the hillside, and they have been half-terraced and leveled as much as possible.

It is not an easy place to make a living. Even the most successful farms—the ones with two-story houses, large pig huts, big cement threshing platforms, and a dozen corn plots carved into the hillside—even these farms speak of the difficulty of growing crops in such a landscape. Every terrace has been shaped by human effort, by successive generations of the same clan, by decades and perhaps centuries of work. All of it consisted of the simple labor of hands and feet and basic tools, and the terrain has been changed so gradually that the work of the peasants seems as inevitable as a force of nature—something as determined and powerful as the river itself. Human history sits heavily on the land, as it so often does in China.

The sun sets. The sky glows orange, the hills darken, the round ball of the sun sends a bright band of light skipping along the boat's wake. And then, behind the western hills, the sun sets.

IN A THIRD-CLASS CABIN a young man and woman arrange their luggage on the floor. They could be eighteen years old or they could be thirty; like many young Chinese, they simply look young. There are eight berths in the cabin, stacked in bunks of two. An old woman sitting on a lower bunk asks the couple if the last two beds are theirs.

"We're sharing a berth," the young woman says. "We were just married."

There is nothing unusual about passengers sharing beds, but the young woman's husband reddens in embarrassment. The woman, pretty with short bobbed hair, smiles and touches his shoulder.

The two women talk politely for a while. They ask each other if they have eaten, and where they are going, and what they were doing in Chongqing. The married couple is returning home to Yichang, the old woman to Wuhan, and none of them has anything good to say about Chongqing.

"It's very backward," says the old woman, shaking her head. "The people's salaries are too low, the cost of living too high."

The young woman agrees, remarking that the Chongqing transportation is inconvenient, and that the city is not as good as Yichang.

Her husband says nothing. He helps his wife slip off her shoes, and then he climbs into bed beside her. By the light of the cabin he reads a magazine while she dozes. The bunk is less than three feet wide but they lounge comfortably.

The nighttime river is peaceful. The summer stars are out

tonight; the Big Dipper glows steady above the gently rocking boat, and a quarter-moon hangs bright in the southern sky. The Yangtze is black except for the lights that streak across its water. By now there are few homes along the banks, and even fewer with their lights on. Most of the light comes from the river—from the low strips of sandstone along shore, faintly luminescent in the evening, and from the dinghies and the shore markers. Red lights blink on the south side of the river, green on the north; the night boats pass between, their searchlights sweeping silently across the water.

At night there are no hydrofoils, no fishing boats, no two-man sampans. Occasionally the *Zhonghua* passes a long flat bank where the smaller boats have docked for the night, pulled onto shore next to bamboo shacks whose windows glow warmly—makeshift restaurants, hotels, mah-jongg parlors. The barge traffic has all but stopped.

Most of the other boats on the river are big passenger ships that pass like floating islands of light. Some have come upstream all the way from Shanghai, traveling through the flats of Anhui province, past the lakes of Hubei, the factories of Wuhan, the cliffs of the Three Gorges, and now, a few hours outside of Chongqing, they are nearly home.

After a while the young woman wakes up. She shifts in the bunk, drawing close to her husband. *"Ni shi shei?"* she says softly, playfully. "Who are you?"

Her husband murmurs something in response and she laughs quietly. The door to the cabin is open, and outside there is the steady hum of the motor and the gentle sound of the river slapping against the hull of the boat. "Who are you?" the woman whispers again. "Who are you?"

FEW PASSENGERS DISEMBARK AT FULING. Most are going another two days through the Gorges to Yichang, or three nights to Wuhan. And so Fuling appears like a break in a dream—the quiet river, the cabins full of travelers drifting off to sleep, the lights of the city rising from the blackness of the Yangtze.

Four hours have passed since Chongqing. Lights cluster on the banks: homes, factories, cars. A newly constructed bridge slips overhead. The boat's loudspeakers crackle, announcing that Fuling is the next stop, and then the dream of the river is over and the city comes into view.

The heart of Fuling is built up around a cove in the river. From the broad arc of this cove the city rises on steep hills like a curtain patchworked with lights—the weak lights of shopkeepers' lamps, the flashing beams of motocab headlights, the steady yellow squares of windows—and this well-lit curtain falls and flickers above the black water of the Yangtze. The *Zhonghua* moves toward the shore, its horn booming, gradually bringing the dock closer. The boat draws southward until it is out of the main current of the river, until the great force of the Yangtze has been left behind, and then it docks.

CHAPTER TWELVE

Upstream

IN LITERATURE CLASS for that last semester we studied Washington Irving, Edgar Allan Poe, Mark Twain, Kate Chopin, Jack London, Robert Frost, and Langston Hughes, and then for the last unit I assigned Amy Tan and some Chinese-American poets. The literature came at the students from far away—Rip Van Winkle and the jumping frog and Hughes's distant rivers—but then suddenly we were watching the end of the *Joy Luck Club* movie, when the Chinese-American narrator comes to China and meets her sisters. It was the first time that China truly entered my literature class; the students had performed Shakespeare with Chinese Characteristics, and they had written about Robin Hood coming to China, but these had only been ways of putting foreign literature into familiar contexts. Now we were really here: the narrator was embracing her long-lost sisters, and all of the girls in my class were crying, and most of the boys were trying hard not to.

Afterward I asked them to write about their families, describing their parents' and grandparents' lives. One student, a girl named Dina, wrote a poem:

Looking Back at My Ancestors

A weak woman,
Sitting in a shabby hut
Spinning yarn again and again

She can't go out
As she was fettered by feudalism deeply

In 1921
The CPC was founded
My grandmother went out for revolution
To Shanghai, to Chongqing
Most of our country had her track.

My mother, a young woman
During the Great Cultural Revolution
Acted as a Red Guard
Denied all the advanced thing
Calling Long Live Chairman Mao.

Many of them, like Linda, wrote about life in the countryside:

My great grandmother was born of a poor family. She had to be as a servant for a landlord. She suffered a lot. She doesn't have enough food to feed in, and doesn't have enough clothes to shelter from cold. She was treated unfairly by her master.

Also, my grandmother's situation didn't improve much. Her feet were also banded with great pain. She had given five children's birth. Unfortunately, three of them dided of hunger. This made my grandmother very sad. She cried and cried for three days. And what was worse her husband dided of illness. She became a widow for thirty years through hardship and difficulties.

My mother's life was a little better than them, since she was born just when the New China was born. My mother was not very tall, but she was very kind and beautiful. She treated us tenderly. Of course, her life was not very satisfactory at all. She had to make a living by hard work. She went out on cold days for getting grass for pigs; carried coal from far away for heat; and she stayed up sewing for us. She contributed her life to her family.

Nearly all of the papers were like that, and I found that I could not grade them—not even a check in the corner. There was nothing about them that I could touch, and some of them I could hardly read, because they were so poignant. In the end I couldn't bring myself to return the stories, and so I kept them, simply telling the students that everybody had done a good job.

Their writings made me think about the future as much as the past. I saw the steady quiet struggle that had taken the students to where they were now, and for the next generation it would probably look much the same. I imagined Linda's own daughter as a young woman—perhaps a college student with a life that was a notch better than her mother's. And I imagined her writing, "My mother was not very tall, but she was very kind and beautiful. . . ."

AFTER CLASS I often walked in the countryside behind campus. I had stopped running and it was pleasant to walk—everything had slowed down; I could talk with the peasants and watch them do their work. Often they asked if I knew the *waiguoren* who ran in the hills, and I told them that it was something I no longer did, which seemed to relieve them. There had never been any point to charging up Raise the Flag Mountain.

In the evenings and on weekends I followed my city routines. Sunday mornings had been refined to perfection—church, the priest, the blacksmiths, the teahouse, and then I ordered dumplings from a restaurant across the street from the South Mountain Gate Park. The dumplings were the best in Fuling and usually I started eating at eleven o'clock sharp, when the twelve-piece brass band began to play in the park. The band was hired almost every Sunday morning for weddings, because a good wedding attracted as much attention as possible—there was big face in that. The band played "Auld Lang Syne" and "Oh Come All Ye Faithful"; and sure enough the stick-stick soldiers always came faithfully, gawking at the bride as she arrived in bright makeup and a full dress.

At the restaurant I usually took one particular seat where I could lean back against the wall and look out at the street and the park. Once the weather turned warm, the parade of everyday life on the sidewalk was even better than the band—peasants with their baskets, families with their children, young couples out for a stroll, old women with umbrellas held against the sunshine.

During the week I often visited Gao Ming and Ma Fulai, two friends whom I had met in the park during the Spring Festival. Gao Ming was an artist; he was twenty-six years old and a few years earlier he had graduated from the Sichuan Institute of Fine Arts. He was quite gifted—his apartment was full of fine oil paintings that he had done in school, mostly in a European style. He owned his own business in Fuling, and his company specialized in massive sheets of frosted glass upon which he painted and etched flowers, bamboo groves, panda bears, and other Chinese motifs. Generally the glass was set into dividers and walls of expensive restaurants and apartments, and Gao Ming was particularly good at this kind of work, which meant that his sheets of frosted glass were particularly tacky. This was no fault of his; he simply painted what people asked him to paint, and usually they asked him to cram as many shapes and colors as possible onto a sheet of frosted glass.

His clientele was the Fuling rich, and sometimes I accompanied him as he went to their apartments to make deliveries or take orders. Every rich person in the city seemed to decorate in precisely the same way, with certain objects that were universally accepted in Fuling as signs of wealth: Gao Ming's style of glasswork, ornate ceiling lights surrounded by baroque constructions of plaster and velvet, odd wooden trellises that were covered with plastic vines and grapes. Another common decoration was an enormous wooden watch that hung on the wall as a clock. And of course they always had top-of-the-line televisions, VCD players, and karaoke machines. These people were what you would call *nouveaux riches* in other countries, but in Fuling such a term was meaningless unless you kept track by the minute. There were no *vieux riches* and I didn't blame them for showing off what they finally had.

I liked going with Gao Ming on his rounds, and none of the rich people seemed to mind, because having a *waiguoren* in your apartment was even classier than a trellis full of fat plastic grapes. But the rich people themselves were the best decorations of all. Invariably the men had big hair-sprayed pompadours and flashy silk shirts, and the women, whose faces were spectacularly made up, wore see-through dresses and lounged on overstuffed couches. I never could figure out what they did all day long, especially the women; they usually looked as if they had just arrived or were getting ready to leave. And yet they always sat there on the couches.

Gao Ming made more than ten thousand yuan a month, but he had constant employee problems and his life was a mess. He had a seven-month-old daughter who lived with his wife, a Chongqing-based artist, and Gao Ming had taken advantage of this job-related separation to find a girlfriend in Fuling. When his wife finally heard about this arrangement, she took the baby off to Henan province, where she found another job. She was threatening to get a divorce, which didn't seem to faze Gao Ming; he was confident that she would return, although at the same time he made no effort to get rid of his girlfriend, who was a classic raspy-voiced Sichuanese *xiaojie* with a sharp wit. Gao Ming simply wasn't one to worry about the future; his goal was to have a good time, and so he gambled, went to karaoke bars, and, I suspected, hired prostitutes—certainly he talked about them a lot. Some days he lost as much as eight hundred yuan playing mah-jongg. He was a lousy mah-jongg player.

He liked talking with me about these problems because he assumed that I understood his lifestyle, which in his opinion was distinctly American. "People's minds in our China still aren't very open," he told me once. "In your country you can have a friend who is a girl, but here it always causes a problem. My wife is like that, because she isn't open-minded." I didn't know how to respond to that—having affairs wasn't exactly my vision of the benefits of Reform and Opening. Usually I said nothing at all; as a *waiguoren* I was often most comfortable when I was listening.

On warm nights Gao Ming sometimes told me about his troubles while we ate hot pot, which was a specialty of eastern Sichuan. It's meaningless to say that hot pot was spicy—everything the people ate in Sichuan was spicy, from breakfast rolls dipped in hot pepper to *kongpao* chicken. Some Peace Corps volunteers developed ulcers from the sheer heat of the food.

But even in such a cuisine, hot pot stood out as particularly spicy: vegetables, meat and noodles cooked in hot oil over an open flame right at your table. People ate it year-round, but it was particularly popular in the summer; the theory was that the hot pot made you sweat, and the sweat made you cool.

Hot pot stands appeared on the Fuling sidewalks during summer evenings, when it became as much a social event as a meal—you sat in front of the bubbling pot, gazing at the pedestrians as they paraded past. Gao Ming and I would eat slowly, watching for *xiaojies*, and if he was in a good mood he talked about things he hoped to buy. Once or twice on bad days he spoke of his possible divorce. But usually he saw the bright side of things, and several times he described the wedding ceremony he'd like to have with his wife if they didn't get divorced first. They had been married for five years, but like many people in Fuling, they had postponed the wedding until they would have enough money to afford an impressive ceremony. Now Gao Ming had the cash but not the wife; fortunately, he was enough of an optimist to overlook this awkward fact, speaking fondly of the magnificent wedding he had in mind. "I'll rent lots of cars," he told me one night. "Ten cars—there will have to be at least ten cars. We'll drive around South Mountain Gate and up to Gaosuntang, and out to the East River district, and then we'll drive back. Everybody out on the street will stop to watch."

In some respects, Gao Ming's friend Ma Fulai was similar: he also had a baby daughter, a wife, and a girlfriend. But he had made the mistake of collecting all of these in Fuling, and he was a tortured soul without any of Gao Ming's blithe hopefulness. Ma Fulai often came to me for advice, partly because he assumed that an American would know how to solve such complications. But I also sensed that he talked with me because he knew that as a *waiguoren* I was outside the loop. A few of my city friends saw me in this light; they knew that I wasn't connected to the local gossip networks, and so they told me their secrets and asked for advice.

One night in late April, Ma Fulai came to my apartment and sat smoking in my living room. I could see that he was upset, but he wouldn't say what was wrong. We talked for a while and then I tried being direct.

"Are you having some problem with your wife?"

He nodded and blew out a cloud of smoke. But still he said nothing.

"Does she have another boyfriend?" I knew this probably wasn't the issue, but it seemed an easy way to open things. He shook his head quickly. "That's not it," he said. "The problem is just that we don't get along. We have nothing in common—no hobbies, no interests, nothing. We fight all the time. It's been like that since we were married."

"Why did you marry?"

"Because of her parents. Her father and mother put pressure on me."

"How did they do that?"

"Maybe you don't understand. Here in our China it's not like it is in your country. Here if you start to have *guanxi* with somebody, with a girl, then you have to get married." He sighed and drew on his cigarette. "What I mean is, once you start sexual *guanxi*, you have to get married. So that's what happened with my wife and me. I was twenty-four and she was twenty-two. So I married her, even though I knew we weren't suitable."

I said nothing. It was seven o'clock on a warm night, and I let him think for a while in the fading twilight.

"I don't know what to do," he said. "Do you have any advice?"

"It's very complicated. Perhaps there's no easy solution."

"All day long I think of this problem. It gives me a headache. All day long, that's what I think about."

"I know that Gao Ming has a girlfriend," I said. "Do you have one?"

There was a pause, and then he nodded.

"Who is it?"

"She's a student here at the college. Remember the girl I come to see sometimes on campus? She's not really my cousin, like I told you before. We get along very well. In all respects I like her better than my wife."

I had assumed that she was his girlfriend; nothing of that sort surprised me. Adam had young male friends in town who were much the same way—divorced or on their way to it, with small children and shifting girlfriends. It didn't seem nearly as common among campus workers, and probably this was also true in other traditional *danweis,* but many of the young people involved in business seemed to be having affairs. They had money, and they weren't tied to an old-style work unit that could influence and even regulate their behavior; yet at the same time they followed the standard Fuling pattern of marrying and having their child as quickly as possible. I asked Ma Fulai if his wife knew about his girlfriend.

"No," he said. "She has no idea."

"Are you sure? Gao Ming's wife was all the way in Chongqing but she still found out about his girlfriend."

"My wife doesn't know; I'm certain of it. If I ever go anywhere with the girl, we go someplace where there aren't any other people."

I wondered where in Fuling that might be, and I thought that I might like to go there myself sometime. Ma Fulai sighed again.

"My marriage is very bad," he said. "The only good thing is my daughter—other than her, we have nothing in common. We never talk and we don't eat together. We sleep in separate beds. You've seen my apartment—each of us has a separate room, and I sleep in the small bed. Her parents and her brothers are like strangers to me. They know I don't love her."

"What does she want to do about it?"

"She doesn't want to do anything."

"Why not?"

"Because she loves me. And maybe she thinks this is the way a marriage should be."

"What do you want to do?"

"I don't know," he said. "Do you have any ideas? What would people do in your country?"

"This problem is the same in my country. It's bad to divorce with a small baby. But if there was no baby of course they'd divorce very quickly."

"It's not the same here," he said. "Divorce isn't very easy, even if you don't have a child. It's because the thought here is still so traditional and closed. It's like it might have been in your country in the 1940s and 1950s. The problem is that women aren't the same as men—they still aren't equal. So a divorce affects them very much. A divorced woman has no face."

"What about a man?"

"It's not very good either; some people will say you're a bad man. But it's not nearly as bad as it is for the woman. All of these ideas are very backward here, like the attitudes toward sex—the way you have to marry somebody if you have sex with her. It's better in your country. I don't like other things about your country, but I wish that in this way China was the same as America."

"In America there are too many divorces," I said. "People think it's too easy. So perhaps it's not good in either place."

We sat in silence for a while. It was nearly dark and I had no advice to give him. I said the same things I always said—move slowly, be patient, think about the baby. He had heard it all before, and he sat there shaking his head.

"Everybody has this problem," he said. "Young people, old people—all of them have the same problem. It's because they have to get married so soon, because there's no sexual freedom. Probably 80 percent of them are unhappy like me. All of my friends are unsatisfied with their marriages, but they know that divorce is difficult, too. Perhaps you don't understand this, but it's a serious problem."

He asked me if he could sit in my apartment for a while, and I said that was fine. I had a literature class review session later, and I prepared my material, thinking about Ma Fulai and other friends like Gao Ming. I doubted that the problem was simply a lack of sexual freedom; rather it seemed that there was just enough freedom to get the trouble started. Later there would be more sexual freedom, but this might not do wonders for the people in Fuling, either. Often I found it hard to explain that certain things were complicated no matter where you lived.

The only honest advice I could ever think of was: Don't get married. But this wasn't particularly realistic and it was easy for me to say; as a *waiguoren* that was yet another way in which I was beyond the pale, because I wasn't going to be married in Fuling. None of those issues touched me directly, and I watched from a distance, the way I did with so many other things. It was like wandering through rich people's apartments, or reading the stories my students wrote, or standing out on my balcony watching the Yangtze boats slip past to unknown destinations. There was a certain power to that, because many things did not touch me, and from this distance there were moments—a trip down the river, a day in the countryside—that stayed with me in all of their vividness and beauty. But often there was helplessness and sometimes there was sadness. Sitting there with Ma Fulai, I knew that there would be something good about bringing this part of my life to a close. I watched him smoke another cigarette, and then he left.

THAT SPRING was Beijing University's hundredth anniversary, which nationwide celebrations combined with the seventy-ninth anniversary of the May Fourth Movement. There was a television special in which Da Shan, the Chinese-speaking Canadian, told jokes and introduced floor shows on a stage in the Beijing campus.

The May Fourth Movement had occurred in 1919, in response to the Versailles Treaty. This agreement rewarded Chinese contributions to the Allied victory by granting former German concessions like Qingdao to the Japanese—an injustice that naturally outraged the Chinese people. The movement began as a student protest, expanding to include a wide range of reform-minded Chinese intellectuals. It was a nationalistic protest that simultaneously reached out to the West; "science" and "democracy" were its catchwords.

The Communist Party claimed that the May Fourth Movement was a predecessor to its own uprising, which was a particularly brazen instance of appropriating history. Indeed, some of the May Fourth leaders were Communist or eventually turned to Communism, but it was a stretch to link their ideals to the attitude of today's Party. As a result, the television special was a surreal mixture of contradictions: Communist Party officials praised the memory of student activists; speeches extolled "science" and "democracy"; and the Beijing University campus proudly commemorated the events of 1919 while tactfully making no mention of what had happened there in 1989. Da Shan told his usual jokes. In its own strange way the event made for gripping television.

Fuling Teachers College joined in the celebration by staging a short play competition to mark the anniversary. Preliminary rounds took place in each department, with the winners performing once more in the campus auditorium. One of my literature classes prepared some scenes from *Romeo and Juliet*, while the other class adapted Kate Chopin's "Désirée's Baby" for the stage. Linda played Désirée and Mo Money was the heartless Armand; I helped them practice, along with the *Romeo and Juliet* group.

Adam's Spanish class went to work on *Don Quixote*. That was a small class—fewer than a dozen students total—and it included some of the liveliest third-year boys. They created their own version of Cervantes's novel, set in Fuling. Don Quixote became an East River noodle shop owner who spent his spare time reading about the fine deeds of Lei Feng, the worker martyr whose selfless dedication to Chairman Mao had made him a propaganda fixture since 1963. Lei Feng Spirit was a Communist-style celebration of the banal: he had been a common soldier who showed no interest in either fame or worldly possessions, preferring to labor in silent anonymity until the day a comrade accidentally backed a truck into a clothesline pole that fell on Lei Feng's head and killed him (it took the driver another twenty-five years before he was finally admitted into the Party).

Reform and Opening had put a damper on Lei Feng Spirit, although there were a few echoes of the old days. Next to the Fuling stock exchange was a building whose original propaganda message, long since removed, was still weather-stained clearly onto the white tile: "Study the Lei Feng Spirit." March was officially Lei Feng Month, although most locals simply laughed if you reminded them of this outdated tradition. But the college still took it seriously, assigning mandatory volunteer work to the students in honor of Lei Feng. In my second year, one of these March events was a cadre-led cleanup of the East River district, which consisted of a television crew filming college officials and students as they pushed dirt to the other side of the street.

The East River cleanup took ten minutes, and Adam and I watched it from the Students' Home noodle restaurant. It was a Friday afternoon and we were eating Sichuan-style spaghetti and drinking local beer. A couple of our students came over and asked us to participate in the volunteer effort, so we could be videotaped working alongside the cadres. The students seemed disappointed when we declined.

"We're eating lunch," Adam said, sipping his beer.

"Anyway, we're already doing volunteer work right now," I said. "We're Peace Corps volunteers."

The scene wasn't exactly Peace Corps brochure material, but it was impossible for us to respond to Lei Feng Spirit with anything other than cynicism. The May Fourth anniversary felt much the same way, a shameless manipulation of idealism, and probably these were the forces that gave birth to the Spanish class's play of *Don Quixote.* But in the end it was impossible to tell exactly where the play came from, because Adam gave the students the basic premise—that Don Quixote was an East River noodle shop owner who admired Lei

Feng—and from there the students took over, writing the dialogue and adding their own details.

On the day of the department competition, they were one of the last groups to perform. The play began with Mo Money sitting in his noodle shop, reading a book. He stared intently at the pages and then shouted:

"How wonderful! Look at all the fine deeds that Lei Feng does—every day he helps so many people! How I wish I could be like Lei Feng!"

He read another page; his eyes grew bigger. He stood up and began to mop his restaurant, thinking hard:

"Why do I spend all of my time working like this? How boring my life is! What good is it to mop my poor noodle shop when I could be a great hero like Lei Feng?"

And then the idea hit him: he could travel across the countryside, performing great deeds for the people. He turned his mop upside down, straddling it like a horse, and he put an old bucket on his head as a helmet. On the wall of the noodle shop was a pinup of a Japanese *xiaojie* in a sundress (you could buy the pictures in downtown Fuling for half a yuan), and Mo Money looked at her in rapture:

"My Dulcinea! I will travel everywhere until I find you!"

He turned the portrait into a banner and trotted off into the countryside. Soon he passed a peasant toiling in his fields, played by a boy named Roger.

"Sancho Panza!" Mo Money shouted. "Would you like to come have adventures with me?"

But Sancho Panza kept working: "No, I have something to do!"

"Aah, you are very *tonto!*" Don Quixote said. "Come have adventures with me. We will go to fight injustice like Lei Feng, saving beautiful maidens, and I will introduce you to my number one girl, Dulcinea! Come on, don't be a yahoo!"

"You are the yahoo! I'm too busy to go with you."

"So *tonto,*" muttered Don Quixote. For a moment he stood there thinking about what to offer the peasant. In the novel, Don Quixote promises that he'll give Sancho Panza the governorship of an island, and Adam had suggested that the student play could use Hainan, the island province in the south of China. But the students had their own ideas about Sancho Panza's reward.

"I must have a servant," Mo Money said. "If you come with me, I will promise you . . . Taiwan Island! I will make you governor of Taiwan Island!"

With that, Sancho Panza grabbed a mop and the two of them rode off together, cantering in perfect time as the audience laughed. Mo Money and Roger were both talented actors, and there was an instant chemistry between them. Roger was the quintessential sidekick, a skinny, wide-eyed boy who weighed perhaps ninety pounds and listened intently to the Don's commands. And Mo Money seemed to have taken lessons from *The Great Dictator,* shouting instructions and carrying an air of mock seriousness.

Together they bumbled through the Sichuan countryside, attacking windmills, fighting tigers, and causing trouble in rural inns. At one point they stopped to rest and Don Quixote commanded his servant to compose a song to Dulcinea. Sancho Panza took his guitar and sang under the Japanese pinup:

Dulcinea!
Dulcineeeeeeeaaaa!
You are so beautiful . . .
Where is my island?
My Taiwan Island . . .

By the time they reached Chongqing, the people had already heard about their exploits. The Chongqing mayor, played by Lewis, presented them with honorary toothbrushes, secretly pasting signs on their backs that said "Tonto," "Yahoo," and "Yashua" (toothbrush). The heroes proudly hung the toothbrushes around their necks, and Don Quixote puffed out his chest and shouted:

"I dedicate all of my good deeds to the beautiful Dulcinea! And I hope that everybody begins to do great things like Lei Feng!"

By now the student audience was in hysterics. Even the department teachers, who sat in the front row as judges for the competition, were laughing helplessly; and the crowd's energy fed the actors, driving them to dash madly across the stage from one adventure to the next. There was no question that it was by far the best play in the department—but also there was no question that the play was treading on risky political ground. Part of the audience reaction seemed to say: I can't believe I'm hearing this. To some degree I felt the same way, and at the end of the performance I found myself watching Party Secretary Zhang. It was hard to tell what he was thinking—he was smiling and laughing softly, but I could see the wheels turning in his head. And in the end he represented the only judge who really mattered.

IT TOOK THE DEPARTMENT authorities a day to react. They banned *Don Quixote;* five other plays were chosen to be performed in the campus auditorium, including "Désirée's Baby." There were never any appeals to decisions like this, and the department made it clear that political issues were involved.

But for some reason the students, who usually kept their grumbling quiet, were openly angry. Even the ones who had produced *Romeo and Juliet* muttered darkly that their play had also been denied for political reasons, because the title actors were real-life boyfriend and girlfriend, which was against the college's anti-romance regulation (the most ignored rule on campus). The strongest reaction, though, was from the Spanish students, who refused to accept the department command. Mo Money angrily confronted the department's assistant political adviser, threatening that if *Don Quixote* was blacklisted he would also pull out of "Désirée's Baby." Quickly it became a serious problem: the authorities didn't want their competition to fall apart, and they liked the politics of the Kate Chopin story, which criticized American racism.

And so it went with the anniversary celebration of the May Fourth Movement. In many ways I felt the department, and by proxy the Party, got exactly what it deserved. If you tried to politicize everything, turning every piece of literature and every scrap of history to your purposes, then at a certain point it was bound to blow up in your face. After two years I was sick of the countless anniversaries and commemorations; I was tired of the twisted history; and I had had enough of our propaganda-laced textbooks.

But at the same time, Adam felt guilty, and even though it wasn't my class I felt the same way, because there was no question that our influence had led the students into trouble. If we hadn't been there, they wouldn't have been performing *Don Quixote* and "Désirée's Baby" (and without our influence there certainly would not have been a Communist Party Member with the English name Mo Money). It was different from the other parts of our lives, in which we watched Fuling from a distance. We had a direct effect on these students, and we had always encouraged them to be open-minded, questioning, and irreverent. Some of this had been intentional—the debates about Robin Hood, the conversations in Chinese—but mostly it was a matter of our fundamental identity. We were *waiguoren,* and we didn't have that voice in the back of our minds that warned us when certain lines were being crossed. We had lived in Fuling long enough to affect some of the people, but not long enough to internalize all of the rules; and this transitional state, like the half-baked history of the May Fourth anniversary, led to risky politics.

It also seemed clear that even though the play had dealt with subjects that usually weren't associated with laughter, the students hadn't intended to be subversive in any serious way. Mo Money, after all, was both a Party Member and the class monitor, and any violation had simply been the result of everybody's losing track of the play as a whole. The subject matter came from too many directions at once: Adam had proposed the references to Lei Feng, and the students had come up with Taiwan, and all of the silly words that they loved had come from many contexts over the course of the year. Probably their biggest mistake was focusing too much on Don Quixote Spirit. They tried to be faithful to Cervantes's novel, applying its satirical bent to Fuling life, and they attempted to be as entertaining as possible. But both satire and entertainment were risky endeavors in a Communist system, which depends on the sort of control that ruins good comedy.

Mostly there was something disappointing about the pettiness. None of it had any larger significance beyond whatever knowledge the students were able to acquire in their enthusiasm, and a counterrevolution was not going to start with *Don Quixote* (although, by coincidence, some of the important dissident meetings of 1989 had taken place under Beijing University's statue of Cervantes). But in any case it seemed clear that if Communist China was going to crumble, the collapse was not going to begin here in Fuling with a group of peasant-students clowning around on mops. It was pathetic that somebody couldn't watch the play and simply laugh; it was unquestionably funny, but even intelligent, well-educated people like Party Secretary Zhang were always listening to that voice in the back of their minds: Should I laugh at this? Is it really funny? Or is it offensive and dangerous? In some ways this was what I had grown to loathe the most about Communism. I could almost bear the falseness and the lies, but I could not forgive its complete absence of humor. China was a grim place once you took the laughter away.

Adam and I encouraged Mo Money and the other students to work things out without causing more problems, but other than that we weren't involved in the negotiations. As the week passed and the students gave us regular reports on these meetings, I began to see why the Don had struck such a chord. He was the perfect Chinese character, the poor knight with his outdated ideals and heart of gold. I saw flashes of him in everybody involved: he was Mo Money and his hopeless play, but at the same time he was also Party Secretary Zhang and his hopeless political faith. When I thought about it, Party Secretary Zhang was just doing whatever he could to hold the line, just as others had held it before him, and probably he didn't enjoy this particular aspect of his job. Earlier in the semester his daughter had died and his wife had just given birth to a son; he had bigger issues to worry about, but regulating the students' politics was his job, and so he did it. Everybody was tilting at windmills and I really couldn't blame any of them.

After a few days they made a compromise. There would be a special final performance of *Don Quixote,* strictly for the English department, with all of the politically sensitive material vetted and purged. This satisfied everybody—"Désirée's Baby" would continue as planned, and the Spanish class would get a final chance to perform in front of their friends, although they weren't allowed to appear in the campus auditorium. Once again Adam helped them practice and rework the script.

At the end of the week, all of us gathered to watch the second performance of *Don Quixote.* In some ways the play was a letdown; it lacked the energy of the original, and a few times the actors became nervous, stumbling over their lines. The problem wasn't so much that important material had been lost, but rather that too much had been added: the play had acquired incredible symbolic weight in the course of a week. During the first staging, nobody had thought too much about what it meant to refer to Lei Feng and Taiwan. Now some of the looseness that makes good comedy was lost; the banned references were conspicuous by their absence, and the students were worn out from a week of negotiating with the authorities.

But nothing could completely ruin the slapstick of the two heroes, and once again the crowd enjoyed it. The play ended in mock sadness, the duo separated by Don Quixote's decision to retire to his noodle restaurant. Mo Money rode his mop slowly home, hanging his head, while the theme song from *Titanic* played mournfully in the background.

William Jefferson Foster was the play's narrator, and after the final scene he stood up to read the postscript. But as he spoke, Adam and I realized that he was departing from the prepared text, reading something that he had written himself. He was always heading off on his own like this; often in class I'd see William Jefferson Foster with his nose buried in the dictionary, and then during the ten-minute break he'd sidle up to me and say, with careful pronunciation, "How is your premature ejaculation?"

Much of his extracurricular studies was along these lines, and he was always trying out some new obscenity or perverted phrase. It was childish, but at the same time he was one of the best students in the class, and I could see that much of his English skill came from the pleasure he gained from manipulating the language. He took English in his own direction, using it as he pleased, and I liked that. I also liked that he had grown up in a poor peasant home not far from Guang'an, Deng Xiaoping's hometown, and yet now he had given himself a ludicrously pretentious WASP name.

At the end of *Don Quixote,* William Jefferson Foster veered off on his own once more. Standing there in front of the department he read his own conclusion:

> Don went back to his noodle shop, and Sancho went back to his farm to raise hogs in order to support his tuition, hoping that he could get the degree in Oxford University. Meanwhile Don taught himself and got the bachelor's degree in Penn University. Later the two crazy men travelled to China and became two English teachers, also the most famous Yahoos in Fuling.

He spoke quickly and none of the cadres caught it. Afterward he looked up at Adam and me, to see if we had understood, and then he grinned. The play was over.

THE NEXT MORNING, Adam and I woke up early to do some filming downtown. For three days we had had access to a video camera, because the Peace Corps medical officer was making a site visit and she had brought the office film equipment. It was the first time anybody from the Peace Corps staff had come to Fuling since the week we arrived in the city.

For three days we tried to capture everything about Fuling that we wanted to remember. We filmed the students' performance of *Don Quixote*, and we made trips to the countryside and the parts of old town that we liked. Much of the tape consisted of short conversations with friends: the family at the Students' Home, the priest, the people who worked in the restaurants, teahouses, and parks where we had spent so much time. We took a cab ride and asked the driver to go as fast as possible while I pointed the camera out the window, filming the traffic as it flashed past in a chorus of honks.

On the morning that the Peace Corps medical officer was leaving, we decided to do one final shooting before returning the camera. We were downtown by seven o'clock, filming a group of elderly people as they did their *taiji* routines in South Mountain Gate Park, and then we took the staircases down toward the docks so we could get some typical street scenes.

It was difficult to film average street life because it always stopped the moment we arrived. The camera was bulky, an expensive model that was essentially the same size as what a television reporter might use, and crowds always gathered and stared. Apart from conversations with friends, much of our Fuling footage consisted of locals and stick-stick soldiers gaping at the camera.

Down near the docks I quickly found myself surrounded by a crowd. Neither Adam nor I had spent much time in this area; there were no teahouses or restaurants where we knew the workers. Many of the people who gathered hadn't seen us before, and we told them that we were local teachers who were filming as a hobby.

Adam decided to create a diversion. He drifted a few feet down the street, stopping to buy a steamed bun from a streetside vendor. They bargained for a while and the crowd started to shift, and then Adam joked with the woman and she laughed, covering her mouth. Slowly I started to move backward, hoping to separate myself from the crowd. Twenty people gathered around Adam, then thirty, forty. A few cabs stopped to stare; traffic backed up. Horns honked. I crossed the street quickly and then I was alone, filming Adam in the center of the crowd. Everybody had forgotten that I was there.

It was the sort of scene that at one point had been terrifying—there was nothing more intimidating during the first year than standing in the center of a mass of people, all of them studying me with incredible intensity. But rarely were these groups anything but curious, and over time, like the other *waiguoren* who lived in rural Sichuan cities, Adam and I learned how to work the crowds. I always smiled and stayed relaxed, usually focusing on a single bystander: he would ask questions and I would answer while the rest of the people listened. Usually I told them my salary, and what I did in Fuling, and I answered their questions about America. To make the crowd laugh, I could use the dialect or refer to myself as a foreign devil. It was like being a politician in a benevolent environment, handling a press conference at which the theme was simply curiosity.

There was a certain power to those moments, because it was a remarkable thing to hold the attention of forty people who had dropped whatever they were doing simply to see you. This morning the crowd continued to swell around Adam. More than fifty people gathered close, laughing at his jokes. He offered a bun to a passing cab. He bought two more buns from the woman and began to juggle. Another battalion of stick-stick soldiers rushed across the street to join the spectators. I zoomed in with the camera, focusing on faces—the smiling bun vendor, the young shopkeepers who had come out into the street, the worn visages of the stick-stick soldiers, their faces broken into grins as they watched the *waiguoren.*

Adam dropped a bun. He picked it up and tossed it across the street toward me. He pointed me out, and the people laughed, turning back to Adam as he told another joke. Slowly I panned across the faces once more, and then suddenly the viewfinder went black.

Something pushed me backward and I took a step to regain my balance. I still had my eye on the viewfinder and it went black once more, and this time I was pushed back harder. I looked up and a man was standing in front of me, waving his leather money bag.

"You can't do this," he said. "You can't film here."

"Who are you?" I asked.

He repeated his command, and I repeated my question. I was still filming, the camera on my shoulder.

"I'm a citizen," he said. "You can't do this. It's illegal."

He swung his bag once more, harder this time, and I felt my anger rise.

"Stop hitting the camera," I said. "Who are you?"

"I'm a citizen," he said again. He had a thick local accent and he stepped close, threateningly. He was a big man with a belly and a shock of greasy hair and a round face that shone with anger. There were certain things about him that I recognized immediately—from his accent I knew that he wasn't educated, and something in the way he dressed and carried himself told me that he had a position of some authority, perhaps as a minor government cadre or a lower-level factory boss. He was in his late forties—of that age group known as the "Lost Generation," because they had grown up during the Cultural Revolution.

"I'm a citizen," he said once more.

"I'm a citizen, too," I said. "I live here in Fuling. I teach at the teachers college. There's nothing illegal about filming here."

He swung again at the camera, hitting it. I stepped forward.

"Leave me alone," I said. "I'm not doing anything wrong. Get out of here. Blow away."

The last phrase caught him. His eyes widened.

"What did you say?"

"I told you to blow away," I said. "Who do you think you are? You can't just come up and hit somebody for no reason at all. Why do you have to be so rude?"

I used the harsh word for rudeness, *culu,* and again it caught him.

"You can't film here," he shouted. "You're not teachers—you're reporters. And you can't throw things on the street like he just did. You should show more respect, and you shouldn't be here."

"I've been here for two years," I said. "We're just teachers, and we're filming because we want to remember Fuling. You shouldn't be so rude."

By now a crowd was gathering around us, murmuring, pressing close. A woman was with the man and she began to shout at me, jabbing her finger in the air. I was still filming but I held the camera low against my side. Adam hurried over from the other side of the street, trying to explain that we were teachers. But by now the woman and the man were shouting angrily, and the crowd's murmurs were growing louder, and I realized that we were in trouble. Nobody was smiling anymore. I turned the camera off. The crowd grew.

OF EVERYTHING THAT HAPPENED during my two years in Fuling, I reviewed that incident the most times. It couldn't be avoided; that was one of the most troubling moments I ever had in the city, and it was on tape.

I did not enjoy watching the video. Every time I saw it, something tensed in my stomach and I could feel my pulse race. I watched the smiling faces as Adam juggled and joked around, and I told myself that the people were obviously happy. I thought about all the days I had spent in the city, all the crowds I had encountered, and all the times nothing had happened. And I remembered the incident when the shoeshine man had bothered me and the people had stood up in my defense.

But always when I watched the video I silently urged it forward, waiting for the man to appear on the screen. He came in from the left, long after Adam had drawn the crowd, but unlike the others the man and his wife stood apart, a few feet away from the pack. They watched Adam for half a minute, and then the man turned to look at me. He crossed the street and walked toward me, striding purposefully off the side of the screen, and then suddenly everything went black.

There was much that the video showed. Most painfully, it showed the mistakes that we had made, starting with drawing a crowd in a part of town that we didn't know well. It also showed that Adam had been too nonchalant, milking the attention, and it showed that he had been disrespectful in tossing the bun across the street. It showed that I was far too quick to anger and use strong language; from the tape it seemed that the man might have left me alone if I hadn't insulted him.

But at the same time there was much missing from the tape, which was probably what made it the most unpleasant to watch. None of the background was there—nothing could show how we had dealt with so many crowds in the past that we were overconfident, and nothing could explain that confidence and looseness were the best ways to deal with that aspect of life in Fuling. The worst reaction was to fear the crowds or wish that they wouldn't appear; you had to accept that you were an anomaly, and that people were going to gather to stare and listen to you talk. If you let this bother you, it would make you miserable, the same way that there was no point in worrying about the noise and the pollution.

And always the key was to avoid taking yourself seriously. To be successful you laughed at yourself, talking of "us foreign devils," and you made a sloppy and hilarious imitation of the dialect. If you felt an urge to juggle, you juggled. It was like something that Adam used to say before he went into town to practice Chinese: "Well, now it's time to be a buffoon for the next two hours."

The tape also said nothing about all of the baggage that accompanied a *waiguoren* holding a camera in China. In 1972, when there were virtually no foreigners in the country, Zhou Enlai invited the Italian filmmaker Michelangelo Antonioni to make a documentary about China. It was a controversial invitation; Mao's wife, Jiang Qing, and other conservatives in the government opposed it, but Zhou believed that a Westerner could make a film about China that would appeal to the outside world. Antonioni was sympathetic to the Chinese government, but his final product enraged officials, who accused him of deliberately trying to make China look poor. Most famously, Jiang Qing pointed out that his shot of the Nanjing Bridge included a workers' laundry line in the foreground.

This was precisely what the Chinese expected of a foreigner—only a *waiguoren* would visit a modern bridge and come away with the image of a clothesline, making the country look poor. Although Antonioni denied strenuously that his intentions had been to criticize China, a 1974 propaganda campaign focused on the incident, turning it into a textbook example of the way *waiguoren* came to China and searched for the negative aspects. I had met older people in Sichuan and Xi'an who were familiar with this story, and as a result I had learned to be careful with my camera in Fuling. More than once somebody had accused me of trying to show the bad side of local life.

But all of our experience failed Adam and me while we videotaped. The camera showed our mistakes with an embarrassing clarity, but it didn't show everything that happened before the man confronted me, and it didn't show what happened after I turned the camera off. And perhaps what bothered me the most was that I watched the tape more than a dozen times, but never could I tell the precise moment when the crowd turned against us. I had always been fascinated by that elusive but definite shift, the quicksilver instant when a Fuling crowd became a mob, but in the end it remained a mystery. Even the camera couldn't capture it.

THE MOB GREW. I turned the camera off. Adam was at my side and both of us were trying to explain at once. The man and his wife were still at the heart of the mob, and I could hear the man saying over and over that we were reporters who had no respect for the city. But by now he wasn't the only one talking. Others pressed forward, shouting and gesturing angrily, and it was hard to understand what they were saying. The buzz of the mob rose, shifting into a roar.

I felt my anger turn to fear, and now Adam and I were trying to be conciliatory, apologizing and emphasizing that we were teachers who meant no harm. But it was too late for explanations; nobody was listening and bystanders were jostling in their effort to see what was happening. Somebody brushed against my back. I wrapped both hands around the camera and held it in front of me. More people were shouting, their faces hard with anger.

"We need to get the hell out of here," I said to Adam. I started to leave, dropping my head and holding the camera carefully, but nobody budged. The man's wife stood directly in front of me. I felt somebody clutching at my arm.

"We're leaving," I said in Chinese. The woman made no reply. She didn't move and now there was a horrible smile on her face—a combination of anger and joy as she saw us get what we deserved.

"Jesus," I said. "They won't let me out."

"Follow me," Adam said. He was carrying the camera case, an enormous metal box, and now he held it before him. Hands grabbed at him, but he shook them off and kept walking, his size and the bulk of the box forcing the mob to give way. Somebody tore at my arm. I cradled the camera as I pressed close to Adam's back. I felt a kick glance off my leg, and then another blow struck me hard on the thigh. We were free of the mob now, starting to run, and I turned quickly to see who had kicked me. But all I saw was a pack of blurred faces. We hurried down the street. I didn't look back again.

NOTHING HAPPENED AS A RESULT of the incident. Somebody called the college to report the confrontation, and the college *waiban* called the Peace Corps. The *waiban* said nothing about whether Adam and I had been in the wrong; they simply asked if the camera was all right, and the Peace Corps said there were no problems. We had told the medical officer about the incident before she left Fuling.

Adam and I talked about it with Noreen and Sunni, but we didn't tell anybody else in Fuling. Together we watched the tape a lot. Nearly all of the footage consisted of pleasant everyday scenes—the rivers and the countryside; our students and our friends—but mostly we watched the part with the crowd. It was as if we were looking for some insight that we could take away from the experience, something that would explain the unpleasantness, but there were no neat revelations. All it showed was a blunt useless truth about life on the streets of Fuling: after two years we were still *waiguoren,* both in the way we acted and in the way the people saw us.

There was nothing to do about that now, and we recovered as best we could. Fortunately we left town for a few days, because there were some Peace Corps administrative matters to take care of in Chengdu, and after returning to Fuling I tried not to think too much about the incident. In some ways avoiding the memory wasn't as hard as I had expected, because already there were many things like that in the river town. You knew they were there, but you tried not to think about them too much.

I went to town during the evenings, just as I always had. I still felt comfortable when people pressed close to see me, and the people were still friendly. Nothing had changed. It was both comforting and disheartening to realize that in some ways things were the same as they always had been.

JUNE WAS A BUSY MONTH, and I tried to start the goodbyes early, so there wouldn't be such a rush at the end.

Qian Manli and Wang Dongmei were two young women from the local Bank of China who had always been particularly helpful, so Adam and I asked them out for hot pot on a Friday night. It was the first date of any sort I'd had in two years of living in Fuling.

We met them on Gaosuntang. Both of them had dressed carefully—very short skirts, very bright makeup, silk blouses, highlights in their hair. We hadn't expected that; Adam and I were wearing T-shirts and baseball caps.

The best hot pot places were on Xinghua Road, winding down toward the center of town, and the four of us walked past the open-air restaurants that lined the sidewalk. It was a warm night, with hundreds of people eating outside, and all of them stared as we walked past. Qian Manli and Wang Dongmei were very pretty women in their mid-twenties, and it was clear that they enjoyed the attention of going out with the *waiguoren*—in fact, this appeared to be why they had prepared themselves so elaborately.

We chose a restaurant and took a table on the sidewalk. There was a hush as we arrived. The women ordered for us, and Adam and I started one of our Chinese routines, referring to each other as foreign devils, running dogs, and Capitalist Roaders. Wang Dongmei and Qian Manli laughed, as everybody always did when we peppered our conversation with Cultural Revolution insults and anti-foreigner remarks. We ordered local beer and it was nice to eat on the sidewalk, chatting and watching the crowd.

The incident with the video camera seemed far away, and I realized that one thing I would never forget about Fuling was its unpredictability—the way things could change so quickly, a bad day followed by a good week. The town wasn't simple, and neither was my role there; it would be wrong to say that I had failed in my efforts to make Fuling a comfortable home, and it would be just as inaccurate to claim that I had been entirely successful. There were good days and there were bad days. To some degree this was what I liked most about Fuling: it was a human place, brightened by decency and scarred by flaws, and a town like that was always engaging. For two years I had never been bored.

Today was one of the good days, and sitting there at the hot pot restaurant I felt completely comfortable with everything, the language and the crowd and the women at our table. It wasn't much different from a Friday night at home, hanging out with friends and joking around. And I liked the fact that Adam and I were also comfortable with each other's Chinese personalities—Ho Wei and Mei Zhiyuan were just as close as our other identities. It seemed ages since our first semester, when we had avoided going into town together because it doubled the harassment.

After an hour I got up to use the bathroom, and I returned to find Adam and Wang Dongmei talking loudly.

"You're not married!" Adam said.

"Yes, I am," she said, laughing. "I was married two months ago."

"You're joking!"

"No, it's true."

"But you never said anything about getting married!"

"You didn't ask."

"You can't be serious—you're lying to me."

But she seemed sincere. I turned to Qian Manli. "Are you married?"

"Yes."

"I don't believe it!"

"It's true," she said, smiling. She had a nice smile and very pretty black eyes, and I realized that in Fuling a woman like this would never make it past twenty-five without marrying. I had been a fool for ever thinking otherwise.

"Where's your husband?" I asked.

"He's at home."

"What's he doing?"

"I don't know. Probably watching television."

It was the same way with Wang Dongmei. Both of them were newlyweds who had left their husbands at home on a Friday night to go out with the *waiguoren.*

I glanced over at Adam. At the beginning of the evening we had promised the women that we wouldn't speak any English, but now we didn't need to; each of us knew what the other was thinking. Regardless of how comfortable certain moments were in the city, life still wasn't normal, and never would be. That had always been part of Fuling's charm and there was no reason to be surprised by it now.

We stayed for another two hours. The best aspect of eating hot pot was that it took so long—it was a slow, lazy meal, perfect for a warm night out on the sidewalk. The restaurant had cold beer and we ordered a few. Everybody had a good time. After dinner we walked the women back to their apartment buildings. I was hoping that they would invite us inside, so we could meet their husbands—sort of like meeting a girl's parents when you went out in high school. But they just smiled and waved goodbye, and we caught a cab back to the college.

TEACHER LIAO WAS PREGNANT; she was due in July. In June she invited Adam and me to a farewell dinner. She gave us some calligraphy that had been written by her father-in-law, who was famous for his brushwork, and we gave her some baby clothes.

A couple of evenings earlier, the college authorities had invited all four of the foreign teachers and our tutors to a banquet. Mr. Wang, the *waiban* representative, had always enjoyed making fun of Adam's and my Chinese, speaking with patronizing slowness and accusing us of not understanding. He sat at my table during the banquet, mocking me mercilessly, until finally Teacher Liao snapped at him.

"Ho Wei understands what you're saying!" she said. "We studied that a year ago. You don't need to talk to him like that!"

Mr. Wang laughed lightly, as he always did; but the point had been made, and I took great pleasure in watching this tiny pregnant woman set the cadre straight. It reminded me of the way she had defended Li Peng during our tutorial a year ago—it was the same fierce pride, and, despite being indirectly linked with Li Peng, I was happy to share in her loyalty.

She knew that I didn't like Mr. Wang because that spring I had been very open with her about my feelings regarding the *waiban* and the English department. Teacher Liao's final assignment had been to summarize my experience in Fuling, and I spent our last two classes doing that. I was blunt—I told her about the things I didn't like, the administration's pettiness and the mocking catcalls in town, and never once did she try to defend any of it. But I spent most of the time talking about the good things that had happened in Fuling, and I said that by far my best experience had been learning Chinese and meeting people in the city. I told her that in particular I respected the way that she and Teacher Kong had extended their friendship as well as their patience; others wouldn't have done the same.

Those classes ended in May, because of her pregnancy. My office was on the sixth floor of the teaching building, and I strongly recommended that for our final tutorials we meet in her apartment, or someplace else that was more convenient. She was not a physically strong woman, and it tired her to climb all the way up to my office.

But until the end she was very Chinese—it was appropriate for us to meet in my office, and so that was where we had class. This had nothing to do with stairs or pregnancy; it was simply how things were done. It was the Chinese way.

In early May we had my last tutorial. She struggled up the steps, gasping for breath, and I gave her a couple of minutes to recover. As was true of so many Chinese women, most of her body remained thin throughout the pregnancy—it was as if somebody had sewn an awkward bundle onto her stomach. Finally she stopped wheezing and we began class.

After thirty minutes she suddenly sat bolt upright, puffed out her cheeks, and rushed out the door. I could hear her getting sick in the spittoon outside my office, and then she hurried down the hallway to the bathroom.

I waited for her to return. A year ago, I would have assumed that she would cancel class, but now I knew better—we would finish the two hours today. I knew exactly how she would act when she returned, and what she would say. And I knew that I would always remember this woman's quiet pride and toughness, and the way it had gone from being infuriating to something whose consistency was admirable and even comforting.

Five minutes later she came back. She smiled, blushed, and said, "*Duibuqi.* Sorry."

"Do you want to stop class?" I asked.

"No. It is nothing—often at this time in the morning I am a little sick."

"Certainly we don't have to finish today if you feel poorly."

"It is nothing," she said firmly. "Now—please continue with what you were saying before I left."

And I did.

I HAD MADE SOME MONEY from a story I had written for the *Los Angeles Times*, and I donated the payment to the Fuling Catholic church. I knew that Father Li had been looking for some extra cash so he could have a mural painted on a new wall in the courtyard, and he thanked me when I made the donation.

"Thank you for your kindness to me," I said, shaking the old man's hand. We were sitting in his office, with the poster of Mao and Deng on the wall. Father Li gripped my hand tightly.

"We'll remember you after you're gone," he said. "I'll say a Mass for you."

"Thank you," I said, and then I thought of something. "Could you also say a Mass for my grandfather?"

"Certainly. Write his name here."

He handed me a piece of paper and I wrote my grandfather's name: Frank Anselm Dietz. Anselm was the holy name that he had chosen when he became a Benedictine monk. I wrote it carefully and gave the paper back to the priest.

"When my grandfather was young, he was a monk in Rome," I said. "He wanted to come here to China." I had told Father Li this before, but for some reason it seemed important that I repeat it now.

"Rome is a very beautiful city," said the priest.

"Yes, it is," I said. "I've been there before."

"I've never gone," he said, chuckling to himself.

"My grandfather didn't become a priest. But I think he would like it very much if you said a Mass for him here in Fuling."

"I'll do that," Father Li said, nodding.

"Thank you very much," I said. "I'll come back sometime and see the new wall."

"You will always be welcome here."

He walked with me into the courtyard, where high walls kept out the noise of the city. Flowers were growing around the Four Modernizations sign. It was a hot afternoon. I was thinking about my grandfather and the old priest, and suddenly I was so sad that I couldn't say anything else. Silently I shook his hand and turned to leave.

"Manman zou," he said. "Go slowly." But I walked quickly out of the courtyard and into the roar of the city.

I GAVE THE LITERATURE STUDENTS their final examination during the last week. Linda's father was very sick now, and she took the test a few hours early so she could catch a noon bus home. I offered to let her take it later, or not at all; she had always been one of the best students and the news about her father had not sounded good. But she insisted on taking the test before leaving Fuling.

Later that afternoon I supervised the rest of the students during the scheduled exam. As always, they were nervous and worked seriously, although I noticed that one girl, Susan, seemed distracted. She was very pale and spent most of the second hour with her head on the desk.

I didn't think much of it until later. It was Adam's birthday and after the exam we had a banquet for all the students at a local restaurant. Everybody drank too much and it was a good night, spilling over to the Students' Home, where Feng Xiaoqin served us more beer.

At some point during the evening, Mo Money told me that Linda's father had died while she was taking my examination. The fortune-tellers had been right; and now I wished that I had insisted she take the test some other time.

The following day Susan disappeared from the college. The story came out gradually, in bits and pieces. Four days earlier she had had an abortion, and the night before the examination she had been taken to the emergency room because of complications. Somehow it had been kept secret up to that point; my impression was that she had found some sort of illegal private doctor, although this wasn't clear. All we knew for certain was that her emergency-room trip had alerted the college authorities, and now they knew the truth, which was why she had left. Students were expelled whenever they were caught having sexual relations, not to mention getting pregnant. And a note was attached to their *dangan*—the dossiers that followed them wherever they went in China. If Susan ever took a *danwei* job of any sort, her superiors would know what had happened to her.

Groups of girl students talked quietly in the hallways, their faces drawn. The night after Susan left, I ran into Sarah and Lisa outside my office. They were serious and we spoke in Chinese, standing on the landing overlooking the city. I asked about Susan, and Lisa looked at me carefully.

"Do you know what happened to her?" she said.

"Yes."

"How do you know?"

"Other students have told me."

"What do you think about it?"

"I think it's very sad, of course. And I think she should be allowed to graduate."

"That won't happen," Lisa said quickly. She was one of the better students and also one of the more thoughtful. I asked her if Susan had gone home, and Lisa shook her head.

"She can't go home," she said. "Her father is very angry."

"How does he know?"

"The college told him. When the authorities found out, at first they agreed not to tell her family. But for some reason they told. This same thing happened to Susan's older sister a few years ago, and when her father found out he beat her. So now Susan will not go home. Her father is very angry—it's a big loss of face for the family. This is the second time they have lost face in such a way."

"Do you think the department should have told him?" I asked.

"I don't think it's their affair. It's a private matter."

I told her that I agreed, and I asked how Susan's boyfriend was treating her.

"He is fine. She has good *guanxi* with his parents and I think they will help her. Perhaps that is where she has gone. But you know, she paid several thousand yuan to get a teaching job in his hometown, but now she won't graduate and she'll lose the job. She'll lose the money, too."

That didn't seem to be the biggest concern—to be honest, I was far more worried about Susan jumping off a bridge. But I said nothing about that.

"This sort of thing happens everywhere," I said. "In America it's very common as well."

"What do people do about the problem there?"

"It's very difficult, just as it is here, but usually it can be kept private. Probably that is the biggest difference."

"That's the way it should be. But here everybody knows—the whole college has heard about it."

"What do most people think?"

"A few people think it's funny; others think she's a bad woman. But most of the students in our class are very sorry for Susan, although we can't help." She shook her head and gazed out on the rivers. *"Mei banfa,"* she said. "There is nothing that can be done."

THE NEXT DAY I turned twenty-nine years old. Always in the past my birthdays had felt like somebody else's—it seemed impossible that I had really gained another year. But this time I knew that I was twenty-nine; in some ways I felt much older. It had been a long two years and during that time I hadn't left western China.

In the morning I went with Adam and Mo Money to the bus station, because Linda had asked us to meet her when she returned. She wore a black armband and her eyes were red. After getting off the bus she tried to smile, one of those brave Chinese smiles that held the emotion at bay, compressed and controlled and pushed to the peripheries—a corner of the mouth, a line across the forehead. But today the sadness was too much; her mouth trembled, and she looked away.

That evening I graded my literature examinations. I thought about how pleasant everything had seemed when I monitored the exam, walking through the rows of students with their heads down, working hard. I liked being surrounded by their silence and concentration, and I liked the way that all of the black-haired heads were bent seriously. There was a simplicity to the scene, and there was a similar simplicity to the examination, which had nothing to do with the complications of life in Fuling, or the political problems in China, or the nationwide struggle of Reform and Opening. It was simply a literature test.

For the final section I asked them to analyze Robert Frost's "Nothing Gold Can Stay":

> Nature's first green is gold,
> Her hardest hue to hold.
> Her early leaf's a flower;
> But only so an hour.
> Then leaf subsides to leaf.
> So Eden sank to grief,
> So dawn goes down to day.
> Nothing gold can stay.

We had studied the poem back in May. I had lectured in detail about its rhythm—I always did that, because the students liked analyzing the sound of the language and you could take a poem apart without boring them. Most of them had understood what I said about Frost, and it was one of those classes that made me feel good about teaching literature. During the exam I felt the same way, walking through the rows and watching them work.

But now I realized that the simplicity had been a mirage. Linda's father had been dying as she took her final exam, and Susan had been struggling with the fear that had now driven her from the college. That was the way so many things in Fuling turned out—even teaching, which seemed to be a straightforward job, was complex and uncertain. There was an unemotional veneer that the people presented to the outside world, especially to *waiguoren,* and this made it harder when you lived there long enough to catch a glimpse of the way things actually worked. Of course, to some degree it was just the difficulties of life anywhere in the world—during my time in Fuling, two students had died; another student had an abortion and was expelled; a father died; a child died; people's marriages crumbled. Those things happened everywhere. But in Fuling it had taken me longer to see that side of life, because at first as a *waiguoren* I was held at a distance, and in a way that distance was hardest to deal with once it was gone. It was like looking at a blank meaningless smile and suddenly recognizing a lifetime of sadness concentrated in the corner.

I had never had any idealistic illusions about my Peace Corps "service" in China; I wasn't there to save anybody or leave an indelible mark on the town. If anything, I was glad that during my two years in Fuling I hadn't built anything, or organized anything, or made any great changes to the place. I had been a teacher, and in my spare time I had tried to learn as much as possible about the city and its people. That was the extent of my work, and I was comfortable with those roles and I recognized their limitations.

But now I found myself wondering if anything would be left from those hours in class. I hoped that my students would remember that Frost poem, or something else that we had studied. It could be something as small as a single character from a story, or a sliver from a Shakespeare sonnet—but I hoped that something would be remembered. I hoped that they would keep it somewhere in the back of their minds, and that they would find something steady and true in its simple beauty. This was the faith I had in literature: its truth was constant, unaffected by the struggles of daily life. But at the same time there was always the issue of relevance, and there were moments when a poem like "Nothing Gold Can Stay" seemed useless against the harsh realities of a place like Fuling.

I thought about that for a while, and then I went back to grading the examinations. I didn't have any answers; in the end I just had to hope for the best. Most of them would be fine, I figured. Certainly Linda would be fine, and Mo Money would be fine, and William Jefferson Foster would be fine, and so would Anne, working down in Shenzhen. Most things in the city would work out all right. The priest would be fine, and my tutors would be fine, and the family at the Students' Home would be fine. Most of the people would continue to make the best of things, and most of the children would have better lives than their parents had. That was really all you could hope for. Perhaps Susan would not be fine, but there was nothing to do about that, just as there hadn't been much to do for Janelle and Rebecca and the others who had lost their way. *Mei banfa.*

A couple of days later, Jimmy gave me a cassette tape and asked if I would make a recording of all the poetry we had studied. He was one of the liveliest boys, but he had never been a particularly good student; usually he sat in the back of the class and muttered "yahoo" and *yashua* whenever anybody said something. But he had always been one of my favorites, and now I was touched by his request.

"Especially I want you to read 'The Raven,'" he said, "and anything by Shakespeare. This is so I can remember your literature class."

I told him that I would make the tape that evening.

"Also, after you finish the poems," he said, grinning, "I want you to say all of the bad words you know in English and put them on the tape. Even if there are some bad words you did not teach us, I want you to say them. I would like that very much. And maybe some of the other students will copy it, too."

It took two long sittings to record all the poetry we had studied. After that was finished, Adam and I spent five minutes shouting obscenities into the recorder, and I returned the tape to Jimmy. He would turn out fine, too. Most of them were that way. They were tough and sweet and funny and sad, and people like that would always survive. It wasn't necessarily gold, but perhaps because of that it would stay.

I LEFT FULING on the fast boat upstream to Chongqing. It was a warm, rainy morning at the end of June—the mist thick on the Yangtze like dirty gray silk. A car from the college drove Adam and me down to the docks. The city rushed past, gray and familiar in the rain.

The evening before, we had eaten for the last time at the Students' Home. They kept the restaurant open late especially for us, because all night we were rushing around saying goodbye to everybody, and it was good to finally sit there and eat our noodles. We kidded the women about the new foreign devils who would come next fall to take our place, and how easily they could be cheated.

A few days earlier, Huang Neng, the grandfather, had talked with me about leaving.

"You know," he said, "when you go back to your America, it won't be like it is here. You won't be able to walk into a restaurant and say, 'I want a bowl of *chaoshou.*' Nobody will understand you!"

"That's true," I said. "And we don't have *chaoshou* in America."

"You'll have to order food in your English language," he said.

"You won't be able to speak our Chinese with the people there." And he laughed—it was a ludicrous concept, a country with neither Chinese nor *chaoshou.* After our last meal the family lined up at the door and waved goodbye, standing stiffly and wearing that tight Chinese smile. I imagined that probably I looked the same way—two years of friendship somehow tucked away in a corner of my mouth.

In the morning we said goodbye to Sunni and Noreen, both of whom had early class, and then we headed down to the docks. A few of the students were free that morning and they came to see us off, along with Dean Fu. Chinese partings were never comfortable—no hugs, few words, tears held back as long as possible. We shook hands awkwardly and boarded the boat.

The hydrofoil was crowded. They played karaoke videos on the television screen while we sat there at the dock for thirty minutes. Outside it was raining, but still the students waited. To show respect for a good friend you would see him off until he was completely and undeniably gone, regardless of the weather.

Most of them were crying as they stared out at the river. Mo Money crouched on a black pylon near the edge of the dock. William Jefferson Foster looked out toward White Flat Mountain, and Roger squatted near a coil of rope. Luke leaned against a wall. There were others—Chuck, Diaz, Lewis, Richard, DJ. Their eyes were red, and they did the best they could to hold their expressions even.

I watched them standing in the rain and wondered what their futures would be like. William Jefferson Foster was going off to teach at a private school in the eastern province of Zhejiang; Mo Money was looking for business jobs in Fuling; Lewis would return to the remote countryside and teach. Luke would be married in October, on National Day. It was an arranged marriage and he had never spent much time with his future wife, but he was a good peasant son who would not oppose his parents' wishes.

The boat pulled out of the harbor. The students stood perfectly still on the dock. Behind them the city rose, gray and dirty-looking in the mist. As always on the river I saw Fuling with an outsider's eyes: it looked big, impersonal, impenetrable. It was hard to believe that for two years this place had been my home. I wondered when I would see it again, and how it would be changed. The boat swung out into the heart of the Yangtze, facing the current.

The river was the same as it always had been. It wasn't like the people, who had changed so much in my eyes over the course of the two years, and who would now go their own separate and unpredictable ways even as they were frozen in my mind, pinned by memory—making *chaoshou,* teaching class, standing motionless on the docks. But it was different out on the river, where my *guanxi* with the Yangtze had always been simple: sometimes I went with the current, and sometimes I went against it. Upstream it was slower and downstream it was faster. That was really all there was to it—we crossed paths, and then we headed off in our own directions.

And finally I stopped worrying about the future or the past, and I simply looked at the city for the last time. The buildings were gray. The mouth of the Wu was wide with the summer rain. A sampan sculled gracefully near the shore. Raise the Flag Mountain was hidden in the mist. Our boat picked up speed and we rushed away against the steady current of the river.

ACKNOWLEDGMENTS

THIS BOOK WOULD NOT HAVE BEEN POSSIBLE without my family. I owe a great deal to all the Hesslers and Gundys who kept in touch during my two years in Sichuan, and thanks for your encouragement and support while I was writing. I promise that someday I'll find subjects closer to home.

From the first trip downriver to the final revision of the manuscript, Adam Meier has been everything I could ask of a friend. In particular, thanks for being such a steadying influence in Fuling, and thanks for all your help with the editing—at times, a difficult and delicate process. We've tilted at our share of windmills together and not for a moment would I have rather been there with anybody else.

I was also fortunate to share the joys and challenges of Fuling life with Sunni Fass and Noreen Finnegan, who were great sitemates. I couldn't have started my time in Sichuan with a better group than Peace Corps China 3: Tamy Chapman, Sean Coady, Mike Goettig, Rose Karkoski, Karen Lauck, Lisa McCallum, Rob Schmitz, Craig Simons, Sarah Telford, Rebecca Steinle Wallihan, Andrew and Molly Watkins, and Adam Weiss. I also want to thank Travis Klingberg, Christopher Marquardt, Mike Meyer, and the Wolken family for their friendship, both in Sichuan and afterwards.

The Peace Corps China staff provided me with a perfect combination of support and freedom while I was in Fuling, especially Dr. William Speidel, Kandice Christian, Don McKay, and Zhan Yimei.

A number of editors helped me with revisions. In particular, I was fortunate to work with Doug Hunt of the University of Missouri, who was always generous with his time and good advice. I appreciated the comments and recommendations of Scott Kramer, Matt Metzger, Angela Hessler, Terzah Ewing of the *Wall Street Journal*, and Ian Johnson of the *Wall Street Journal*'s Beijing bureau. I benefited from the recommendations of a former Fuling student who read the manuscript and gave me a local's reaction—I won't name you here, but I very much appreciate your help. And I want to thank John McPhee of Princeton University for both guidance and friendship; your encouragement while I was living in Fuling helped get this book started.

Thanks to Tim Duggan, my editor at HarperCollins, and William Clark, my agent, for your enthusiasm and support for this project.

My largest debt of gratitude is to my friends in Fuling. I hope that my stories reflect your generosity, patience, and understanding. In particular I want to thank my former students, who are now working all across China, from the highlands of Tibet to southern boom towns like Shenzhen. Most of you are now teachers, and many of you are living in your own Sichuanese river towns, along the Yangtze, the Wu, the Longxi, the Changtou, the Meixi, the Yancang, the Quxi, the Daxi—all of the small and remote rivers that run through eastern Sichuan, where the schools are simple and the classes crowded but the teachers do the best they can. I hope that you are blessed with students as wonderful as mine.